Learn WatchKit
for iOS

Kim Topley

Apress®

Learn WatchKit for iOS

ISBN-13 (pbk): 978-1-4842-1026-0

ISBN-13 (electronic): 978-1-4842-1025-3

Managing Director: Welmoed Spahr
Lead Editor: Michelle Lowman
Technical Reviewer: Jeff Tang
Editorial Board: Steve Anglin, Gary Cornell, Louise Corrigan, James T. DeWolf,
     Jonathan Gennick, Robert Hutchinson, Michelle Lowman, James Markham,
     Matthew Moodie, Jeffrey Pepper, Douglas Pundick, Ben Renow-Clarke,
     Gwenan Spearing, Matt Wade, Steve Weiss
Coordinating Editor: Kevin Walter
Copy Editor: Corbin Collins
Compositor: SPi Global
Indexer: SPi Global
Artist: SPi Global
Cover Photo: Michelle Lowman

Distributed to the book trade worldwide by Springer Science+Business Media New York, 233 Spring Street, 6th Floor, New York, NY 10013. Phone 1-800-SPRINGER, fax (201) 348-4505, e-mail orders-ny@springer-sbm.com, or visit www.springeronline.com. Apress Media, LLC is a California LLC and the sole member (owner) is Springer Science + Business Media Finance Inc (SSBM Finance Inc). SSBM Finance Inc is a Delaware corporation.

For information on translations, please e-mail rights@apress.com, or visit www.apress.com.

Apress and friends of ED books may be purchased in bulk for academic, corporate, or promotional use. eBook versions and licenses are also available for most titles. For more information, reference our Special Bulk Sales–eBook Licensing web page at www.apress.com/bulk-sales.

Any source code or other supplementary material referenced by the author in this text is available to readers at www.apress.com. For detailed information about how to locate your book's source code, go to www.apress.com/source-code/.

To the engineers at Apple who keep us coming back every year for more and the staff at the Astronaut Scholarship Foundation for making it possible for me to meet my boyhood heroes.

Contents at a Glance

Contents

About the Author

Kim Topley is a software engineer with more than 30 years of experience, ranging from mainframe microcode and the UNIX kernel to graphical user interfaces and mobile applications. He is the author of five books on various aspects of Java and JavaFX and is coauthor of *Beginning iPhone Development with Swift*.

About the Technical Reviewer

Jeff Tang worked on enterprise and web app development for many years before reinventing himself to focus on building great iOS and Android apps. He's had an Apple-featured, top-selling iOS app with millions of users and was recognized by Google as a Top Android Market Developer. He's the author of *Beginning Google Glass Development published* by Apress in 2014. His favorite quote is The Man in the Arena. Jeff loves simplicity, solving puzzles, and AI. His LinkedIn profile is www.linkedin.com/profile/view?id=1539384. He can be reached at jeffxtang@gmail.com.

Acknowledgments

Writing a book is always a long and often frustrating process, and this one has been no exception. Apple released the first SDK for the Apple Watch in November 2014, but didn't give us hardware to test with for another five months. During that period, developers had to create applications using a bare bones simulator that didn't let them test everything that they would normally expect to. There is no doubt that some of those developers had their fingers firmly crossed when they submitted their work for App Store approval. As an author, I was fortunate that my deadline was a little later than launch day for the Apple Watch, and I have at least been able to make sure that everything in this book is up to date and all the example source code works.

Of course, the tight deadlines involved in writing a book don't only apply to the author. There's a whole team at Apress who have to do much of their work as I was finishing mine. You'll find their names on the second page of this book. I would like to give special thanks to Michelle Lowman for accepting my proposal for this book only a couple days after the first version of Xcode with WatchKit included was shipped, to Kevin Walter and Jim Markham for steering the book through the review and production process at Apress, and to Jeff Tang for a great technical review (and for not complaining about the ratio of the number of pages in Chapter 7 to the number of days available to read and comment on it!). Finally, I would like to thank the engineers at Apple for making my life over the last six months interesting (in some sense of that word) again, as they seem to manage to do every year.

Welcome to the Apple Watch

When I learned to program computers more years ago than I care to remember, the hardware that I used literally filled a room. Ten years later, it was possible to build a computer that was small enough and cheap enough to have in your home or on your desk at work. Today, we think nothing of carrying in our pockets computers that are more powerful than the ones that were used back in the "good old days" to run a business or navigate a spacecraft to the moon and back. We use them to schedule our lives, read books, listen to music, send and receive e-mails, and even make phone calls. Over the last 15 or so years, several companies have experimented with the idea of making it possible to wear your phone or personal computing device instead of carrying it in your pocket. By 2014, Samsung, Sony, Motorola, and others had taken this idea to its logical conclusion by developing and marketing a range of *smartwatches*—devices that are basically wearable computers packaged as wristwatches—with varying degrees of success. In 2015, Apple released its own wearable computing device called the Apple Watch. It remains to be seen whether it will be as popular as the company's other consumer products. If it is, then it represents a major new opportunity for iOS developers to profit by extending their existing applications to work with the Apple Watch and to write new applications that make use of its unique features.

As you'll see in the first few chapters of this book, an Apple Watch application is really just an extension of an application written to run on an iPhone, so you'll need to know how to write iPhone applications. This book does not teach iPhone programming from scratch—I assume you already have some experience of developing for iOS using the Swift programming language. If you don't, then you'll need to first learn the basics by reading an introductory iOS programming book, such as *Beginning iPhone Development with Swift: Exploring the iOS SDK* by David Mark, Jack Nutting, Kim Topley, Fredrik Olsson, and Jeff LaMarche (Apress, 2014—see www.apress.com/9781484204108).

Your First Watch Application

Let's dive straight in and write our first watch application. Like iPhone and iPad applications, Apple Watch applications are developed using Xcode and can be debugged using both the iOS simulator and a real device. At the time of writing (May 2015), the simulator does not let you test the complete lifecycle of a watch application—for example, the simulator does not show the home screen of the watch, so you can't see your application's icon and launch it from there. You also can't configure glances or test how your application handles local notifications (glances and notifications are covered in Chapters 8 and 9, respectively). Although the simulator is useful for debugging, testing on a real device is important before releasing your application to the App Store.

The classes that you'll use to build Watch applications are included in the *WatchKit framework*, which is included in the iOS SDK starting with version 8.2. You can build Apple Watch applications with version 6.2 or higher of Xcode. The examples in this book use version 1.2 of the Swift language (which was introduced with Xcode 6.3 and is not completely compatible with the version of the language supported by Xcode 6.2) and were tested with Xcode 6.3 and 6.4. I assume that you are already an iOS developer, so you should have Xcode installed. If you don't have the most recent version, you can get it from Apple's developer web site at https://developer.apple.com/xcode/downloads.

EXAMPLE SOURCE CODE

The source code for the examples in this book can be downloaded from the book's page on the Apress website at www.apress.com/9781484210260. Once you have downloaded the source code archive and unpacked it, you'll see that each example has a separate folder with a name that includes the number of the chapter to which it relates. These folders contain the completed application. You'll also find folders that contain images and other resources that you'll need when following the step-by-step instructions to construct each example from scratch.

Creating a WatchKit Application

Fire up Xcode and let's create our first WatchKit application. As an experienced iOS developer, you already know how to create a project for a new application—just go to the Xcode menu bar and open the New Project dialog by selecting **File ➤ New ➤ Project...** and then choose the appropriate template from the iOS section. Try that now. Unfortunately, you'll find that there is no template for a WatchKit application. That's because you can't just build a WatchKit application and release it to the App Store. An application for the Apple Watch is supposed to be an add-on to an existing iOS application, so you first have to create an iOS application and then add a WatchKit application to it. This makes a lot of sense—the Apple Watch is smaller and less powerful and has a much smaller screen than the iPhone to which it is paired. It can't really support full-fledged applications (at least not yet). Instead, you'll need to decide which parts of your application's functionality, if any, make sense in the context of a watch and implement those features using WatchKit. Later in this book, you'll see a practical example of this—we'll take an iPhone weather application and add the ability for the user to view weather forecasts on Apple Watch. However, in most of the examples in this book, the iOS application does nothing.

So, how do we start writing our add-on WatchKit application? It's easy. First we need to create the hosting iOS app. Select **File ➤ New ➤ Project...** and then choose **Single View Application** from the **iOS Application** section of the template chooser (see Figure 1-1).

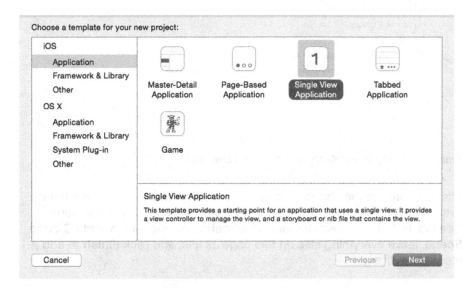

Figure 1-1. Creating a host application for a WatchKit app. Notice there is no WatchKit app project template

Click **Next** and then enter HelloWatch in the **Product Name** field. Enter the same values that you would use for other iOS projects in the **Organization Name** and **Organization Identifer** fields. Select Swift as the **Language**, Universal for **Devices**, and leave the **Core Data** check box unchecked. Press **Next** and choose the save location for the project.

> **Note** You can use Objective-C to write a WatchKit application if you prefer. All the source code in this book is written in Swift.

To add a WatchKit application to the project, you need to add a new target. From the menu bar, select **File ➤ New ➤ Target…**. In the template chooser that appears, select **WatchKit App** from the **iOS Apple Watch** section, as shown in Figure 1-2, then click **Next**.

Figure 1-2. Adding a WatchKit app target to an iOS application

The next page of the chooser contains various options, most of which have fixed values derived from the name and identifier of the host application (see Figure 1-3). Uncheck **Include Notification Scene** and **Include Glance Scene**, leave everything else on this page as it is, and click **Finish** to add the WatchKit target.

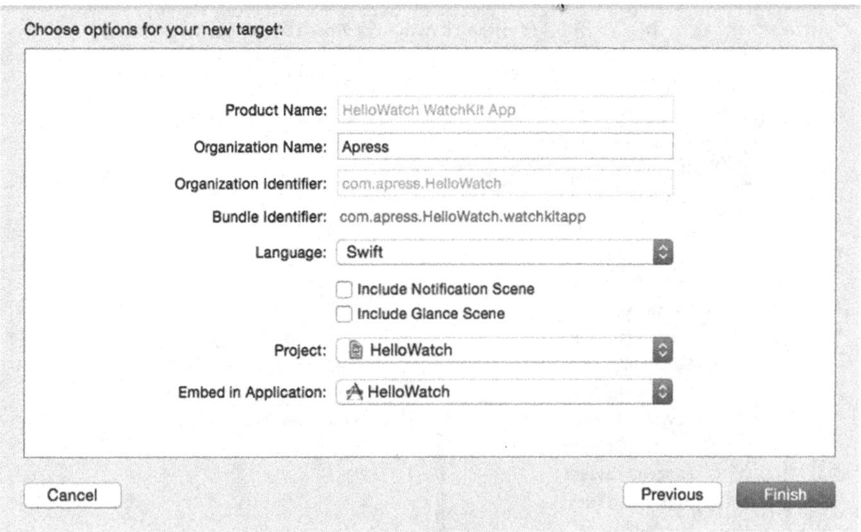

Choose options for your new target:

Product Name:	HelloWatch WatchKit App
Organization Name:	Apress
Organization Identifier:	com.apress.HelloWatch
Bundle Identifier:	com.apress.HelloWatch.watchkitapp
Language:	Swift

☐ Include Notification Scene
☐ Include Glance Scene

Project:	📄 HelloWatch
Embed in Application:	🅰 HelloWatch

Cancel   Previous   Finish

Figure 1-3. Completing the addition of the WatchKit app target

Xcode prompts you to confirm that you want a scheme that will allow you to run your WatchKit application to be activated. Check the **Do not show this message again** checkbox and then click **Activate** to activate the scheme.

In addition to this new scheme, Xcode adds two new groups and two new targets to your project. Let's take a look at what's in the new groups. Select the Project Navigator tab if it's not already selected (a quick way to do this is to press ⌘1) and you'll see that the new groups are called HelloWatch WatchKit Extension and HelloWatch WatchKit App (see Figure 1-4).

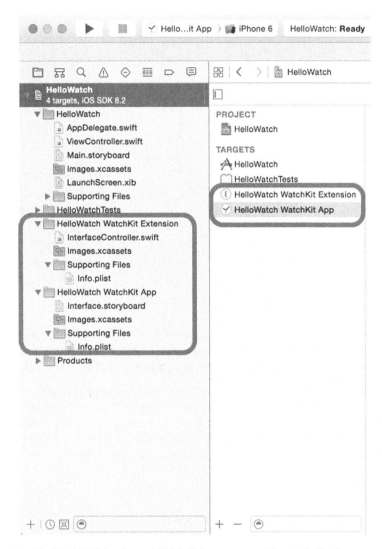

Figure 1-4. The WatchKit Extension and WatchKit App groups and targets in Xcode

The HelloWatch Watchkit App group contains a storyboard and an asset catalog that you'll use to create the user interface for your WatchKit application. You'll notice that it does not contain any .swift files—that's because all the code for the application is in the WatchKit Extension, not in the WatchKit application itself.

Now let's look at the HelloWorld WatchKit Extension group. As you can see in Figure 1-4, Xcode created a file called InterfaceController.swift in this group. Select this file in the Project Navigator so that you can see what it contains (Figure 1-5).

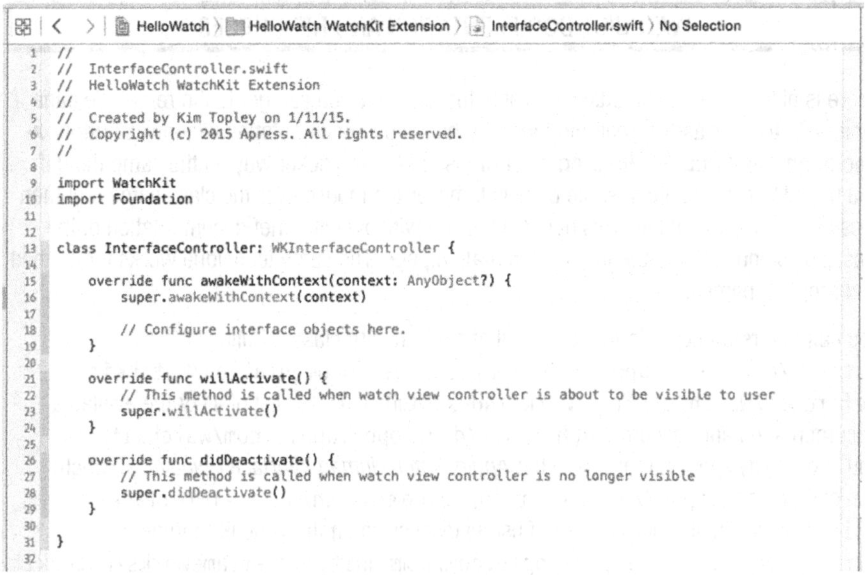

```
88 | < > | HelloWatch > HelloWatch WatchKit Extension > InterfaceController.swift > No Selection
1  //
2  //  InterfaceController.swift
3  //  HelloWatch WatchKit Extension
4  //
5  //  Created by Kim Topley on 1/11/15.
6  //  Copyright (c) 2015 Apress. All rights reserved.
7  //
8
9  import WatchKit
10 import Foundation
11
12
13 class InterfaceController: WKInterfaceController {
14
15     override func awakeWithContext(context: AnyObject?) {
16         super.awakeWithContext(context)
17
18         // Configure interface objects here.
19     }
20
21     override func willActivate() {
22         // This method is called when watch view controller is about to be visible to user
23         super.willActivate()
24     }
25
26     override func didDeactivate() {
27         // This method is called when watch view controller is no longer visible
28         super.didDeactivate()
29     }
30
31 }
32
```

Figure 1-5. The skeleton interface controller for a WatchKit application

As you can see, InterfaceController is a subclass of the WatchKit class WKInterfaceController (the names of all of the WatchKit classes begin with the letters WK). WKInterfaceController is WatchKit's version of the UIViewController class in UIKit—it contains the controller code for your application's user interface. The Xcode template gives you just a single controller class that manages the screen that the user sees when your application launches. For some applications, that's all you need, but for more complex applications, WatchKit provides mechanisms that allow you to navigate from screen to screen, including segues that are similar to the ones that you are familiar with from UIKit. There is one WKInterfaceController for each screen in your application, so if your application requires more than one screen, you'll need to have more than one WKInterfaceController. Chapter 5 talks more about interface controllers, including how to write applications with more than one interface controller.

WATCHKIT DOCUMENTATION AND RESOURCES

There is plenty of documentation available for WatchKit. You can get to the reference page for any WatchKit class by searching for it in the Xcode documentation window (**Window ➤ Documentation and API Reference**, or press ⇧⌘0). A quicker way do the same thing if you have the class name in some code is to hover the mouse over the class name and then press the ⌥ (option) key. This opens a pop-up window with brief documentation of the class, including a link to the full documentation page. The same technique works for method and property names.

You can find reference information for all of the WatchKit classes online at `https://developer.apple.com/library/ios/documentation/WatchKit/ Reference/WatchKit_framework/index.html` and a full list of all of the available documentation and resources at `https://developer.apple.com/watchkit`. You should pay special attention to the *Apple Watch Human Interface Guidelines*, which you can find at `https://developer.apple.com/watch/human-interface- guidelines`. Finally, there is a lot of useful discussion on the WatchKit forum at `https://forums.developer.apple.com/community/app-frameworks/watchkit`.

It is important to note that the code for a WatchKit application runs in the WatchKit app extension on the iPhone, not on the Apple Watch itself. That's so important that I'll say it again: **None of your WatchKit application's code runs on the Apple Watch—it executes in an extension on the paired iPhone**. That means you don't have direct access to the Apple Watch hardware. Instead, you have to rely on the WatchKit classes to draw your user interface on the screen, react to user input, tap the user's wrist when required, and so on. You can find out more about what your WatchKit application can and can't do in the section "Some Things That a WatchKit Application Can and Can't Do" at the end of this chapter.

All of your application's code files will be in the WatchKit Extension group and will be assigned to the WatchKit Extension target. The exception to this rule is any code that you need to share between the WatchKit app extension and the iOS application, which you should put into a shared framework. I discuss this in detail in Chapter 7.

> **Caution**   Do not add any code to the Hello WatchKit App group or target—all the code for the WatchKit application *must* be in the group and target that Xcode created for your WatchKit app's extension.

EXTENSION PROGRAMMING

Don't be concerned if you're not familiar with writing iOS extensions. For the most part, coding an extension is the same as coding an application. The main thing you need to be aware of is that some APIs are not available to code running in an extension. I'll point out some of the differences as we progress through the book. Usually, you can work around the limitations by delegating work to your iOS application and you'll see exactly how to do that in Chapter 7. You can read about extensions in the *App Extension Programming Guide*, which you'll find at `https://developer.apple.com/library/ios/documentation/General/Conceptual/ExtensibilityPG/index.html`.

Building the User Interface

There are three ways to construct the user interface for an iOS application: you can create it entirely in code, you can build it from nib files, or you can use a storyboard. By contrast, there is only one way to build the user interface for a WatchKit application—you have to use the storyboard that Xcode created when you added the WatchKit application target. Select the `Interface.storyboard` file in the WatchKit App target to open it in the editor area. Right now, the storyboard contains a single empty screen, as shown in Figure 1-6.

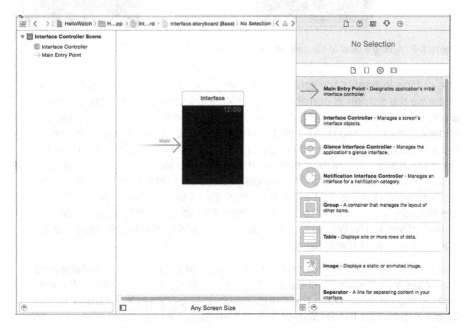

Figure 1-6. The WatchKit application's storyboard and the Object Library

To the right of the editor area, you'll find the Object Library (use **View ➤ Utilities ➤ Show Object Library** to make it visible if necessary). While you are editing a WatchKit application storyboard, the Object Library contains WatchKit *user interface objects*, which are roughly equivalent to views in UIKit. As you can see, there are far fewer of these than there are UIKit views. Take the opportunity to scroll through the list to see what's available—Chapters 3 through 6 talk in detail about them all.

Our first WatchKit application is very simple, consisting of just a label and an image. Let's start with the label. Locate a Label object in the Object Library and drag it over the watch screen in the storyboard. As you do so, the cursor changes, and a blue outline appears on the watch screen, as shown on the left in Figure 1-7.

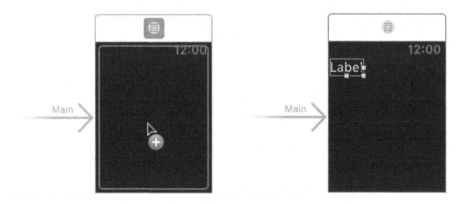

Figure 1-7. Adding a label to the user interface

The outline indicates the area in which you can drop the label. In this case, because the screen is currently empty, Xcode indicates that you can drop it anywhere. With the label positioned anywhere over the watch screen, release the mouse to drop it and you'll see that it instantly snaps to the top left corner (see the right image in Figure 1-7). Unlike UIKit, WatchKit does not have a sophisticated layout mechanism like Auto Layout. In fact, pretty much all you can do is arrange your user interface objects in a row or a column. Objects that are added directly to the watch screen (which are actually being added to the screen's interface controller) are always arranged vertically, one above the other. That's why the label was placed right at the top of the screen.

Make sure the label is selected, which is indicated by the blue outline and the white resize handles shown in Figure 1-7. If it's not currently selected, just click on it. Now open the Attributes Inspector (**View ➤ Utilities ➤ Show Attributes Inspector**) to see the attributes of the label that you can set (see Figure 1-8).

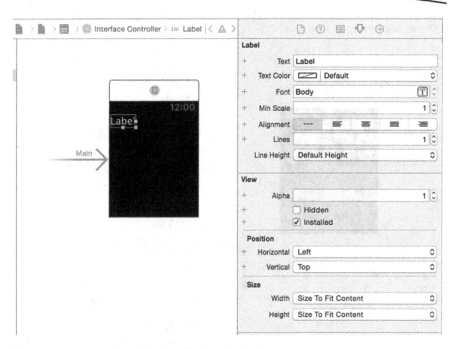

Figure 1-8. Inspecting the attributes of the Label object

Use the Attributes Inspector to change the label text from Label to Hello
Watch. Next, use the Font control to change the text font from Body to
Headline. As you can see, the label resizes automatically to fit its new
content. Let's also horizontally center the text on the screen. A little below
the Text field is a segmented control labeled Alignment, which sets the
position of the text within the label itself. You can click the third segment
from the left to center the text within the label itself, but that doesn't do what
we want—we actually need to reposition the label relative to the interface
controller. For that, you need to use the controls in the Position section of
the Attributes Inspector. Click the Horizontal selector and choose Center.
You'll see that the label repositions itself horizontally while remaining at the
top of the screen, as shown in Figure 1-9.

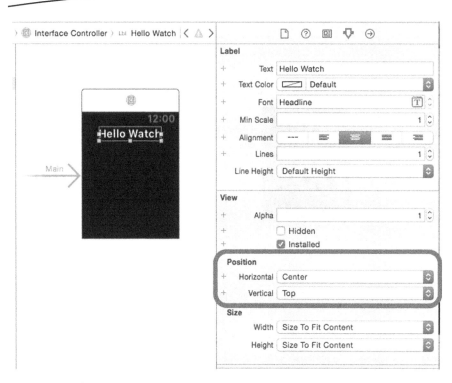

Figure 1-9. Horizontally centering the label

Now let's add an image below the label. Drag an Image object from the Object Library and drop it onto the storyboard. It doesn't matter where you release the mouse as long as it's over the watch screen and somewhere below the label—the image will be positioned underneath the label, up against the left edge of the screen.

The Image object is empty until you give it something to display. In the 1 - HelloWatch Icon folder of the book's example source code archive, you'll find a suitable image. In the Project Navigator, select Image.xcassets from the HelloWatch WatchKit App group to open the WatchKit app's asset catalog and then drag the image into the editor area and drop it (see Figure 1-10).

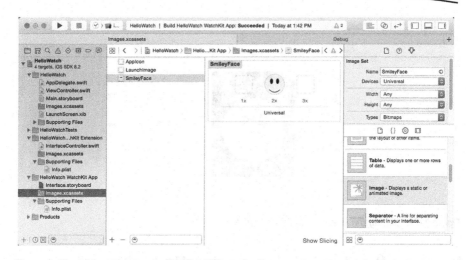

Figure 1-10. Adding an image to the WatchKit application

> **Note**   The images that you plan to use in the WatchKit application should be added to the asset catalog of the WatchKit application itself. As you'll see later, it is possible to programmatically install images from WatchKit extension's asset catalog, but images configured in the storyboard *must* come from the WatchKit application's asset catalog.

The image came from a file called SmileyFace@2x.png and it was added to the 2x section of the entry in the asset catalog. The Apple Watch has a Retina screen, so all images must be prepared at double the required point size. In this case, the image is a 206-pixel square, which maps to a 103-point square from the point of view of the WatchKit software.

Back in the storyboard, make sure the Attributes Inspector is open, select the Image object, and then choose SmileyFace from the Image selector. The smiley face image appears in the storyboard, but it's still aligned to the left of the screen. You can center the image using the Horizontal selector from the Position section, as you did with the label.

Before running the application, let's give it a title. To do this, select the interface controller by clicking it in the Document Outline and then enter Hello in the Title field in the Attributes Inspector. Press the Return button, and the title appears at the top left of the watch screen (see Figure 1-11).

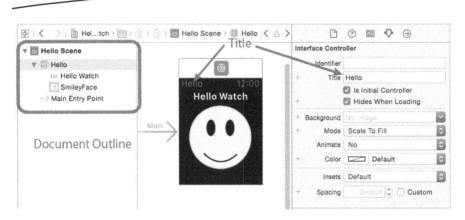

Figure 1-11. Setting the interface controller's title

Running the Application on the Simulator

When you added the WatchKit application target to your project, Xcode also added a scheme that you can use to run it on the simulator (or a real Apple Watch). Open the scheme selector and you'll see that there are two schemes for HelloWatch (shown in Figure 1-12).

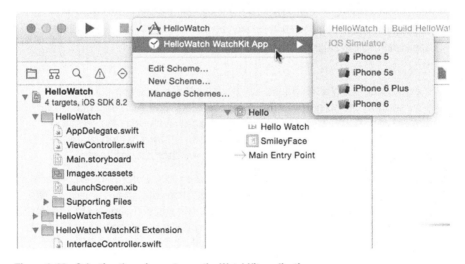

Figure 1-12. Selecting the scheme to run the WatchKit application

The scheme labeled HelloWatch runs the HelloWatch iOS application, which is just an empty shell because we didn't add anything to it. The second scheme, labeled HelloWatch WatchKit App, is the one that you need to launch the WatchKit application. Select this scheme and then choose one of the iPhone simulators. You need to select an iPhone simulator because when you start your WatchKit application, the code in the HelloWatch WatchKit extension is actually run on the iPhone simulator. In a real application, the code in the extension would perform initialization and prepare the interface controller to be displayed. For this simple example, we don't need any initialization, so the extension doesn't do anything useful.

The user interface of the WatchKit application is not displayed on the iPhone simulator—instead, it's shown on an external display. To make this possible, you need to select an appropriate simulated external display. To do that, with the HelloWatch WatchKit App scheme selected, build and run the WatchKit application in the usual way using **Product ➤ Run** from the menu bar or the keyboard shortcut ⌘R. When the iOS simulator starts, select **Hardware ➤ External Displays** from its menu bar and you'll see a menu of external displays, as shown in Figure 1-13.

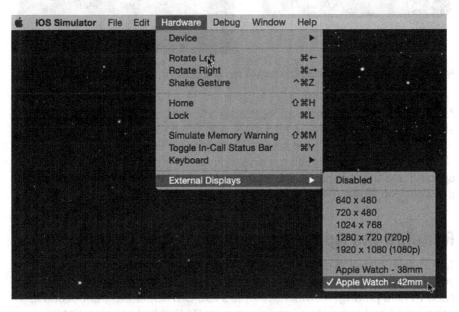

Figure 1-13. Choosing an external display for the Apple Watch

Select the 38mm Apple Watch screen and a separate empty window will open. Now stop and rerun the WatchKit application and you should see the user interface from your storyboard in this window. Next, select the 42mm screen and run the application again to see how it looks on the larger screen. The results are shown in Figure 1-14.

Figure 1-14. Running the HelloWatch WatchKit app on the 38mm (left) and 42mm (right) screens

As you can see, this simple application works well on both sizes of screen, although you might prefer to add more vertical spacing to get a more balanced view on the 42mm screen. In Chapter 2, you'll see that it is possible to do that by creating a single design in the storyboard that has spacing and other attribute values that depend on the size of the screen of the watch on which the application is run.

Running the Application on an Apple Watch

To run an application on a real Apple Watch, the watch must be paired to your iPhone and the iPhone must be connected to your computer. You'll also need to be a paid-up member of Apple's iOS Developer program because Xcode will need to create a provisioning profile that includes the watch.

Before we run our example on the Apple Watch, let's give it a home screen icon. You need to provide several icons for a production WatchKit application. You can see what they are by selecting Images.xcassets in the HelloWatch WatchKit App group in the Project Navigator and selecting the AppIcon image set (see Figure 1-15).

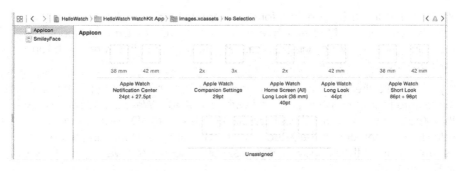

Figure 1-15. The full set of application icons for a WatchKit icon

For most of the examples in this book, we won't supply any of these icons, and for this example, we're only going to include the home screen icon. You should, of course, design an appropriate set of icons for any application that you intend to release to the App Store.

> **Note** You'll see warnings in Xcode if you don't supply all the icons that Xcode thinks you need to include. Click on the warning indicator (the yellow triangle in the Activity View at the top of the Xcode window) to see which icons are missing.

Below each group of icons, you'll see a description of what each icon is used for and its size. The slot for the Home Screen icon, which is in the middle in Figure 1-15, shows that the icon needs to be a 40 pt. square (all Apple Watch icons are square). Because the Apple Watch screen is a 2x Retina display (which means that 1 point is equivalent to 2 pixels), you actually need to create an image that's 80 pixels square. Some icons need to be sized differently for the 38mm and 42mm watches. For example, the Short Look Notification icon (you'll find out what this is used for in Chapter 9) is 86 points on the 38mm device and 98 points on the 42mm device.

> **Tip** Apple provides design guidelines for icons (and for all aspects of building Apple Watch applications) in its document *Apple Watch Human Interface Guidelines*, where you'll find links to a set of resource files that include Photoshop templates that you can use as the basis for your icon designs.

You'll find a Home Screen icon for our example in the `1 - HelloWatch Home Screen Icon` folder of the example source code archive. Drop the icon onto the Home Screen slot of `Images.xcassets`, and you're almost ready to run the application on the watch.

If you haven't already done so, connect your iPhone to your computer and make sure that the iPhone is paired with your Apple Watch. You can check that Xcode has recognized your watch by opening the Devices window (**Window ➤ Devices** in the Xcode menu). Select your iPhone in the device list on the left of the window and you should also see the watch, as shown in Figure 1-16.

Figure 1-16. The Apple Watch in the Xcode Devices window

To run the application, go the scheme selector in Xcode, select the HelloWatch WatchKit App scheme, and choose your iPhone as the target device (see Figure 1-17). Then click the `Run` button.

Figure 1-17. Choosing the scheme and target to run the example on your watch

The first time you do this, you'll probably see a dialog box reporting that Xcode failed to sign the WatchKit application. That's because you need to add the watch to your account at the Developer Portal and create a provisioning profile that includes it. You can do this manually, if you prefer (you'll find the identifier for the watch in the Devices screen, as shown in Figure 1-16), but it's much easier to allow Xcode to do it for you. Click the **Fix Issue** button in the dialog, and Xcode will try again. The HelloWatch application will be installed on your iPhone, and the watch application will be sent to the watch—if you have your watch screen unlocked and are showing the home screen, you'll see this happen. The application's icon should appear on the watch home screen. You can see the application's icon at the bottom right in Figure 1-18.

Figure 1-18. The HelloWatch application installed on the Apple Watch

---

Tip   To take a screenshot of the watch, press and hold the side button and then click the digital crown. The screen should flash, and the screenshot will be stored in the Camera Roll on the paired iPhone.

Even though you clicked the Run button in Xcode, the application doesn't automatically run on the watch—you need to tap on its icon to launch it. When you do that, you'll see a launch screen with the application's name and a progress indicator for a short while, and then the application's main screen appears (see Figure 1-19).

Figure 1-19. Launching the HelloWatch application on the Apple Watch

Note   Sometimes launching the application for the first time appears to stall. Wait for a few seconds. If it still doesn't work, click the digital crown to return to the home screen and try again.

The application remains installed until you do one of three things:

■ Delete it on the watch by pressing and holding your finger on the screen and clicking the delete icon that appears, just as you would to delete an application from your iPhone. This is not recommended because the application does not get reinstalled if you run it again from Xcode. To fix this, delete the application from the iPhone (or the iPhone simulator) and run it again.

■ Open the Apple Watch application on your iPhone, find the entry for HelloWatch, and switch off the Show App on Apple Watch setting. You can reinstall the application just by toggling the switch back to the on position.

■ Delete the HelloWatch application from your iPhone. When you do this, the watch application is uninstalled from the watch.

For normal development, you don't need to manually delete the application from either the watch or the iPhone—if you make changes to the application and run it again from Xcode, it gets reinstalled automatically.

Congratulations! You just successfully built and ran your first Apple Watch application. Now let's take a quick look at what you can and can't do with the WatchKit framework.

Some Things That a WatchKit Application Can and Can't Do

WatchKit lets you build simple applications for the Apple Watch. You can create very useful extensions for your iPhone applications, like the weather application that you'll build in Chapter 7 of this book. However, you can't do everything that the Apple's own native Apple Watch applications can do. Here's a list of some of the things that you can and can't do with WatchKit:

■ Your application can include a glance, which is a single screen that you can use to present useful information relating to your application. The user can configure which glances are available when by swiping up from the bottom of the Apple Watch screen. Chapter 8 adds a glance to the weather application from Chapter 7.

■ You can handle local and remote notifications from your iPhone application on the watch, if the user allows it. You can choose to let the system display the notification using a default presentation, or you can build one of your own. We'll talk more about that in Chapter 9.

- You can't install or run any code on the Apple Watch itself. Only your storyboard and image resources are sent to the watch. The application logic is implemented in an extension that runs on the iPhone and uses WatchKit APIs to communicate with the software on the watch.

- WatchKit user interfaces are restricted to very simple layouts, as you'll see in Chapter 2. You can't create the equivalent of custom UIViews, and there is nothing equivalent to Core Graphics, so you can't draw directly (or indirectly) to the screen.

- Animations in WatchKit are limited to animated image frames. There is nothing like Core Animation, and the delay between an operation being performed in your extension and the result appearing on the watch means that it is not really feasible to create fluid animations that are driven from code in the extension. One consequence of this, along with the lack of direct drawing on the Apple Watch, is that you can't really create a custom watch face.

- There is no way to detect when the user interacts with the screen—for example, you don't get notified when the user taps or swipes across your user interface. You have to rely on WatchKit user interface objects such as buttons and sliders to detect the user's gestures and translate them into calls to code in your extension.

- Apple Watch has a built-in heart rate sensor, an accelerometer, a speaker, a microphone, Bluetooth, and WiFi. Unfortunately, you don't have direct access to any of this hardware. You can get speech input through a specially designed controller that uses the microphone on the watch, and you can use the Core Location framework in your application's extension to present location-based information to the user. However, you can't detect orientation changes, monitor the user's movement or heart rate, or play audio on the watch itself.

That may sound like a lot of restrictions, but as you'll see as you progress through this book, you can still build some very useful and appealing WatchKit applications. You'll find some of the applications that have already been built on Apple's website at https://www.apple.com/watch/app-store-apps.

IMPORTANT NOTE

Sometimes you may find that an example from this book fails to build. Most likely, you'll see an error from the link phase of the build. A typical manifestation of the problem looks like this:

```
ld: framework not found SharedCode for architecture x86_64
clang: error: linker command failed with exit code 1 (use -v to see
invocation)
```

This is not a problem with the example source code—it's an Xcode problem. To fix it, hold down the option key, select **Product ➤ Clean Build Folder. . .** from Xcode's menu then try again. If this doesn't work, quit Xcode, restart it and try again. You may have to repeat these steps more than once, but eventually you will find that the example will build and run.

Summary

In this chapter, you had a first look at the Apple Watch and at the tools in Xcode that you can use to build applications for it. You also built and ran a very basic application on the iOS simulator and on a real Apple Watch (assuming, of course, that you are lucky enough to have one!). Chapter 2 takes a closer look at the components that make up a WatchKit application. We'll look in more detail at using the Xcode storyboard editor to design its user interface.

Interface Controllers and Layout

Chapter 1 introduced the basic building blocks of WatchKit and helped you create a very simple application. This chapter looks in detail at *interface controllers*, the WatchKit equivalent of UIKit's view controllers. We start by discussing the lifecycle of an interface controller and how it relates to the lifecycle of your WatchKit application's extension. We then cover in some detail the way in which interface controllers handle layout and the storyboard tools you can use to construct layouts that adapt to the different screens of the 38mm and 42mm Apple Watch devices.

Interface Controllers

As you saw in Chapter 1, interface controllers contain the logic for your WatchKit application. Every interface controller must be configured in the storyboard and connected to a subclass of `WKInterfaceController`. Xcode packages your interface controllers (and any other files in your WatchKit Extension group in Xcode) as an application extension, which is installed on the iPhone as part of your iOS application when it is downloaded from the App Store or run from Xcode. The storyboard and any resources in the WatchKit App group (usually images or custom fonts) are packaged into a separate bundle and installed on the Apple Watch that is paired to the user's iPhone. In this section, we examine the lifecycle and configuration of an interface controller.

Interface Controller Lifecycle

When the user launches your WatchKit application, its storyboard is loaded from the WatchKit application bundle (which is stored on the watch), and the user interface for the controller indicated by the main entry point arrow (see Figure 1-6 in Chapter 1) is loaded on the watch. On the iPhone, WatchKit then loads and runs the extension associated with your WatchKit application (from the WatchKit application's extension bundle) and initiates the lifecycle of the interface controller class that is linked to the initial interface controller that was loaded from the storyboard on the watch.

> **Note**   As emphasized in Chapter 1, it is important to keep in mind at all times that the user interface that you design in your storyboard is loaded by Apple's software running on the Apple Watch, but the interface controllers and all of the executable code in your application are part of the extension and execute on the iPhone, not the Watch.

Let's examine the interface controller lifecycle by running a WatchKit application on the simulator. Start by making a copy of the project from Chapter 1, leaving the project name and everything else unchanged.

> **Note**   You'll find the completed version of this project in the folder
> 2 - Controller Lifecycle in the source code archive.

Open the project in Xcode and select Interface.storyboard in the HelloWatch WatchKit App group in the Project Navigator. In the storyboard, select the interface controller and then open the Attributes Inspector, as shown in Figure 2-1.

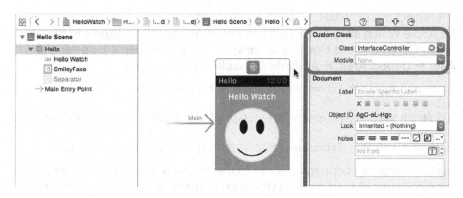

Figure 2-1. The initial interface controller in the storyboard

The link between the initial interface controller in the storyboard and the class that implements it is made by the value of the **Class** field in the **Custom Class** section of the controller's attributes. Here, the initial interface controller class is called `InterfaceController`. Back in the Project Navigator, you'll find the source for this class in the file `InterfaceController.swift` in the `HelloWatch WatchKit Extension` group. Select this file and add the following code shown in bold to it.

```swift
class InterfaceController: WKInterfaceController {

    override init() {
        super.init()
        NSLog("InterfaceController init() called")
    }

    override func awakeWithContext(context: AnyObject?) {
        super.awakeWithContext(context)

        // Configure interface objects here.
        NSLog("awakeWithContext() called with context \(context)")
    }

    override func willActivate() {
        // This method is called when watch view controller
        // is about to be visible to user
        super.willActivate()
        NSLog("willActivate() called")
    }

    override func didDeactivate() {
        // This method is called when watch view controller
        // is no longer visible
        super.didDeactivate()
        NSLog("didDeactivate() called")
    }

}
```

Now select the HelloWatch WatchKit App schema and run the example on the Apple Watch simulator. You'll see the following output appear in the Xcode Console (if this Console is not visible, you can open it by selecting **View ➤ Debug Area ➤ Activate Console** in the menu bar):

```
HelloWatch WatchKit Extension[87630:25575085] InterfaceController init()
called
HelloWatch WatchKit Extension[87630:25575085] awakeWithContext() called with
context nil
HelloWatch WatchKit Extension[87630:25575085] willActivate() called
```

The first thing that happens is a call to the interface controller's initializer, followed by a call to its awakeWithContext() method. You can use either of these methods to perform one-time initialization. The awakeWithContext() method has an optional argument of type AnyObject?. In the case of the initial interface controller, this argument is always nil (as you can see from the Console output), but when you create an interface controller programmatically, as you will in Chapter 5, you can use this argument to pass contextual information that the controller can use to configure itself. Next, the controller's willActivate() method is called. This happens just before the interface controller becomes visible on the Apple Watch.

Apple recommends that you use these methods as follows:

- Use the init() method to perform one-time initialization of data and user interface objects that does not require the initial context and the awakeWithContext() method to incorporate state from the context object, if there is one. You can use either of these methods to populate the user interface with initial values that you didn't set in the storyboard and to make any necessary adjustments to the storyboard layout. As you'll see, however, you don't have much control over the layout at run time over and above what is available in Xcode at design time.

- Use the willActivate() method to allocate resources and start timers that are required only while the controller is visible. It is possible to update the user interface in this method too, but that should be done only if it has to be done each time the controller becomes active.

While the user is interacting with your application on the Apple Watch, its extension will continue to run on the iPhone. However, as soon as the user switches to another application or lowers his wrist, the extension is suspended and it may be terminated immediately or at some later time. This means that you can really only do useful work while the user is interacting with your application on the watch, which could be only a few seconds.

> **Note**   It is possible to configure the watch so that it does not activate and deactivate your extension when the user raises and lowers his wrist. In that case, the extension will be deactivated when the screen times out and goes blank and will be reactivated (if it hasn't been terminated) when the user taps the screen to wake up the watch. This behavior is controlled by the `Activate on Wrist Raise` setting in the Settings application on the watch itself. For the sake of simplicity, this book assumes that this setting is at its default value.

Before your extension is suspended, the active interface controller's `didDeactivate()` method is called to give it an opportunity to release any resources or stop any timers that it no longer needs. It is not possible to simulate switching to another application on the simulator, but you can trigger the execution of the `didDeactivate()` method for testing purposes by locking the screen of the iPhone simulator. To do this, click on the simulator and then select **Hardware ➤ Lock** from the menu bar, or use the keyboard shortcut ⌘**L**. You'll see the following appear in the Console, indicating that the interface controller is no longer active:

```
HelloWatch WatchKit Extension[87630:25575085] didDeactivate() called
```

If you now unlock the iPhone using the slider on the lock screen, the interface controller is activated again:

```
HelloWatch WatchKit Extension[87630:25575085] willActivate() called
```

Notice that the `init()` and `awakeWithContext()` methods were not called when the screen was unlocked. That's because the interface controller instance that was in use when the screen was locked was still available when the screen was unlocked. However, on a real device, it is possible for the WatchKit application extension to be terminated while it is not active. In that case, the next time the user interacts with your application, a new interface controller instance would be created and its `init()` and `awakeWithContext()` methods called before it is activated.

> **Tip**   You can use the example application to explore when the extension's lifecycle methods are called by running it on a real Apple Watch. Select your iPhone as the target in the scheme selector, install the application by pressing the Run button, and then start it by tapping its icon on the home screen. You'll see the output from the `println()` statements in the Xcode console, just as you did when using the simulator. Try lowering and raising your wrist, letting the display time out and go blank and then using the digital crown to switch back to the home screen to see what lifecycle events are generated. You can also place breakpoints in your code in the same way that you would when debugging an iOS application or when running in the simulator.

Navigation and Lifecycle Events

Navigation between interface controllers is another reason for a controller to be activated or deactivated. Applications that require more than one interface controller can use either of two different types of navigation between the controllers. In a *page-based* application, two or more controllers are logically placed side-by-side with the user interface of only one controller on screen at any given time. To navigate between controllers, the user swipes left or right, just like the home screen of an iPhone or iPad, or when navigating the pages of a UIPageViewController in UIKit. By contrast, a *hierarchical* application has a single root interface controller onto which other controllers can be pushed to form a stack, like UIKit's UINavigationController.

You choose at design time whether your application uses page-based or hierarchical navigation, and your choice is reflected in the storyboard, as you'll see in Chapter 5. Only one navigation style can be used in an application—it is not possible to use hierarchical navigation style and then push an interface controller that uses page-based navigation or vice versa. However, you can *present* an interface controller that is page-based even if your application uses hierarchical navigation.

All forms of navigation cause the willActivate() and didDeactivate() methods of the interface controllers concerned to be called:

- In a page-based application, when the user swipes left or right, the didDeactivate() method of the outgoing controller is called, followed by the willActivate() method of the incoming one.

- In a hierarchical application, when one controller is pushed on another, the didDeactivate() method of the controller that is being hidden is called before the willActivate() method of the controller being pushed.

- When an interface controller is presented, the didDeactivate() method of the presenting controller is called, followed by the willActivate() method of the controller being presented. The sequence is reversed when the presented view controller is dismissed.

- An interface controller is also deactivated when the user uses the force touch gesture (a firm press on the screen) to trigger the controller's menu, if there is one. It is reactivated when the menu is closed.

You'll find a detailed discussion of interface controller navigation in Chapter 5.

Lifecycle of the WatchKit App Extension

The willActivate() and didDeactivate() methods notify events in the lifecycle of an interface controller, but these methods tell you nothing about the lifecycle of your WatchKit application's extension. As noted earlier, the extension is started whenever it's required—typically because the user launched your application—and is suspended (or terminated) when the user stops interacting with the application.

Unlike iOS applications, there are no lifecycle methods for extensions. Your extension also does not have a UIApplication object or a UIApplicationDelegate. This means that there is no way to get control when the extension is started, suspended or terminated. In the special case that your application has only one interface controller, you can probably assume that the extension is about to be suspended if your controller's didDeactivate() method is called.

Incidentally, the fact that the WatchKit application's code executes in an extension and not as a fully-fledged iOS application has several consequences for the way in which you code the application. Here are some things to keep in mind:

- The extension runs only while the user is interacting with your WatchKit application. This interaction might last for only a few seconds, so you may not have time to start and complete long-running activaties, such as fetching data from the Internet. To do this, you need the assistance of your iOS application. WatchKit and iOS provide mechanisms that let you coordinate activity between your WatchKit extension and the iOS application, which you'll use in Chapter 7 to allow an extension to fetch weather forecast data from the Internet and display it on the Apple Watch.

- Code in extensions is not allowed to run in background mode. That means you can't do things like periodically refresh cached data by running a background fetch, or use Core Location to continuously monitor the user's position. Again, the solution is to use the techniques that you'll see in Chapter 7 to enlist the help of the iOS application to obtain the data that's required and share it with the WatchKit extension.

▓ Extensions of other types (like Today extensions) that are linked to a `UIViewController` have access to an `NSExtensionContext` object via the view controller's `extensionContext` property. The `NSExtensionContext` makes it possible for code in the extension to open a URL even though it does not have access to a `UIApplication` object. The `WKInterfaceController` class does not have a similar property, so WatchKit application extension classes do not have an `NSExtensionContext`.

It's possible for the user to run your WatchKit application without ever having started the iOS application that installed it—in fact, this is exactly what happened when you run the example in Chapter 1 on your watch. It's also possible for the WatchKit application (and hence your extension) to be running when the iOS application is not running. This is what happens when you run the WatchKit app in the iOS simulator.

Debugging the WatchKit App Extension and the iOS Application Together

Sometimes it is useful to be able to run and debug the WatchKit app and the iOS application at the same time. If you try to do this by running them individually in the simulator, you'll find that you can't. Try it out for yourself. If you start the HelloWatch WatchKit application in the usual way and then try to run the iOS application by using the HelloWatch scheme, Xcode will tell you that the simulator is already in use. The same thing happens if you run the iOS application first and then try to start the WatchKit application. To have both applications available for debugging in the simulator at the same time, do the following:

1. Use the HelloWatch WatchKit App scheme to run the WatchKit app. This installs both applications in the simulator.

2. In the home screen of the iOS simulator, find the icon for the HelloWatch iOS application and tap it. This launches the iOS application. Now both applications are running, but the Xcode debugger is connected only to the WatchKit application extension.

3. To connect the debugger to the iOS application, select **Debug ➤ Attach to Process** from the Xcode menu bar. Hover the mouse for a few seconds, and a list of all of the processes running on the simulator will appear, as shown in Figure 2-2. Click on `HelloWatch` to connect the debugger to the iOS application.

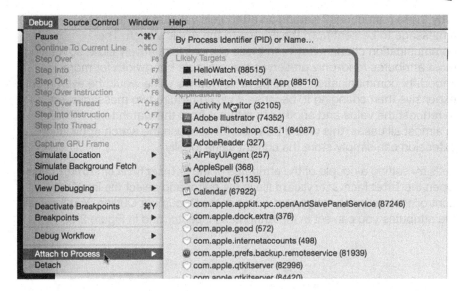

Figure 2-2. Debugging a WatchKit application and its iOS application at the same time

In the Xcode Debug Navigator (which you can open by pressing ⌘6), you should now see that both the WatchKit application and the iOS application are available for debugging.

The same technique works when running on real hardware—run the WatchKit application using Xcode in the usual way, start the iOS application by tapping its icon on the iPhone home screen, and attach to it using the **Attach To Process** menu item shown in Figure 2-2.

Interface Controller Attributes

Interface controllers have ten settable attributes. You'll find descriptions of these attributes on the documentation page for the WKInterfaceController class, which you can find from the **Documentation and API Reference** window in Xcode. The rest of this chapter discusses some of these attributes.

Most WatchKit attributes have the following things in common:

- They can only be set in the storyboard. That means they have fixed values at run time, because you can't change them programmatically.

- There is no way to read the current value of an attribute—you are assumed to know what the current value is. In the case of attributes that can be changed at run time, you are expected to keep track of the last value that you set.

Why these restrictions? Setting an attribute's value at run time requires a message to be sent from the iPhone to the Apple Watch. The communication channel between these devices is relatively slow, so making most attributes read-only preserves the available bandwidth for more important communication. Reading an attribute's value would be even more expensive than changing it, because it would require two messages—one to request the value and another to return it from the watch to the iPhone. In almost all cases, this would be wasteful because the watch application extension can simply store the current value locally.

Let's try setting a couple of the attributes of the WKInterfaceController class. Open the Interface.storyboard file in the editor and select the interface controller class in the storyboard editor or the Document Outline. You'll see all the attributes you can set in the Attributes Inspector and in Figure 2-3.

Figure 2-3. Interface Controller attributes

Setting the Background Color

The Color attribute sets the background color of the interface controller, which is, of course, the background color of your application. Initially, the background is black. Use the Color selector to change the background color to light gray. The color change is reflected in storyboard as soon as you set it (see Figure 2-4). Notice that the color of the status bar at the top of the watch screen does not change—it remains black. There is no way to change this. In fact, Apple recommends that you use black as the background color for your application if at all possible to avoid a large contrast between it and the black edges of the device.

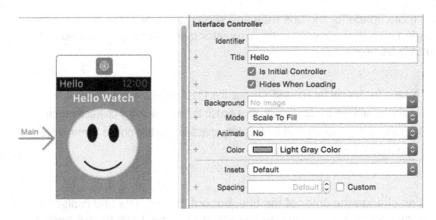

Figure 2-4. Changing the background color of an interface controller

You can also use an image to set the background, or a combination of an image and a color. If you set both, the image is drawn on top of the color that you specify, which means that the color will only be seen in places where the image has translucent pixels. You'll see how to use an image as the background in Chapter 3, where you'll also make use of the Mode and Animate attributes shown in Figure 2-4.

At the top of the Attributes Inspector you'll see a group containing two attributes called Identifier and Title. The Identifier attribute can be used to refer to an interface controller in code, which you'll need to do when pushing or presenting that controller, for example. We'll use this attribute in Chapter 5. You don't need to supply an identifier for the initial controller because you will never need to reference it in code. WatchKit identifies that this is the initial controller because the Is Initial Controller checkbox in Figure 2-4 is checked, and the Main arrow next to the controller in the storyboard is a more obvious visual cue for you.

Setting the Application Title

You used the Title attribute to set the application's title in Chapter 1. The title appears at the top left of the status bar. Because space in the status bar is at a premium, you should try to keep the title short so it doesn't get truncated. It's worth noting, though, that on a real device you would normally have more space for the title than you see on the simulator, because the charging icon that appears in the simulator (see Figure 1-14) would not normally be present.

> **Note** Try this out for yourself. Change the `Title` attribute in the Attributes Inspector and run the application on a watch to see how many characters you can use. Note, however, that there is less space for the title on the 38mm screen than there is on the 42mm one.

You can change the color of the title, but not its font. The title is also the only interface controller attribute you can set at run time. Let's try out both of these features.

There is no attribute that specifically sets the color of the title. Instead, there is an application-wide attribute called the *Global Tint* (which you may also see referred to as the application's *key color*). To set this attribute, select the storyboard in the Project Navigator and then open the File Inspector using **View ➤ Utilities ➤ Show File Inspector** from the menu bar or by pressing ⌥⌘1. There's a selector for the Global Tint attribute in the **Interface Builder Document** section. Use it to change the title color to yellow (see Figure 2-5).

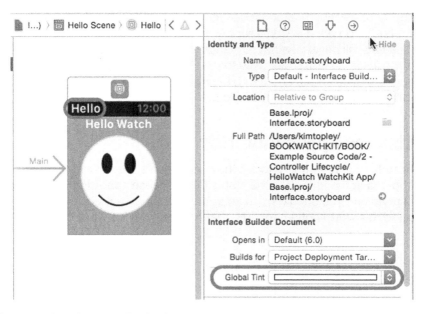

Figure 2-5. Changing the application title color

Now let's change the title in code. Select InterfaceController.swift in the Project Navigator and make the changes shown in bold to the init() method:

```
override init() {
    super.init()
    NSLog("InterfaceController init() called")

    setTitle("Hi!")
}
```

When the interface controller is initialized, the new title replaces the value set in the storyboard. Run the application now and you'll see the new title, as shown in Figure 2-6.

Figure 2-6. Setting the application title in code

In general, if an attribute value can be changed at run time, you can set its value whenever the controller is active, not just when it's being initialized. However, there are a couple of things to keep in mind:

- As noted earlier, changing an attribute value requires the iPhone to send a message containing the new value to the Apple Watch. This takes time and communication bandwidth, so you should take care to do this only when necessary. In particular, try to avoid setting the attribute to its current value. However, because you can't read the current values of attributes, you need to keep track of the last value you set, so it should be easy to detect whether the current and new values are the same.

- If you change the values of several attributes, WatchKit may combine the changes into a single message to minimize the overhead. However, you should not rely on this.

Interface Controller Layout

Layout in WatchKit is much simpler than it is in UIKit. Whereas UIKit allows you complete control over the size and position of any view, WatchKit only allows interface objects to be arranged in rows or columns. Also, even though you can specify the size of most user interface objects, you don't have fine-grained control over positioning.

Once you've designed the layout you want in the storyboard, WatchKit takes care of constructing the user interface at run time. The only real problem you're likely to encounter with layout is the need to support the two slightly different screen sizes shown in Figure 2-7.

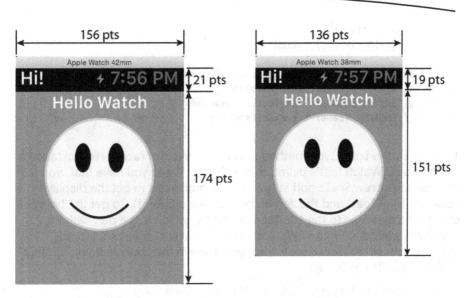

Figure 2-7. Dimensions of the 42mm and 38mm Apple Watch Screens

The overall screen size of the 42mm device is 156 pts by 195 pts, a little taller and wider than the 38mm device, which is 136 pts by 170 pts. The status bar of the 42mm device is also a couple of points taller than that of the smaller version.

> **Note** A UIKit application can choose to increase the available screen space by hiding the iPhone's status bar. A WatchKit application does not have this luxury—you can't hide or reduce the height of the status bar.

Notice that the dimensions in Figure 2-7 are all given in points (pts). Like all the most recent iPhones and iPads, the Apple Watch has a Retina screen, so you need to think in terms of (logical) points instead of hardware pixels. The display scale factor is 2, so a point maps to 2 pixels along each axis. Throughout this book, whenever we refer to sizes and coordinates, we use points, not pixels, unless explicitly stated to the contrary.

You can get the display scale factor and the screen dimensions at run time from the WKInterfaceDevice class. Let's try that out. In the Project Navigator, select InterfaceController.swift and add the following code shown in bold to the willActivate() method:

```
override func willActivate() {
    // This method is called when watch view controller
    // is about to be visible to user
```

```
    super.willActivate()
    NSLog("willActivate() called")

    let device = WKInterfaceDevice.currentDevice()
    NSLog("Scale: \(device.screenScale)")
    NSLog("Screen bounds: \(device.screenBounds)")
    NSLog("Content frame: \(contentFrame)")
}
```

The currentDevice() type method returns the WKInterfaceDevice instance for the Apple Watch that's paired to the iPhone. Once you have that, you can use the screenScale and screenBounds properties to get the display scale (as a CGFloat) and the screen bounds (as a CGRect). To get the bounds of the area available to the interface controller (which is the part with the gray background in Figure 2-7), you use the contentFrame property of WKInterfaceController. Here's what you'll see in the console if you run this code on the 42mm screen:

```
HelloWatch WatchKit Extension[93510:27376874] Scale: 2.0
HelloWatch WatchKit Extension[93510:27376874] Screen bounds:
(0.0,0.0,156.0,195.0)
HelloWatch WatchKit Extension[93510:27376874] Content frame:
(0.0,21.0,156.0,174.0)
```

On the 38mm device, the results look like this:

```
HelloWatch WatchKit Extension[7538:28690257] Scale: 2.0
HelloWatch WatchKit Extension[7538:28690257] Screen bounds:
(0.0,0.0,136.0,170.0)
HelloWatch WatchKit Extension[7538:28690257] Content frame:
(0.0,19.0,136.0,151.0)
```

You can see that the values match the dimensions shown in Figure 2-7.

Spacing, Insets, and Screen-Dependent Layout

Although the size differences between the 38mm and 42mm screens are relatively small, it's still important to take them into account when designing your application. This is well illustrated by the unused space at the bottom of the screenshot on the left in Figure 2-7. Clearly, we need to improve this example to make better use of the larger screen. In fact, there is scope to improve the layout for both devices. We'll start by improving the layout on the 38mm device and then fine-tune the result to get the best result for the 42mm screen.

While we're making these changes, it would be useful to see both layouts at the same time. We can do that by previewing the results in the Assistant Editor. Start by showing the Assistant Editor using **View ➤ Assistant Editor ➤ Show Assistant Editor** in the menu bar. Then in the jump bar at the top, select **Preview** followed by **Interface.storyboard (Preview)** (see Figure 2-8).

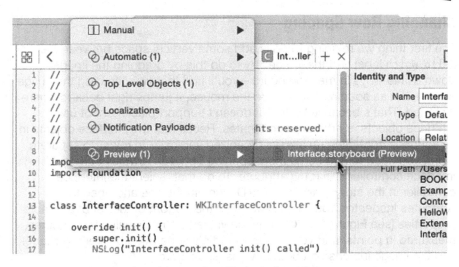

Figure 2-8. Opening a preview of the storyboard in the Assistant Editor

At this point, you'll see a preview of the 38mm screen in the Asssistant Editor, as shown on the left in Figure 2-9.

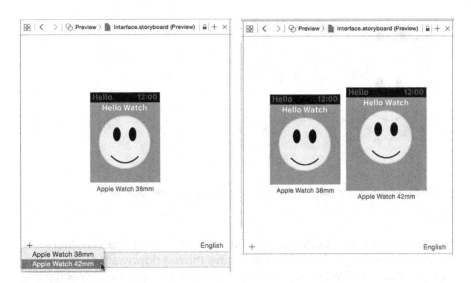

Figure 2-9. Previewing the 38mm screen and adding a preview of the 42mm device

To add the 42mm device, click the **+** icon at the bottom left of the preview area and select **Apple Watch 42mm**. You should now have previews of both screen sizes, side by side, as shown on the right in Figure 2-9.

Changing Row Spacing

The first thing we're going to do is add some vertical space between the Hello Watch label and the image. Try to do this by dragging the image down a little ways in the storyboard—you'll find that you can drag the image around, but as soon as you release the mouse, it jumps right back to where it started. That's because WatchKit doesn't support placement of user interface objects at arbitrary coordinates. Recall that the interface objects in an interface controller are always organized vertically, in rows. To separate them, you need to add some more spacing between rows by setting the interface controller's Spacing attribute. To do that, select the interface controller in the storyboard or in the Document Outline and open the Attributes Inspector. You'll find Spacing at the bottom of the list of available properties (see Figure 2-3). Change the value to 10 (this value is, of course, measured in points) and you'll see the vertical separation between the label and the image increase on both devices (see Figure 2-10).

Figure 2-10. *Increasing the space between rows of the interface controller layout*

The spacing is applied between each pair of rows, so if we had another label below the image, that label would have moved downward by the same distance relative to the image—you can't set different spacing for each pair of rows.

Setting the Interface Controller Insets

Notice that this change did not affect the distance between the top of the interface controller and the label. To change that, we need to adjust the value of the interface controller's Insets attribute, which determines how much space at the top, bottom, left, and right of the controller is not available for layout. Changing this attribute effectively creates an empty border around the edge of the interface controller, like the margins on the pages of a book.

We'd like to add 8 points of space above the label, which means we need to set the interface controller's top inset to 8, leaving the other values unchanged. In the Attributes Inspector, change the value in the Insets selector from Default to Custom and four input fields containing the current inset values appear. Change the value in the Top field to 8 (see the left of Figure 2-11), and you'll see that the label moves further away from the top of the screen, as shown on the right in Figure 2-11.

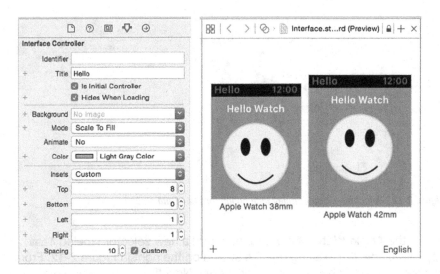

Figure 2-11. Setting the interface controller's top inset

Making an Attribute Value Depend on Screen Size

With these changes, the user interface looks more balanced on the 38mm screen, but there is still a problem on the 42mm device—there is too much empty space around the image. The most obvious ways to deal with this are to use a larger image when the application is running on the larger screen or to stretch the existing one to take up the additional space. Stretching an image reduces its quality, so it's better to create a larger version and use that when the application is running on the 42mm device. Together, Xcode and WatchKit make it very easy to do that.

In the Project Navigator, select Images.xcassets in the Hello WatchKit App group and then drag and drop the file SmileyFaceLarge@2x.png from the folder 2 - Controller Lifecycle Icon in the example source code archive onto the asset catalog editor. You should now have two smiley face icons in the asset catalog. Next, select the image object in the storyboard, open the Attributes Inspector, and click in the Image field. You'll see that there are now two images to choose from. We need to use SmileyFace when the application is running on the 38mm device, but SmileyFaceLarge for the 42mm screen. To do that, click on the small **+** sign to the left of the Image field to open a pop-up that lets you add screen size customizations for the Image attribute, as shown on the left in Figure 2-12.

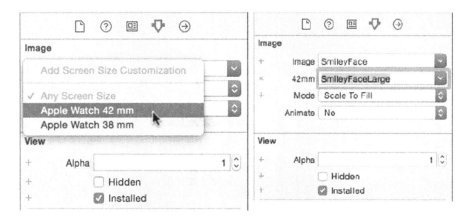

Figure 2-12. Selecting a larger smiley face image for the 42mm screen

Select the **Apple Watch 42 mm** option, and a new selector labeled 42mm appears below the existing one, as shown on the right in Figure 2-12. From this new selector, choose SmileyFaceLarge. Now the SmileyFaceLarge image will be used on the 42mm device, and the original SmileyFace image otherwise. Look back at the preview area and you'll see that the 42mm device is using the larger image, whereas the 38mm device still has the smaller one (see Figure 2-13). Run the application on the simulator with both screen sizes to verify that this really works.

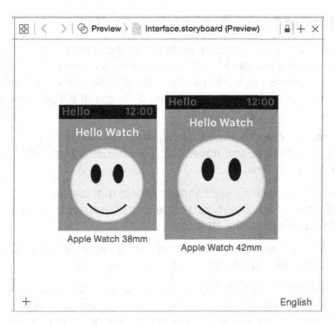

Figure 2-13. The HelloWatch application, customized for both screen sizes

You may have noticed that the selector that was added for the 42mm screen doesn't have a + icon—it has a cross icon instead, as you can see on the right in Figure 2-12. The X icon lets you delete the 42mm version of the selector, reverting the layout to just a single image for both screen sizes. This is a general pattern that applies everywhere in the Attributes Inspector for a WatchKit interface controller or user interface object: whenever you add an input field for a specific screen size, you get a delete control to allow you to remove it again.

All of the settable properties in the Attributes Inspector have a + icon, which means that you can set different values for any of them based on the screen size.

> **Note** There is another way to arrange for the 38mm and 42mm devices to use different images without having to configure them separately in the Attributes Inspector. You'll see how to do that when we discuss menus in Chapter 6. Either method works, and you can use whichever you prefer.

Making Layout Depend on the Screen Size

WatchKit layouts are almost completely static and can only be built in a storyboard—*there is no way to add or remove user interface objects at run time*. If you're used to the flexibility that UIKit gives you, this probably comes as something of a shock. There are a couple of things you can do to customize your layout:

- You can create separate designs for the 38mm and 42mm devices and have WatchKit choose the correct one at run time.

- You can make a user interface object that is already defined in the storyboard appear or disappear by setting its hidden or alpha attribute.

Let's see how to customize the layout based on the screen size; Chapter 4 talks more about using the hidden and alpha attributes.

The key to making the layout depend on the screen size is the control at the bottom of the storyboard editor that is currently labeled Any Screen Size. You can see this control at the bottom of the screenshot in Figure 1-6. If you click this control, a pop-up appears with the three choices shown in Figure 2-14.

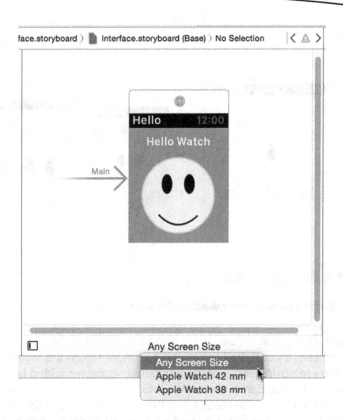

Figure 2-14. Selecting the screen size for the design in the storyboard

When Any Screen Size is selected, you see the parts of the design that are common to both screen sizes. It's recommended that you do most of your design in this mode and then make adjustments for a specific screen size by selecting either Apple Watch 38 mm or Apple Watch 42 mm. Let's see how this works by adding a separator between the label and the image, but only for the 42mm screen.

Start by selecting Apple Watch 42 mm and then find a separator object in the Object Library. Drag the separator onto the storyboard and drop it in the space between the label and the image, as shown in Figure 2-15.

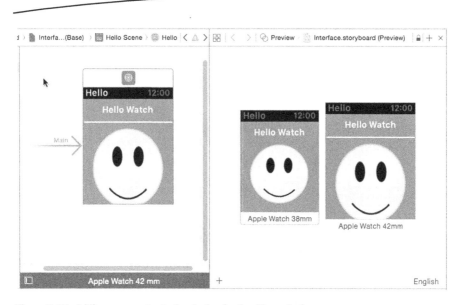

Figure 2-15. Adding a separator to the design for the 42mm device

The preview shows that the separator appears only for the 42mm device. You can also see, though, that the image no longer fits on the screen. We can fix that by removing some of the additional space we added between the rows of the layout. Earlier we set the interface controller's Spacing attribute to 10 points, which means that there is now a gap of this size both above and below the separator. To make the image fit on the screen again, we need to change the Spacing attribute value for the 42mm device to 5 points. To do that, select the interface controller in the storyboard and open the Attributes Inspector. Click the + icon next to the Spacing attribute and select Apple Watch 42 mm to create a second input field and then set its value to 5. Check the preview and you'll see that the image moves back up onto the screen. Notice also that the 38mm screen layout does not change (see Figure 2-16).

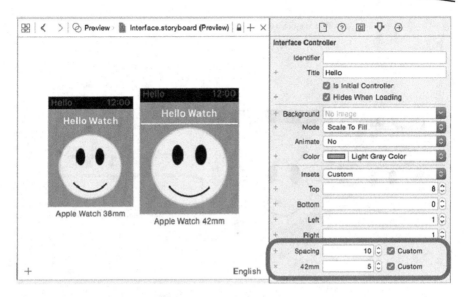

Figure 2-16. Adjusting row spacing for the 42mm device

This looks better, but it's not quite perfect—there's still too much space above the label at the top of the screen. We can reduce that by changing the value of the top inset. Make sure the interface controller is selected in the storyboard, click the + icon next to the Top attribute in the Attributes Inspector, and select Apple Watch 42 mm. This adds extra input fields for each of the four inset values. Change the value of the 42mm Top input field from 8 to 4 and you'll see that everything the 42mm layout in the preview moves up, as shown in Figure 2-17. Notice again that the 38mm layout was not affected.

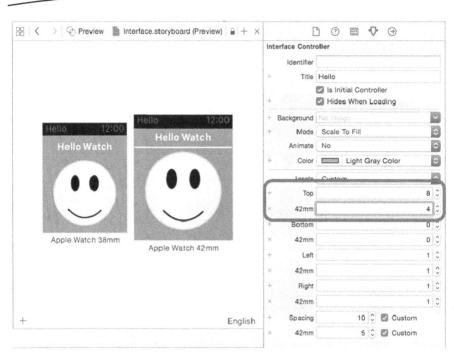

Figure 2-17. Adjusting insets for the 42mm device

Now set the screen size selector back to Any Screen Size.

> **Caution**   Remember to always set the screen size selector back to Any
> Screen Size when you have finished making adjustments. If you forget to
> do that, you'll find that any additional changes you make will only apply to the
> device that is selected.

The tools that Xcode provides for adapting your design so that it works well
for both screens sizes are both powerful and easy to use. It's worthwhile
spending some time experimenting to see what you can do with them.

Controlling Position

As you have seen, the interface controller has a very simple layout policy—it
arranges the objects that it contains in a single-column grid, with one row
per object. You have also seen that you can modify this behavior slightly by
using the interface controller's Insets and Spacing attributes. In this section,
you'll see how to get better control over the sizes of your interface objects
and their positions within their respective rows.

Let's start by creating a new project. Use the Single View Application project template and name the project Position And Size. Then add a WatchKit application to it, just as you did when creating the Hello Watch application in Chapter 1. Remember to deselect the option to include a notification scene, since we don't need one for this example.

> **Note** From this point onward, when creating a new project, unless otherwise specified, use the Single View Application template and uncheck the Notification scene check box—we won't need to handle notifications until Chapter 9.

Open the Position And Size WatchKit App group in the Project Navigator and select the file Interface.storyboard. Next, drag three labels from the Object Library onto the interface controller. Given what you have learned so far, it should not surprise you to find that the labels arrange themselves into three rows at the top of the interface controller. Now select each label in turn and use the Attributes Inspector to change their Text attributes to Label1, Label2, and Label3. Alternatively, double-click the labels in the storyboard and change the text in-place. At this point, your storyboard should look like Figure 2-18.

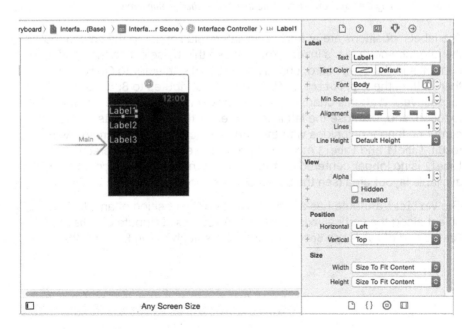

Figure 2-18. Preparing to experiment with layout

The positions of the labels are determined by their Horizontal and Vertical attributes, which you'll find in the Position group in the Attributes Inspector (see Figure 2-18). Initially, these attributes are set to Left and Top respectively, which is why the labels are grouped together at the top left of the layout. Use the Attributes Inspector to change the Horizontal attribute of Label2 to Center and of Label3 to Right. Changing this attribute causes the interface controller to move the affected labels to the center and right of their rows, as shown on the left in Figure 2-19.

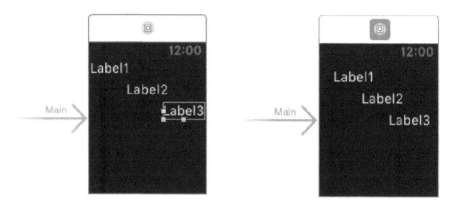

Figure 2-19. Using the Horizontal attribute to position labels within a row

The labels' positions are actually calculated relative not to the screen, but to the interface controller's insets. You can see this by selecting the interface controller in the storyboard, changing the Insets selector to Custom, and then setting the Top, Bottom, Left, and Right attributes to 8, 8, 16, and 8 respectively. With this change, the area in which the labels are positioned is reduced, and, because the left inset is greater than the right, its horizontal center no longer coincides with the horizontal center of the screen. As a result, Label1 and Label3 move away from the edges of the screen, and Label2 is no longer centered on the screen, although it is still centered in the available layout area (see the screenshot on the right in Figure 2-19).

The Vertical attribute has a similar effect on the position of an interface object along the vertical axis. Change the Vertical attribute of Label2 to Center and of Label3 to Bottom to get the result shown in Figure 2-20.

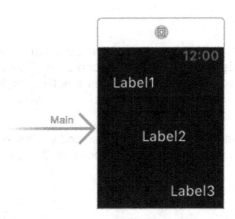

Figure 2-20. Using the Vertical attribute to position labels vertically

Drag another label onto the storyboard and drop it onto the interface controller. As noted earlier, whenever an interface object is created, its Vertical attribute defaults to Top. As a result, this label gets placed at the top of the layout, just below Label1, which has the same Vertical attribute value, as shown on the left in Figure 2-21.

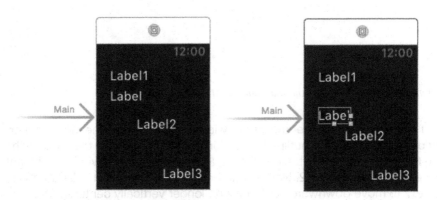

Figure 2-21. The Vertical attributes results in objects being positioned in groups

Now change the Vertical attribute of the new label to Center. As you can see on the right in Figure 2-21, it is repositioned just above Label2, and Label2 itself moves down a little way. What's happening here? As it turns out, interface objects that have the same Vertical attribute value are grouped together and then the group is positioned based on the attribute value. So in this case, the group consisting of the new label and Label2 is vertically centered. Finally, delete the new label from the layout by selecting it and pressing the Delete key, since we don't need it any more.

Adjusting Size

So much for position—what about size? The size of an object is determined by its Width and Height attributes. As you can see in Figure 2-18, these both default to Size To Fit Content, which does exactly what it says. There are two other possible values: Fixed and Relative to Container. Let's look at what these do.

Change the Width attribute of Label1 to Fixed and you'll see that an input field appears, initialized with the value 100, as shown on the left in Figure 2-22.

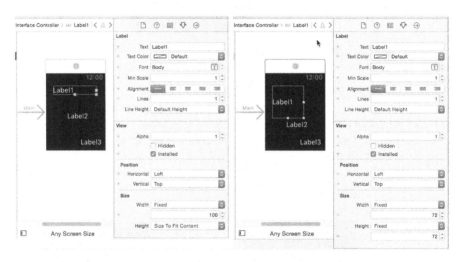

Figure 2-22. Manually setting the width and height of label

You can now manually set the label's width either by using the input field or by dragging the label's outline in the storyboard. You can do the same with the Height attribute. On the right of Figure 2-22, the label's width and height have both been set to 72. Notice that the increased height of Label1 causes Label2 to move downward so that it's no longer vertically centered. It is, however, as close to the vertical center as it can be.

The value Relative To Container lets you set the width or height of the object as a proportion of the available horizontal or vertical space in the interface controller. We'll illustrate this setting by sharing the interface controller's vertical space equally between the three labels. To do this, first select Label1 and change its Height attribute to Relative To Container. A new input field appears, into which you can enter a value between 0 and 1. Enter the value 0.333 to allocate a third of the available height to this label. Do the same with the other two labels and you should get the result shown in Figure 2-23.

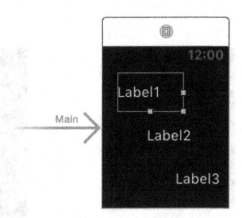

Figure 2-23. Using Relative To Container to allocate vertical space equally between the three labels

> **Note**   The available vertical space does not include the space required by the interface controller's insets Top and Bottom attributes, as you can see by selecting the interface controller and changing the value of these attributes.

Below the first input field there is another one labeled Adjustment. You can use this field to increase or decrease the allocated width or height by a specified number of points—use a positive value to increase it and a negative value to decrease it. Try this out by selecting Label3 and entering -16 in the Adjustment field and you'll see that the height of the label is reduced accordingly, as shown on the left in Figure 2-24. Now change the Adjustment value to 32 and the label's height will be increased by 32 points above its originally allocated value, as shown on the right in Figure 2-24.

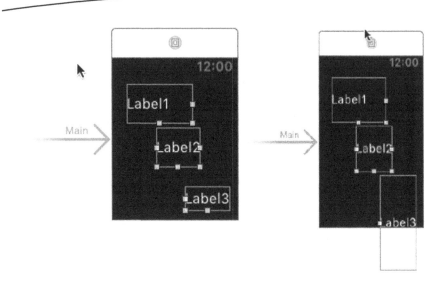

Figure 2-24. *The effect of the* Adjustment *field*

As you can see from its outline, Label3's height is now so large that it no longer fits on the screen. If you run this example in the simulator, you'll find that Label3 is clipped (see Figure 2-25), but if you click the mouse over the simulated screen and drag upwards, you can scroll to bring Label3 completely into view. This demonstrates that it is possible to produce a layout that is taller than the screen. On a real device, the user can scroll vertically either by swiping up and down with a finger or by turning the digital crown. Note, however, that Apple Watch does not support horizontal scrolling, so you should ensure that your layout fits within the width of the screen.

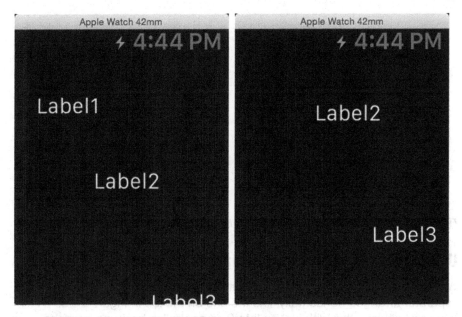

Figure 2-25. *The screen can be scrolled vertically to show all of* Label3

The width and height of a user interface object can be changed at run time. You'll see an example that does this in Chapter 3.

Groups

You now know almost everything there is to know about WatchKit layout. There's only one important thing left to discuss: groups. A *group* (represented by the WKInterfaceGroup class) is a user interface object that acts as a container for other user interface objects, much like the interface controller does. However, whereas an interface controller allows only vertical layout, a group lets you choose whether you want its nested objects to be laid out vertically or horizontally. A group is itself a user interface object, so you can nest a group inside another group.

In the rest of this chapter, you'll see how to use groups to create more interesting user interfaces than can be created with just an interface controller. In Chapter 3, you'll see some of the other features that groups share with interface controllers, including the ability to use an animated image for the background.

Start by creating a new project called Groups and add a WatchKit target to it. Figure 2-26 shows the simple application we are going to create to experiment with groups.

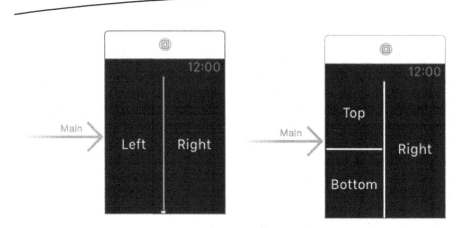

Figure 2-26. Using groups to create a layout with both rows and columns

Using a Group to Create a Horizontal Layout

We're going to start by creating a layout consisting of two labels and a separator arranged horizontally, like the one on the left in Figure 2-26. You can't achieve this with just an interface controller, because interface controllers do not support horizontal layout. Once we've done that, we'll replace the label on the left with a nested group containing two labels and a separator arranged vertically, as shown on the right in Figure 2-26. Layouts like this that combine horizontal and vertical layout are very common and always require the use of nested groups.

As always, start by selecting Interface.storyboard in the Project Navigator and open the Object Library. Locate a Group object in the library then drag and drop it onto the interface controller. By default, the group takes up a position at the top of the interface controller, as shown in Figure 2-27 (as an exercise, check the group's attributes in the Attributes Inspector to see why it is positioned and sized as it is). We need to make it occupy all of the available space on the screen.

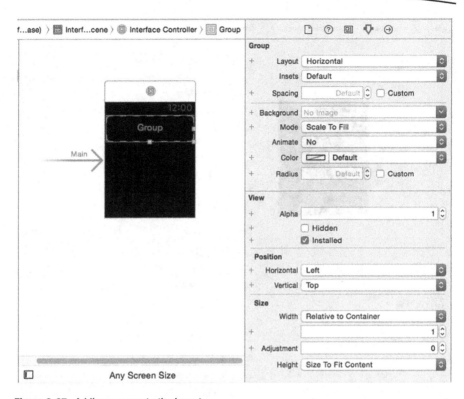

Figure 2-27. Adding a group to the layout

> **Note**   If you look carefully at the outline of the group in Figure 2-27, you'll see
> that it has rounded corners. You can make the corners more or less rounded
> by setting the `Radius` attribute, which you can see in Figure 2-27. By default,
> the corner radius is 6 points. All the corners have the same radius. Rounded
> corners can enhance the visual appeal of your layout, especially if you change
> the group's background color or use a background image (see Chapter 3), since
> these effects are both clipped by the corners.

To make the group fill all of the available space on the screen, change the
`Height` attribute from `Size To Fit Content` to `Relative to Container`. The
height value is automatically set to 1, and the group resizes to fill all of the
available space, as shown in Figure 2-28.

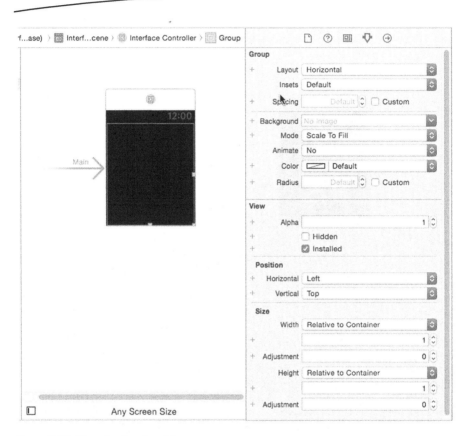

Figure 2-28. Changing the size of the group

The group has an attribute called Layout that determines whether it arranges nested objects horizontally or vertically. To achieve the layout shown on the left in Figure 2-26, we need a horizontal layout, so we need to set this attribute to Horizontal. It turns out that this is the default (as you can see in the Attributes Inspector in Figure 2-28), so we don't actually need to do anything.

Now let's add two labels and a separator to the group. Drag first a label, then a separator, and then another label and drop them on the group. You'll see that these objects are arranged horizontally (because the Layout attribute has the value Horizontal) and that they are initially aligned on the left of the group, as shown in Figure 2-29.

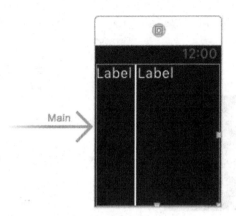

Figure 2-29. Adding two labels and a separator to the group

Note   Notice that in this example, the separator is drawn as a vertical line, whereas in our HelloWatch example it was horizontal (see Figure 2-15). You don't need to set an attribute to get this behavior—the separator figures out what it needs to do automatically.

We need to make a couple of adjustments to this layout—we need to move the separator to the center and then align the labels both horizontally and vertically in their respective areas. You do this by setting the Position and Size attributes of all three objects to appropriate values. Start with the following steps:

■ Select the label on the left and change its Text property to Left.

■ Change the label's Width attribute to Relative to Container and change the width value from 1 to 0.49. This allocates 49% of the available width to this label and resizes it to fill that space.

■ Change the label's Vertical position attribute from Top to Center. This moves the label down from the top of the group to the vertical center.

■ Finally, we need to move the text to the center of the label. To do that, find the segmented control for the Alignment property and click the third segment from the left.

At this point, your layout should look like Figure 2-30. If it doesn't, go back and correct it.

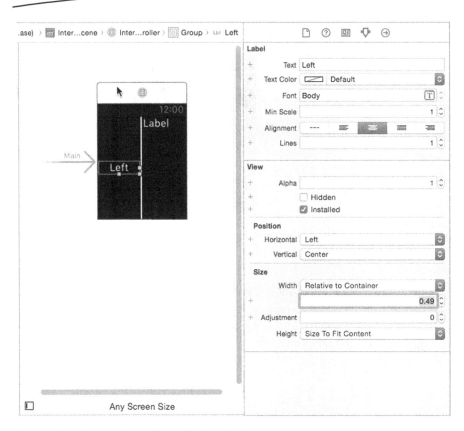

Figure 2-30. Adjusting the position of the first label

Next, we need to do the same thing for the label on the right. Select it and do the following:

- Change its `Text` property to `Right`.

- Change its `Width` attribute to `Relative to Container` and change the width value from 1 to 0.49. Notice that when you do this, the separator moves over to the center of the layout.

- Change its `Vertical` position attribute from `Top` to `Center`.

- Click the third segment from the left in the `Alignment` property to center the text in the label.

That's it—your layout should now look like the left screenshot in Figure 2-26. Run the application on the simulator to see that it looks correct on both the 38mm and 42mm devices.

You may be wondering where the magic 49% width value that we used to set the width of the labels came from. Why not 47% or 48%? It turns out that there is no scientific way to get the correct value. I got the 49% value by experimentation.

Notice that we didn't need to specify the separator's width—it automatically gets the 2% of the screen width that is left over. In fact, we can't specify the width of a vertical separator because it does not have a Width attribute—you can verify this by selecting the separator and checking the available attributes in the Attributes Inspector.

Using a Nested Group

Now we're going to change the layout a little to make it look like the screenshot on the right in Figure 2-26. The label on the left in our current layout needs to be replaced by a vertical layout containing another two labels and a separator. Whenever you see layout in two different directions like this, you can be sure that there is a nested group involved, because on their own, groups and interface controllers only support layout along one axis.

Start by deleting the left label from the layout. When you do this, the separator and the other label will jump over to the left. Next, we need to place a new group object on the left of the separator. It's quite difficult to do this by dragging the group over the interface controller, because the space into which you are trying to drop it is very small. Instead, it's easier to use the Document Outline (which is the hierarchical control to the left of the storyboard) to position the group. Start by making sure that the icon for the existing group in the Document Outline is expanded so you can see both the separator and the label. Next, grab a group object from the Object Library, drag it over the Document Outline, and drop it when the blue line that indicates its position is between the existing group and the separator, as shown on the left in Figure 2-31.

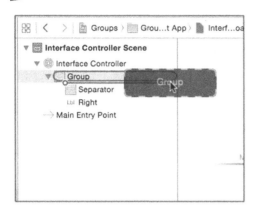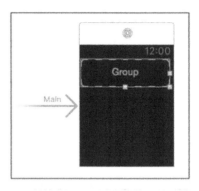

Figure 2-31. Positioning the second group to the left of the separator

Initially, as you can see on the right in Figure 2-31, the group takes up all the available width but does not fill all the vertical space. To fix this, make sure the group is selected in the storyboard and do the following in the Attributes Inspector:

▓ Change the value of the group's Width attribute from 1 to 0.49. This allocates to it the same width that was previously allocated to the label that was deleted. The separator and the second label should now reappear.

▓ Change the Height attribute to Relative to Container. Because the default height value is 1, the group expands to fill the left column of the layout.

Your layout should now look like Figure 2-32.

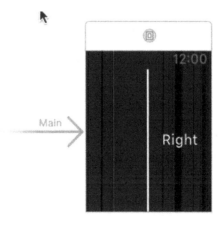

Figure 2-32. Although you can't see it, the left column is occupied by a nested group

As you saw earlier, the default value of a group's Layout attribute is
Horizontal. We need a vertical layout, so, with the group selected in the
storyboard, change the Layout attribute in the Attributes Inspector to
Vertical. Next, drag a label, a separator, and another label into the new
group. Then change the Text attributes of the top and bottom labels to
Top and Bottom respectively. At this point, your storyboard should look like
Figure 2-33.

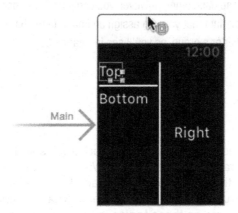

Figure 2-33. Adding the three objects for the left side of the layout

The remaining steps are very similar to the ones we used to create the first
part of the layout. You should find them very straightforward:

- Select the top label and change its Width attribute to
  Relative to Container. Do the same for the bottom
  label. This causes both labels to expand to fill all the
  horizontal space in the group.

- Use the Alignment field for both labels to center their
  text.

- Change the Height attributes of both the top and
  bottom labels to Relative to Container and set the
  height value to 0.49. The vertical space is now divided
  equally between the two labels, leaving space for the
  separator between them.

You have now completed the layout shown on the right in Figure 2-26. Feel free to change any of the attributes of the groups or the labels to see how the layout is affected. If you are feeling a little more adventurous, design a layout of your own that requires nested groups and see if you can reproduce it in the storyboard.

> **Tip** Interface controllers and groups do not allow you to position user objects so that they overlap each other. However, you can sometimes get a similar effect by using the fact that you can assign an image to the background of an interface controller or a group, as you'll see in Chapter 3.

Summary

This chapter focused entirely on interface controllers and layout. You have seen how user interaction with the Apple Watch causes your interface controllers to be activated or deactivated, and how the fact that your application's code runs in an extension affects what it is able to do. We concentrate much more on these topics in the chapters that follow. You also saw how layout is handled in WatchKit and how much simpler it is than its iOS equivalent.

Now that you know how to create a WatchKit application and how to position things on the screen, it's time to find out more about the relatively small selection of user interface objects that WatchKit offers. We cover the most basic of these in Chapter 3, followed by some more complex ones in Chapter 4. Finally, we discuss tables, which are almost as useful in WatchKit as they are in iOS, in Chapter 6.

Watch User Interface Objects

In Chapter 2, you learned how to add user interface objects to your storyboard and how to use features of the WKInterfaceController and WKInterfaceGroup classes to control the size and positioning of those objects. In this chapter, we discuss in some detail two user interface objects that you'll use very frequently—WKInterfaceLabel and WKInterfaceImage. Along the way, you'll find out more about how to control the layout of text, how to use the built-in fonts and custom fonts, and how to work with both static and animated images.

Overview

All of the WatchKit user interface objects are based on the WKInterfaceObject class, which declares a small number of common attributes. You have already seen some of the attributes that are used in layout, such as Width, Height, Horizontal, and Vertical. You'll find the documentation for all these attributes in the reference page for the WKInterfaceObject class on the Apple developer website or in the Xcode documentation set for WatchKit.

Most of the attributes of WKInterfaceObject can only be set in the storyboard. There are a few exceptions that can be modified at run time—specifically, there are six attributes that provide accessibility information and four attributes that let you change the size or visibility of the object, which we'll use in the course of this chapter and the next. For reasons discussed in Chapter 2, all of the attributes of WKInterfaceObject are write-only, so it is your responsibility to record the last value that you set if you need to make use of it later.

Table 3-1 lists the user interface objects that are available, together with the chapter that discusses them.

Table 3-1. WatchKit User Interface Objects

Class	Description	Reference
WKInterfaceButton	A push button that triggers an action when pressed.	Chapter 4
WKInterfaceDate	Displays the current date and/or time.	Chapter 4
WKInterfaceGroup	A container that positions user interface objects either horizontally or vertically.	Chapter 2
WKInterfaceImage	Displays a static or animated image.	Chapter 3
WKInterfaceLabel	Displays single- or multi-line text.	Chapter 3
WKInterfaceMap	A map showing a region around a given point.	Chapter 4
WKInterfaceSeparator	A straight line providing visual separation between regions of a layout	Chapter 2
WKInterfaceSlider	An input control that allows the user to choose a value from a bounded range.	Chapter 4
WKInterfaceSwitch	A control that has an on/off state allowing the user to make a choice from two alternatives.	Chapter 4
WKInterfaceTable	A single-column, multi-row table that allows dynamic content to be displayed.	Chapter 6
WKInterfaceTimer	Displays a timer that counts down or up.	Chapter 4

One important item that's missing from Table 3-1 is a text input control. That's because there is no user interface object that lets the user enter text—instead, there is a separate interface controller that you present whenever you need text input. The controller allows the user to select from a fixed set of suggestions, choose an emoji icon, or speak the required text. Chapter 5 covers text input.

The only way to add a user interface object to your application is to drag it from the Xcode Object Library to your storyboard. When (for example) you drag a Label object onto the storyboard, Xcode includes the object and its attribute values in the compiled version of the storyboard, and an instance of the WKInterfaceLabel class is created in the WatchKit extension at run time as part of the initialization of the user interface controller. The mapping from storyboard object to user interface object class is fixed, so you cannot substitute your own classes. This means you cannot subclass any of the `WKInterfaceObject` classes to modify their behavior or create completely new, custom user interface objects. You can check this for yourself by opening the `HelloWatch` project from Chapter 1, clicking the `Hello Watch` label, and opening the Identity Inspector. You'll see that the object class is `WKInterfaceLabel`, but the selector is read-only, so you can't replace it with your own subclass (see Figure 3-1).

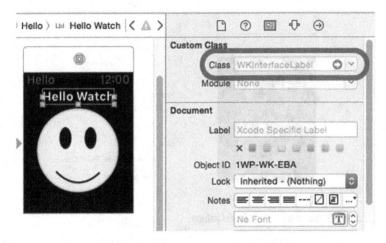

Figure 3-1. The class selector for an object in the storyboard is read-only

Labels

Labels are used to display text. You can set the label's text and text color attributes both in the storyboard and at run time, and there are several other attributes that can only be set in the storyboard.

Text Layout

We need a new project to work with, so create one, name it `Labels`, and add a Watch App target to it. Select the file `Interface.storyboard` in the WatchKit App group and then drag a label from the Object Library and drop it on the interface controller in the storyboard. Now open the Attributes Inspector and you'll see the attributes you can use to configure a label, as shown in Figure 3-2.

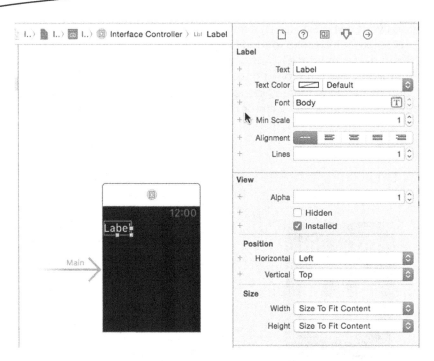

Figure 3-2. Label attributes with their initial values

The label is initially sized to exactly fit the text that it's displaying. That's because its Width and Height attributes are both set to Size To Fit Content, which is usually the setting you want. You can change the text by using the Text field in the Attributes Inspector or by double-clicking the label in the storyboard and typing directly into it (as you'll see later in this chapter, you can also change the text at run time). Change the text to something else, such as Hello World, and you'll see that the label grows so that the text fits exactly (if you are using the Text field in the Attributes Inspector, you'll need to press the Return key to install the new text). Now change the Width attribute to Relative to Container, and the label expands to fit the whole width of the interface controller.

When the text is narrower than the label, you can use the Alignment attribute to determine where it's placed relative to the label's bounds. By default, it's aligned to the leading edge of the label. You can use the Alignment segmented control to change the value of this attribute. The segments in the Alignment control, which is shown in Figure 3-3, map to leading alignment, left alignment, center alignment, justify, and right alignment respectively. In Figure 3-3, the text has been centered in the label.

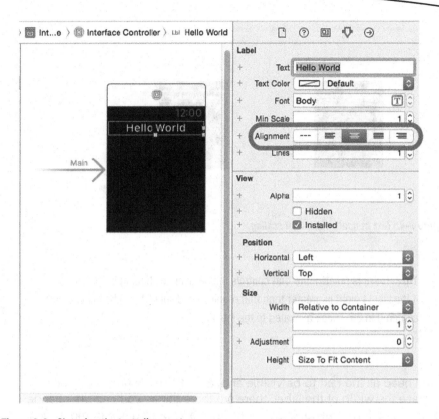

Figure 3-3. Changing the text alignment

Change the text to *This text is too wide to fit* and you'll see that when the text is wider than the available space, it is truncated and ellipses are added to indicate that this has happened, as shown on the left in Figure 3-4.

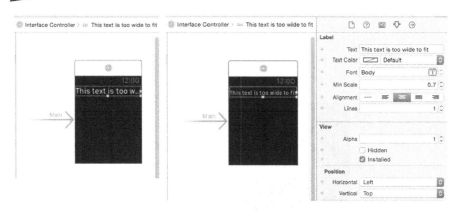

Figure 3-4. Text truncation and font scaling

> **Tip**   There is no attribute that controls the vertical positioning of the text.
> If the label height is greater than that required to display it, the text is vertically
> centered in the space allocated to the label.

If you need all the text to be visible and, as is the case here, you can't
increase the width of the label, there are three things you can do: change
the font, use font scaling, or allow the text to flow onto two or more lines.
Changing to a different font is discussed later in this chapter, so let's look at
the other two options.

Font scaling allows the label to automatically change the font size to reduce
the width of the text until it fits. You can set the minimum font scaling factor
using the Min Scale attribute in the Attributes Inspector. The default value is
1, which does not allow any reduction in font size. In this case, to make the
text fit on the 38mm device, you need to set the Min Scale attribute to 0.7,
as shown on the right in Figure 3-4.

> **Caution**   The WatchKit documentation says that setting a Min Scale value of 0
> is equivalent to using the value 0.8. At the time of writing, however, the value 0
> causes the text to scale down by as much as is necessary to make it fit, which
> may result in very small text!

If the text still doesn't fit after the font has been scaled to its minimum
permitted size, it is displayed at the smallest font size, with ellipses.

If your layout permits it, you can allow a label to grow vertically to accommodate its content. To do that, you need to change the value of the Lines attribute. By default, this attribute has value 1, allowing only a single line of text. Use a positive value to allow the label to grow to a fixed maximum number of lines, or 0 to allow as many lines as are required to fit all of the text. Change the value of the Lines attribute in the Attributes Inspector to 2, and the text overflows onto a second line, as shown on the left in Figure 3-5. Notice that the text alignment (in this case, center alignment) applies to each line of text.

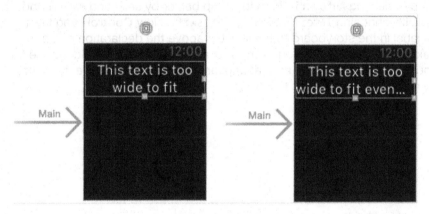

Figure 3-5. Allowing a label to flow onto more than one line

If you compare Figure 3-5 with Figure 3-4, you'll see that font scaling is no longer in effect. If you add enough additional text so that two lines are no longer enough, as shown on the right in Figure 3-5, you'll see that the text is truncated again and no font scaling takes place. Font scaling applies only to single-line labels. To make the text fit again, change the Lines attribute to 3. If you need to set the text at run time and you don't know how long it will be, consider changing this attribute to 0, allowing the label to use as many lines as it needs, subject to other layout constraints (for example, you might have fixed the label's height to 0.5 of the the interface controller's height). Whether or not this is practical depends on the details of your layout.

> **Tip**   You can enter text that contains embedded newlines in the Text attribute field by typing **Control-Return** for each newline. Of course, the text is displayed correctly only if the Lines attribute is set appropriately.

Text, Text Color, and Attributed Text

You can set the Text and Text Color attributes of a label either in the storyboard or at run time. Let's add some code to set both attributes programmatically. To set the attributes of a user interface object at run time, we need to create an outlet for it in the interface controller class. You do that in the same way as you would create an outlet for a UIKit object. Select Interface.storyboard in the Project Navigator so that the storyboard is open in the editor, then open the Assistant Editor (press ⌥⌘**Return**) and use its jump bar to open InterfaceController.swift. You can do this by selecting Automatic from the jump bar, or by selecting Manual and explicitly choosing InterfaceController.swift. Now **Control**-drag from the label in the storyboard to the line just above the declaration of the awakeWithContext() method in InterfaceController.swift and release the mouse button. In the pop-up that appears (see Figure 3-6), give the outlet the name label and press **Connect**.

Figure 3-6. Creating an outlet for the label

You should now have an outlet for the label in your class file:

```
import WatchKit
import Foundation

class InterfaceController: WKInterfaceController {
    @IBOutlet weak var label: WKInterfaceLabel!
```

We're going to add some code to this class that displays the current time in yellow text whenever the view controller is activated. To do that, we'll need an NSDateFormatter object. Add the code shown in bold to InterfaceController.swift:

```
class InterfaceController: WKInterfaceController {
    @IBOutlet weak var label: WKInterfaceLabel!
    private var formatter: NSDateFormatter

    override init() {
        formatter = NSDateFormatter()
        formatter.dateStyle = .NoStyle
        formatter.timeStyle = .ShortStyle
        super.init()
    }
```

You can use an NSDateFormatter instance more than once, so we create it in the init() method and assign it to an instance variable. The date formatter is initialized to give us a short form of the time, with no date. Now whenever the interface controller is activated, we can use it to format the time. Add the code in bold to the willActivate() method:

```
override func willActivate() {
    // This method is called when watch view
    // controller is about to be visible to user
    super.willActivate()

    let timeString = formatter.stringFromDate(NSDate())
    label.setText(timeString)
    label.setTextColor(UIColor.yellowColor())
}
```

Notice that we used methods called setText() and setTextColor() to set the label's attributes. That's because the attributes are not properties of the WKInterfaceLabel class, so we can't use the label.textColor form that you are probably familiar with from your experience with UIKit. The same is true of all WatchKit attributes.

Now if you run the WatchKit application, you'll see the current time appear in yellow, as shown in Figure 3-7. If you lock the simulator's screen, leave it locked for a minute, and then unlock it, you'll see the time update. That's because we are updating the label in the willActivate() method.

Figure 3-7. Setting a label's text and text color at run time

In reality, you should consider saving the last value that you wrote to both the Text and Text Color attributes and update them only if the new value is different. That's too complicated for this simple example, but in a more complex application, you should seriously consider whether doing so would improve the perceived performance of your application.

> **Caution** You can only update attributes of a user interface controller or a user interface from the time when the willActivate() method is called to the time when the controller is deactivated and didDeactivate() is called. Any changes made to attributes at other times (including in didDeactivate()) have no effect. It is easy to make this mistake, especially when using hierarchical or presented controllers (both of which are discussed in Chapter 5).

When you call setTextColor(), the color is applied to all of the label's text. If you need to change the color of part of the text, create an NSMutableAttributedString and use the NSForegroundColorAttributeName attribute to set the color for the required range or ranges. The rest of the text will use the default color. You need to use the setAttributedText() method instead of setText() when using an attributed string. To see this in action, make the changes shown in bold to the willActivate() method:

```
override func willActivate() {
    // This method is called when watch view
    // controller is about to be visible to user
    super.willActivate()

    let timeString = formatter.stringFromDate(NSDate())
    label.setText(timeString)
    label.setTextColor(UIColor.yellowColor())

    let plainText: NSString = "Red text, Green text"
    let text = NSMutableAttributedString(string: plainText as String)

    let redRange = plainText.rangeOfString("Red")
    let greenRange = plainText.rangeOfString("Green")
    text.addAttribute(NSForegroundColorAttributeName,
                    value: UIColor.redColor(), range: redRange)
    text.addAttribute(NSForegroundColorAttributeName,
                    value: UIColor.greenColor(), range: greenRange)
    label.setAttributedText(text)
}
```

This code creates an NSMutableAttributedString initialized with the plain text Red text, Green text, then gets NSRange objects that correspond to the substrings Red and Green, and sets the foreground color for these ranges to red and green respectively. If you run this example, you should get the result shown Figure 3-8—except, of course, that you can't see the actual colors used if you are reading the printed version of this book.

Figure 3-8. Using the WKInterfaceLabel setAttributedText() method

The setAttributedText() method doesn't limit you to just changing text color—you can use it to adjust fonts (as you'll see later in this chapter) and to apply most of the other attributes that you can use with UIKit text views. If you're not familiar with attributed strings, read the *Attributed String Programming Guide* and the reference pages for NSAttributedString, NSMutableAttributedString, and the NSAttributedString UIKit Additions Reference, all of which can be found from the Xcode Documentation and API Reference window.

> **Caution** If you call both setText() and setAttributedText(), whichever method is called second wins. Similarly, if you call setTextColor() before calling setAttributedText(), the color set with setTextColor() applies only to those characters that do not have their foreground set in the attributed string, whereas if you call setAttributedText() and then setTextColor(), the colors in the attributed string are overwritten.

Fonts

You can change the font of a label (and all the other user interface components that display text) by setting the Font property in the Attributes Inspector. The preferred approach is to use one of the standard text style fonts in the Text Styles section of the pop-up for the Font attribute, shown on the left in Figure 3-9.

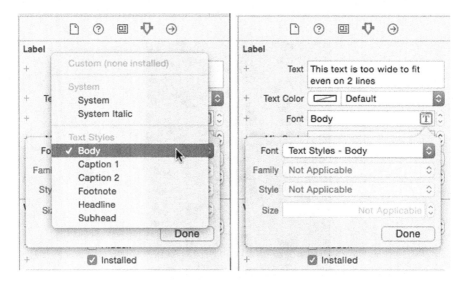

Figure 3-9. Choosing a font in the Attributes Inspector

Using the Standard Text Styles

You can open the list of standard text styles by clicking on the T button in the Font input field and then clicking in the font selector. As you can see in Figure 3-9, there are six text styles to choose from. You should use the style that best represents the role that the text plays in your user interface. Generally, text should be Body style, unless it clearly falls into one of the other categories. If you are familiar with Dynamic Text in iOS, you'll already have realized that these styles are the same ones that are available to iOS applications that support Dynamic Text. If you select a text style, you'll see that the Family, Style, and Size fields in the font pop-up (shown on the right in Figure 3-9) are all disabled. That's because a text style corresponds to a fixed combination of all of these attributes, so there is no need to specify them explicitly. These fields are, however, used when working directly with system or customs fonts, as you'll see shortly.

> **Note**   The Dynamic Text feature in iOS allows users to have some control over the size of the fonts used by applications that use it. Instead of specifying fixed font names and sizes, a conforming application uses a font style such as Headline, Body, and so on. At run time, iOS uses the font style together with the user's preferences to choose an actual font and text size. It's good practice to use this feature whenever possible, and it is the default for WatchKit applications.

We need a new project to experiment with fonts, so go ahead and create one using the Single View Application template, name it Fonts, and add a WatchKit application target to it. Open the WatchKit App storyboard in the editor, drag six labels from the Object Library, and drop them onto the user interface controller. Change the Width attribute of each label to Relative to Container and the Alignment attribute to Center.

> **Tip**   There's an easy way to set an attribute of several user interface components to the same value. Select all the labels by holding down the **Shift** key while clicking each of them in turn and then set the attribute values in the Attribute Inspector. The same value will be set for all of the labels.

When you've done this, you should have six labels that stretch across the entire width of the screen and with centered text, as shown on the left in Figure 3-10.

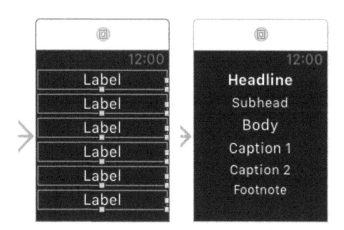

Figure 3-10. *Using the built-in text styles*

Now change the text of the top label to Headline and apply the Headline text style to it. Repeat for all the other labels, but instead of Headline, use Subhead, Body, Caption 1, Caption 2, and Footnote for both the text and the text style. You should now be able to see all the standard text styles together (see the screenshot on the right in Figure 3-10).

Using the System and System Italic Fonts

If you need more flexibility than the six fixed standard text styles, you can use the System and System Italic fonts instead. When you choose either of the system fonts, you're actually using the same font as the one used by the standard text styles, but you are allowed to modify the Style and Size attributes. Select the Headline label in the storyboard, open the pop-up for the Font attribute, choose System from the System section, and then open the Style selector, shown in Figure 3-11.

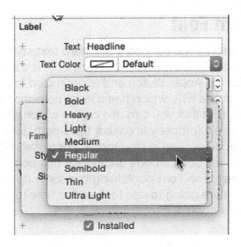

Figure 3-11. The style values for the system fonts

You'll see that there are nine choices, each of which corresponds to a different font weight, ranging from Black (the most heavyweight) to Ultra Light. Experiment with each of these to see how they affect the appearance of the text. The top three labels in Figure 3-12 have the Black, Medium, and Thin styles.

Figure 3-12. Applying different styles and sizes

If you need italic text, choose System Italic instead of System. The bottom three labels in Figure 3-12 all use a System Italic font, and I've also used the Size attribute to change the size of the text. Experiment with different font styles and sizes to see what's available.

Using a Custom Font

The font that's used when you choose a standard text style or specify the System or System Bold font is called San Francisco. It was developed by Apple specifically for the Apple Watch and is optimized for readability on very small devices. Unlike iOS, which has a large collection of fonts, San Francisco is the only font that you can use on the watch, unless you create one of your own or use a (properly licensed) third-party font. One place to get fonts that you can freely use is the Google Fonts web site at google.com/fonts. In the source code archive for this book, you'll find a folder called 3 - Tangerine Font containing two fonts downloaded from Google Fonts that we are going to use to illustrate how to include custom fonts in your WatchKit application.

> **Note**   Custom fonts cannot not be used in Glances (see Chapter 8) or Notifications (Chapter 9).

To import custom fonts, you first need to add them to the Fonts WatchKit App group and target in Xcode. To do this, select both fonts in the 3 - Tangerine Font folder in the Finder, then drag and drop them into the Fonts WatchKit App group in Xcode. In the pop-up that appears when you drop the fonts, select Copy items if needed and check Fonts WatchKit App in the Add to Targets list, as shown in Figure 3-13.

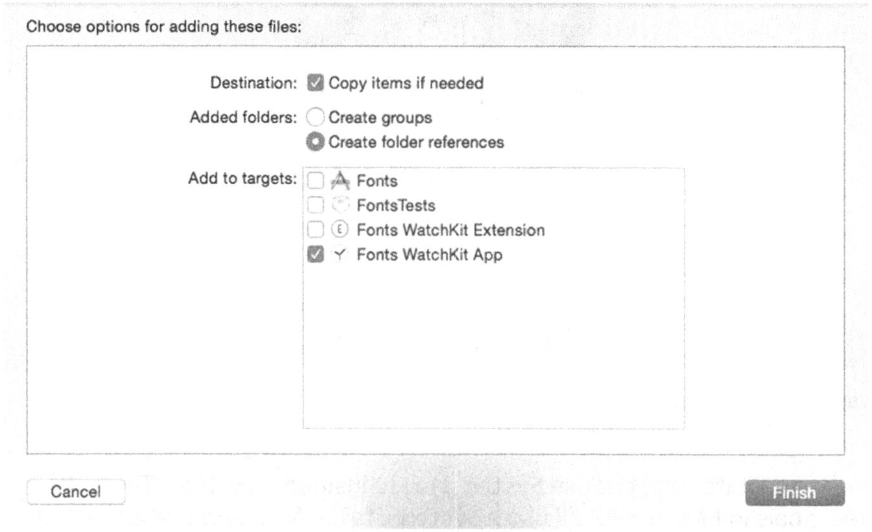

Figure 3-13. Adding custom fonts to a WatchKit application

Next, the fonts need to be added to the Info.plist file, which you'll find in the Font WatchKit App's Supporting Files folder. Select it so that it opens in the editor.

> **Caution** Be sure to select the correct Info.plist file. There are three files called Info.plist in your Xcode project—make sure you select the one in the Font WatchKit App.

Hover your mouse over the left column of the last row of the table in the editor, and two buttons labeled + and – appear. Press the + button to add a new row, and a pop-up opens to allow you to select a key. Choose Fonts provided by application (see Figure 3-14).

Figure 3-14. Adding custom fonts to the Info.plist file

The value of this key needs to be an array of strings, where each string is the name of a custom font file. Click the exposure triangle on the newly added row and you'll see that it already has one array entry called Item 0. Double-click the value column for the Item 0 row and enter the file name Tangerine_Bold.ttf. To add a second row, hover the mouse over Item 0 and click the + button that appears. The new row is given the key Item 1. Change its value to Tangerine_Regular.ttf. Your Info.plist file should now look like Figure 3-15.

Figure 3-15. Custom fonts added to the `Info.plist` *file*

The two custom fonts are now available for use in the storyboard. Select
`Interface.storyboard` in the Project Navigator and then select the top label
in the interface controller. Then in the Attributes Inspector, click the T in the
`Font` attribute field to open the font chooser pop-up again. Click in the `Font`
selector to open the next pop-up and choose `Custom`, as shown on the left
in Figure 3-16. The font chooser pop-up is now populated with the two
custom fonts you just added. The `Family` field should be pre-populated with
`Tangerine`, and the Style field should contain `Bold`. If you click in the `Style`
field, you'll see that the regular variant of the font is also available. Leave
`Bold` selected and change the `Size` field to 20, as shown on the right in
Figure 3-16. Click **Done** to close the pop-up. Use the Text attribute field to
change the label's text from `Black` to `Tangerine Bold`.

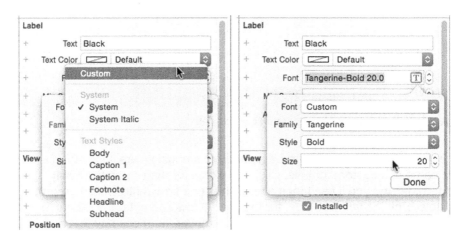

Figure 3-16. Selecting the Tangerine Bold font

Now select the second label in the interface controller and use the same
steps to change its font to Tangerine Regular and its title from `Medium` to
`Tangerine Regular`. When you've done this, the new text and fonts should
appear in the storyboard editor. When you run the application on the
simulator, you should get the result shown in Figure 3-17.

Figure 3-17. Custom fonts in the simulator

Setting Fonts in Code

A font that you set in the storyboard applies to all of the label's text. If you want to use a different font for parts of the text, you need to create an attributed string and apply the `NSFontAttributeName` attribute to those parts of the text for which the font should be changed. The value of the attribute is a `UIFont` object for the font to be applied. Any regions of the text for which the `NSFontAttributeName` attribute is not set continue to use the font set in the storyboard.

Before we can start experimenting with setting fonts programmatically, we need to create outlets for some of the labels in the storyboard. Select `Interface.storyboard` in the Project Navigator and then open `InterfaceController.swift` in the Assistant Editor, just as you did in "Text, Text Color, and Attributed Text" earlier in this chapter. Control-drag from the top label (with text `Tangerine Bold`) to the top of the class definition and create an outlet called `label1`. Repeat with the three labels below it to create outlets called `label2`, `label3`, and `label4`. You should now have the outlets, shown in bold in the following code, at the top of the class definition:

```
class InterfaceController: WKInterfaceController {
    @IBOutlet weak var label1: WKInterfaceLabel!
    @IBOutlet weak var label2: WKInterfaceLabel!
    @IBOutlet weak var label3: WKInterfaceLabel!
    @IBOutlet weak var label4: WKInterfaceLabel!
```

To get a font that represents one of the standard text styles, use the `UIFont.preferredFontForTextStyle()` method, passing the required text style as the argument. You can find a list of constants that represent the available text styles (which are the same as the ones that you can select for the Font field in the Attributes Inspector and which are shown in Figure 3-10) in the Text Styles section of the documentation page for the `UIFontDescriptor` class at `developer.apple.com/library/ios/documentation/UIKit/Reference/UIFontDescriptor_Class/index.html`.

Add the following code in bold to the `awakeWithContext()` method in `InterfaceController.swift` to apply the `Headline` and `Footnote` styles to parts of the text in the topmost label:

```
override func awakeWithContext(context: AnyObject?) {
    super.awakeWithContext(context)

    // Configure interface objects here.
    let headlineFont = UIFont.preferredFontForTextStyle(
                            UIFontTextStyleHeadline)
    let footnoteFont = UIFont.preferredFontForTextStyle(
                            UIFontTextStyleFootnote)
    let text1 = NSMutableAttributedString(string: "Tangerine Bold")
    text1.addAttribute(NSFontAttributeName,
                    value: headlineFont, range: NSMakeRange(0, 3))
    text1.addAttribute(NSFontAttributeName,
                    value: footnoteFont, range: NSMakeRange(3, 3))
    label1.setAttributedText(text1)
}
```

You can see the result of running this code in Figure 3-18. The first three characters of the label are in the `Headline` text style, and the next three are in the `Footer` style. The rest of the text uses the font set in the storyboard.

Figure 3-18. Adding standard text styles programmatically

You can get a variant of the system font with a given size and weight by using the `UIFont.systemFontOfSize()` and `UIFont.systemFontOfSize(_:weight:)` methods. The first method returns a font that has regular weight, whereas the second returns a font with the weight specified using one of the Font Weight constants defined in the documentation of the `UIFontDescriptor` class. To see how these methods work, add the following code shown in bold to the `awakeWithContext()` method:

```
    label1.setAttributedText(text1)

    let regularFont = UIFont.systemFontOfSize(24)
    let heavyFont = UIFont.systemFontOfSize(24, weight: UIFontWeightHeavy)
    let text2 = NSMutableAttributedString(string: "Tangerine Regular")
    text2.addAttribute(NSFontAttributeName,
                        value: regularFont, range: NSMakeRange(0, 3))
    text2.addAttribute(NSFontAttributeName,
                        value: heavyFont, range: NSMakeRange(3, 3))
    label2.setAttributedText(text2)
}
```

This code gets a 24-point system font of regular weight and applies it to the first three characters of the second label and then uses a heavy variant of the same font for the next three characters, as shown in Figure 3-19.

Figure 3-19. Setting system fonts with different weights in code

How about custom fonts? You can use a custom font in an attributed string provided that you first add it to the Fonts WatchKit Extension target and to the Fonts WatchKit Extension's Info.plist file, as well as to the Fonts WatchKit App target and Info.plist file. Because we've already added the Tangerine fonts to the Fonts WatchKit App target, adding them to the Fonts WatchKit Extension target is a simple matter of checking a couple of boxes. In the Project Navigator, select both Tangerine_Bold.ttf and Tangerine_Regular.ttf and then open the File Inspector (⌥⌘1) and check Fonts WatchKit Extension in the Target Membership section, as shown in Figure 3-20.

Target Membership
☐ ⒶＦonts
☐ ▢ FontsTests
☑ Ⓔ Fonts WatchKit Extension
☑ Ⓨ Fonts WatchKit App

Figure 3-20. Adding custom fonts to the extension's target

Adding the fonts to the Fonts WatchKit Extension's Info.plist file is also straightforward—you can either follow the same steps that we used earlier or you can do the following:

- Open the Info.plist file in the Fonts WatchKit App group.

- Select the row containing the Fonts provided by application key.

- Copy it (⌘C) to the clipboard.

- Open the Info.plist file in the Fonts WatchKit Extension group.

- Paste the Fonts provided by application key and its associated values from the clipboard (⌘V).

> **Note**   Custom fonts always need to be included in the WatchKit App target and its Info.plist file. This allows you to refer to them in the storyboard and results in them being installed on the watch with your application. If you need to refer to them in code, you must also add them to the WatchKit Extension target and its Info.plist file.

To get a UIFont object for a custom font, use the initializer that requires a font name and a size. Add the following code in bold to the awakeWithContext() method to set the font of the third label to Tangerine Bold with size 20 points:

```
label2.setAttributedText(text2)

let text3 = NSMutableAttributedString(string: "Tangerine Bold (Code)")
if let tangerineBoldFont = UIFont(name: "Tangerine-Bold", size: 20) {
    text3.addAttribute(NSFontAttributeName,
                value: tangerineBoldFont, range: NSMakeRange(0, 21))
}
label3.setAttributedText(text3)
}
```

Take note of the line of code that was used to create the UIFont instance:

```
if let tangerineBoldFont = UIFont(name: "Tangerine-Bold", size: 20) {
```

The init(_:size:) initializer is failable because a font with the given name may not exist. To protect against the possibility that the font is not found, the code that uses it is bracketed in an if let statement.

The value of the name argument is the font's *PostScript name*, which is not necessarily the same as its file name. The easiest way to get the PostScript name of a font is to use the OS X FontBook application. Here are the steps:

- Start the FontBook application, located in the Applications folder of your Mac.

- In the left column, select User (see Figure 3-21).

- In the menu, select File ➤ Add Fonts... or press ⌘O.

- Navigate to and select the files Tangerine_Bold.ttf and Tangerine_Regular.ttf and click **Open**.

- The Tangerine font family should now appear in the FontBook window. Select it and click the exposure triangle, then click on Bold.

The details of the Tangerine Bold font appear in the right-hand section of the FontBook window (see Figure 3-21). The font's PostScript name appears at the top—in this case, it is Tangerine-Bold.

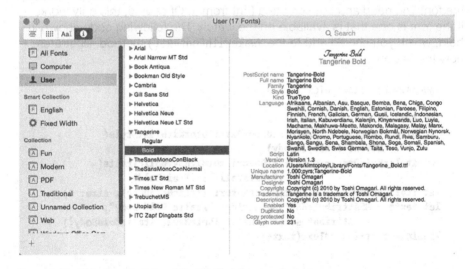

Figure 3-21. Using FontBook to get the PostScript name of a font

If you run the example now, you'll see that the third label is using the Tangerine Bold font, as shown in Figure 3-22.

Figure 3-22. *Using the Tangerine Bold font in code*

You can use the UIFont methods boldSystemFontOfSize() and
italicSystemFontOfSize() to get bold and italic variants of the system font
with a given size. What if you want a variant that's both bold and italic? How
could you get a bold and italic variant of a font that represents a text style,
such as Body? There are no methods that directly return either of those
fonts, but there is a way to get them: create a font descriptor that describes
the font you need and then create a font from it. Of course, this only works
if the font is one that is available on the watch. The following code shown in
bold, which you should add to the awakeWithContext() method, illustrates
how this is done:

```
    label3.setAttributedText(text3)

    let desc =
        UIFontDescriptor.preferredFontDescriptorWithTextStyle(
            UIFontTextStyleBody)
    let italicBoldDesc = desc.fontDescriptorWithSymbolicTraits(
                            .TraitItalic | .TraitBold)
    let italicBoldBody = UIFont(descriptor: italicBoldDesc!, size: 0)
    let text4 = NSAttributedString(string: "Italic Bold Body",
                    attributes: [NSFontAttributeName: italicBoldBody])
    label4.setAttributedText(text4)
}
```

The preferredFontDescriptorWithTextStyle() method of the
UIFontDescriptor class returns a font descriptor for the font that maps to a
given text style—in this case, Body. We need a bold and italic variant of this
font. Bold and italic are both examples of symbolic traits that can be added
to a font descriptor; you can find the full list of possible traits in the Symbolic
Font Traits section of the documentation page for UIFontDescriptor.
The fontDescriptorWithSymbolicTraits() method creates and returns
a new font descriptor that has the specified traits added to those in the
source descriptor. Traits are represented by integer raw values of the

UIFontDescriptorSymbolicTraits enumeration that can be OR'ed together to form a bitmask of all the required traits. Here, we pass the argument .TraitItalic|.TraitBold to request both the italic and bold traits. To get a font from the resulting font descriptor, we use a UIFont initializer that accepts the font descriptor and the required font size:

```
let italicBoldBody = UIFont(descriptor: italicBoldDesc!, size: 0)
```

A size value of 0 means that the font should have the size specified by the font descriptor, which in this case means the size of the Body text style font. Having obtained the font, we apply it to an attributed string, which we use to set the text of the fourth label. Run the example and you'll see that the label has the correct font (see Figure 3-23).

Figure 3-23. Using a UIFontDescriptor to derive one font from another

Here, we started with a font descriptor for a particular font. If instead you already have a font that you want to use as a starting point, you can get its font descriptor and then derive a new font from that, like this:

```
let bodyFont = UIFont.preferredFontForTextStyle(
                UIFontTextStyleBody) // Get Body font
let desc = bodyFont.fontDescriptor()  // Get Body font descriptor
let italicBoldDesc = desc.fontDescriptorWithSymbolicTraits(
                .TraitItalic | .TraitBold)
```

Images

They say a picture is worth a thousand words, and that's certainly true when you need to fit those words onto the small screen of an Apple Watch. You're likely to need to use images frequently, often in places where you might use words in an iOS application, simply because there's not enough room for a lot of text. WatchKit has an interface object that displays an image, and you can also use an image as the background of an interface controller or a group. Images are also the only way to create animations on the watch, since there is no equivalent of the Core Animation framework in iOS.

Using an Image as a Background

Let's first look at using an image as a background for an interface controller. Create a new project called ControllerImage and add a WatchKit application target to it. In the Project Navigator, select Images.xcassets in the ControllerImage WatchKit App group and drag the image SmallSun@2x.png from the folder 3 - Images in the example source code archive into the assets catalog. The image file contains a 128 × 128-pixel graphic of the Sun. Because the Apple Watch has a Retina display, the image file name has the usual @2x suffix, and WatchKit treats it as a 64-point square. If you created an image of this size and omitted the @2x suffix, WatchKit would assume that the image is intended to be 128 × 128 points, which is probably not what you intended.

We added the image to the WatchKit application's assets catalog because we're going to reference it from the storyboard. Images in this asset catalog can be used in the storyboard and are installed on the watch along with the application. You can't reference images that are part of the WatchKit App extension or the iOS application from the storyboard, although it is possible to access those images at run time, as you'll see in the section "Sending Images to the Apple Watch" later in this chapter.

In the Project Navigator, select Interface.storyboard. Select the interface controller in the storyboard editor and open the Attributes Inspector (⌥⌘4). In the Interface Controller section, you'll see four fields that you can use to configure the controller's background, as shown in Figure 3-24. We'll discuss three of these attributes here and cover the Animate attribute in the section "Animating Images" later in this chapter.

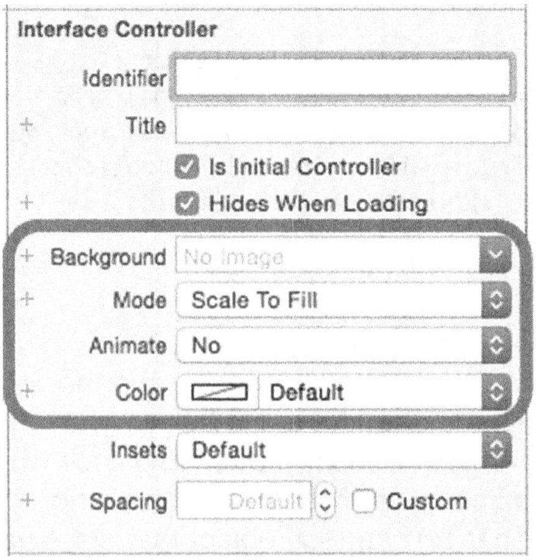

Figure 3-24. Configuring the background of an interface controller

Xcode adds references to all the images in the WatchKit App's assets catalog to the Background selector. Click to open it and choose SmallSun, which is the only entry. Next, use the Color selector to change the controller's background color to blue. The image appears as the controller's background in the storyboard, drawn over the blue color specified in the Color selector, as shown in Figure 3-25.

Figure 3-25. Using an image as the interface controller's background

You'll get the same result if you run the Controller WatchKit App on the simulator and you should also be able to see more clearly that the image is fuzzy—it has lost its sharp edges. That's because the original image is 64 × 64 points, but WatchKit has scaled it up to fill the background of the controller. The scaling happens because the controller's Mode attribute is set to Scale To Fill, which is the default (see Figure 3-24). To get the best results, you should supply a background image that's the same size as the interface controller itself and set the Mode attribute to Center. In fact, you'll probably need to create two slightly different images, one sized for the 38mm watch, the other for the 42mm version, and use the + icon to the left of the Background selector to specify the correct image for each device.

If you open the Mode selector, you'll see that there are 13 possible selections. Experiment with each of them to see the effect that they have on the position and scaling of the image. Figure 3-26 shows four of these modes.

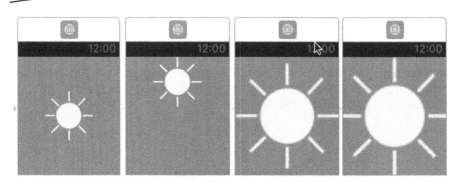

Figure 3-26. Four different background image modes

The image on the left in Figure 3-26 uses the Center mode, which preserves the original size of the image and centers it in the available space. There are eight other modes that preserve the image size but give rise to different positioning. One example is Top, which is the mode used for the second image in Figure 3-26.

The Aspect Fit, Aspect Fill, and Scale To Fill modes all resize the image in some way. Aspect Fit and Aspect Fill preserve the image's aspect ratio, whereas Scale To Fill does not. The third image in Figure 3-26 uses Aspect Fit, which resizes the image so that the smaller axis, in this case the horizontal axis, is filled, while ensuring the whole image remains visible. As you can see, there are gaps above and below the image on the vertical axis. Aspect Fill, used for the rightmost image in Figure 3-26, scales the image so that both axes are filled with the image. In this case, the result is that the left and right edges of the image are clipped. The Scale To Fit mode scales the image so that it exactly fits the screen, without preserving the aspect ratio. If you look carefully at Figure 3-25, where this mode is used, you'll see that the Sun is no longer circular because the image has been stretched more along the vertical axis than along the horizontal axis.

> **Note** The Redraw mode behaves the same as Scale To Fill, so it's not really of any use in WatchKit applications. Its origin is with the contentMode property of the UIView class in UIKit, where Redraw is used by custom views that need to redraw their content whenever the view itself is resized.

Now let's use an image as the background for a group. Create another new project called GroupImage and add a WatchKit App extension to it. Select the asset catalog in the GroupImage WatchKit App group in the Project Navigator and drag the files SpeechBubble38mm@2x.png and SpeechBubble42mm@2x.png into it. We'll use these images as the background for a group on the 38mm and 42mm devices, respectively. The application we're aiming to create is shown in Figure 3-27.

Figure 3-27. Using an image as the background for a group

We'll create the user interface in Figure 3-27 by adding a label containing the text to a group and adding the group to the interface controller. The speech bubble is the group's background image.

Let's start by adding the group. Select Interface.storyboard in the Project Navigator, open the Object Library, and drag and drop a group onto the interface controller. The group positions itself at the top of the interface controller, but we need it to cover all of the available space. With the group selected, open the Attributes Inspector and change the group's Height attribute to Relative to Container. The group should now take up the whole screen.

Next, click the + icon next to the Background field, and add an extra field for the 42mm device. Click in the Background field and select SpeechBubble38mm, then repeat with the 42mm device field, selecting SpeechBubble42mm instead. Change the Mode attribute to Center so that the image is centered in the group and is given its actual size. If you want to see how this looks on both devices, create a preview for both screen sizes as you did in Chapter 2, or switch the control at the bottom of the storyboard to select each screen size, remembering to switch back to Any Screen Size when you are finished.

> **Caution**   As noted in Chapter 2, when designing, you should keep the storyboard in Any Screen Size mode whenever possible. It's easy to forget to do this and accidentally create some or all of your design with the storyboard targeted for just one device. If you find that some of your design doesn't appear on both devices, this is the first thing to check for.

At this point, a preview for both devices would look like Figure 3-28.

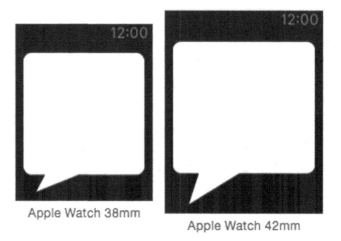

Apple Watch 38mm

Apple Watch 42mm

Figure 3-28.   Creating a speech bubble using a group background image

> **Note**   Although you can't see it in this example, an image used as the background for a group will be clipped by the group's rounded corners. This is a useful technique to use if you actually want to make an image that has square corners appear to have rounded corners.

Now let's add the label. Drag a label from the Object Library and drop it onto the group in the storyboard. Then change its Width and Height attributes to Relative to Container, so that it covers the whole group. Change the Text Color attribute to black, the Alignment attribute to Center, and the Lines attribute to 0 to allow the text to flow onto as many lines as required. Next, type some text into the Text field—something like "That's one small step for man, one giant leap for mankind"—and press Return. Your preview should now look like Figure 3-29.

Apple Watch 38mm

Apple Watch 42mm

Figure 3-29. Adding text to the speech bubble

You are almost finished. All that remains to be done is to arrange for the text to be completely inside the speech bubble. To do that, you need to arrange for the group to move the edges of the label so that they're over the background image. That's the function of the group's Insets attribute. Select the group in the storyboard (or in the Document Outline) and change the value of its Insets attribute in the Attributes Inspector to Custom. Change both the Left and Right values to 16 to move the left and right edges of the text inside the bubble. To adjust the vertical position, change the Bottom attribute to 14. This moves the text up to the correct position for the 38mm device, but it's still not quite correct for the 42mm screen. To fix that, click the + icon next to the Bottom attribute and add a field for the 42mm device and then change its value to 26. Run the application on the simulator to confirm that you get the result shown in Figure 3-27.

The Image Interface Object

You can add images to your user interface by using the WKInterfaceImage class. An instance of this class is created at run time when you include an image object from the Object Library in your storyboard. Let's see how this works by using an image in conjunction with a label. Create a new project called ImageAndLabel and add a WatchKit App target to it. Select the asset catalog in the ImageAndLabel WatchKit App target and drag the file VerySmallSun@2x.png from the folder 3 - Images onto it.

Next, open `Interface.storyboard` in the storyboard editor, drag a group from the Object Library, and drop it onto the interface controller. We'll be using the group to place an image and a label next to each other. Find an image object in the Object Library and drag it into the group. The group resizes to match the size of the image object, which is currently set to a default value. Now drag a label from the Object Library and drop it onto the right edge of the group—you'll see a blue vertical bar appear when the label is in the right place. Your layout should now look like Figure 3-30.

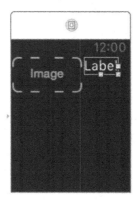

Figure 3-30. Building a group from an image and a label—part 1

Select the image object and open the Attributes Inspector. You'll see that image objects have attributes called `Image` and `Mode` that work just like those of the group and interface controller objects. Click the `Image` selector and choose `VerySmallSun`. Immediately, the image appears in the storyboard, and the image object resizes itself to match the image size. Next, select the label and change its `Text` attribute to `Sunny`. You should now have a storyboard that looks like Figure 3-31.

Figure 3-31. Building a group from an image and a label—part 2

This is almost what we want. The only problem is that the text is not properly aligned with the label. That's because the label's height is set from that of the text that it contains. To fix that, select the label and change its Height property to Relative to Container. Now the label's height matches that of the image, giving a much nicer result (see Figure 3-32). You can also adjust the horizontal distance between the label and the image by changing the value of the Spacing attribute of the group.

Figure 3-32. Building a group from an image and a label—complete

Animation

Animating WatchKit objects is not as simple as animating UIKit views because WatchKit does not have an equivalent of the iOS Core Animation framework. If you need to animate something, you have only two choices:

- Set up a timer in your extension. When the timer fires, change the value of an interface object attribute.
- Use an animated image.

Using a timer has the advantage that you can animate any attribute of any user interface object that you can set at run time, although, as you have seen, there aren't many of these. The downside of this approach is that each animation step requires a message to be sent from the iPhone to the Apple Watch, which takes time and uses up network bandwidth. It's unlikely that this approach will lead to a completely smooth animation. Animated images, on the other hand, are animated on the watch itself (provided that the image frames are installed on the watch) and are therefore more efficient and will almost certainly give a better visual result. The disadvantage is that watch-based animation only works with images. Let's look at both techniques.

Animation Using a Timer

Create a new project called ManualAnimation and add a WatchKit App target to it. Open the WatchKit App's asset catalog and drag the file VeryLargeSun@2x.png from the 3 - Images folder onto it. We're going to manually animate this image from zero size up to a 120-point square in increments of 10 points and then animate it back down to zero size and repeat the cycle.

To create this animation, we're going to use a group that covers the whole interface controller, in the center of which we'll add an image object. We'll then animate the width and height of that image object, which will cause the image itself to grow or shrink while staying centered on the interface controller.

Start by dragging a group from the Object Library onto the interface controller and set its Height property to Relative to Container. Next, drag an image object and drop it onto the group and then set its Horizontal and Vertical attributes to Center, so that it's centered in the group. Use the Image selector to set the image to VeryLargeSun and set the value of the Mode attribute to Scale to Fit, so that the image content is scaled to fit the changing size of the image object.

Next, show the Assistant Editor (⌥⌘**Return**) and use its jump bar to open InterfaceController.swift. Control-drag from the image object in the storyboard to the top of the class definition to create an outlet to the image called image and then add these additional lines of code shown in bold:

```
class InterfaceController: WKInterfaceController {
    @IBOutlet weak var image: WKInterfaceImage!
    private var timer: NSTimer?
    private var size: CGFloat = 0.0
    private var expanding = true
    private let delta: CGFloat = 10
```

The size variable will hold the current size of the image object, in points. We'll update this variable every time the NSTimer, referenced by the timer variable, fires. We'll use the expanding variable to keep track of whether we are increasing or decreasing the image width. The delta value is the amount (in points) by which we will adjust the image size each time the timer fires.

Next, add code in bold to the willActivate() method:

```
override func willActivate() {
    super.willActivate()

    size = delta
    image.setWidth(size)
    image.setHeight(size)
    expanding = true
```

```
timer = NSTimer.scheduledTimerWithTimeInterval(0.1,
    target: self, selector: "timerFired:",
    userInfo: nil, repeats: true)
}
```

Here, we are setting the initial width and height of the image to the delta value by calling its setWidth() and setHeight() methods. Because the image is always going to be square, we only need a single variable to keep track of its size. We then create an NSTimer that will call the timerFired() method in this class repeatedly every 0.1 seconds and schedule it on the run loop of the main thread. Because we have created and scheduled a timer, we need to invalidate it when the interface controller is deactivated. To do that, add the following code to the didDeactivate() method:

```
override func didDeactivate() {
    super.didDeactivate()
    timer?.invalidate()
    timer = nil
}
```

Finally, we need to implement the code that's executed when the timer fires. Add the following method to the InterfaceController class:

```
func timerFired(timer: NSTimer) -> Void {
    let maxSize: CGFloat = 120.0
    let delta: CGFloat = 10.0
    if (expanding) {
        if (size >= maxSize) {
            expanding = false
            size -= delta;
        } else {
            size += delta
        }
    } else {
        if (size <= delta) {
            expanding = true
            size += delta
        } else {
            size -= delta
        }
    }
    image.setWidth(size)
    image.setHeight(size)
}
```

This code either adds a delta to or subtracts a delta from the size variable, depending on the value of the expanding variable, and flips the expanding state if size reaches its maximum or minimum value. The new size value is then used to set the image's width and height.

If you run this code on the simulator, you'll see that the image does indeed start from a very small size and grow to its maximum, then shrinks again, and so on. You'll probably notice immediately that the animation is not very smooth and you may also find that it appears to be skipping frames. If you run this on a real watch, you'll see that the result is slightly better. However, as noted earlier, animating images from the WatchKit extension is not a particularly good idea—it's usually better to use WatchKit's support for animation images on the watch itself, which we'll now discuss.

Animating Images

In the example you have just seen, we started with a single graphic of the Sun and gave the impression of an animation by drawing it at different sizes, from 10 points up to full size and back to 10 points again. At each stage, WatchKit had to scale the image to match the size of the WKInterfaceImage object on which it was being drawn. This is inefficient and wastes battery power. There is a much better way to do this: create a separate image for each frame of the animation, install the images on the watch, and have WatchKit perform the animation by displaying the frames one after the other. Let's see how that works.

Create a new project called ImageAnimation1 and add a WatchKit App extension to it. Then open the asset catalog in the ImageAnimation1 WatchKit App group and then drag the 12 images that you'll find in the folder 3 - Sun Image Frames into the asset catalog. Each image contains one frame of the animation that's similar to the one that we created in the previous example. In the first frame, which comes from the file sun0@2x.png, the Sun has zero size. In the second frame (in the file sun1@2x.png) it has grown to 20 points (or 40 pixels), in the third frame (which comes from the file sun2@2x.png), it's 40 points across, and so on until frame 7 (sun6@2x.png), when it reaches its maximum size of 120 points. In frame 8, the size is reduced to 100 points, and finally in frame 11 it's back to 20 points. Notice the naming convention that has been applied to the file name—sunX@2x.png, where X is the frame number from 0 to 11 inclusive. When WatchKit sees a sequence of image file names like this, it assumes that they form the frames of an animation. If you assign the base name of the image sequence (by which is meant the part of the file name that appears before the frame number) to a WKInterfaceImage object, or as the background image of an interface controller or a group, WatchKit automatically displays the image frames in sequence and repeats the animation until you explicitly stop it by calling the stopAnimating() method, an example of which you'll see in "Programmatic Control of Image Animation" later in this chapter.

> **Tip** It's important to note that the image frames are installed in the asset
> catalog of the WatchKit App, not the WatchKit extension. This follows the same
> rule that applies to custom fonts—resources that are referenced from the
> storyboard must be packaged with the WatchKit app, whereas those that are
> used by your code must be in the WatchKit extension.

Open the storyboard and drag an image from the Object Library onto the
interface controller. Then, in the Attributes Inspector, change its Width and
Height attributes to Relative to Container so that it occupies all of the
available space. To make the image object display the animation, type the
base name of the image files (sun) into the Image field. You'll need to be
careful when doing this, because Xcode will try to autocomplete the name
to sun0. If it does this, delete the trailing 0 (if you open the pop-up for the
Image input field, you'll see that it contains the names of all 12 image frames,
but not the base name of the animation sequence). Next, set the Mode
attribute to Center. This is necessary because otherwise the image frames
would be scaled to the full size of the image object, which is not what we
want. Set the Animate attribute to Yes to reveal the Duration field. Set the
Duration attribute to 1 to specify that the animation sequence would take
one second, after which it is repeated until you explicitly stop it. Finally,
leave the Animate on Load check box checked so that the animation starts
automatically when the user interface controller is loaded. If you uncheck
this box, you'll need to explicitly start the animation yourself. You'll see how
to do that shortly.

The correct attribute settings for the image object are shown in Figure 3-33.

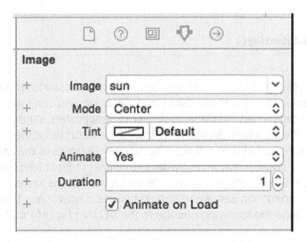

Figure 3-33. An image object configured to perform an image animation

Run the application and you'll see the animation running. You should notice that it is much smoother than the one in the previous example and it does not skip frames. That's because the animation is being performed on the watch, with no intervention from the extension running on the iPhone.

Programmatic Control of Image Animation

If you don't want an animation to begin when the interface controller is loaded, you can use API provided by the WKInterfaceImage class to start it at a later point. Let's modify the example to do that. First, select the image object in the storyboard and uncheck Animate on Load in the Attributes Inspector. If you run the example again now, you'll see just the first frame of the animation, which is empty.

Open InterfaceController.swift in the Assistant Editor and Control-drag from the image object in the storyboard to the top of the class to create an outlet called image, like this:

```
class InterfaceController: WKInterfaceController {
    @IBOutlet weak var image: WKInterfaceImage!
```

Now add the following code shown in bold to the willActivate() and didDeactivate() methods in InterfaceController.swift:

```
override func willActivate() {
    super.willActivate()

    image.startAnimating()
}

override func didDeactivate() {
    super.didDeactivate()

    image.stopAnimating()
}
```

Run the example again and you'll see that the animation starts when the interface controller becomes visible and, although you can't see this happening, it stops when interface controller is deactivated. When you explicitly start the animation in this way, it uses the Duration attribute set in the storyboard and repeats forever. If you need more control over the animation, you can use the startAnimatingWithImagesInRange(_:duration:repeatCount:) method, which allows you to choose which frames are to be animated, how long each animation sequence should take, and how many times it should be repeated. Make the following change to the willActivate() method:

```
override func willActivate() {
    super.willActivate()

    image.startAnimating()
    image.startAnimatingWithImagesInRange(
            NSMakeRange(0, 12), duration: 5,
            repeatCount: 0)
}
```

This code runs the first 12 frames of the animation (which is actually the whole animation) over a period of 5 seconds (instead of the 1 second configured in the storyboard) and repeats it indefinitely (which is the meaning of a repeatCount of zero).

Now try this:

```
override func willActivate() {
    super.willActivate()

    image.startAnimatingWithImagesInRange(
            NSMakeRange(0, 12), duration: 5,
            repeatCount: 0)
    image.startAnimatingWithImagesInRange(
            NSMakeRange(0, 6), duration: 1,
            repeatCount: 1)
}
```

Now you'll see only the first 6 frames of the animation over a period of 1 second, with no repeats (a repeatCount of 1 means to run the animation once)—the animation stops when the sixth frame has been drawn.

You don't have to start from the first animation frame. This code runs the last 6 frames twice, over half a second:

```
override func willActivate() {
    super.willActivate()

    image.startAnimatingWithImagesInRange(
            NSMakeRange(0, 6), duration: 1,
            repeatCount: 1)
    image.startAnimatingWithImagesInRange(
            NSMakeRange(6, 6), duration: 0.5,
            repeatCount: 2)
}
```

If you want to run some or all of your animation backwards, use a negative time value, like this:

```
override func willActivate() {
    super.willActivate()

    image.startAnimatingWithImagesInRange(
            NSMakeRange(6, 6), duration: 0.5,
            repeatCount: 2)
    image.startAnimatingWithImagesInRange(
            NSMakeRange(6, 6), duration: -5,
            repeatCount: 1)
}
```

When the duration is negative, the frames specified by the range argument are animated in reverse order, so the preceding code runs frames 11, 10, 9, 8, 7, and 6 over a period of 5 seconds (the absolute value of the duration) and then stops (because repeatCount is 1). You can repeat the cycle any number of times by setting repeatCount to the required value.

As noted earlier, you can also use an image as the background of a group or an interface controller. Use the Background property to set the background image (animated or single frame) and, in the case of a group, you can use methods with the same names as the ones you have just seen to start and stop animation of the image.

Dynamic Image Content

Packaging images in the WatchKit application bundle is the most efficient approach, but it's not always possible. You might need to display an image downloaded from the Internet or a graphic containing data that's been processed by the owning iOS application. In cases like this, you need to be able to send images to the watch at run time and have them appear in your WatchKit application's user interface.

Sending Images to the Watch

The easiest way to incorporate an image at run time is to use the setImage() and setImageData() methods of the WKInterfaceImage class or the setBackgroundImage() and setBackgroundImageData() methods of WKInterfaceGroup. These methods let you supply the image to be used as either a UIImage object or as data encoded in one of the supported image formats. Invoking one of these methods with a non-nil argument replaces any existing image, while passing nil removes the image. Depending on how the Width and Height attributes of the WKInterfaceImage or WKInterfaceGroup object are configured, changing or removing the image content might cause the host object to change size.

Let's explore how these methods work by sending an image at run time to an image object on the watch. To keep things simple, and because it makes no difference to the way in which the WKInterfaceImage API is used, instead of fetching the image data over the network or creating it on the fly, we'll use an image that's in the WatchKit extension's bundle.

By now, you should be getting used to creating simple WatchKit applications and you should be very familiar with what we're about to do. Start by creating a new project called ImageUpload and adding a WatchKit application target to it. Open Interface.storyboard in the storyboard editor, drag an image object from the Object Library, drop it onto the interface controller. Set the image object's Horizontal and Vertical attributes to Center, so that its center is pegged to the center of the interface controller's visible area and its Mode object to Center. We don't need to worry about setting the image object's size, because it will automatically resize itself to fit the size of the image when it's installed. We're going to install the image when the interface controller is created, so we need an outlet for the image object. Open InterfaceController.swift in the Assistant Editor and then Control-drag from the image object in the storyboard to the top of the class definition to create an outlet called image.

Because we're going to send an image to the watch by using code in the WatchKit extension, the image needs to be in the extension's asset catalog, not the asset catalog in the WatchKit application. Open the WatchKit extension's asset catalog by clicking it in the Project Navigator and drag the file VeryLargeSun@2x.png from the folder 3 – Images onto it.

To send the image to the watch, add the following code in bold to the awakeWithContext() method of InterfaceController.swift:

```
override func awakeWithContext(context: AnyObject?) {
    super.awakeWithContext(context)

    // Configure interface objects here.
    let sunImage = UIImage(named: "VeryLargeSun")
    image?.setImage(sunImage)
}
```

The UIImage(named:) initializer loads the image by name from the WatchKit application's asset catalog and creates a UIImage object wrapping it. To make the image appear in the user interface, you just need to call the setImage() method of the WKInterfaceImage object.

Run the example now and you'll see the image appear on the screen. When you call setImage(), WatchKit sends the image data from the iPhone to the watch. This process takes time, so there may be a small delay before it appears on the screen. This delay will be incurred every time the interface controller is created—but, as you'll see shortly, there is a way to minimize this delay once the interface controller has been created for the first time.

If you have raw image data instead of a UIImage object, you can either create a UIImage from it or you can send the data directly to the watch using the setImageData() method of WKInterfaceImage or the setBackgroundImageData() method of WKInterfaceGroup. We'll illustrate the second approach by using image data loaded from a file in the extension's bundle. In reality, of course, you would be more likely to get the image data from the Internet or to create it using Core Graphics APIs. Drag the file SmallSun@2x.png from the folder 3 – Images and drop it in the WatchKit Extension group in the Project Navigator, ensuring that the image is added to that WatchKit Extension target.

To load the data and send it to the watch, replace the code in awakeWithContext() with the following code in bold:

```
override func awakeWithContext(context: AnyObject?) {
    super.awakeWithContext(context)

    // Configure interface objects here.
    let sunImage = UIImage(named: "VeryLargeSun")
    image?.setImage(sunImage)
    if let url = NSBundle.mainBundle().URLForResource(
                    "SmallSun@2x", withExtension: "png") {
        let data = NSData(contentsOfURL: url)
        image?.setImageData(data)
    }
}
```

We load the image data by getting a URL for its location in the main bundle and then using the URL to initialize an NSData object. Once we have the data, we use the setImageData() method to send it to the watch. Because the image data may (theoretically) be absent, the URL may be nil, so we wrap the code where the NSData object is initialized and used in an if let construction. Run the example again and you'll see a slightly smaller Sun appear in the space occupied by the image object.

> **Caution**   Because this code is running in the WatchKit extension, its main bundle is the extension's bundle. By contrast, the main bundle for code executing in the iOS application is the application's own bundle, which is built from code and resources in the iOS application's target. Do not confuse these two different bundles.

Everything that you have just seen also applies to the setBackgroundImage() and setBackgroundImageData() methods of WKInterfaceGroup. As an exercise, you should replace the WKInterfaceImage object in the storyboard with a WKInterfaceGroup and modify the code in awakeWithContext() to verify that these two methods work as described. Ensure that you set the Mode attribute of the group to Center to avoid distortion of the image.

Caching Images on the Watch

Sending images to the watch is expensive. If you're likely to need to use the same image more than once, you can have it cached on the watch so that subsequent uses do not incur the overhead of transmitting the image data from the paired iPhone. The API to manage the image cache is provided by the WKInterfaceDevice class. To see how this API works, create a new project called CachingImages and, as usual, add a WatchKit extension to it. Follow the same steps that we used to create the ImageUpload project in the previous section: drag an image onto the storyboard, center it, set its Mode attribute to Center, and create an outlet for it called image in the InterfaceController class.

Installing an image in the cache is almost the same as programmatically installing it in a WKInterfaceImage object or as the background of a group or interface controller—the image needs to be in the WatchKit extension bundle and it needs to be loaded into either a UIImage or NSData object. Open the WatchKit extension's asset catalog and drag the file VeryLargeSun@2x.png from the folder 3 - Images into it. Add the following code shown in bold to the awakeWithContext() method of InterfaceController.swift:

```
override func awakeWithContext(context: AnyObject?) {
    super.awakeWithContext(context)

    // Configure interface objects here.
    let device = WKInterfaceDevice.currentDevice()
    let cacheKey = "CachedVeryLargeSun"
    if device.cachedImages[cacheKey] == nil {
        if let sunImage = UIImage(named: "VeryLargeSun") {
            if !device.addCachedImage(sunImage, name: cacheKey) {
                println("Unable to add image to cache");
            }
        }
    }
    image?.setImageNamed(cacheKey)

    println(device.cachedImages)
}
```

What we're aiming to do with this code is install the image in the watch image cache under the name CachedVeryLargeSun and then use the setImageNamed() method of WKInterfaceImage to display the cached copy of the image. The cache is persistent over restarts of the watch application, so once the image is installed, it remains available until you explicitly remove it. The first two lines get a reference to the WKInterfaceDevice instance for the paired watch and declare the name under which the image will be cached:

```
let device = WKInterfaceDevice.currentDevice()
let cacheKey = "CachedVeryLargeSun"
```

Next, we check whether the image is already cached:

```
if device.cachedImages[cacheKey] == nil {
```

The cachedImages property of WKInterfaceDevice is a map in which the keys are the names of the cached images and the value stored for each key is the size of the corresponding image. To test whether the image is already present, we look for the key CachedVeryLargeSun and skip the image upload if we find it. If the key is not found, we attempt to load the image and add it to the cache:

```
if let sunImage = UIImage(named: "VeryLargeSun") {
    if !device.addCachedImage(sunImage, name: cacheKey) {
        println("Unable to add image to cache");
    }
}
```

The WKInterfaceDevice addCachedImage(_:name:) method (and likewise addCachedImageWidthData(_:name:)) adds the image to the cache using the given name, or replaces it if it's already present. Here, we have already ensured that the image is not in the cache so that we wouldn't waste time uploading it again. Each application can store up to five megabytes of image data in the cache. If adding the image would exceed the capacity of the cache, the operation fails, and addCachedImage(_:name:) returns false. In this example, we just print a message to the console if this happens (of course, it won't because we are only adding a single small image). In a real application, you need to keep track of what's in the cache and remove images that you no longer need, or remove all cached images, when there is no spare capacity.

Finally, we install the image from the cache in the WKInterfaceImage object using its setImageNamed() method and print the content of the cache to the console using the cachedImages property of WKInterfaceDevice:

```
    }
    image?.setImageNamed(cacheKey)

    println(device.cachedImages)
}
```

If you run this example, you'll see the Sun image on the screen and the following output will appear in the Xcode console, indicating that there is a single cached image called CachedVeryLargeSun of size 5843 bytes:

```
[CachedVeryLargeSun: 5843]
```

To remove an image from the cache, use the `removeCachedImageWithName()` method as shown in the following code, which removes the Sun image:

```
device.removeCachedImageWithName("CachedVeryLargeSun")
```

To remove all images that are cached by your WatchKit application, use `removeAllCachedImages()`:

```
device.removeAllCachedImages()
```

Caching Image Animations

The example you have just seen demonstrates how to cache single-frame images on the watch. You can also create and cache image animations, although you need to use a slightly different technique than the one we used when specifying the animation in the storyboard in the section "Animating Images" earlier in this chapter. There, we added 12 image frames called sun0, sun1, and so forth to the WatchKit application's asset catalog, added a WKInterfaceImage object to the storyboard, set its image name attribute to sun, and told it to animate the image sequence. Let's try to do a similar thing while caching the images on the watch. We're going to find that it doesn't work and then we're going to modify the code to do something different that *does* work.

Create another WatchKit app project called `ImageAnimation2` with a centered image on the storyboard and an outlet for it in the `InterfaceController`. swift file by following the same steps as you did to create the `CachingImages` example. Instead of adding the large Sun image to the WatchKit extension's asset catalog, add the 12 image frames from the folder 3 – Sun Image Frames. Now add the following code shown in bold to the `awakeWithContext()` method of `InterfaceController.swift`:

```
override func awakeWithContext(context: AnyObject?) {
    super.awakeWithContext(context)

    // Configure interface objects here.
    let device = WKInterfaceDevice.currentDevice()
    for i in 0...11 {
        if let image = UIImage(named: "sun\(i).png") {
            device.addCachedImage(image, name: "sun\(i)")
        }
    }
    println(device.cachedImages)

    image.setImageNamed("sun")
    image.startAnimating()
}
```

The for loop in this code installs each of the 12 image frames in the watch image cache and then prints the cache content to the console for verification. Then, by analogy to what we did with the storyboard version of this example, we use sun as the name of the image to be displayed and tell the image to start animating. If you run this example, you won't see an animating image, but you will see the following output in the console:

```
[sun11: 2613, sun6: 5303, sun2: 3204, sun9: 3760, sun5: 4932, sun1: 2613,
sun8: 4451, sun10: 3204, sun0: 1905, sun4: 4451, sun7: 4932, sun3: 3760]
ImageAnimation2 WatchKit Extension[18508:6717336] Unable to find image named
"sun" on Watch
```

This confirms that the images were cached correctly. However, it seems that WatchKit cannot animate a sequence of image frames from the image cache in the same way as it does when the images are in the WatchKit application bundle.

Fortunately, there is a way around this. Instead of uploading the individual frames, we construct an animated image in the WatchKit extension, cache it on the watch, and tell the WKInterfaceImage object to animate it. To do that, remove all the code that you added to the awakeWithContext() method and replace it with the following code in bold:

```
override func awakeWithContext(context: AnyObject?) {
    super.awakeWithContext(context)

    // Configure interface objects here.
    let device = WKInterfaceDevice.currentDevice()
    let cacheKey = "AnimatedSun"
    if device.cachedImages[cacheKey] == nil {
        var images = Array<UIImage>()
        for i in 0...11 {
            if let image = UIImage(named: "sun\(i).png") {
                images.append(image)
            }
        }
        let animatedImage =
            UIImage.animatedImageWithImages(images, duration: 1.0)
        device.addCachedImage(animatedImage, name: cacheKey)
    }

    image.setImageNamed(cacheKey)
}
```

The first part of this code checks whether the animated image is already installed in the image cache. If it's not, it loads the 12 image frames into an array and then combines them into an animated image by using the UIImage animatedImageWithImages(_:duration:) method, specifying that each cycle of the animation should take one second. The animated image (which is also a UIImage object) is then uploaded in the WatchKit image cache. The last line of code installs the image in the WKInterfaceImage object. To start and stop the animation, add the following code to the willActivate() and didDeactivate() methods:

```
override func willActivate() {
    super.willActivate()
    image.startAnimating()
}

override func didDeactivate() {
    super.didDeactivate()
    image.stopAnimating()
}
```

Run the example to see the Sun image animating.

The startAnimating() method plays the whole animation in the forward direction and repeats it indefinitely. To play only a part of the animation, play it backwards, or change the repeat count or the duration, use the startAn imatingWithImagesInRange(_:duration:repeatCount:) method, which we discussed in the section "Programmatic Control of Image Animation" earlier in this chapter. As an example, replace the startAnimating() call with the following:

```
image.startAnimatingWithImagesInRange(NSMakeRange(0, 6),
                        duration: 5, repeatCount: 2)
```

Run the example again and you'll see the first part of the animation played twice, each time over a period of five seconds instead of the one second specified in the image itself.

Summary

In this chapter, you saw how to use all the features of the WatchKit WKInterfaceLabel and WKInterfaceImage classes. You also learned how to work with the Apple Watch system font and how to install and use fonts of your own. Everything you read about fonts in this chapter also applies to the other user interface objects that use text, some of which are covered in the next chapter. The second half of the chapter covered the use of both static and animated images and how to use an image as the background of a group or an interface controller. The next chapter covers most of the remaining user interface objects. After reading it, you should be able to create a simple WatchKit application including some basic user interaction.

Chapter 4

More Watch User Interface Objects

In Chapter 3, we looked at two of the simplest user interface objects: WKInterfaceLabel and WKInterfaceImage. This chapter covers six more, starting with three objects (buttons, sliders, and switches) the user can interact with that cause code in your WatchKit Extension to be invoked when their state changes. We'll also look in detail at three more objects you can use to present information to the user: the WKInterfaceDate object, which displays dates and times, the WKInterfaceTimer object, which is a count-down or count-up timer, and WKInterfaceMap, a simple, non-interactive map. By the time you reach the end of this chapter, you will have seen all the objects you can use to build WatchKit user interfaces (except tables, which are covered in Chapter 6).

Buttons

Buttons allow the user to interact with your WatchKit application. A button is linked to an action method in the interface controller, so that when the user clicks on the button, the action method is called. As you'll see in Chapter 5, a button can also be used as the trigger for a segue that causes a transition to another interface controller. Buttons are instances of the WKInterfaceButton class.

Creating and Configuring Buttons

Create a new project called `Buttons` and add a WatchKit application target to it. Select `Interface.storyboard` in the `Buttons WatchKit App` target to open it in the editor. Then locate a button object in the Object Library and drag it onto the interface controller. You'll see that the button expands to fill all of the available width. That's because Apple recommends that, whenever possible, you use only one button per row. To encourage this, when you drop a button onto a storyboard, its `Width` attribute is set to `Relative to Container` with a value of 1, as shown in Figure 4-1.

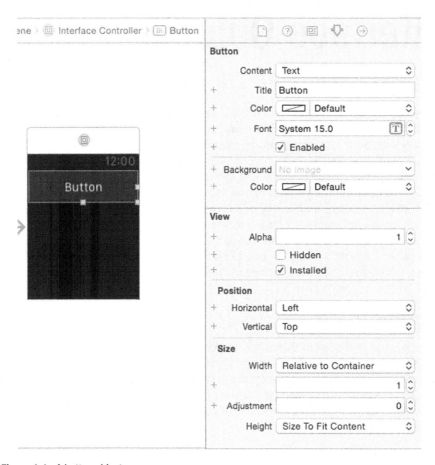

Figure 4-1. A button object

In the storyboard, the button looks transparent and rectangular, but that's not the case. Select the interface controller in the storyboard, change its Background attribute to blue, and then run the example on the simulator. You should see that the button actually has a translucent white background and rounded corners (see Figure 4-2).

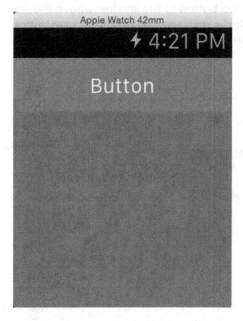

Figure 4-2. Buttons have a translucent white background and rounded corners

You can change the background color and the color of the text in the Attributes Inspector. Referring back to Figure 4-1, the Color attribute below the Title attribute sets the color of the text, while the other Color attribute, below the Background attribute, changes its background color. The Background attribute itself allows you to add an image to the button's background. Typically you would use a background image to give the button a distinctive appearance. It isn't possible to control the mode used to display the image—it is always scaled to fit the button's width and height. There is also no way to change the radius of the button's rounded corners.

You can set the button's title and font in the storyboard using the Title attribute and Font attribute respectively. The title can also be changed at run time using the setTitle() method or the setAttributedTitle() method, which lets you set the title using an NSAttributedString. These methods work in the same way as the setText() and setAttributedText() methods of the WKInterfaceLabel class, discussed in Chapter 3. Unlike labels, the text in a button is always horizontally centered.

Actions and State

To respond to a button press, you need to link the button to an action in your interface controller. Select the button in the storyboard and then open the Assistant Editor (⌥⌘↩). The file InterfaceController.swift should appear in the Assistant Editor; if it does not, use the jump bar to open it. Control-drag from the button to the line just above the final closing brace in InterfaceController.swift and release the mouse button. In the pop-up that appears, change the Connection type to Action and the Name to buttonClicked, as shown in Figure 4-3.

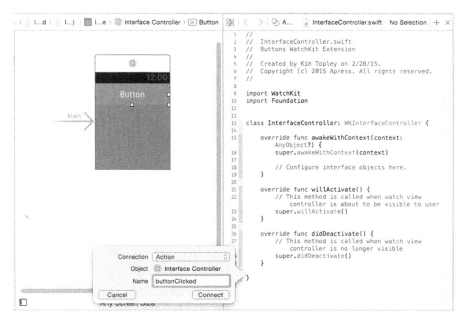

Figure 4-3. Creating an action method for a button

Click **Connect**, and the following code shown in bold will be added to InterfaceController.swift:

```
@IBAction func buttonClicked() {
}
}
```

Notice that the buttonClicked() method does not have any arguments, so you don't get a reference to the button that was clicked. If you have multiple buttons in your user interface, you'll need to create a separate action method for each button. This is different to UIKit, where you can use a single action method to respond to clicks from any number of buttons. Make the following change shown in bold to the buttonClicked() method and then run the example and click the button—you should see the text Button clicked appear in the Xcode console:

```
@IBAction func buttonClicked() {
    println("Button clicked")
    }
}
```

By default, buttons are enabled, which means they respond to clicks. If you don't want a button to be enabled, perhaps because you need the user to supply some information before the button's action can be perfomed, call the setEnabled() method with argument false. To enable the button again, call setEnabled(true). To see how this works, drag another button from the Object Library and drop it on the storyboard below the first one. Control-drag from both buttons to the top of the InterfaceController class in the Assistant Editor to create outlets called button1 for the top button and button2 for the second button. Create an action method called button2Clicked() for the second button using the same steps that you used to create the button1Clicked() method.

We're going to use the second button to control the enabled state of the first. Select the second button in the storyboard and set its Title attribute to Disable Button 1, to indicate what will happen when the button is clicked. We can't get the enabled state of a button at run time, so we'll need to keep track of it in our interface controller. To do that, add a variable called button1Enabled to the InterfaceController class:

```
class InterfaceController: WKInterfaceController {
    @IBOutlet weak var button1: WKInterfaceButton!
    @IBOutlet weak var button2: WKInterfaceButton!
    var button1Enabled = true
```

The variable is initialized to true because buttons are enabled by default. Now add the following code shown in bold to the button2Clicked() method:

```
@IBAction func button2Clicked() {
    button1Enabled = !button1Enabled
    button1.setEnabled(button1Enabled)
    button2.setTitle(button1Enabled ? "Disable Button 1"
                                    : "Enable Button 1")

}
```

Select the interface controller in the storyboard, set its Color attribute back to Default, and then run the example. You'll see both buttons, with the top button initially enabled, as shown on the left in Figure 4-4.

Now click the bottom button to disable the top button, as shown on the right in Figure 4-4. You should see a slight change in its background color (the background color of the interface controller was changed to make this a little easier to see), and it no longer responds when clicked. Click the bottom button again to re-enable it.

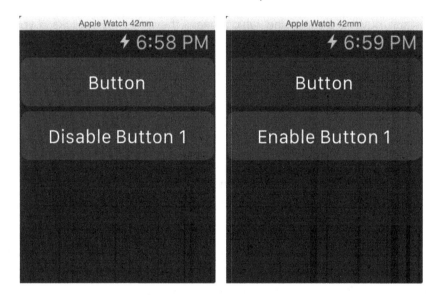

Figure 4-4. Enabling and disabling a button

Using a Group as the Content of a Button

Select either of the buttons in the previous example and look at its Content attribute in the storyboard (see Figure 4-1). By default, this is set to Text, but there is another value: Group. When you select this value, the button's title disappears, to be replaced by an empty group. The button no longer looks like a button, but it still responds to taps. You can add user interface objects to this group to make almost any region of your user interface a tappable area. You could, for example, add an image and a label to create a layout similar to that shown in Figure 3-1 nested inside a button. In this section, we'll create a button with a nested image and use it to show how to use the hidden and alpha attributes of user interface objects—which were mentioned in Chapter 2 but not covered in detail—to make parts of your layout appear and disappear. The application we're going to create initially consists of four buttons, as shown on the left in Figure 4-5.

Figure 4-5. Embedding an image in a group inside a button

When one of the buttons is tapped, it disappears, revealing part of an image that's hidden behind the buttons, as shown on the right in Figure 4-5. If you tap a different button, the first button reappears, and the button you just tapped vanishes, to show another part of the image.

Start by creating a new project called ImageButtons and add a WatchKit application target to it. Select the asset catalog in the ImageButtons WatchKit App target and drag the two images from the folder 4 - Button Images into it. These images are the application's background and the question mark image that we'll use for the buttons.

The layout shown in Figure 4-5 is a grid of four equal squares. To create it, we're going to add two groups to the interface controller, one above the other, each covering half of the available height. We're then going to split each of these groups into two horizontally to form the four grid squares. Drag a group from the Object Library and drop it onto the interface controller in the storyboard. In the Attributes Inspector, change the group's Height attribute to Relative to Container and set the associated value to 0.5, so that the group covers the top half of the interface controller, as shown at the top in Figure 4-6.

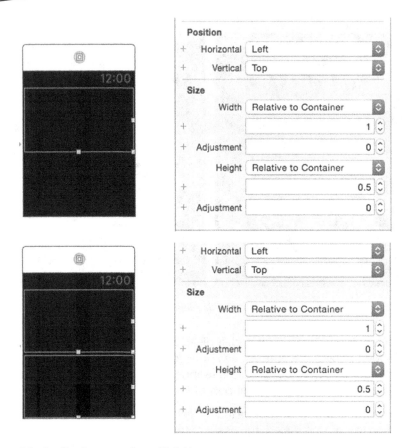

Figure 4-6. Creating two rows of equal height

We need another group for the second row. We could drag it from the Object Library to the storyboard and set its Height attribute, just as we did with the first row, but there is an easier way. Because the second group has the same attribute values as the first one, we can use a shortcut by just making a copy of the group we just added. To do that, hold down the ⌥ key (the option key), drag the first group downward, and drop it into the empty space. You should now have two equal rows, as shown on the bottom in Figure 4-6.

When we add the buttons to these groups, we need them to completely cover the interface controller. At the moment, they won't because there is a small vertical gap between the two rows, which you can see in Figure 4-6. This is caused by the Spacing attribute of the interface controller, which leaves a 4-point vertical gap between its child objects. Select the interface controller in the storyboard and change the Spacing attribute to 0 (zero) to remove the vertical gap. While you have the interface controller selected, use its

Background attribute to set BackgroundImage as its background and change the Mode attribute to Center. You should now be able to see (Figure 4-7) the background image behind the two groups that we just added. The image is visible because groups are transparent by default.

Figure 4-7. The background image behind the two group rows

The idea is for the background image to be hidden by the four buttons. Let's add a couple of buttons to the bottom row to make sure this is going to work. Drag a button from the Object Library and drop it onto the bottom row. Initially, it expands to fill the whole row. Set its Width attribute value to 0.5 and its Height attribute to Relative to Container. The button now covers the bottom left corner of the interface controller, but you can still see the image through it, because buttons are translucent by default. To fix that, set the button's background color to black. We need another copy of the button to cover the bottom right corner, so ⌥–drag a copy of the first button and drop it to the right of the first one. If you look carefully at the storyboard, you'll see a small gap between the two buttons. To remove that, select the bottom group and set its Spacing attribute to 0. You may find it difficult to select the group in the storyboard, so select it in the Document Outline (the tree structure to the left of the storyboard editor) instead. Now run the example on the simulator to see how it looks (see Figure 4-8).

Figure 4-8. The background image partially hidden by two buttons

As you can see, this doesn't quite work—some parts of the background are visible at the bottom corners and the bottom center. That's because the buttons and the group they are nested in have rounded corners. Unfortunately, you can't change the radius of the buttons' corners, but you can change the radius of the rounded corners of a group. To make sure that every pixel of the background is covered, we're going to nest each button inside a group of its own and make sure those groups have squared-off corners. We'll also set the background color of those groups to black, so that they hide everything that's behind them. That's not quite enough, though—those groups will be nested inside the top and bottom groups that are already present and which also have rounded corners, which will clip their content. To stop that happening, we need to make sure our existing groups have square corners too. To do that, delete both of the buttons you just added and select both groups. Then in the Attributes Inspector, change the Radius attribute to 0, which makes the corners square instead of circular arcs. With both groups still selected, set the Spacing property for both of them to 0 so there is no horizontal gap between the groups that will hold the buttons.

Now let's add the first of the four groups that we need as background for each button. Drag one group from the Object Library and drop it in the top group. Sets its Width attribute value to 0.5 so that it covers half the width of the top row and change its Height attribute to Relative to Container so that its height is the same as that of the top row. Set its Radius attribute to 0 to eliminate the rounded corners and the Color attribute to black to hide the interface controller's background image. At this point, the storyboard and Attributes Inspector should look like Figure 4-9.

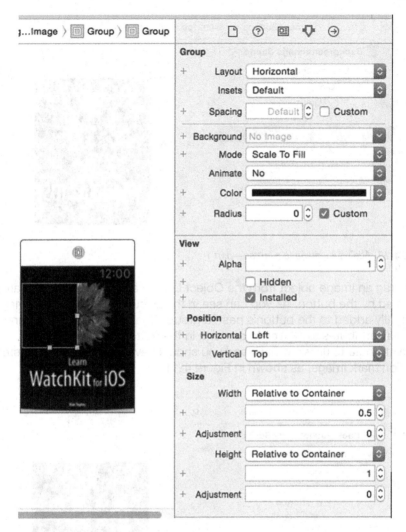

Figure 4-9. Adding the first button background group

The next step is to add a button to the group. Drag a button from the Object Library, drop it into the group, and then use the Attributes Inspector to change its Height value to Relative to Container. The result will be that the button now completely fills the space occupied by the group. Now we need to add the question mark image to the button. To do that, first change the Content attribute of the button from Text to Group and look at the Document Outline. You'll see that there is a disclosure triangle next to the button. Click that triangle and you'll see that there is a group nested inside the button, as shown in Figure 4-10.

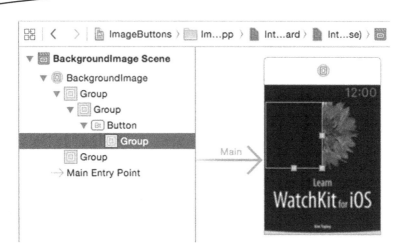

Figure 4-10. Adding an image to a button—part 1

Now drag an image object from the Object Library and drop it onto the area occupied by the button. As you can see in the Document Outline, the image is actually added to the button's nested group. Change its Horizontal and Vertical attributes to Center to center it in the button. Now change its Image attribute to QuestionMark and you should have a button with a nested question mark image, as shown in Figure 4-11.

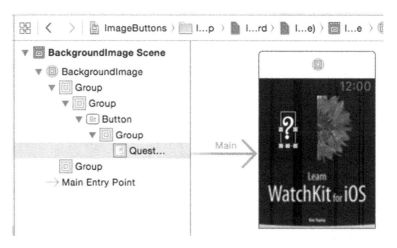

Figure 4-11. Adding an image to a button—part 2

Now you need to make three copies of the group that contains the button. To do that, first select the group in the Document Outline. Make sure you select the group that is the immediate parent of the button, as shown in Figure 4-12.

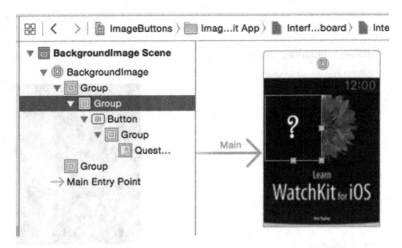

Figure 4-12. Making three copies of the image button—stage 1

With the correct group selected, go back to the storyboard and ⌥-drag the group and its content to the right and drop it. You should now have two copies of the button in the top row. Repeat the process to create another two copies of the button and its enclosing group in the bottom row. When you've done that, your Document Outline and storyboard should look like Figure 4-13.

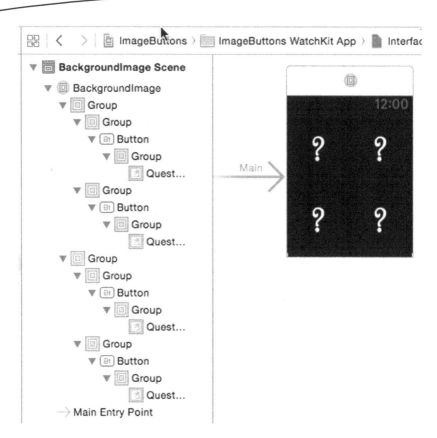

Figure 4-13. Making three copies of the image button—completed

With the storyboard complete, we now need to implement the simple logic of this application. When the user taps any of the four buttons, we need to make that button disappear and make sure that the other three buttons are visible. To hide a button and make the background image visible, we actually need to hide the group that the button is wrapped in. To do that, we need outlets for all four of those groups. Open `InterfaceController.swift` in the Assistant Editor and `Control`-drag from the group that contains the first button (the button at the top in the Document Outline in Figure 4-13) to the top of the class definition. Then release the mouse button and create an outlet called `group1`. Figure 4-14 shows the process of creating this outlet—be sure that you select and drag from the correct group—it must be the group that is the immediate parent of the button.

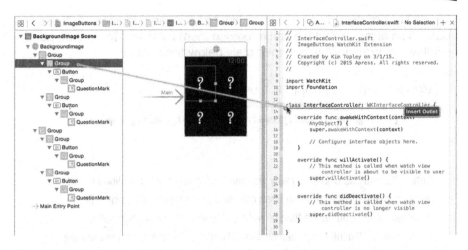

Figure 4-14. Creating an outlet for the group wrapping the first button

This line shown in bold should have been added to the interface controller class:

```
class InterfaceController: WKInterfaceController {
    @IBOutlet weak var group1: WKInterfaceGroup!
```

Repeat this process for the group wrapping the second button on the top row, naming the outlet group2. Do the same for the group wrapping the leftmost button on the bottom row (naming it group3) and the group wrapping the rightmost button on the bottom row (naming it group4), giving you four outlets:

```
class InterfaceController: WKInterfaceController {
    @IBOutlet weak var group1: WKInterfaceGroup!
    @IBOutlet weak var group2: WKInterfaceGroup!
    @IBOutlet weak var group3: WKInterfaceGroup!
    @IBOutlet weak var group4: WKInterfaceGroup!
```

As you'll see shortly, it is more convenient to keep the references to these groups in an array so that we can reference them by index. To do that, add the following array definition immediately below the outlets:

```
@IBOutlet weak var group4: WKInterfaceGroup!
lazy var groups: [WKInterfaceGroup] =
      [self.group1, self.group2, self.group3, self.group4]
```

> **Note**   You may be wondering why we aren't using an outlet collection instead of four individual outlets that are then collected into an array. That would be the ideal solution, but at the time of writing, Xcode does not support outlet collections for WatchKit applications. Should outlet collections become available, the code can easily be converted by deleting `group1` to `group4`, changing the declaration of groups to look like this: `@IBOutlet weak var groups:` `[WKInterfaceGroup]`! Then connect each of the groups in the storyboard directly to the `groups` outlet collection, in the same order as they are currently connected to the individual outlets. The rest of the code would remain unchanged.

We also need to create an action method in the interface controller for each of the four buttons. Again, it is easier to use the Document Outline than the storyboard when doing this, to ensure that you are dragging from the correct source object. In the Document Outline, select the topmost button and `Control`-drag to the line above the closing brace in `InterfaceController.swift`, as shown in Figure 4-15.

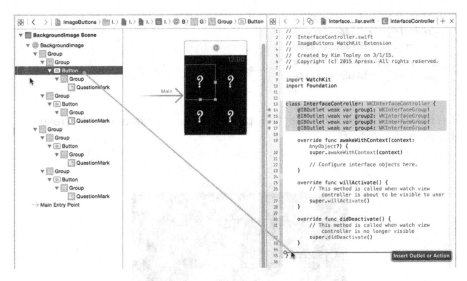

Figure 4-15. Creating an action method for first button

Release the mouse button, change the Connection type to Action, and use button1Clicked as the method name. Do the same thing for the second button down, naming the action method button2Clicked. Repeat for the third and fourth buttons, using the names button3Clicked and button4Clicked respectively. You should now have four empty action methods in the interface controller:

```
@IBAction func button1Clicked() {
}
@IBAction func button2Clicked() {
}
@IBAction func button3Clicked() {
}
@IBAction func button4Clicked() {
}
}
```

In the button1Clicked() method, we need to make the group wrapping the top left button disappear and we need to make sure that the other three groups are visible (since we could already have pressed one of the others buttons). There are two WKInterfaceObject methods that affect the visibility of an interface object: setHidden() and setAlpha(). Let's try the more obvious of the two first. Add the following code shown in bold to the button1Clicked() method:

```
@IBAction func button1Clicked() {
    groups[0].setHidden(true)
    groups[1].setHidden(false)
    groups[2].setHidden(false)
    groups[3].setHidden(false)
}
```

Run the example and click on the top left button. You should get the result shown in Figure 4-16.

Figure 4-16. Making the wrong button disappear

It looks like the wrong button has disappeared, but that's not actually what has happened. When you make an interface object invisible, the group (or interface controller) no longer allocates space for it. In this case, we made the top-left button invisible, so the group that manages the top row of the layout allocated its space to the other button in that row. In other words, the button that you see at the top left in Figure 4-16 is actually the one that was initially at the top right. We need to hide the group for the top left button but still have the group for the row allocate space for it. That's exactly what setAlpha() does when called with argument 0. The setAlpha() method changes the translucency of the object on which it is called—just like changing the alpha value of a UIColor or CGColorRef. When called with argument 1, it makes the object completely opaque, which is the default state. When called with argument 0, it makes the object invisible. Values between 0 and 1 cause the pixels of the object to be blended with those of its background, with smaller values causing more of the background to show through. With this in mind, change the implementation of the button1Clicked() method to this:

```
@IBAction func button1Clicked() {
    groups[0].setAlpha(0)
    groups[1].setAlpha(1)
    groups[2].setAlpha(1)
    groups[3].setAlpha(1)
}
```

Now run the example again and click on the top left button. This time it should disappear, leaving the other three buttons intact, as shown in Figure 4-17.

Figure 4-17. Making the correct button disappear

The implementation of the other three action methods is very similar. In fact, we can save some code by observing that in the action method for button N, we need to set the alpha value for group N to 0, and for all the other groups to 0, and that this code can easily be factored out into a common method. To do this, modify the `InterfaceController.swift` class as shown in bold in the following code snippet:

```
@IBAction func button1Clicked() {
    hideButton(0)
}

@IBAction func button2Clicked() {
    hideButton(1)
}

@IBAction func button3Clicked() {
    hideButton(2)
}

@IBAction func button4Clicked() {
    hideButton(3)
}

private func hideButton(index: Int) -> Void {
    for i in 0..<groups.count {
        groups[i].setAlpha(i == index ? 0 : 1)
    }
}
}
```

If you now run the application, you'll see that if you click any of the buttons, it disappears. Click any other button and that button disappears while the hidden one reappears. This should make clear the distinction between `setHidden()` and `setAlpha()`—use the former when you want the object's layout space to be reused by other objects and the latter when you do not. Of course, you can also use `setAlpha()` with a value between 0 and 1 if you just want to make an object translucent.

Sliders

The slider allows the user to choose a value from a given bounded range. The minimum and maximum values are set in the storyboard and cannot be changed, but the current value and the number of available values in the slider's range can be changed at run time. Let's experiment a little with the slider control. Create a new project called `Sliders` and add a WatchKit app target to it. Select `Interface.storyboard` in the Project Navigator. Then locate a slider in the Object library and drag one onto the storyboard, as shown in Figure 4-18, where you can also see the slider's configurable attributes.

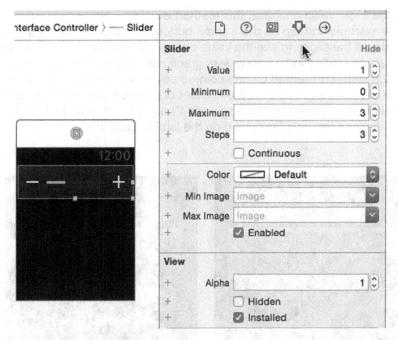

Figure 4-18. A slider and its configurable attributes

The slider has a bar and two buttons that the user can tap to change the slider's value, which is a floating-point number. Tapping to the left of the slider's center or on the minus button decrements the value by one step; tapping to the right or on the plus button increments by one step. The slider does not respond to dragging.

As you can see in Figure 4-18, the default minimum value is 0, and the default maximum is 3. The Steps attribute determines how much the value changes by each time the user taps. To calculate the step value, subtract the minimum from the maximum and divide by the value of the Steps attribute. In this case, each tap changes the slider's value by $(3 - 0) / 3 = 1$.

You can track the slider's value as it changes by linking it to an action method in your interface controller. Open InterfaceController.swift in the Assistant Editor, Control-drag from the slider in the storyboard to the bottom of class, and release the mouse button. In the pop-up that appears, change the Connection to Action and set the name to onSliderValueChanged. Then add a line of code to print the current value, as shown in bold:

```
@IBAction func onSliderValueChanged(value: Float) {
    println("Slider value is \(value)")
}
```

When the slider value changes, this method is called with the new value. Run the example and tap on the + and - buttons, or to the left and right of the center of the slider, to see the value change in the console. As you tap, the slider bar is filled with more or less green color to reflect the new value, with each step represented by one colored segment. You can increase the number of steps, and therefore the number of segments, by changing the Steps attribute in the Attributes Inspector. Changing this value to 6 doubles the number of segments, as shown on the left in Figure 4-19.

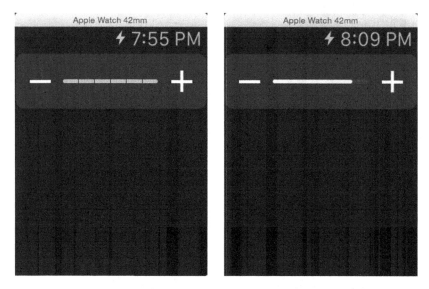

Figure 4-19. A slider with 6 steps and with its Continuous attribute off (on the left) and on (on the right)

With Steps set to 6, the slider value changes by 0.5 for each tap. If you need to change the number of steps at run time, you can do so by calling the setNumberOfSteps() method with an integer argument specifying the new step count.

You can change the slider's current value by calling setValue() with a new value. These changes are not reported to your action method and they don't need to be multiples of the step value either. Here, for example, even though the step value is 0.5, it is perfectly legal to call setValue(2.25). If you try to set a value that's larger than the maximum or smaller than the minimum, you get the maximum or minimum instead.

If you prefer to see a solid bar instead of discrete segments, check the Continuous checkbox in the slider's attributes. You can also change the color used to draw the slider bar by setting the Color attribute. Check the Continuous checkbox and change the Color attribute to yellow; then run the example again to get the result shown on the right in Figure 4-19.

A solid bar and the subtle animation that takes place when you tap it give the impression that the value is varying continuously, but in fact the effect is entirely visual—as you can easily verify, in this example the value still changes in steps of 0.5.

You can change the images used for the + and – buttons by setting the Max Image and Min Image attributes. Open the WatchKit app's asset catalog and drag the image files SliderMax@2x.png and SliderMin@2x.png from the folder 4 – Slider Images onto it. Now set the Max Image attribute to SliderMax and the Min Image attribute to SliderMin. Then run the example again to get the result shown in Figure 4-20.

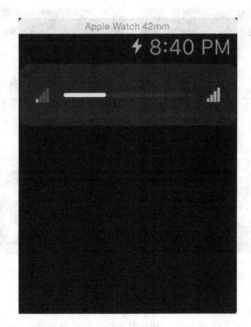

Figure 4-20. Using custom images for the slider's buttons

You can disable a slider if you don't want the user to be able to change its value. To demonstrate that, let's add a switch to our example application.

Switches

A switch gives the user a way to make a yes or no choice. You can set the state of the switch, its title, and its title color both in the storyboard and at run time, and you can enable or disable it. To track the current state of the switch, you need to link it to an action method in your interface controller.

Locate a switch in the Object Library and drag it onto the storyboard, dropping it underneath the slider. In the Attributes Inspector, change the Title attribute to Enable Slider. You'll notice when you do this that the title automatically wraps, and slider's height increases to accommodate it. The Color attribute sets the color of the title, while the Tint attribute changes the fill color of the switch itself. Figure 4-21 shows the switch with its default green tint on the left and with a blue tint on the right.

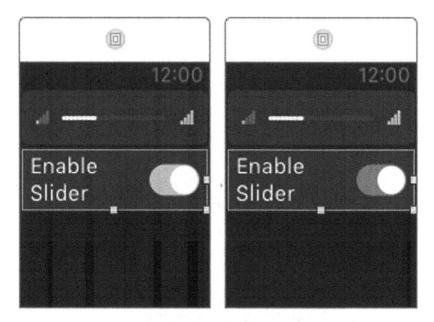

Figure 4-21. Changing the tint color of a switch

The title can be set at run time using the setTitle() and setAttributedTitle() methods, which work just like the setText() and setAttributedText() methods of WKInterfaceLabel that Chapter 3 discusses in detail.

To link the switch to the interface controller, open InterfaceController. swift in the Assistant Editor and Control-drag from the switch to a point just below the onSliderValueChanged() method. Release the mouse button, change the Connection type to Action, and use onSwitchValueChanged as the method name. The action method gets the current value of the switch as its argument, as a boolean value. We want to use this value to set the enabled property of the slider, so we also need an outlet for the slider. Control-drag from the slider to the top of the class to add an outlet called slider and then add the code shown in bold to the onSwitchValueChanged() method:

```
class InterfaceController: WKInterfaceController {
    @IBOutlet weak var slider: WKInterfaceSlider!

    // Code removed

    @IBAction func onSliderValueChanged(value: Float) {
        println("Slider value is \(value)")
    }

    @IBAction func onSwitchValueChanged(value: Bool) {
        println("Switch value is \(value)")
        slider.setEnabled(value)
    }
}
```

Now run the example and toggle the switch to see the slider change between its enabled and disabled states, as shown in Figure 4-22. It's worth running this example just to see the subtle animation that occurs when the slider changes state.

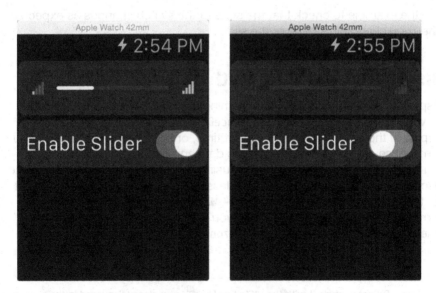

Figure 4-22. Using a switch to control the enabled state of a slider

You can change the state of the switch programmatically by calling the setOn() method. As with the slider, these state changes are not reported to the switch's action method. Let's link the value of the slider to the state of the switch, so that the switch is on when the slider value is less than 2 and off when it's greater than or equal to 2. We'll need an outlet for the switch, which you can create in the usual way by Control-dragging from the switch in the storyboard to the top of the class and naming the outlet switch:

```
class InterfaceController: WKInterfaceController {
    @IBOutlet weak var slider: WKInterfaceSlider!
    @IBOutlet weak var `switch`: WKInterfaceSwitch!
```

> **Note**   You can see that Xcode automatically quoted the outlet name, because
> switch is a Swift language keyword and we're using it here as the name of an
> instance variable.

Now add the following line of code in bold to the onSliderValueChanged()
method:

```
@IBAction func onSliderValueChanged(value: Float) {
    println("Slider value is \(value)")
    `switch`.setOn(value < 2)
}
```

Run the example to check that the state of the switch changes as expected
when you change the value of the slider.

Displaying the Date and Time

Displaying the time and date is something that's likely to be very important
for watch applications. The WKInterfaceDate class provides an analog
display of the current date, the current time, or both. In the storyboard, you
can choose exactly how you want the date and time to be formatted and
you can control the layout of the text using the same options you saw in the
discussion of the WKInterfaceLabel class in Chapter 3. Note that you can't
set the date and time to be displayed—WKInterfaceDate always uses the
current time. However, as you'll see, you can change the way in which the
time is interpreted by setting the Timezone and Calendar attributes.

> **Note**   Despite its name, WKInterfaceDate handles display of both date and
> time. Do not confuse it with the WKInterfaceTimer class (discussed in the
> next section), which is a count-down or count-up timer that has nothing to do
> with the current date and time.

Basic Usage

Create a new project called DateDisplay, add a WatchKit application target to it, and then select Interface.storyboard in the Project Navigator. Find a date object in the Object Library and drag it onto the storyboard. Initially, the WKInterfaceDate object displays a fixed date and time in short format, but if you run the example on the simulator, you'll see that it shows the current date and time, as shown in Figure 4-23. The displayed date and time update automatically as the time changes.

Figure 4-23. Default date and time display in the storyboard (left) and on the simulator (right)

The attributes you can use to configure WKInterfaceDate are shown in Figure 4-24.

Figure 4-24. Storyboard attributes for the WKInterfaceDate class

As you can see, the attributes are divided into two groups. The lower group is concerned with controlling how the date/time text is displayed. They are the same as those provided by WKInterfaceLabel and you can use them to change the color and font, font scaling, and horizontal alignment, and to allow the text to wrap onto subsequent lines. Given the limited amount of space available on the watch screen, it's likely that you'll need more than one line when using anything but the most compact date and time representations. The upper group contains the formatting options for the date and time. By default, both the date and time are shown in short format (which is what you see in Figure 4-23). The Preview attribute is somewhat misnamed because (at least at the time of writing) it doesn't update when you change the formatting options. However, this field is editable, so you can use it to change the date and time that's used in the storyboard and in the preview pane in the Assistant Editor.

The selectors for the Date and Time attributes let you individually control the formatting for the date and time parts respectively. Choosing the value None in either selector causes the corresponding part to be omitted—to display only the time, for example, set the Date attribute to None. The other possible values and the results that they produce are shown in Table 4-1.

Table 4-1. Date and Time Formatting Options

Format	Date Example	Time Example
Short	9/9/14	1:09 PM
Medium	Sep 9, 2014	1:09:00 PM
Long	September 9, 2014	1:09:00 PM EDT
Full	Tuesday, September 9, 2014	1:09:00 PM Eastern Daylight Time

You can use the project that we just created to experiment with these settings. As noted earlier, in most cases, to get a usable result you'll need to change the Lines attribute to at least 2, or to 0 to allow the WKInterfaceDate object to take as much vertical space as it needs. Some typical examples are shown in Figure 4-25.

Figure 4-25. Various date and time formats

The screenshot on the left has the Date attribute set to None and Time set to Short, to show just the time. Similarly, in the center screenshot, Time is None and Date is Medium. In the final screenshot, Date is Long and Time is Medium; note that in this case (and also when Date is Full), the parts are linked by the word *at*. When the Date format is Short or Medium, a comma separator is used instead.

Custom Formatting

If the standard date and time formatting options don't give you what you need, you can supply a custom formatting string using formatting patterns described in Apple's *Data Formatting Guide*, which you'll find at https://developer.apple.com/library/ios/documentation/Cocoa/ Conceptual/DataFormatting/Articles/dfDateFormatting10_4.html#// apple_ref/doc/uid/TP40002369-SW1.

Suppose, for example, that you want to show just the day of the week and the current time. There is no combination of standard date and time options that let you do this, but it can be done with a custom format pattern. Start by selecting the WKInterfaceDate object in the storyboard and set its Format attribute to Custom. This reveals an input field that you can use to set the pattern, as shown in Figure 4-26.

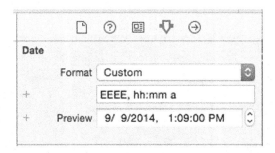

Figure 4-26. Setting a custom date and time format in the storyboard

The format string in this example is made up of three parts:

- 'EEEE' produces the day of the week in long form—for example, Sunday. To get the abbreviated version, use fewer letters, such as EEE, which gives Sun.

- 'hh:mm' gives the current time in hours and minutes, separated by a colon. A lower case h formats the time according to a 12-hour clock. Use H to use a 24-hour clock.

- 'a' is replaced by either AM or PM, depending on the time of day.

You'll find a reference to the document that describes all of the formatting characters that are accepted, and their meanings, in the *Data Formatting Guide*. If you run this example, you'll get the result shown in Figure 4-27.

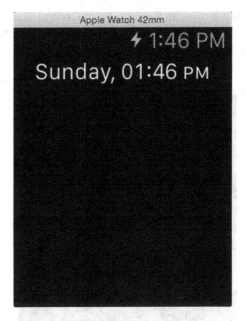

Figure 4-27. Using a custom date and time format

Changing the Timezone and Calendar

By default, the text representation of the current time shown by
WKInterfaceDate is based on the user's configured timezone. That means that
if the user is on the east coast of the United States, the time that she sees is
correct for the EST timezone, whereas if she is on the west coast, she sees
the time as it is in the PST timezone. Usually, this is exactly what you want.
But if you need to display the time as it would be in a different timezone, you
can do so by setting the TimeZone attribute using the setTimeZone() method.

To see how this works, make sure Interface.storyboard is selected in the
Project Navigator, open InterfaceController.swift in the Assistant Editor,
and Control-drag from the WKInterfaceDate object in the storyboard to the
top of InterfaceController.swift to create an outlet called date. Next,
change the format string to 'EEEE, hh:mm: a zzz' to add the timezone to
the formatted result. Finally, add the following code shown in bold to the
awakeWithContext() method and run the example again:

```
override func awakeWithContext(context: AnyObject?) {
    super.awakeWithContext(context)

    // Configure interface objects here.
    let timezone = NSTimeZone(abbreviation: "CST")
    date.setTimeZone(timezone)
}
```

You should now see the time as it would be in Central Standard Time, as shown in Figure 4-28. (If you happen to be in the CST timezone, use some other timezone abbreviation, such as EST instead.)

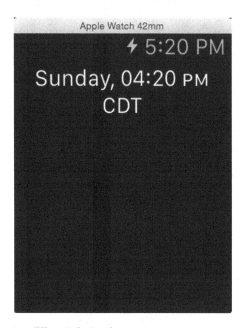

Figure 4-28. Switching to a different display timezone

Notice that the displayed timezone is CDT, not CST. That's because, at the time of writing, daylight savings is active, so the prevailing timezone is actually CDT.

Calling setTimeZone() with a nil argument restores the user's default timezone.

In some cases, you may want to change the calendar used to convert the time into individual day, month, and year components. Again, by default, the active calendar is set by the user. Much of the world uses the Gregorian calendar, but you may want to show the date and time relative to, say, the Hebrew calendar. You can do this by setting the Calendar attribute using the setCalendar() method.

You can find a list of the available calendars on the documentation page for the NSLocale class. As an example, add the following code shown in bold to the awakeWithContext() method to use the Hebrew calendar:

```
override func awakeWithContext(context: AnyObject?) {
    super.awakeWithContext(context)

    // Configure interface objects here.
    let timezone = NSTimeZone(abbreviation: "CST")
    date.setTimeZone(timezone)

    date.setCalendar(NSCalendar(identifier: NSCalendarIdentifierHebrew))
}
```

Now change the Format attribute back to Standard and the Date and Time attributes to Medium. Then run the example again to see the date and time relative to the Hebrew calendar (Figure 4-29).

Figure 4-29. Using the Hebrew calendar

To revert to the user's default calendar, call setCalendar(nil).

Displaying a Timer

The WKInterfaceTimer class implements a count-up or count-down timer. Understanding how this object works really ought to be simple, but it seems (at least to me) to be somewhat counterintuitive. The easiest way to explain what this class does is to set up an example and experiment with it, so create a new project called Timer and add a WatchKit extension to it. Select Interface.storyboard in the Project Navigator and then drag a Timer object from the Object Library and drop it onto the interface controller. Like WKInterfaceDate, WKInterfaceTimer acts like a label and you can set all the usual label options. Change the Width attribute to Relative to Container, set Lines to 0 so that the content can wrap onto as many lines as it needs to, and set the Alignment to Center. At this point, your storyboard and Attributes Inspector should look like Figure 4-30.

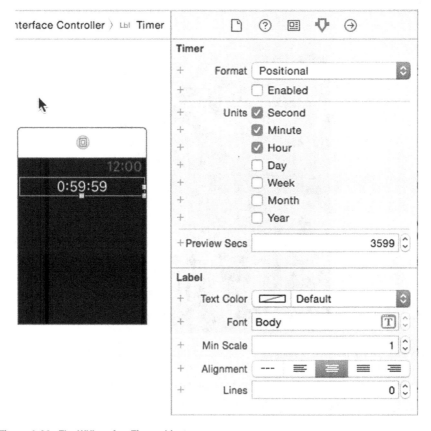

Figure 4-30. The WKInterfaceTimer object

Timer Formatting Options

Before we look at the timer's behavior, let's examine the formatting options that are available. Formatting is set using the controls in the top three sections of the Attribute Inspector. First, you can use the Preview attribute to set a time interval that's used only so that you can see the effect of your selected formatting options in the storyboard. The value you set here is not used at run time. By default, this attribute is set to 3599 seconds and it's displayed as 0:59:59, as shown in Figure 4-30. The Units checkboxes in the second group specify which time units are displayed. The Format control in the top group determines how they are formatted. Open the Format selector and you'll see that there are five options available: Positional, Abbreviated, Short, Full, and Spelled Out. Experiment with these to see what they do. The Positional option is used in Figure 4-30, and Figure 4-31 shows the Abbreviated (left), Short (center), and Spelled Out (right) options.

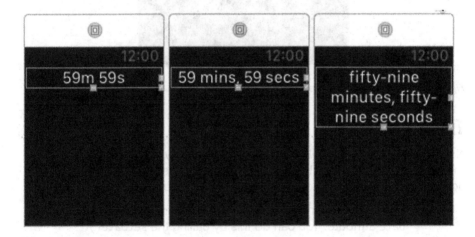

Figure 4-31. Three of the available timer formatting options

Toggle the Units checkboxes to show or hide the various parts of the time. Changing the visible units may have an effect on the way the value is displayed. For example, change the Format attribute to Abbreviated and clear all the Unit checkboxes apart from Second. Because the hour and minute values can no longer be shown, the preview value must be displayed as 3,599s instead of 59 m 59s, leading to the result shown in Figure 4-32.

Figure 4-32. The effect of changing the Units *attribute*

Timer Behavior

Now let's talk about what WKInterfaceTimer actually does. It does two things: it counts time and it updates its display. These two things are actually independent of each other. Here's how it works:

- The time-counting behavior starts once you set the Date attribute. You can do this by calling the setDate() method.

- If you call setDate() with a time that's in the future, the timer counts *down* until it reaches that time, then stops.

- If you call setDate() with the current time or a time that's in the past, the timer counts *up* from that time and does not stop.

- If you don't call setDate() at all, that's equivalent to calling it with the current time, and the timer counts up from zero and does not stop.

That all sounds straightforward, so let's try it out to see how it works. Set the Format attribute to Positional. Then select the Second, Minute, and Hour checkboxes and run the example on the simulator. You'll see the result shown on the left in Figure 4-33.

Figure 4-33. *The* WKInterfaceTimer *class in action*

The timer displays 0:00:00 and doesn't change. When, as here, you don't call setDate(), the timer initializes itself to count up from the current time, but it actually displays the difference between the current time and the initial time. The initial time *is* the current time, so the difference is zero, and that's the value that is displayed.

The timer display isn't changing because the Enabled attribute is false in the storyboard. Check the Enabled attribute, which you'll find in the top group of attributes in the Attributes Inspector (see Figure 4-30) and run the example again. This time, you'll see the timer counting upwards from 0:00:00, as shown in the second screenshot in Figure 4-33.

Now let's try setting the Date attribute. We'll first need to create an outlet for the timer object. Open InterfaceController.swift in the Assistant Editor, Control-drag from the timer in the storyboard to the top of the class to create an outlet called timer, and then add the following code shown in bold to the willActivate() method:

```
override func willActivate() {
    super.willActivate()
    timer.setDate(NSDate(timeIntervalSinceNow: 60))
}
```

We've initialized the timer with a time that is one minute in the future. As I said earlier, the timer deals with the difference between the time that was set and the current time. Here, the difference is one minute, so that's what the timer initially displays. Because the time is in the future, it then counts down—effectively, you are asking the timer to count down to the future time that you set. After seven seconds, you'll see the result shown in the third screenshot in Figure 4-33. Once the timer reaches zero (at the time that you set with setDate()), it stops.

Now change the code in willActivate() as shown here and run the
example again:

```
override func willActivate() {
    super.willActivate()
    timer.setDate(NSDate(timeIntervalSinceNow: -120))

}
```

This time, the date that's set is two minutes in the past. The timer now
initializes itself to show two minutes, but this time it counts up, as shown on
the right in Figure 4-33—you've asked it to count forward from the past time
that you set.

Once you've remembered the relationship between the time difference and
the counting direction, this all seems reasonable. But that's not the end
of the story. Remember that the timer didn't update itself until we set the
Enabled attribute? You may have thought that's because the timer doesn't
start unless Enabled is true, but that's not the case. It starts as soon as its
Date attribute is set—what the Enabled attribute actually controls is *whether
the timer updates itself on the screen*. When we first ran this example, the
time display did not update because Enabled was false, but the timer was
still running.

Let's modify our example to make it easier to see that the timer updates
itself independently of what you see on the screen. Make sure Interface.
storyboard is selected in the Project Navigator and drag three buttons onto
the storyboard, placing them one above the other and below the timer.
Change the button titles to Start, Stop, and Reset, as shown in Figure 4-34.

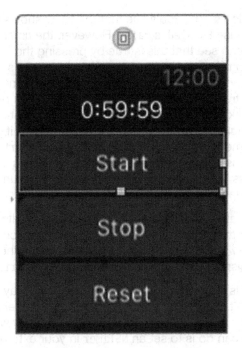

Figure 4-34. Using buttons to control a WKInterfaceTimer object

Now Control-drag from the Start, Stop, and Reset buttons in turn to the
InterfaceController class in the Assistant Editor to create action methods
called onStart(), onStop(), and onReset() respectively and add the code
shown in bold here to these methods:

```
@IBAction func onStart() {
    timer.start()
}

@IBAction func onStop() {
    timer.stop()
}

@IBAction func onReset() {
    timer.setDate(NSDate(timeIntervalSinceNow: -120))
}

}
```

Finally, select the timer object in the storyboard, uncheck its Enabled
attribute in the Attributes Inspector, and run the example again.

When the application starts, you'll see that the timer shows 0:02:00 and it's not updating, because Enabled is false. However, the timer is still counting upwards and you can see that this is true by pressing the Start button to call the timer's start() method. The start() method does not start the timer—*it starts timer updates to the screen* (it's the run-time equivalent of setting Enabled to true). If you wait one minute before you press Start, you'll see that the timer skips from 0:02:00 to 0:03:00, demonstrating that it was running even through the display was not changing. Now if you press the Stop button, the timer's stop() method is called. Like start(), this does not stop the timer—it just stops the screen updates. So press Stop, wait a few seconds, and press Start again, and you'll see the time jump forward when the display starts updating again.

The Reset button causes the Date attribute to be reset to its initial value. If you press this button, you'll see the time value on the screen update immediately, even if you've pressed the Stop button, but the timer is still running, and the display won't update until you press Start.

WKInterfaceTimer is a purely visual object—there is no way to get its current value, and you can't link it to an action method in your interface controller. If you initialize a timer to count down and you want to know when it's reached zero, the best you can do is to set an NSTimer in your extension and take any required action when it fires. Keep in mind, though, that there may be a slight time difference between the timer reaching zero and your extension's timer firing—and, if the user stops interacting with your application, your extension may be terminated and the timer will be destroyed with it.

WatchKit Maps

The WatchKit WKInterfaceMap object is a highly simplified version of MapKit's MKMapView control. Like MKMapView, it displays a map, and you can add annotations to it, but unlike MKMapView it is almost completely static—for example, you can't pan and zoom the map. The only interaction that it supports is a touch, which opens the watch's native Map application.

Displaying a Map

Create a new project called Map and add a WatchKit extension to it. Select Interface.storyboard in the Project Navigator and then drag and drop a Map object from the Object Library onto the interface controller. Although the WKInterfaceMap object does not have built-in support for zooming, we can still implement it ourselves and we're going to do that here to illustrate the effect of setting different size values for the map's Region attribute. Drag a slider from the Object Library and drop it below the map. At this point, your storyboard should be as shown on the left in Figure 4-35.

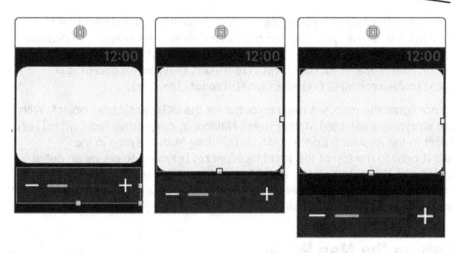

Figure 4-35. Using a map with a slider

We'd like to show as much of the map as the screen size will allow, but, as you can see, there is currently a gap below the slider. We need to move the slider to the bottom of the screen and then resize the map to occupy the rest of the space. We can move the slider to the bottom of the screen by selecting it and setting its Vertical position attribute to Bottom. Making the map occupy all the remaining space is not quite so simple, however. WatchKit does not have auto layout, so there is no way to link the bottom of the map to the top of the slider—instead, we have to do it manually. So use the mouse to select the map in the storyboard and drag its lower edge down until it meets the top edge of the slider. You'll know you've reached this point because the slider will start moving downwards—when this happens, nudge the bottom of the map up a little so that the map and slider together exactly fill the screen, as shown in the center in Figure 4-35. Unfortunately, that's not all you need to do. The design in the storyboard will work on the 38mm Watch, but not on the larger version. Use the control at the bottom of the storyboard editor to switch the layout display from Any Screen Size to Apple Watch 42 mm and you'll see that there's still a gap between the map and the slider, as shown on the right in Figure 4-35. As before, drag the bottom of the map down until it reaches the slider and then set the storyboard back to Any Screen Size.

Your layout now works for both screen sizes, which you can confirm by running the example on the simulator. When you do that, you'll see that the map is blank, as it is in Figure 4-35. The map doesn't show anything until you set the location and size of the area that you'd like it to display. You can do that using either the setRegion() or setVisibleMapRect() method. Which of these methods you use depends on whether you prefer to think in terms of degrees of latitude and longitude, or the more abstract map units. Personally, I prefer the former, so we'll use the setRegion() method in this example. You can read about map units in Apple's *Location and Maps Programming Guide*, which you'll find at https://developer. apple.com/library/mac/documentation/UserExperience/Conceptual/ LocationAwarenessPG/Introduction/Introduction.html.

To configure the map, we need an outlet for the WKInterfaceMap object. With the storyboard selected in the Project Navigator, open InterfaceController. swift in the Assistant Editor and Control-drag from the map in the storyboard to the top of the InterfaceController class to create an outlet called map. While we're here, we'll also add an action method for the slider. Control-drag from the slider to the bottom of the InterfaceController class and add an action method called onSliderValueChanged().

Setting the Map Region

To set the location and size of the region that we want the map to display, we need to create an MKCoordinateRegion structure. MKCoordinateRegion is part of the MapKit framework and it uses two other structures: MKCoordinateSpan specifies the size of an area, and CLLocationCoordinate2D is part of the Core Location framework and represents a coordinate pair. Let's add to our interface controller a variable that represents the coordinates of the center of the region displayed by the map and the scale factor that we want to use. Initially, this will be 1, but later we'll link it to the value of the slider, so that we can zoom in to show more and more detail. Add the following lines shown in bold to InterfaceController.swift:

```
import WatchKit
import Foundation
import CoreLocation
import MapKit

class InterfaceController: WKInterfaceController {
    @IBOutlet weak var map: WKInterfaceMap!
    private var coords: CLLocationCoordinate2D!
    private var scaleFactor = 1.0
```

What do we use for the location coordinates? Of course, it depends on what we want to show in the map. The most natural thing to do would be to use the user's current location, and we'll do that later in this section, but for now let's just use a hard-coded value so that we can get something working. Add this code in bold to the awakeWithContent() method:

```
override func awakeWithContext(context: AnyObject?) {
    super.awakeWithContext(context)
```

```
    // Configure interface objects here.
    coords = CLLocationCoordinate2DMake(37.33233141,-122.03121860)
}
```

The `CLLocationCoordinate2dMake()` function returns a
`CLLocationCoordinate2d` object for a point given its latitude and longitude.
The values we're using here are not random—they are the coordinates
of Apple's HQ building. Now lets add a method that uses the coords and
scaleFactor variables to set the map's visible region:

```
func updateMap() -> Void {
    if coords != nil {
        let areaSize = 1 / scaleFactor
        let region = MKCoordinateRegionMake(coords!,
                            MKCoordinateSpanMake(areaSize, areaSize))
        map.setRegion(region)
    }
}
```

The `MKCoordinateRegionMake` function requires two arguments: the
coordinates of the center of the region and an `MKCoordinateSpan` object that
specifies the region's latitude and longitude deltas. Initially, we want the map
to show an area that covers 1 degree of latitude and 1 degree of longitude.
However, we'd like to be able to change this using the slider, so we've
incorporated the value of the scaleFactor variable:

```
let areaSize = 1 / scaleFactor
```

We initialized the scaleFactor variable to 1, so areaSize starts out being 1
as well. As we increase the value of scaleFactor, the value of areaSize will
get smaller, meaning that the area covered by the map will also get smaller.
Because the map's size is constant, however, it will display progressively
smaller areas in the same space, in effect zooming in on the center
coordinate.

Finally, add the following line of code to the willActivate() method to
configure the map when the interface controller is shown and then run the
example. You should get the result shown in Figure 4-36.

```
override func willActivate() {
    super.willActivate()
    updateMap()
}
```

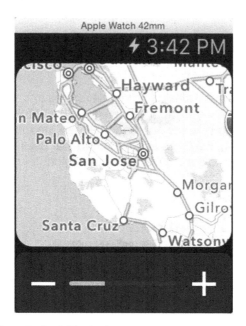

Figure 4-36. California on the Apple Watch simulator

A one degree-square region covers a lot of territory! What we'd really like to do is use a pinch gesture to zoom in to see Apple's HQ, but the map doesn't support that, and the slider is currently not connected. Let's fix that now.

Select the slider in the storyboard, open the Attributes Inspector, and set its attributes, as shown in Figure 4-37.

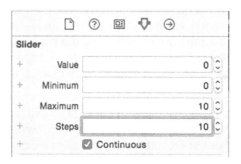

Figure 4-37. Configuring the slider to allow the map to be zoomed

These settings allow the slider to range in value from 0 to 10 through 10 intermediate steps, starting from 0. Now add the following code shown in bold to the onSliderValueChanged() method:

```
@IBAction func onSliderValueChanged(value: Float) {
    scaleFactor = pow(2, Double(value))
    updateMap()
}
```

The effect of this code is to double (or halve) the value of the scaleFactor variable each time the value of the slider increases (or decreases) by one step. Once we've set the new value, we call updateMap() to calculate the new span of the region to be displayed and redraw the map. Now run the example and you'll see that as you change the slider value, the map zooms in or out to let you see more or less detail. Figure 4-38 shows a couple of examples at different levels of zoom.

Figure 4-38. Using a slider to zoom the map

You'll notice that the map zooms quite slowly. Updating map tiles is an expensive process, so although this makes an interesting example, you may not want to allow the user to do much of this in a real application.

Adding an Annotation

You can add an annotation to a map by specifying the coordinates of the location to be annotated. You can choose to use a standard pin annotation with a choice of color (red, green, or purple) or you can create a custom annotation with an image of your own. Let's add a green pin to our map to mark the exact location of Apple's campus. To do that, add the following code in bold to the awakeWithContext() method:

```
override func awakeWithContext(context: AnyObject?) {
    super.awakeWithContext(context)

    coords = CLLocationCoordinate2DMake(37.33233141,-122.03121860)
    map.addAnnotation(coords, withPinColor: .Green)
}
```

Run the example and you'll see the green pin, as shown in Figure 4-39 where the map has been zoomed in to show the Apple campus.

Figure 4-39. Adding an annotation to the map

To create a custom annotation, use the addAnnotation(_:withImage:cent erOffset:) or addAnnotation(_:withImageNamed:centerOffset:) method. The former requires the image in the form of a UIImage object which is sent from the iPhone to the Watch at run time, whereas the latter uses an image that's either in the WatchKit App bundle or has been preloaded into the image cache on the watch. The centerOffset argument lets you control the exact point of the image that's placed over the annotated location. You can remove all annotations from the map by calling the removeAllAnnotations() method.

Using Core Location to Get the User's Location

To close our discussion of the WKInterfaceMap class, we're going to enhance the Map application to show the user's current location—or whatever the simulator is configured to return when asked for the user's location. Doing this won't demonstrate anything new about WKInterfaceMap itself (in fact, all we're going to be doing is setting the coords variable in a different way), but it does illustrate something important about writing extensions which we'll revisit in Chapter 7: sometimes, the extension needs to get help from its owning application.

To get the user's location, you need to use the Core Location standard location service. Before you can do that, you need to get the user's permission to do so. When you make the API call to get that permission, iOS displays a pop-up on the iPhone (*not* on the watch) to which the user can respond either yes or no. You can certainly make this API call from your WatchKit Extension (and I encourage you to try it once you've seen the code shortly), but Apple strongly recommends that you don't. The reason is simple: the pop-up appears immediately, whatever the user is doing. If the user is actually using the iPhone to do something else, the appearance of an unrelated pop-up requesting permission to use his location might be surprising and, in these days where everyone is security-aware, downright suspicious. Or, more likely, the user is using your WatchKit app and looking at the watch, with the iPhone on a table somewhere or in a pocket, and the pop-up will go unnoticed. The recommended approach is for your iOS application to ask for permission to use the user's location at some convenient point in its lifecycle, when the user is actually interacting with it. Once the iOS application has permission, any extension in that application inherits it.

Let's start by adding the code to get the user's permission to use Core Location services to the iOS application. Because this is just an example and the iOS application isn't doing anything useful, we'll do this in the simplest possible way, by adding the code to the view controller's viewDidLoad() method. In a real application, you would find a more natural place to put this code. Select the file ViewController.swift on the Map group in the Project Navigator and add the code shown in bold to it:

```
import UIKit
import CoreLocation

class ViewController: UIViewController, CLLocationManagerDelegate {
    private var locationMgr: CLLocationManager!

    override func viewDidLoad() {
        super.viewDidLoad()

        if CLLocationManager.locationServicesEnabled()
                && CLLocationManager.authorizationStatus() ==
.NotDeterminded {
            locationMgr = CLLocationManager()
            locationMgr.delegate = self
            locationMgr.requestWhenInUseAuthorization()
        }
    }

    func locationManager(manager: CLLocationManager!,
            didChangeAuthorizationStatus status: CLAuthorizationStatus) {
        println("Location manager auth status changed to \(status.
rawValue)")
    }

}
```

The code in the viewDidLoad() method first checks that location services have not been disabled and that permission to use the user's location has not already been requested (and possibly denied). It then creates an instance of CLLocationManager, makes the view controller its delegate, and requests permission to use location services while the application itself is in use. Asking for in-use permission is enough if your application just needs to know the user's current location while it is active, because the application is deemed to be active if only the extension is running. The result of the request is delivered at some later point to the view controller's implementation of the locationManager(_:didChangeAuthorizationStatus:) method, where we just print the result to the console.

Before running this example, open the application's Info.plist file and add a new key called NSLocationWhenInUseUsageDescription, as shown in Figure 4-40.

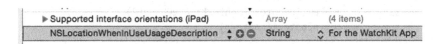

| ▶ Supported interface orientations (iPad) | ↕ | Array | (4 items) |
| NSLocationWhenInUseUsageDescription | ↕ ⊕ ⊖ | String | ⬦ For the WatchKit App |

Figure 4-40. This key in the Info.plist file is required before a request for permission to use Core Location services can be made

The value of this key is a message that is shown to the user in the permission request pop-up. If this key is not present, the permission request is not made. Run the iOS application in the simulator by using the Map scheme in the Scheme selector in Xcode and click Allow in the pop-up that appears (see Figure 4-41).

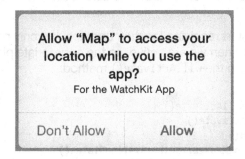

Allow "Map" to access your location while you use the app?
For the WatchKit App

| Don't Allow | Allow |

Figure 4-41. Requesting permission to use Core Location services

You should see the following message in the Xcode console, indicating that permission has been granted:

Location manager auth status changed to 4

Now let's add the code that we need in the WatchKit extension. To be notified of the user's location, the extension needs to create a CLLocationManager instance, become its delegate, and then ask it to start reporting the user's position. To do this, open InterfaceController.swift and make the changes shown in bold:

```
class InterfaceController: WKInterfaceController, CLLocationManagerDelegate
{
    private var locationMgr: CLLocationManager!
    @IBOutlet weak var map: WKInterfaceMap!
    private var coords: CLLocationCoordinate2D!
    private var lastCoords: CLLocationCoordinate2D!
    private var scaleFactor = 1.0
```

```
     override func awakeWithContext(context: AnyObject?) {
         super.awakeWithContext(context)

//          coords = CLLocationCoordinate2DMake(37.33233141,-122.03121860)
//          map.addAnnotation(coords, withPinColor: .Green)
         locationMgr = CLLocationManager()
         locationMgr.delegate = self
     }
```

This code is similar to the code we added to the iOS application. In the interface controller's awakeWithContext() method, we create a CLLocationManager instance and make the interface controller its delegate. We also remove the code that we used earlier to hard-code the location to be used in the map. We also added a variable called lastCoords that we'll use later.

Next, we need to start receiving location updates. We only need to know the user's location when we are active, so the appropriate place to request location updates is in the willActivate() method:

```
     override func willActivate() {
         super.willActivate()
//          updateMap()
         if CLLocationManager.authorizationStatus()
             == .AuthorizedWhenInUse {
             locationMgr.startUpdatingLocation()
         }
     }
```

Notice that we only ask for location updates if the user has granted permission for us to receive them. By the way, it's possible for the user to revoke this permission at any time. We don't handle that case here, but in a real application you would need to consider what you should do if that happens.

We need to stop receiving updates when our interface controller is not active. To do that, add the code in bold to the didDeactivate() method:

```
     override func didDeactivate() {
         super.didDeactivate()
         locationMgr.stopUpdatingLocation()
     }
```

Location updates are delivered to the delegate's locationManager(_:didUp
dateLocations:) method. Add the following implementation of that method
to InterfaceController.swift:

```
func locationManager(manager: CLLocationManager!,
                     didUpdateLocations locations: [AnyObject]!) {
    if let location =
            locations[locations.count - 1] as? CLLocation {
        lastCoords = coords
        coords = location.coordinate
        if coords != nil && (lastCoords == nil
                || coords?.latitude != lastCoords?.latitude
                || coords?.longitude != lastCoords?.longitude) {
            updateMap()
        }
    }
}
```

The locations array that is passed to this method contains one or more
CLLocation objects, each representing the user's location at some time in
the recent past. The newest position is the one at the end of the list, so we
retrieve it, checking that it is indeed a CLLocation object, and get the user's
coordinates from its coordinate property. We then use this value to update the
coords property and call updateMap() to set the region to be drawn by the map.

It's possible that we'll get frequent updates that report the same user
location. The map performs a fade animation whenever its Region attribute
is changed, so if we were to update it each time we get a new location,
it would appear to flash. To minimize this effect, we save each reported
location in the lastCoords property and only update the map if the new
location differs from what is stored in lastCoords.

Now if you run this example on the simulator, you'll see that the map shows
whatever location the simulator is configured to return in response to
location update requests. You can change this location from the simulator's
Debug ➤ Locations menu. If you run this on a device, you should be able to
watch your own position updating on the map as you move.

Summary

In this chapter, you saw how to use three different types of user interface object that can be linked to action methods in your WatchKit extension-buttons, sliders, and switches. You also saw how to use the date object to format dates and times, how to use the timer object to display a countdown, and how to display location information in a map. In the course of learning how to use the map, you discovered that, because of restrictions on what extensions can do, it is sometimes necessary for a WatchKit application to get help from its owning iOS application. This is a topic that Capter 7 discusses in much greater detail.

You have now seen almost all of the WatchKit user interface objects and how to use them to build simple applications that have only one screen. Most applications, however, are more sophisticated than that. In the next chapter, you'll see how to build applications that require more than one screen and how to navigate from screen to screen.

Chapter 5

Controller Navigation

Over the course of the last three chapters, you have been introduced to the building blocks that you can use to create a simple, single-screen application. This chapter takes the next logical step and looks at how to create multi-screen applications. In UIKit, each screen is built around a view controller, and similarly in WatchKit, each screen is mapped to an interface controller. UIKit offers you several ways to combine view controllers—for example, you can use a `UITabBarController` to create a tabbed user interface, a `UINavigationController` to build a hierarchical application, or a `UIPageViewController` if your application has pages of similar information that you want to be able to swipe through. You are completely free to mix all these different view controllers together or create navigation schemes of your own if you need to.

WatchKit is not nearly as flexible. In fact, your choices are very limited. At design time, you can take one of two approaches:

- You can create a root interface controller and then push additional controllers onto it, much like UIKit's `UINavigationController`.

- You can build your application as a set of sibling pages, like UIKit's `UIPageViewController`.

Once you've made your choice, you have to stick with it. You can't create an application that mixes the hierarchical navigation style with the paged style—it's all hierarchical, or all paged-based. To make that clearer, here are a couple of things that you are allowed to do in UIKIt that you can't do with WatchKit:

- If you choose the hierarchical style, none of the interface controllers that you push are allowed to be paged-based.

- Similarly, if you choose the page-based style, none of the pages can be a hierarchical interface controller.

The only exception to these rules comes when you present an interface controller. A presented interface controller must be either a single object or be part of a paged-based interface, but it can be presented by both hierarchical and page-based interface controllers. Interface controller navigation is the subject of the first part of this chapter, followed by a discussion of interface controller presentation.

Hierarchical Navigation

To build a hierarchical interface, you start with a root controller and then push another controller onto it. WatchKit animates the new interface controller onto the screen, replacing the existing one. The new controller can push further controllers if required, although it's unlikely that a WatchKit application will need to create a deep hierarchy of screens. Later, you can pop controllers off of the stack one by one, or remove them all at the same time and jump directly back to the root controller.

You can either push a new controller manually or create a segue in the storyboard and let WatchKit take care of it for you. This section illustrates both approaches.

Manual Controller Navigation

Let's start by creating a project that we can use to explore hierarchical navigation. Call the project HierarchicalNavigation, add a WatchKit target to it, and select Interface.storyboard in the Project Navigator to open the storyboard in the editor. As with all of our earlier examples, we have a single interface controller—the root controller—which is the entry point to the WatchKit application. In this example, we're going to add a second controller that we'll push onto the root controller to create a very simple hierarchical user interface.

Creating the Second Interface Controller

To create the second controller, we need to do two things: first, add an interface controller object to the storyboard, and then create a WKInterfaceController subclass that will contain the controller's logic. Locate an interface controller object in the Object Library, drag it onto the storyboard, and drop it somewhere near the root controller. Next, select the HierarchicalNavigation WatchKit Extension group in the Project Navigator. Click File ➤ New ➤ File… in Xcode's menu or press ⌘N to open the New File dialog. In the iOS Source section, select Cocoa Touch Class and click **Next**. On the next page, name the class ImageController and make it a subclass of WKInterfaceController. Click **Next** and save the new class file in your project, making sure it's part of the HierarchicalNavigation WatchKit Extension group and the target of the same name. You should now have two interface controller files in your project—InterfaceController.swift and ImageController.swift—and the second one should be open in the editor.

> **Note** At this point, you may notice that Xcode is complaining that you have an unreachable controller in your storyboard. Don't worry about this—we'll fix it shortly.

Now we need to link the new controller in the storyboard to the class that we just created for it. Select Interface.storyboard in the Project Navigator, click on the interface controller that you added earlier, and open the Identify Inspector (⌥⌘3). To create the link, click the Class selector in the Custom Class section of the Identity Inspector and select ImageController, as shown in Figure 5-1.

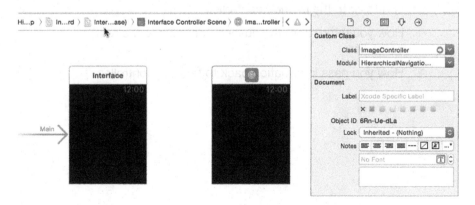

Figure 5-1. Linking the interface controller class to the controller in the storyboard

The application you're going to build is shown in Figure 5-2.

Figure 5-2. Using hierarchical interface controller navigation

On the left is the root interface controller, which contains two buttons and a label. Tapping either of the buttons pushes the second interface controller, which displays an image that depends on which button was pressed and another pair of buttons with which you can either like or dislike the image. When one of these buttons is pressed, the interface controller will be popped, revealing the root view controller again, with its label updated to show whether you liked the image or not.

This is a very simple application, but it illustrates the basic features of an application that uses hierarchical navigation, namely:

- How you trigger the switch from one interface controller to another.

- How you pass information from the root interface controller to the pushed controller.

- How you return from the pushed controller to the root controller.

- How you pass information back to the root controller.

Building the Controllers' User Interfaces

Before we look in detail at each of these aspects of the application, we first need to create the user interfaces for both controllers. By now, you should find this to be very straightforward. Start by dragging two buttons and a label from the Object Library and dropping them onto the root view controller, with the label at the bottom, and then do the following:

- Change the title of the top button to Image 1 and of the bottom button to Image 2.

- Open the Attributes Inspector (⌥⌘4), select the label, and change its Vertical attribute to Bottom and its Width attribute to Relative to Container. This makes the width of the label match that of the interface controller and moves it to the bottom. Change the label text to Press a Button, its Alignment to center, and its Lines attribute to 0.

- The label is too close to the bottom of the screen, so let's move it up a little. To do that, select the interface controller, change its Insets attribute to Custom, and then set the Bottom attribute to 8.

At this point, the root interface controller should be as shown on the left in Figure 5-3.

Figure 5-3. Constructing the interface controllers

Now let's populate the second interface controller. Here, we want an image at the top and two buttons underneath, arranged as shown in Figure 5-2. An interface controller positions its child objects vertically, so to create a single row containing two buttons side-by-side, we need to add a horizontal group underneath the image and place the buttons in that group. Here are the steps required to create the layout shown on the right in Figure 5-3:

1. Drag an image object from the Object Library, drop it onto the second interface controller, and then drop a group underneath it.

2. Select the group and change its Vertical attribute to Bottom.

3. Drag a button from the Object Library and drop it inside the group. We need to make the button occupy half the width of the group, so select it and change the value in the input field below the Width attribute from 1.0 to 0.5. Change its Title attribute to Like.

4. Now drag a second button and drop it to the right of the first one. Change its Width attribute to 0.5 and change its Title attribute to Dislike. You should now have two buttons of equal width.

5. Select the image object and change its Mode attribute to Aspect Fit so that the image will be scaled to fit the space available, but without any distortion. Also change the Width attribute to Relative to Container.

6. Finally, drag the bottom of the image down until it just touches the top of the group containing the buttons. Switch the storyboard to Apple Watch 42 mm and do the same again. Switch the storyboard back to Any Screen Size.

You also need to give the second interface controller an identifier so you can refer to it when you navigate from the main interface controller. Select the ImageController in the storyboard or in the Document Outline. In the Attributes Inspector, locate the Identifier field in the Interface Controller section and enter the name ImageController. You can use any name you like here, as long as you use the same name when writing the code to push the interface controller, which we'll see shortly.

> **Note**   Now that you've given this interface controller a name, the Xcode
> warning about an unreachable controller should go away. You didn't need to give
> the first interface controller a name, because it's tagged as the initial controller
> and gets loaded automatically when the application starts running.

The second interface controller should now be as shown on the right in
Figure 5-3.

Finally, we need a couple of images to display when the second interface
controller is pushed. You'll find these in the 5 - Navigation Example Images
folder of the example source code archive. Open the asset catalog in the
HierarchicalNavigation WatchKit App Group and drag the files image1@2x.
png and image2@2x.png into it. That completes the initial storyboard for this
application.

Creating Outlets and Action Methods

Now you need to create the outlets and action methods that connect the
user interface objects in the storyboard to the two interface controllers. Let's
start with the root controller. Here, you need an action method for each of
the buttons and an outlet for the label:

- Open InterfaceController.swift in the Assistant
  Editor and Control-drag from the top button in the root
  controller to the bottom of the class definition to create
  an action method called onImage1ButtonClicked().
  Repeat with the other button to create an action method
  called onImage2ButtonClicked(). We need two action
  methods because we need to know which button was
  pressed. As you have already seen, WatchKit action
  methods do not have an argument that indicates which
  object triggered them, so you can't connect more than
  one button (or slider, switch etc) to the same action
  method if you need to know which button was pressed,
  as we do in this case.

- Control-drag from the label to the top of the class
  definition and create an outlet called label.

At this point, the InterfaceController class should be as shown in the following code, with the code just added in bold. You should also add the println() statements in the willActivate() and didDeactivate() methods:

```
class InterfaceController: WKInterfaceController {
    @IBOutlet weak var label: WKInterfaceLabel!

    override func awakeWithContext(context: AnyObject?) {
        super.awakeWithContext(context)

        // Configure interface objects here.
    }

    override func willActivate() {
        super.willActivate()
        println("InterfaceController willActivate() called")
    }

    override func didDeactivate() {
        super.didDeactivate()
        println("InterfaceController didDeactivate() called")
    }

    @IBAction func onImage1ButtonClicked() {
    }

    @IBAction func onImage2ButtonClicked() {
    }
}
```

Now select the second interface controller in the storyboard and open ImageController.swift in the Assistant Editor. Control-drag from the image object to the top of the class definition to create an outlet called image. Then Control-drag from the two buttons in turn to create action methods called onLikeButtonClicked() and onDislikeButtonClicked(). The changes to the ImageController class are shown in bold in the following code. As before, add the println() calls in the awakeWithContext(), willActivate(), and didDeactivate() methods:

```
class ImageController: WKInterfaceController {
    @IBOutlet weak var image: WKInterfaceImage!

    override func awakeWithContext(context: AnyObject?) {
        super.awakeWithContext(context)
        println("ImageController awakeWithContext() called: \(context)")
    }
```

```
override func willActivate() {
    super.willActivate()
    println("ImageController willActivate() called")
}

override func didDeactivate() {
    super.didDeactivate()
    println("ImageController didDeactivate() called")
}

@IBAction func onLikeButtonClicked() {
}

@IBAction func onDislikeButtonClicked() {
}
}
```

Navigating to the Second Interface Controller

When the user clicks either of the buttons on the screen of the initial interface controller, we need to push an instance of the second interface controller and tell it which image should be displayed. We do that by calling the pushControllerWithName(_:context:) method of the main interface controller. The first argument of this function is the name of the interface controller to be pushed, which is the identifier (ImageController) that we assigned to that controller in the storyboard. The second argument is an object that gets passed to the pushed interface controller's awakeWithContext() method. You can use this object to pass any information that the controller needs to do its job. We need to tell the controller which image to display, so we can simply pass it the image name, like this:

```
pushControllerWithName("ImageController", context: "image1")
```

Let's try that out. Make the following changes to the onImage1ButtonClicked() and onImage2ButtonClicked() methods in InterfaceController.swift:

```
@IBAction func onImage1ButtonClicked() {
    pushControllerWithName("ImageController", context: "image1")
}

@IBAction func onImage2ButtonClicked() {
    pushControllerWithName("ImageController", context: "image2")
}
}
```

Now make sure that the Xcode console is visible (⇧⌘C), run the application, and click either of the buttons. You should see that the original interface controller is replaced by an instance of the `ImageController`, although the image is currently missing and the two buttons at the bottom of the screen don't do anything. Also, at the top left of the screen, you'll see a < symbol. If you click this, the `ImageController` is removed, and the original interface controller reappears. Let's take a look at exactly what happened here. Run the application again and pay attention to the console output. When the application starts, you'll see that `InterfaceController` is activated:

```
InterfaceController willActivate() called
```

Now press one of the buttons to push `ImageController` and you'll see the following output in the console:

```
ImageController awakeWithContext() called: Optional(image1)
ImageController willActivate() called
InterfaceController didDeactivate() called
```

When the button was pressed, the `pushControllerWithName(_:context:)` method was called with the name argument set to `ImageController`. WatchKit looked in the storyboard for an interface controller with this identifier and found the `ImageController` class. It then created an instance of `ImageController` and called its `init()` method (which we did not override) followed by its `awakeWithContext()` method, passing it the value of the `context` argument of the `pushControllerWithName(_:context:)` call, which is the image name. Notice that the context is wrapped in an `Optional`, because the argument type is `AnyObject?` to allow a `nil` context to be passed if required. Finally, the `ImageController` instance is activated, and the original controller is deactivated because it is no longer visible.

Now press the < symbol at the top left of the screen and you'll see that the original controller is activated and the outgoing controller is deactivated:

```
InterfaceController willActivate() called
ImageController didDeactivate() called
```

So far, so good. Now we need to install the correct image in the `WKInterfaceImage` object in the second interface controller. Because we pass the image name as the context object, all we need to do is make use of it. To do that, add the code shown in bold to the `awakeWithContext()` method of the `ImageController` class:

```
override func awakeWithContext(context: AnyObject?) {
    super.awakeWithContext(context)
    println("ImageController awakeWithContext() called: \(context)")
```

```
    if let imageName = context as? String {
        image.setImageNamed(imageName)
    }
}
```

Run the application again, press one of the buttons, and you should now see an image when the second interface controller appears, as shown back in Figure 5-2.

Returning to the First Interface Controller

When the user presses the Like or Dislike button, we need to return to the initial interface controller and display the result, which depends on which button was pressed, in the label at the bottom of the screen. There are two problems with this:

- To return to the initial interface controller, we need to call the popController() method of ImageController (or, because the initial interface controller is the root of the hierarchy, we could also call popToRootController()). This method does not accept any arguments, so there is no way to use it to pass back any information.

- You have already seen that you can return to the first interface controller by pressing the ‹ symbol at the top left of the screen. When this happens, WatchKit itself calls popController() without notifying any application code, meaning there is no way to know that ImageController is being removed from the screen until it has been deactivated. There is no way to disable this, so you can't stop the user returning to the initial controller without pressing either the Like or Dislike button.

Let's first tackle the problem of how to tell the initial interface controller which button was pressed. There are several ways to share information between interface controllers. I illustrate one approach here, and you'll see another in a discussion of how to work with page-based user interfaces.

We can't pass any information with the popController() method, but we could call a method in the initial interface controller to tell it which button was pressed, if we had a reference to the controller available. Unfortunately, there is no way to get such a reference from code executing in the second interface controller, but we could pass the reference as part of the context information when we push the second interface controller. The downside to this is that the second interface controller needs to know the type of the interface controller that activated it, or at least know that it conforms to a protocol with a method that would be used to return results. Although that would work for this simple example, in general it is not a good pattern to adopt. It would be better to just pass the second controller some code, in the form of a closure, that it can execute just before it is removed from the screen. Passing a closure decouples the second controller from whatever pushed it—all it needs to know is the signature of the closure.

With this approach, we need to use the context to pass both the name of the image and the closure. Instead of passing a string as the context, we'll define a class to contain both pieces of information and pass that as the second argument to pushControllerWithName(_:context:). In fact, we can also include in the context class a title for the second interface controller to display. Where should this class be declared? You could make it a top-level class, but it seems more logical to declare it inside the second interface controller, since it is something that you need to know about to make use of that controller and therefore is part of its API. To do that, add the following code shown in bold to the top of the ImageController class:

```
class ImageController: WKInterfaceController {
    class ImageControllerContext {
        let imageName: String
        let title: String
        let callback: (liked: Bool) -> Void

        init(imageName: String, title: String,
                callback: (liked: Bool) -> Void) {
            self.imageName = imageName
            self.title = title
            self.callback = callback
        }
    }
    var context: ImageControllerContext?
    @IBOutlet weak var image: WKInterfaceImage!
```

The ImageControllerContext class contains the name of the image, the title that should be displayed, and the closure that should be called to return the result to whatever activated the controller. The context variable is used to save the context information until it's time to call the callback method. The callback closure has a single boolean argument that will be true if the user pressed the Like button and false for Dislike.

Let's start using the new context type. First, modify the awakeWithContext() method of ImageController to handle the change of type of its context argument:

```
override func awakeWithContext(context: AnyObject?) {
    super.awakeWithContext(context)
    println("ImageController awakeWithContext() called: \(context)")

    if let imageName = context as? String {
        image.setImageNamed(imageName)
    }
    if let contextStructure = context as? ImageControllerContext {
        self.context = contextStructure
        setTitle(contextStructure.title)
        image.setImageNamed(contextStructure.imageName)
    }
}
```

Next, add code to the onLikeButtonClicked() and onDislikeButtonClicked() methods to invoke the callback function and pop the second interface controller when either button is pressed:

```
    @IBAction func onLikeButtonClicked() {
        context?.callback(liked: true)
        popController()
    }

    @IBAction func onDislikeButtonClicked() {
        context?.callback(liked: false)
        popController()
    }
}
```

Finally, modify InterfaceController to pass an instance of ImageControllerContext when pushing the second interface controller. Make the following changes to the InterfaceController class:

```
    @IBAction func onImage1ButtonClicked() {
        pushControllerWithName("ImageController", context: "image1")
        pushImageControllerWithImageName("image1", title: "Image 1")
    }

    @IBAction func onImage2ButtonClicked() {
        pushControllerWithName("ImageController", context: "image2")
        pushImageControllerWithImageName("image2", title: "Image 2")
    }
```

```
        private func pushImageControllerWithImageName(imageName: String,
                                                      title: String) {
            let context = ImageController.ImageControllerContext(
                imageName: imageName, title: title,
                callback: { (liked) in
                    self.label.setText(liked ? "Liked \(title)"
                                             : "Disliked \(title)")
                })
            pushControllerWithName("ImageController", context: context)
        }
    }
}
```

When either the Image 1 or Image 2 button is pressed, the pushImageCon
trollerWithName(:title:) method is called. This method constructs an
ImageControllerContext object initialized with the name of the image to
display, a title, and the closure to call when the user presses the Like or
Dislike button. It then pushes the second interface controller, passing the
ImageControllerContext object as the context.

Now run the example again. Press either the Image 1 or Image 2 button to
push the second interface controller. Notice that the title is now set to the
value set in the ImageControllerContext object. Press Like or Dislike and
you'll see that the first controller reappears as expected, but the label at the
bottom of the screen is unchanged—it has apparently not been updated by
the closure in the pushImageControllerWithName(:title:) method. Place a
breakpoint in the closure and try again, to convince yourself that the closure
is being called with the correct argument. The breakpoint will be hit, so why
doesn't this work?

The problem is that the closure is called while the initial interface controller
is not active—it was deactivated when the second controller was pushed
and it won't be activated again until some time after the popController()
call completes. While an interface controller is inactive, you can't update any
of its user interface objects. As a result, the call to the WKInterfaceLabel's
setText() method to change the label's text is ignored. How do we fix this?
We have to defer the update by storing the new value for the label's Text
attribute so that we can update it in the willActivate() method. To do that,
add the following code shown in bold to the InterfaceController class:

```
class InterfaceController: WKInterfaceController {
    @IBOutlet weak var label: WKInterfaceLabel!
    var labelText: String?

    override func awakeWithContext(context: AnyObject?) {
        super.awakeWithContext(context)

        // Configure interface objects here.
    }
```

```
override func willActivate() {
    super.willActivate()
    println("InterfaceController willActivate() called")
    if labelText != nil {
        label.setText(labelText!)
        labelText = nil
    }
}
```

The labelText variable will hold the new text for the label. If its value is not nil when willActivate() is called, we update the label and clear the variable. The variable's type is String? because it needs to be nil when the willActivate() method is called as the interface controller is being shown for the first time. Now we need to change the closure in the pushImageCont rollerWithName(:title:) method to set the labelText variable instead of trying to update the label directly:

```
private func pushImageControllerWithImageName(imageName: String,
                                              title: String) {
    let context = ImageController.ImageControllerContext(
        imageName: imageName,
        title: title, callback: { (liked) in
            self.label.setText(liked ? "Liked \(title)"
                                     : "Disliked \(title)")
            self.labelText = liked ? "Liked \(title)"
                                   : "Disliked \(title)"
    })
    pushControllerWithName("ImageController", context: context)
}
```

Run the example again and this time you'll see that the label on the initial interface controller updates correctly (see Figure 5-4).

Figure 5-4. The result of passing data from one interface controller to another

Structuring interface controllers so that they update themselves in this way is something that you'll need to do any time you pass information from one controller to another, if the new information results in a change to something in the user interface and it is received while the controller is not active.

We've dealt with the first of the two issues we identified earlier—namely, how to pass a result back from an interface controller to the controller that pushed it. The second problem we need to deal with is what to do when the user dismisses the pushed controller by pressing the < symbol. In this case, there is no way to invoke the callback function, so the label on the initial screen will not be updated—try it and see. We'd prefer to update the label to say something like "Neither liked nor disliked". Although we can't do this when the second controller is popped, we can achieve the same effect by assigning this value to the labelText variable before the second controller is pushed. This works because if neither the Like nor the Dislike button is pressed, the labelText variable will not be overwritten and its value will be used to update the label when the first controller is reactivated. To do this, make the change shown in bold:

```
private func pushImageControllerWithImageName(imageName: String,
                                              title: String) {
    let context = ImageController.ImageControllerContext(
        imageName: imageName,
        title: title, callback: { (liked) in
            self.labelText = liked ? "Liked \(title)"
                                   : "Disliked \(title)"
    })
    labelText = "Neither liked nor disliked"
    pushControllerWithName("ImageController", context: context)
}
```

Run the example one more time, press the Image 1 or Image 2 button, and then press the < symbol at the top left of the second interface controller's screen to dismiss it. You should see the label on the first screen update correctly, as shown in Figure 5-5.

Figure 5-5. *Handling the case where the user dismisses the pushed interface controller without pressing one of our buttons*

Using a Segue to Push a Controller

You've seen how easy it is to manually push an interface controller by calling the pushControllerWithName(_:context:) method. There is another way to do the same thing—you can create a segue in your storyboard and let WatchKit push the target controller for you. Let's do that now. You'll need to make some changes to both the storyboard and the main interface controller, so first take a copy of the HierarchicalNavigation project to use as a starting point.

> **Note**   In the example source code archive, you'll find the code for this section in the folder 5 - SegueNavigation, although the Xcode project is still called HierarchicalNavigation.

We're currently triggering the transition to the second view controller from action methods that are connected to the Image 1 and Image 2 buttons. What we're now going to do is create a segue from each of those buttons to the second interface controller—but before we do that, we need to unlink the buttons from their action methods. Open Interface.storyboard and right click on the Image 1 button. In the pop-up that appears, you'll see the linkage from the button to onImage1ButtonClicked() method in the interface controller (see Figure 5-6).

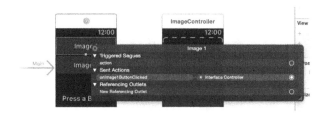

Figure 5-6. *Unlinking the buttons from their action methods*

Click the small x button to remove the link. Do the same for the Image 2 button. Next, open InterfaceController.swift and delete the onImage1ButtonClicked() and onImage2ButtonClicked() methods because they are no longer required.

Now let's create the segues. Go back to Interface.storyboard and select the main interface controller. Control-drag from the Image 1 button over to the second interface controller. Release the mouse button and you'll see a pop-up that offers you the choice of creating a push or modal segue, as shown in Figure 5-7.

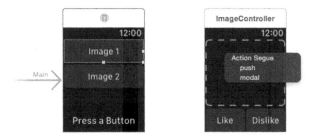

Figure 5-7. *Creating a push segue from a button to an interface controller*

The section "Presenting an Interface Controller" later in this chapter discusses modal segues. Here, we need a push segue, so click on push to create one. Repeat the process by dragging from the Image 2 button to the second interface controller. When you're done, your storyboard should look like Figure 5-8.

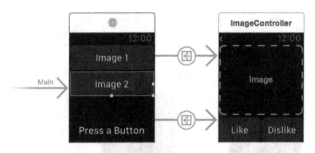

Figure 5-8. Two push segues to the same interface controller

Although we're not yet finished, we already have enough to see the segues in action. Run the application and click one of the buttons. You should see that the second interface controller is pushed, but there is no image and no title. If you look at the Xcode console, you'll see why:

```
InterfaceController willActivate() called
ImageController awakeWithContext() called: nil
ImageController willActivate() called
InterfaceController didDeactivate() called
```

The second interface controller's awakeWithContext() method was called with a nil argument, but it's expecting an ImageControllerContext object. In the first version of this application, we created this object in the button's action method and passed it to the pushControllerWithName(_:context:) method. Now, however, the action method doesn't exist, and WatchKit is calling pushControllerWithName(_:context:) for us, passing a nil context. What we need to be able to do is give it the context object. We can do that by overriding the contextForSegueWithIdentifier() method, which is defined like this:

```
func contextForSegueWithIdentifier(_ segueIdent: String) -> AnyObject?
```

The segueIdent argument allows us to distinguish between the two segues that originate from our interface controller. Our implementation of this method needs to create and return an ImageControllerContext object populated with the appropriate values for the segue that has been triggered. Before we implement this method, though, we need to assign identifiers to our segues.

In the storyboard, click the segue from the Image 1 button and open the Attributes Inspector. In the Identifier field, type Image1, as shown in Figure 5-9.

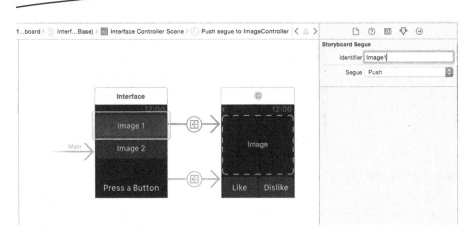

Figure 5-9. Assigning an identifier to a push segue

Next, do the same with the other segue, assigning it the identifier Image2. Save the storyboard file.

Now select InterfaceController.swift in the Project Navigator and add the following code shown in bold:

```
override func contextForSegueWithIdentifier(segueIdent: String)
                 -> AnyObject? {
    labelText = "Neither liked nor disliked"
    var imageName: String!
    var title: String!

    switch segueIdent {
    case "Image1":
        imageName = "image1"
        title = "Image 1"

    case "Image2":
        imageName = "image2"
        title = "Image 2"

    default:
        println("Invalid segue ideintifier: \(segueIdent)")
        abort()
    }

    let context = ImageController.ImageControllerContext(
        imageName: imageName,
        title: title, callback: { (liked) in
            self.labelText = liked ? "Liked \(title)"
                                   : "Disliked \(title)"
```

```
    })
    return context
  }

  private func pushImageControllerWithImageName(imageName: String,
                                                title: String) {
    let context = ImageController.ImageControllerContext(
        imageName: imageName,
        title: title, callback: { (liked) in
            self.labelText = liked ? "Liked \(title)"
                                   : "Disliked \(title)"
        })
    labelText = "Neither liked nor disliked"
    pushControllerWithName("ImageController", context: context)
  }
}
```

Our override of the contextForSegueWithIdentifier() method uses a switch statement to set the imageName and title variables based on the identifier of the segue that has been triggered and then uses the values of these variables to create an ImageControllerContext object. We are actually using exactly the same code to create the ImageControllerContext object that is in the pushImageControllerWithImageName(_:title:) method from our previous example—in fact, you can simply copy that code directly into the new method and then delete pushImageControllerWithImageName(_:title:), as shown in the preceding code. Notice that we also set the labelText variable to "Neither liked nor disliked" in this method. Previously, we did that while handling the button click, but we now need to do it here because it's the only point at which we have control while the segue from the first to the second interface controller is in progress.

Place a breakpoint on the contextForSegueWithIdentifier() method and run the example again. When you click either of the buttons, you'll see that this method is called with the correct segue identifier as its argument. Restart the application and you should find that the image and title are now displayed properly.

Whether you use the pushControllerWithName(_:context:) method or configure a segue in your storyboard is really just a matter of taste. As you can see, there is very little to choose between them in terms of code size and complexity. It makes no difference to the pushed controller either, as you can see from this example, because we didn't need to modify the ImageController class at all to switch from manually pushing it to using a segue. Lastly, notice that we still need to use the popController() method to manually return to the initial interface controller—WatchKit does not have the concept of an unwind segue.

Page-Based Navigation

Some applications are naturally hierarchical, while others work better if they are implemented as a series of sibling pages that the user can navigate through by swiping left and right. WatchKit supports page-based navigation with either a fixed set of pages, which you can construct in the storyboard, or with a variable collection of pages that is constructed at run time. You'll see examples of both in this section.

Constructing a Page-Based Application in the Storyboard

Let's create a simple application that lets the user page through a fixed set of images. Create a new Xcode project called FixedPageNavigation and add a WatchKit extension to it. Now select Images.xcassets in the FixedPageNavigation WatchKit App group in the Project Navigator and drag the images from the folder 5 - Fixed Page Navigation Images into it. These are the same two images that we used in the previous example.

Select Interface.storyboard to reveal the initial interface controller. Drag a label from the Object Library and drop it on the controller. In the Attributes Inspector, change the label's text to Swipe to View Images and change the Lines attribute to 0 to allow the text to flow onto a second line. We want the label's text to be horizontally centered near the top of the screen, so change the Alignment attribute to Center, the Horizontal attribute to Center, leave the Vertical attribute set to Top and change the Width attribute to Relative to Container.

Next, we need to add one interface controller for each image. Drag a new interface controller from the Object Library and drop it to the right of the main controller. Then drag an image object and drop it onto the new controller. Select the image object and change the Image attribute to image1, the Mode attribute to Aspect Fit, the Width to Relative to Container with the default value of 1, and the Height to Relative to Container with a value of 0.8. At this point, your storyboard should look like Figure 5-10.

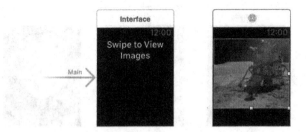

Figure 5-10. Constructing a page-based application, part 1

We need another identical interface controller to display the second image. We could create it manually by following the same steps again, but there is a quicker way. In the Document Outline (the area to the left of the storyboard), click on the interface controller that you just created and then Option-drag downwards, as shown on the left in Figure 5-11.

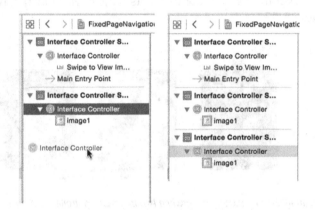

Figure 5-11. Making a copy of an interface controller

This action creates a copy of the interface controller with the image. Drop the copy by releasing the mouse button, and it will position itself underneath the second controller in the Document Outline, as shown on the right in Figure 5-11. Although you now have three interface controllers, only two are visible on the storyboard. That's because the interface controller you just created is positioned right on top of the one that you copied it from. Click on the new image controller in the storyboard and drag it a little way to the right. Then select its image and change its Image attribute in the Attributes Inspector to image2. Your storyboard should now look like Figure 5-12.

Figure 5-12. Constructing a page-based application, part 2

Now we need to link these three controllers together using *next page* segues, so that the user can swipe horizontally to navigate between them. To create a next page segue between the first two controllers, Control-drag from the first controller to the second one, making sure that you start dragging somewhere outside the label in the first view controller. As the mouse moves over the second controller, its outline will highlight in blue, as shown in Figure 5-13.

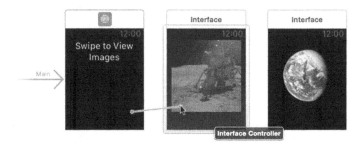

Figure 5-13. Creating a next page segue between two interface controllers—step 1

> **Tip** If you can't get the second controller to highlight, you probably started the drag in the label instead of the controller itself. Try dragging from the controller's title area instead.

When you release the mouse button, a pop-up appears, offering to create a next page segue (see Figure 5-14). Click on the pop-up, and the segue will be created.

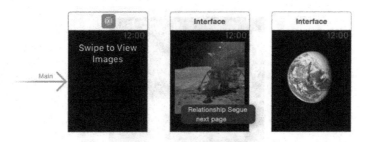

Figure 5-14. *Creating a next page segue between two interface controllers—step 2*

To add the second segue, Control-drag from the second controller to the third, again making sure you start the drag operation inside the controller but not on the image. Release the mouse button and create the seque as you did before. You should now have a page segue between each pair of controllers, as shown in Figure 5-15.

Figure 5-15. *All three controllers are now linked with next page segues*

Now run the application and swipe from right to left. As you do so, the second interface controller is dragged in from the right side of the screen, as shown in Figure 5-16, followed by the third one, and you can swipe left to return to the initial controller.

Figure 5-16. Swiping from right to left to reveal the second interface controller

Note   It's not possible to create a segue from the third interface controller back to the first one, to allow the user to cycle through the pages by continually swiping to the right. Try it and see. Xcode will let you add the segue, but you'll get an error because you have created a relationship cycle. To get rid of the segue, select it and press the `Delete` key.

As you can see, it's easy to create a fixed page layout in the storyboard. We didn't even need to create interface controller subclasses for this simple example. There are, however, some things that you can't do by using this approach. For example, you can't determine the number of pages at run time and you can't pass context information to any of the interface controllers. To do either of these things, you need to write some code. Let's now look at how you can do both of these things by creating the page linkage at run time.

> **Note** At the bottom of Figure 5-16, you see three white circles that correspond to the three interface controllers. You can't control where these circles appear and you can't change their color or size. Depending on your user interface, you may or may not be able to let its content flow all the way to the bottom of the screen behind the white circles without making it difficult or impossible for the user to see them. Here, we made sure that the images do not cover the whole screen so that the circles are easily seen. This is important, because they may be the only visual cue that tells the user that there is more to be seen to the right or left of the current screen.

Using Pages Constructed at Run Time

Static user interfaces are easy to build, but they only get you so far. In this section, we're going to build an application that lets the user page through a set of images and either like or dislike them. This time, we're going to define the linkage between the pages in code instead of in the storyboard. This technique is useful if you don't know until runtime how many pages you need or what needs to be displayed on those pages. We'll also see how to programmatically move between pages and how to jump from anywhere back to the initial page (or to any other page).

Figure 5-17 shows three screenshots from this application.

Figure 5-17. The main page and the image page of the dynamic page navigation application

The screenshot on the left shows the application in its initial state. The six dots at the bottom indicate that there are five more pages. Each of the following pages contains an image and a pair of Like and Dislike buttons, as shown in the center in Figure 5-17. To get from the initial page to the first image, the user has to swipe to the left. Subsequently, when the user clicks either the Like or Dislike button for an image, the application automatically moves to the next page, but if the user chooses to swipe to the left or right instead of pressing a button, it is assumed that he neither likes nor dislikes the image. When the last image has been viewed, pressing the Like or Dislike button causes the application to return to the initial page, where the totals of likes, dislikes, and pages that the user swiped through are displayed, as shown on the right in Figure 5-17.

Creating the Storyboard

This application has two interface controllers: the initial controller, which is the one on the left and right in Figure 5-17, and the controller in the center of the figure that displays an image. We're going to display five different images, so we need five image controller pages in addition to the page for the initial controller—but unlike our previous example, we only need to build one instance of the image interface controller in the storyboard because we're going to tell WatchKit to create five different instances of it at run time and link them together, with the initial controller as the first page. Let's get started by creating the project and building the storyboard.

Create a new project called DynamicPageNavigation and add a WatchKit App target to it. Then open the DynamicPageNavigation WatchKit App's asset catalog and drag the five images from the 5 - Dynamic Page Navigation Images folder into it. Now select Interface.storyboard in the Project Navigator to open the storyboard. The main interface controller has two parts: the label that tells the user to swipe to show the first image, seen on the left in Figure 5-17, and another label that summarizes the users likes and dislikes, shown on the right in that same figure. Only one of these labels will be visible at any given time.

To create the initial controller interface, drag two labels from the Object Library and drop them onto the controller. Select both labels (hold down the Shift key while clicking first one, then the other) and then, in the Attributes Inspector, set the Alignment attribute to Center, the Lines attribute to 0, and the Width attribute to Relative to Container. Now select the top label only, set its Text attribute to Swipe to Begin, and change its Font attribute to Headline. Select the bottom label and set its Vertical attribute to Center and make sure its Height attribute has value Size To Fit Content.

Next, we need to create outlets for the two labels. To do that, open InterfaceController.swift in the Preview Assistant. Then Control-drag from the top label to the top of the class definition to create an outlet called startLabel and from the bottom label to the class definition to create an outlet called summaryLabel. At this point, the top of the InterfaceController class definition should look like this:

```
class InterfaceController: WKInterfaceController {
    @IBOutlet weak var startLabel: WKInterfaceLabel!
    @IBOutlet weak var summaryLabel: WKInterfaceLabel!

    override func awakeWithContext(context: AnyObject?) {
```

To complete the user interface for the initial controller, you need to make the bottom label disappear. To do that, select it in the storyboard and check its Hidden attribute in the Attributes Inspector. You should also clear the text from its Text attribute, because we're going to set its content programmatically later.

The second interface controller for this application is the same as the one we built for our hierarchical navigation example. Drag an interface controller from the Object Library to the storyboard and then follow the steps for building the second interface controller in the section "Building the Controllers' User Interfaces" earlier in this chapter to create the interface shown on the right in Figure 5-3. Return here after setting the interface controller's identifier to ImageController.

We need an interface controller subclass to manage the controller's user interface. Create a new subclass of WKInterfaceController called ImageController in the DynamicPageNavigation WatchKit Extension group. Link it to the interface controller by selecting the second interface controller in the storyboard, opening the Identity Inspector, and setting its Class attribute to ImageController. You're also going to need an outlet for the image object and action methods for the two buttons. To do that, select ImageController in the storyboard and then open the ImageController class in the Assistant Editor. Control-drag from the image object to the top of the class definition to create an outlet called image and then Control-drag from each button in turn to the bottom of the class definition to create action methods called onLikeButtonClicked() and onDislikeButtonClicked() respectively, just as you did for the hierarchical navigation example earlier in this chapter.

Building the Controller Linkage in Code

When the application starts, the user will see the main interface controller. Swiping right should reveal an instance of the image controller showing the first image. Swiping right again should show another image controller instance with the second image. And so on. For our previous example, we created the linkage between the controllers in the storyboard. This time, we're going to do the same thing in code, which has the advantage that you can determine the number of pages and the page order at run time instead of at design time. That's perfect if you need to display content based on information that can't be known in advance, perhaps because you need to connect to a server to get it.

To do that, you'll use the `reloadRootControllersWithNames(_:contexts:)` method of `WKInterfaceController`. This method requires two arguments: an array of interface controller identifiers and an array of context objects. When this method is called, each identifier in the first array is used to find a controller definition in the storyboard. An instance of that controller is created, and the corresponding object in the second array is passed to its `awakeWithContext()` method. The two arrays must have the same number of elements, and the order of identifiers in the first array determines the page order of the controllers.

For this example, we need the main controller to appear first, followed by five instances of the image controller, so the identifier array must be initialized with the main controller's identifier and five instances of the image controller's identifier. We assigned an identifier to the image controller when we added it to the storyboard, but the main controller doesn't yet have one. Let's fix that now—select the main interface controller in the storyboard ad then use the Attributes Inspector to set its `Identifier` attribute to `MainController`. Now add the following code shown in bold to the `awakeWithContext()` method of the `InterfaceController` class:

```
override func awakeWithContext(context: AnyObject?) {
    super.awakeWithContext(context)

    // Configure interface objects here.
    if context == nil {
        var identifiers = ["MainController"]
        var contexts = [0]

        for pageNumber in 1...pageCount {
            identifiers.append("ImageController")
            contexts.append(pageNumber)
        }

        WKInterfaceController.reloadRootControllersWithNames(
                identifiers, contexts: contexts)
    }
}
```

This code initializes the `identifiers` array with the identifier for the main controller followed by five instances of the image controller's identifier. At the same time, we initialize the `contexts` array with the number of each page, counting the main controller as page zero. We do this to allow each page controller instance to display its page index in its title and select the image to be displayed—although, as you'll see shortly, we'll need to give it more information than that when we implement the functionality of the Like and Dislike buttons.

You may be wondering why we need the if context == nil test in this code. When the application starts, an instance of the main interface controller is created, and its init() and awakeWithContext() methods are called. In the latter method, we call reloadRootControllersWithNa mes(_:contexts:), which causes an instance of each controller in the identifiers array to be created. That means that a second instance of the main controller will be created (because its identifier is the first element of the array), and its init() and awakeWithContext() method will be called, executing the preceding code again. This triggers a never-ending sequence in which we perpetually replace the main controller and every page controller instance with new ones. We can avoid this problem by noting that when the main controller is created from the storyboard as the application is launched, the context argument passed to awakeWithContext() is nil, but when it's created as a result of our call to reloadRootControllersWithName s(_:contexts:), its awakeWithContext() method is called with the value 0 (since that's the first value in the contexts array).

Next, we need to add some code to the ImageController's awakeWithContext() method. Select ImageController in the Project Navigator and add the following code shown in bold:

```
class ImageController: WKInterfaceController {
    @IBOutlet weak var image: WKInterfaceImage!

    override func awakeWithContext(context: AnyObject?) {
        super.awakeWithContext(context)

        // Configure interface objects here.
        let pageIndex = context! as! Int
        setTitle("Page \(pageIndex)")
        image.setImageNamed("image\(pageIndex)")
    }
```

The context object that we're passing to this controller is an Int that represents the controller's page index, from 1 to 5. We use this value to set the controller's title and install the correct image for the page. You should now be able to run the application and see the initial controller, as shown on the left in Figure 5-17, and then scroll right to reveal each of the five images in turn.

At this point, the Like and Dislike buttons don't do anything. We need them to register whether the user likes or dislikes the image on the current page, and we also want them to automatically scroll right to reveal the next page, or return to the main page if the user is already viewing the last image. Let's implement these features separately.

Implementing the Like and Dislike Counts

When the user presses the Like or Dislike button, we need to record that he or she likes or dislikes the image on the current page. When we return to the main controller, we want to display how many likes and dislikes there are and on how many pages the user did not press either button. To store this information, we'll create another class, which we'll call the SharedModel class, where we'll keep a set containing the page indices of the images that the users liked and another set with the page indices of the images that the user disliked. We'll create a single instance of this class in the main interface controller and pass it as part of the context information to each image controller.

Click **File ➤ New ➤ File…** from Xcode's menu and then in the iOS Source section of the new file dialog, select Swift File and click **Next**. Name the file Model.swift and save it in the location that Xcode suggests, making sure that's it in the DynamicPageNavigation WatchKit Extension group and target. We're going to add a couple of classes to this file, starting with the SharedModel class. Add the following code shown in bold:

```
import Foundation

class SharedModel {
    private var likedImages = Set<Int>()
    private var dislikedImages = Set<Int>()
    var likedImageCount: Int {
        get {
            return likedImages.count
        }
    }
    var dislikedImageCount: Int {
        get {
            return dislikedImages.count
        }
    }

    func likeImage(pageIndex: Int) {
        likedImages.insert(pageIndex)
        dislikedImages.remove(pageIndex)
    }
```

```
    func dislikeImage(pageIndex: Int) {
        dislikedImages.insert(pageIndex)
        likedImages.remove(pageIndex)
    }
}
```

This code is very straightforward. The likedImages and dislikedImages properties hold the page indices of the pages that the user liked and disliked, respectively. When the user presses the Like button, we'll call the likeImage() method, which adds the page index that it's given to the likedImages set and removes it from the dislikedImages set (allowing the user to have a change of heart) and similarly for the Dislike button and the dislikeImage() method. To find out how many images have been liked (or disliked), just use the likedImageCount (or dislikedImageCount) computed property, which simply returns the number of elements in the likedImages set (or the dislikedImages set).

Now let's add the code to create an instance of this class and pass it as part of an image controller's context information. We're currently using the context object to pass a page index and we still need to do that. Since we can only pass one context object to a controller, we'll create a new class to contain both the receiving controller's page index and the reference to the SharedModel instance and use an instance of that class as the context object. Add the following code to the Model.swift file:

```
class ControllerContext {
    let model: SharedModel
    let pageIndex: Int

    init(model: SharedModel, pageIndex: Int) {
        self.model = model
        self.pageIndex = pageIndex
    }
}
```

Note It would be really nice if ControllerContext could be a struct instead of a class, because we wouldn't have to write an initializer. Unfortunately, we can't use a struct as a context object, because a context has to be of type AnyObject?, which a struct is not.

Next, modify the InterfaceController class as shown here:

```
class InterfaceController: WKInterfaceController {
    private let pageCount = 5
    @IBOutlet weak var startLabel: WKInterfaceLabel!
    @IBOutlet weak var summaryLabel: WKInterfaceLabel!
    private var model: SharedModel!

    override func awakeWithContext(context: AnyObject?) {
        super.awakeWithContext(context)

        // Configure interface objects here.
        if context == nil {
            // This case is application launch
            model = SharedModel()

            var identifiers = ["MainController"]
            var contexts = [0]
            var contexts = [ControllerContext(model: model, pageIndex: 0)]

            for pageNumber in 1...pageCount {
                identifiers.append("ImageController")
                contexts.append(pageNumber)
                contexts.append(
                    ControllerContext(model: model, pageIndex: pageNumber))
            }

            WKInterfaceController.reloadRootControllersWithNames(
                    identifiers, contexts: contexts)
        } else {
            // Created by reloadRootControllersWithNames(_:contexts:)
            let controllerContext = context as! ControllerContext
            model = controllerContext.model
        }
    }
}
```

The first two changes add a constant that represents the mumber of pages and a property that will hold a reference to the SharedModel instance. Moving on to the awakeWithContext() method, when the application is launched, we enter the first branch of the if statement, where we now create an instance of ControllerContext as the context for each image controller, initialized with the reference to the SharedModel instance and the controller's page index. When we call reloadControllersWithNames (_:contexts:), a new instance of the InterfaceController class will be created along with the ImageController instances for the image controllers, and this InterfaceController instance will be discarded. The new InterfaceController instance needs access to the SharedModel object, so we also create a ControllerContext for the main controller and store it as the first element in the contexts array. The second branch of the if statement handles this case—all we need to do here is cast the context object to ControllerContext and initialize the model property from it.

Now we need to move over to the ImageController class and make a small change there because the context object passed to its awakeWithContext() method has changed from Int to ControllerContext. Make the code changes shown here in bold:

```
class ImageController: WKInterfaceController {
    private var controllerContext: ControllerContext!
    @IBOutlet weak var image: WKInterfaceImage!

    override func awakeWithContext(context: AnyObject?) {
        super.awakeWithContext(context)

        // Configure interface objects here.
        let pageIndex = context! as! Int
        controllerContext = context! as! ControllerContext
        let pageIndex = controllerContext.pageIndex
        setTitle("Page \(pageIndex)")
        image.setImageNamed("image\(pageIndex)")
    }
```

Here we cast the context object to type ControllerContext and save it to the controllerContext property for later use. Then, we get the controller's page index from the ControllerContext and use it as we did before. At this point, you can run the example again and get the same results as before.

What we were really trying to achieve with these latest changes is make the Like and Dislike buttons work. Now that we have a reference to the ControllerContext, we can use that reference to get access to the SharedModel object, which implements the methods that let us change the sets of liked and disliked images when either of the buttons is pressed. We've already connected the buttons to action methods in the ImageController class, so let's go ahead and implement those methods by adding the code in bold:

```
    @IBAction func onLikeButtonClicked() {
        controllerContext.model.likeImage(controllerContext.pageIndex)
    }

    @IBAction func onDislikeButtonClicked() {
        controllerContext.model.dislikeImage(controllerContext.pageIndex)
    }
}
```

As you can see, all you have to do is call the appropriate method of the SharedModel class to register the user's opinion of the image on the current page.

Showing Results in the Initial Interface Controller

We're now maintaining the liked and disliked image sets correctly, but there's no way for us to see the results yet. What we need to do is update the initial controller's user interface to show the results when we return to it. You may remember that we added a label to the storyboard so that we could display our results. Initially, this label is empty and hidden. We need to update it and then make it visible when the initial interface controller is activated. However, we can't do this on the first activation, because the user won't yet have seen any of the images. So we make the first activation a special case by adding a property that we can check in the willActivate() method. Switch back to the InterfaceController class and add this property, as shown here:

```
class InterfaceController: WKInterfaceController {
    private let pageCount = 5
    @IBOutlet weak var startLabel: WKInterfaceLabel!
    @IBOutlet weak var summaryLabel: WKInterfaceLabel!
    private var model: SharedModel!
    private var firstActivation = true
```

Now add the code in bold to the willActivate() method:

```
override func willActivate() {
    super.willActivate()

    if (firstActivation) {
        firstActivation = false
    } else {
        startLabel.setHidden(true)
        summaryLabel.setHidden(false)
        let likedImageCount = model.likedImageCount;
        let dislikedImageCount = model.dislikedImageCount
        let noCommentImageCount =
            pageCount - likedImageCount - dislikedImageCount
        summaryLabel.setText(
            "Likes: \(likedImageCount)\n"
            + "Dislikes: \(dislikedImageCount)\n"
            + "No comment: \(noCommentImageCount)")
    }
}
```

The first time this method is called, we simply set firstActivation to false. On all subsequent calls, we hide the label at the top of the interface that invites the user to swipe to see the images, and then show the results summary label and update it using the counts of liked and disliked images from the model. If the sum of these two values is not the same as the page count, the user must have swiped past an image without clicking either of the buttons, and we calculate the number of those pages too.

Now run the application again and swipe through the images, clicking the Like or Dislike buttons as you go. At the end, keep swiping to the left until you reach the initial controller, and you should see a summary, as shown on the right back in Figure 5-17.

Automatically Scrolling between Pages

At this point, the application works, but having to manually swipe to the next image after pressing the Like or Dislike button is not very user-friendly. So we're going to go the extra mile and scroll automatically to the next page when either button is pressed. To scroll from one controller to the next, the current controller needs to call the becomeCurrentPage() method of the next controller. It's as simple as that. The only problem is that none of the controllers has a reference to the next controller in the page sequence, and there is no API that lets you get it. Fortunately, there is a way to work around this—we can have each image controller store a reference to itself in the SharedModel object when its awakeWithContext() method is called. If we save the controller references in an array indexed by page number, any controller can get a reference to any other controller. If we have the initial controller do the same thing, we can even make the Like and Dislike buttons on the last page scroll all the way back to the first page using the same code that we'll create to move from controller to controller.

Let's start by adding the controller's array to the SharedModel object. To do that, we need to know how many pages there are going to be. We'll pass the page count to the model's initializer.

> **Note** We could just create an empty array and have each controller append to that array a reference to itself when its awakeWithContext() method is called. However, that assumes that the controllers are initialized in page order, and there is no reason to believe that this will be the case because Apple's documentation does not specify any given order of initialization. Instead, we create an array of the correct size that's initialized with nils and let each controller add itself at the correct position in the array.

Open Model.swift and add the two lines shown here in bold to the SharedModel class to declare the controllers array:

```
import Foundation
import WatchKit

class SharedModel {
    var controllers: [WKInterfaceController?]
    private var likedImages = Set<Int>()
    private var dislikedImages = Set<Int>()
```

Next, we add an initializer that allocates the array and initializes it with a nil value for each page and an extra one, at index 0, for the main controller:

```
init(pageCount: Int) {
    controllers = Array<WKInterfaceController?>(
                    count: pageCount + 1, repeatedValue: nil)
}

func likeImage(pageIndex: Int) {
```

Now in the InterfaceController class where we create the SharedModel instance, we supply the page count and install the main interface controller at index 0 of the controllers array:

```
override func awakeWithContext(context: AnyObject?) {
    super.awakeWithContext(context)

    // Configure interface objects here.
    if context == nil {
        // This case is application launch
        model = SharedModel()
        model = SharedModel(pageCount: pageCount)

        var identifiers = ["MainController"]
        var contexts = [ControllerContext(model: model, pageIndex: 0)]

        for pageNumber in 1...pageCount {
            identifiers.append("ImageController")
            contexts.append(
                ControllerContext(model: model, pageIndex: pageNumber))
        }

        WKInterfaceController.reloadRootControllersWithNames(
                    identifiers, contexts: contexts)
    } else {
```

```
    // Created by reloadRootControllersWithNames(_:contexts:)
    let controllerContext = context as! ControllerContext
    model = controllerContext.model
    model.controllers[0] = self
  }
}
```

Notice that we install the initial controller reference in the else branch of the if, which is entered when the second instance of the controller is created, because this is the instance that the user will actually see.

In the awakeWithContext() method of each image controller, we need to assign the controller reference to the correct entry of the controllers array. To do that, make the change shown here in bold in the ImageController class:

```
override func awakeWithContext(context: AnyObject?) {
    super.awakeWithContext(context)

    // Configure interface objects here.
    controllerContext = context! as! ControllerContext
    let pageIndex = controllerContext.pageIndex
    controllerContext.model.controllers[pageIndex] = self

    setTitle("Page \(pageIndex)")
    image.setImageNamed("image\(pageIndex)")
}
```

With the data structures set up, we now just need a method that lets us move from the current controller to the next one. Here's the method we need—add it to the ImageController class:

```
func moveToNextPage() {
    let pageIndex = controllerContext.pageIndex
    let totalPages = controllerContext.model.controllers.count
    let nextIndex = (pageIndex + 1) % totalPages
    let nextController =
            controllerContext.model.controllers[nextIndex]!
    nextController.becomeCurrentPage()
}
```

The controller gets the index of the next controller by adding one to its own page index, which it gets from its ControllerContext. When we are on the last page, however, we want to move back to the initial controller. Because we added a reference to the initial controller at index 0 of the controllers array, all we need to do is wrap back to 0 when the next page index equals the total number of pages. That's what the following line of code does, by using the modulo operator:

```
let nextIndex = (pageIndex + 1) % totalPages
```

Once we have the correct index, we find the next controller by accessing its entry in the controllers array and then call its becomeCurrentPage() method:

```
let nextController =
    controllerContext.model.controllers[nextIndex]!
nextController.becomeCurrentPage()
```

We need to invoke this method when either of the buttons is pressed, so add calls to the onLikeButtonClicked() and onDislikeButtonClicked() methods:

```
@IBAction func onLikeButtonClicked() {
    controllerContext.model.likeImage(controllerContext.pageIndex)
    moveToNextPage()
}

@IBAction func onDislikeButtonClicked() {
    controllerContext.model.dislikeImage(controllerContext.pageIndex)
    moveToNextPage()
}
```

That's it! Now run the example again and check that the Like and Dislike buttons behave as they should. Notice also the nice animation that occurs to bring the initial controller back into view when you press either button on the last page.

Presenting an Interface Controller

So far in this chapter, you have seen two forms of interface controller navigation: hierarchical and page-based. To close the chapter, we'll look at the third option: modal presentation. As on iOS, you typically present a controller when you need to get input from the user before you can continue with an operation that's being performed in another controller. When you present a controller, it animates into view from the bottom of the screen and completely covers the interface of the controller that presents it. WatchKit provides a prebuilt interface controller that you can present to get text input from the user. You can also present your own controller, which can be built either programmatically or in the storyboard. You'll see examples of all three options in this section.

Getting Text Input

The only way to get text input on the watch is to present WatchKit's text input controller using the following WKInterfaceController method:

```
func presentTextInputControllerWithSuggestions(
        _ suggestions: [AnyObject]?,
        allowedInputMode inputMode: WKTextInputMode,
        completion completion: ([AnyObject]!) -> Void)
```

The user sees a full-screen presentation that consists of a list of suggested inputs taken from the suggestions argument (which is optional), a microphone button to enable spoken input, and possibly a button that presents a selection of emoji characters. You use the allowedInputMode argument, of type WKTextInputMode, to control what the input can consist of. WKTextInputMode is an enumeration with three possible values:

- .Plain allows the user to use the microphone or the suggestions that appear on the screen.

- .AllowEmoji is the same as .Plain plus non-animating emoji characters.

- .AllowAnimatedAmoji is the same as .AllowEmoji plus animated emoji characters.

At some point shortly after the presentTextInputControllerWithSuggest ions(_:allowedInputMode:completion:) method is called, the presenting interface controller is deactivated, and the input controller is animated into view from the bottom of the screen. When the user has finished composing input or cancelled the interaction, the input controller animates itself off the screen, the presenting controller is reactivated, and the closure passed using the completion argument is called to allow the input to be processed. The user's input is passed to the completion handler as an array, or nil if the user cancelled input. If it's not nil, the array always has one element, which is either a text string or an NSData object containing an emoji image.

Let's build a simple application that uses the input controller. Create a new project called TextInput and add a WatchKit app target to it. Open Interface.storyboard and drag a label onto the interface controller. Use the Attributes Inspector to change the label's Text attribute to Text Appears Here, its Alignment to center, its Lines attribute to 0, and its Width attribute to Relative to Container. Drag an image object and drop it below the label and then set its Horizontal attribute to Center and its Mode attribute to Center as well. Finally, drag a button onto the storyboard and drop it below the label, and then change its Title attribute of the top button to Change Text (see Figure 5-18).

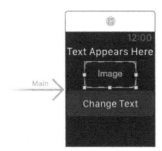

Figure 5-18. Building an application that uses the text input controller

We don't want the image object to be visible when the application starts (we're going to make it visible if the user selects an emoji icon), so select it in the storyboard and check the Hidden check box in the Attributes Inspector.

We're going to link the button to an action method that will present an input controller that will allow the user to pick one of three pre-defined text strings that will replace the label's text, speak some replacement text of their own using the microphone, or chose an emoji icon. Open InterfaceController.swift in the Assistant Editor, Control-drag from the button to the bottom of the class definition and create an action method called onChangeTextButtonClicked(). We also need outlets for the label and the image. Control-drag from the label to the top of the class definition and create an outlet with the name label. Then do the same for the image to create an outlet called image.

Now let's add the code that we need to show the text input controller. Start by adding the three suggested text strings to the top of the InterfaceController class definition:

```
class InterfaceController: WKInterfaceController {
    @IBOutlet weak var label: WKInterfaceLabel!
    @IBOutlet weak var image: WKInterfaceImage!
    let suggestions = ["Hello, World", "Hello, Watch",
                       "To be or not to be, that is the question"]
```

Next, add the completion method that is called when the input controller is closed:

```
@IBAction func onChangeTextButtonClicked() {
}

private func onTextInputComplete(results: [AnyObject]!) -> Void {
    if results != nil && !results.isEmpty {
        if let text = results[0] as? String {
```

```
            label.setText(text)
            image.setHidden(true)
            label.setHidden(false)
        } else if let data = results[0] as? NSData {
            let emojiImage = UIImage(data: data)
            image.setImage(emojiImage)
            image.setHidden(false)
            label.setHidden(true)
        }
    }
}
```

The results argument would be nil if the user cancelled the interaction. Otherwise, it contains a string or an NSData object containing an emoji image. If the array contains a string, we use it to set the text property of the label and hide the image. If the array contains an NSData object, we convert it to an image and display it, hiding the label.

Finally, add the code to present the text input controller when the button is clicked:

```
@IBAction func onChangeTextButtonClicked() {
    presentTextInputControllerWithSuggestions(suggestions,
                    allowedInputMode: .AllowAnimatedEmoji,
                    completion: onTextInputComplete)
}
```

Notice that we're allowing the user to select an emoji or animated emoji character as well as provide plain text input.

Run the example and click the Change Text button. You'll see the text input controller scroll into view from the bottom, covering the whole screen, as shown in Figure 5-19.

Figure 5-19. The presented text input controller

If you look first at the top of the screen, you'll see that the presented controller replaces the title bar with one of its own that contains the text Cancel and does not show the current time. If you tap anywhere in the title bar, the controller is dismissed, and the completion method will be called with a nil argument. If you tap on one of the suggested strings instead, the input controller disappears and you should see that the label in the initial interface controller is updated. That's all you can do in the simulator. However, if you run this on a real device, you can use the two buttons at the bottom of the screen.

First tap on the microphone button. This shows the same screen that Siri uses for voice input, as shown on the left in Figure 5-20.

Figure 5-20. Microphone input (left) and emoji input (right)

Dictate some text and press the Done button, and you'll see the text appear in the label on the application's main screen. Now press the Change Text button again and this time tap the emoji button. You'll see a new paged interface controller from which you can choose either an animated or a fixed emoji icon. Each animated icon has its own page, whereas the static ones are grouped into a single page, as shown in the center and on the right in Figure 5-20. Select an icon from either of these pages and you'll see that it appears in the image object in the application instead of the label.

> **Tip**   If you want the user to go directly to dictated input without having to press the microphone button, present the text input controller with the suggestions argument set to nil and allowedInputMode set to .Plain.

Presenting a Controller Programmatically

Presenting a controller programmatically is very similar to the process of pushing a controller that we covered in the first part of this chapter. You build the controller in the same way and you pass information to it and get results from it using the context object passed to its awakeWithContext() method. The only difference is that you use different methods to present and dismiss the controller.

As usual, we'll illustrate the process with an example. Because you're already familiar with how to navigate and pass information between interface controllers, this is just going to be a bare-bones example that demonstrates the mechanics of controller presentation, and we're not going to add anything more to the interface. You'll see a more complete example of controller presentation in Chapter 6.

Create a new project called ControllerPresentation and add a WatchKit App target to it. Open Interface.storyboard and drag a button onto it. We're going to use this button to trigger the presentation of a second interface controller, so change its Title attribute to Present Controller. We need to link the button to an action method, so open InterfaceController.swift in the Assistant Editor and Control-drag from the button to the bottom of the class to create an action method called onPresentControllerButtonClicked().

Next, drag a second interface controller onto the storyboard. This is the controller that we are going to present. With the controller selected in the storyboard, use the Attributes Inspector to set its Identifier attribute to PresentedController. We'll use this identifier when we write the code to present the controller. Now drag a label and a button from the Object Library and drop them onto the controller. Change the label's Width attribute to

Relative To Container, its Lines attribute to 0, and its Alignment attribute to Center, and then set the button's Title attribute to Close.

We need to link the label to an outlet and the Close button to an action method, but we don't have an interface controller class for this controller yet. To fix that, right-click on the ControllerPresentation WatchKit Extension group in the Project Navigator and select New File... then, in the dialog that appears, select Cocoa Touch Class from the iOS Source section and click **Next**. Name the class PresentedInterfaceController, make it a subclass of WKInterfaceController, and save it. Open Interface.storyboard again, select the new interface controller, and change the Class attribute in the Identity Inspector (⌥⌘3) to PresentedInterfaceController. To create the button's action method, open PresentedInterfaceController in the Assistant Editor and Control-drag from the Close button to the bottom of the class definition. Name the action method onCloseButtonClicked(). Finally, Control-drag from the label to the top of the class definition and create an outlet called label.

With both controllers constructed, you can now write the code to have the first controller present the second. To present a controller, use one of the following WKInterfaceController methods:

```
func presentControllerWithName(_ name: String, context: AnyObject?)
func presentControllersWithNames(_ names: [AnyObject],
                                 contexts: [AnyObject]?)
```

The first method presents the single controller with the identifier given by its first argument, passing the second argument as its context. The second method presents a set of controller pages, where the first argument is an array of controller identifiers and the second contains the controller contexts. Because we're only presenting one controller, we'll use the first method. Add the following code shown in bold to the onPresentControllerButtonClicked() method in the presenting controller in InterfaceController.swift:

```
@IBAction func onPresentControllerButtonClicked() {
    presentControllerWithName("PresentedController",
                              context: "Presented Controller")
}
```

To dismiss a presented controller, you call its dismissController() method. We want the controller to be dismissed when we press the Close button, so add the following code in bold to the onCloseButtonClicked() method in PresentedInterfaceController.swift:

```
@IBAction func onCloseButtonClicked() {
    dismissController()
}
```

In a real application, we would probably want to pass some information from the presented controller back to the presenting controller. To do that, we would use the mechanism discussed earlier in this chapter—that is, pass a reference to a closure in the presented controller's context and invoke the closure before calling the dismissController() method. We'll do exactly that in an example that you'll see in Chapter 6. In this simple example, of course, there is nothing to return, and the context is just a string that we'll use to set the Text property of the label. To do that, add the following code to the awakeWithContext() method:

```
override func awakeWithContext(context: AnyObject?) {
    super.awakeWithContext(context)

    // Configure interface objects here.
    let text = context! as! String
    label.setText(text)
}
```

Run the example and you should see the initial controller, as shown on the left in Figure 5-21.

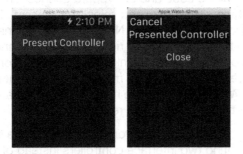

Figure 5-21. Presenting an interface controller

Click the Present Controller button and the second controller will animate into view from the bottom of the screen, as shown on the right in Figure 5-21. If you press the Close button, the presented controller's onCloseButtonClicked() method calls dismissController() to dismiss itself.

You can also return to the presented interface controller by touching the title bar. As you can see in Figure 5-21, when it presents a controller, WatchKit replaces the title bar of the presenting controller with one that contains a Cancel label. When the user dismisses the controller by touching the title bar, you do not get an opportunity to return information to the presented controller, so this is effectively a cancel operation, as the default title suggests. If necessary, you can change the title bar text in the normal way, by setting the `Title` attribute of the presented interface controller in the storyboard or by calling its `setTitle()` method.

> **Note**   A presented interface controller can itself present another controller (or a set of controller pages), but you cannot push a controller onto a presented controller.

Presenting a Controller from the Storyboard

You can present a single controller (or set of controller pages) by configuring a modal segue from the presenting controller to the first (or only) presented controller in the storyboard. To demonstrate, we'll convert our last example to use a segue instead of explicitly calling the `presentControllerWithName (_:context:)` method.

Start by taking a copy of the project folder to a new folder called `StoryboardControllerPresentation` and open the copied project in Xcode. Our first task is to remove code and storyboard connections that we don't need. Open `Interface.storyboard` and select the `Present Controller` button in the main interface controller. Next, open the Connections Inspector (⌥⌘5) and click on the small x, on the right side of the connection in `Sent Actions` section, to remove the link between the button and the `onPresentControllerButtonClicked()` method. We don't need this method anymore because WatchKit is going to handle the presentation for us, so open `InterfaceController.swift` and remove it.

This example is going to be different from the previous one in two ways. First, we'll be presenting two interface controllers instead of one, and second, we'll use a segue instead of code to initiate the presentation. Both of these changes require updates to the storyboard.

Let's start by adding the second presented controller, which will be a copy of the first one. To do that, select `PresentedController` in the storyboard Document Outline and `Option`-drag downward, as shown in Figure 5-22, and then release the mouse button. You should see a second copy of the controller appear in the Document Outline. If you can't make this work, select the controller in the Document Outline and press ⌘C followed by ⌘V.

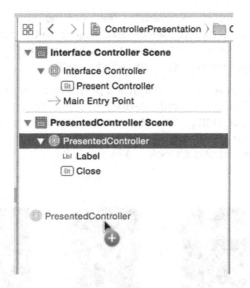

Figure 5-22. Creating a copy of an interface controller

Even though there are two copies of the presented controller, you can probably see only one in the storyboard, because the second one is directly above the first, so use the mouse to drag them apart so you can see them both. Your storyboard should now look like Figure 5-23.

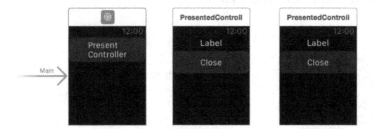

Figure 5-23. Storyboard with two presented controllers

At this point, you should see that Xcode is reporting an error because there are two interface controllers with the identifier `PresentedController`. Let's fix that before continuing. Select the presented controller instance on the left, open the Attributes Inspector, and change its identifier to `PresentedController1`. Do the same with the controller on the right, changing its identifier to `PresentedController2`. The error should now be gone.

The next step is to link the two presented controllers so that they appear as pages when they are presented. `Control-drag` from the first presented controller to the second one, making sure that the mouse pointer starts at a point that is in the interface controller itself, not the label or the button. Release the mouse button and select next page from the pop-up that appears. If you don't see a pop-up like the one shown in Figure 5-14, you started the drag with the mouse in the wrong place.

Now we need to create the segue that will present our two interface controller pages. To do that, Control-drag from the Present Controller button in the main controller to the leftmost presented controller and release the mouse button. Then select modal from the pop-up. With these two segues in place, your storyboard should look like Figure 5-24.

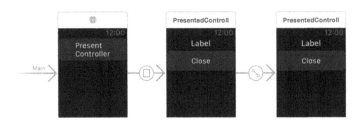

Figure 5-24. *Storyboard with segues added*

At this point, with all the required linkage in place, run the example. When the initial interface controller appears, press the Present Controller button. Unfortunately, instead of presenting the second controller, the application crashes, as shown in Figure 5-25.

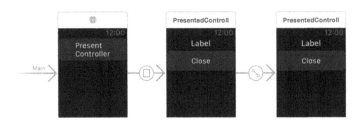

Figure 5-25. *Crash while presenting a controller*

What went wrong? The presented controller expects its awakeWithContext() method to be called with a context object that is the text for its label. In our previous example, this worked because we explicitly called the pres entControllerWithName(_:context:) method, passing the label's text as the context argument. Now, though, WatchKit is presenting the controller, so how do we arrange for the presented controller's awakeWithContext() method to be called with the correct argument? You may remember a similar situation earlier in this chapter when we pushed an interface controller using a push segue in the storyboard. There, the solution was to override the contextForSegueWithIdentifier() method in the source controller to return the context object for the pushed controller. The same technique works when presenting a controller, but here we are actually presenting two interface controllers, so we need to override this method instead:

```
func contextsForSegueWithIdentifer(_ segueIdentifier: String)
        -> [AnyObject]?
```

To fix the problem, open InterfaceController.swift and add the following code:

```
override func contextsForSegueWithIdentifier(segueIdentifier: String)
        -> [AnyObject]? {
    return ["Presented Controller #1", "Presented Controller #2"]
}
```

This method returns two strings, the first of which is used as the context object for the first presented controller and the other for the second presented controller. Run the example one more time and press the Present Controller button. This time, you'll see the first presented controller appear (see Figure 5-26).

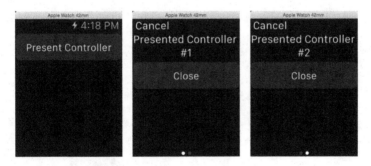

Figure 5-26. Interface controllers presented from a storyboard

If you swipe to the right, the second presented controller appears. Pressing either Close button or tapping the title bar of either controller dismisses both of them and returns to the initial controller.

Summary

We've reached the end of our discussion of interface controller navigation. There was a quite a lot of material to absorb, but the principles are straightforward, and the behavior is very similar to what you are used to when working with UIKit view controllers. As you'll see, you can also perform controller navigation from the rows of a WatchKit table. The table is probably the most powerful WatchKit interface element and it is the subject of the next chapter, along with menus. So turn the page, and let's get started.

Chapter 6

Tables and Menus

In Chapter 2, you learned that when building WatchKit user interfaces, you have to know at design time which user interface objects you need and you must include them all in the storyboard. In some cases, this just isn't possible. Suppose, for example, that you wanted to display the results of a database query in rows, with one row (and hence one group of user interface objects) for each query result. In general, you can't know in advance how many query results there will be. You could try to work around this by adding a fixed number of groups to the storyboard and then, at run time, hiding any that you find you don't need. You might be able to make that approach work in some cases, but it's wasteful of scarce resources on the watch and doesn't really work if you need to display different query results in different ways.

Fortunately, there is a better solution: you can use a WatchKit table. Tables work like vertical groups, except that they let you decide at run time what nested user interface objects you need. The first part of this chapter will develop an example that uses several of the features of the table class—and in Chapter 7 you'll see how to use tables to build a more complex application.

The second part of this chapter discusses WatchKit menus. Menus allow you to save space on the screen by providing a place to keep functionality that the user does not always need access to. A menu can contain up to four menu items that act like buttons. It is invisible until the user presses on the screen with a little more than the usual amount of force. When the watch detects this *Force Touch* gesture, it overlays the menu on the screen allowing the user to see the available actions.

WatchKit Tables

WatchKit tables are instances of the WKInterfaceTable class. Like UITableView, WatchKit tables can have rows that are all of the same type or a mixture of different types. A typical table might have one row type that is used for table data and another for section headers. You declare the row types that you need, along with the user interface components that define their content, in the storyboard. Each row type also needs a *row controller* class containing outlets that are linked to its user interface components and possibly data that is associated with that particular row and action methods for any active objects (such as buttons) in the row.

Defining a row controller object is very similar to creating a prototype table cell for a UITableView. However, unlike UITableView, the rows of a WatchKit table are not created as they are about to appear on the screen. Instead, a row controller object for every row is created when you configure the table at run time, usually in the init() or awakeWithContext() method of its owning user interface controller. WatchKit is forced to do this because using the UITableView approach of configuring rows as the table scrolls would require a round trip from the watch to the WatchKit App extension running on the iPhone for each row, which would lead to very bad performance. Of course, creating all of the rows immediately means that the memory required to manage the table is proportional to the total number of rows in the table, not to the number that are currently visible (as it is in UIKit). As a result, you really shouldn't try to create large WatchKit tables. In fact, Apple recommends that you limit yourself to around 20 rows. If the data you need to display requires more rows, you need to provide some kind of paging mechanism to allow the user to see the next block of rows by reconfiguring the ones that are currently visible.

The first example application for this chapter uses a table to build an interface that looks a little like the iOS Settings application. We'll construct the example step by step, as usual, but let's first run the completed version to see what it does, after which it will be easier to understand the implementation.

Fire up Xcode and open and run the project in the 6 - Configuration Table folder of the book's example source code archive. When the application starts, you see a label and a Configure button, as shown on the left in Figure 6-1.

Figure 6-1. Using a WatchKit Table

When you press the button, a new controller containing a table and a Save button is presented, as shown in the middle two screenshots in Figure 6-1. There are two different types of row in this table: the first and fourth rows act as section headers for the other six rows, which contain the useful information in the table. The rows in the first section represent colors and the rows in the second section represent font styles. The idea is that the user can tap on a row in the first section to choose a color and a row in the second column to select a font. The rows that correspond to the current color and font are indicated by a green check mark. Because there are two different types of row, the table uses two row controller objects.

Pressing the Save button dismisses the presented controller and applies the new color and font to the text in the first interface controller, as shown on the right in Figure 6-1.

This example demonstrates the following:

- How to add a table to an interface controller

- How to specify the number of different row controllers that a table requires

- How to build the layout for each row controller in the storyboard

- How to build the table by adding row controller instances when the table first appears

- How to respond to the user tapping on a table row

- How to pass information to and from a presented controller, using the techniques from Chapter 5

Let's get started with this example. Begin, as usual, by creating a new Xcode project. Name the project Configuration Table and add a WatchKit application target to it. Now select Interface.storyboard in the Project Navigator so that we can start building the user interface.

Adding the Controllers and the Table to the Storyboard

For the main controller, we need a label and a button. Drag a label and a button from the Object Library and drop them onto the main controller in the storyboard. Select the button and change its Vertical attribute to Bottom and its Title attribute to Configure. Select the label and then change its Width attribute to Relative To Container, its Alignment attribute to Center, and its Lines attribute to 0. At this point, the main controller should be as shown on the left in Figure 6-1, apart from the label text, which we'll set programmatically. To do that, we'll need an outlet for the label, so open InterfaceController.swift in the Assistant Editor and Control-drag from the label to the top of the class definition to create an outlet called label, like this:

```
class InterfaceController: WKInterfaceController {
    @IBOutlet weak var label: WKInterfaceLabel!
```

Now let's build the second controller. Drag an interface controller from the Object Library and drop it onto the storyboard. We want to present this controller when the user taps the Configure button in the main interface controller, so Control-drag from that button to the new controller, release the mouse button, and choose **modal** from the pop-up that appears.

Next, drag a table from the Object Library and drop it onto the second controller. You'll notice that the table initially contains one row. That's a little misleading; if you were to run the example at this point, you would see an empty table (try it and see). What the table actually contains is one *row controller prototype*. We actually need two row prototypes, so select the table in the storyboard or in the Document Outline and use the Attributes Inspector to set its Rows attribute to 2.

> **Tip** A table's Rows attribute represents the number of row controllers (row prototypes) that the table has, not the number of rows that will appear in the table at run time.

Drag a separator and a button from the Object Library and drop them below the table. Then use the Attributes Inspector to change the button's Title attribute to Save. At this point, your storyboard should look like Figure 6-2.

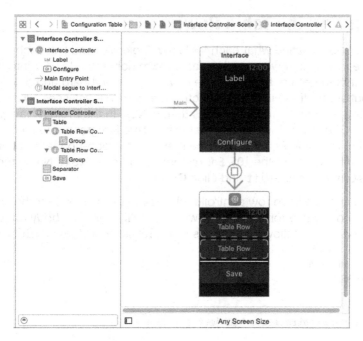

Figure 6-2. *Building the Configuration Table user interface*

The initial interface controller in the storyboard is already associated with
the InterfaceController class, which was supplied by the Xcode project
template. We also need a class to contain the logic for the presented
interface controller. Select the Configuration Table WatchKit Extension
group in the Project Navigator and then click on File ➤ New ➤ File... in
the Xcode menu. From the iOS Source section of the dialog that opens,
choose Cocoa Touch Class, press **Next**, and then name the new class
ConfigurationController, making it a subclass of WKInterfaceController.
Press **Next** and save the new class, making sure that it goes into the
Configuration Table WatchKit Extension group. In the storyboard, select
the second controller (the one at the bottom in Figure 6-2) and use the
Identity Inspector to set its Class attribute to ConfigurationController.
We'll add some code to this class in a while, after we've configured the rows
for the controller's table. That code will need an outlet for the table, which
we'll create now. Select the table in the Document Outline (it's quite hard to
select it in the storyboard—try it and see) and then open the Assistant Editor.
You should see the ConfigurationController class in the Assistant Editor,
but if you don't, select it manually from the jump bar. Control-drag from the
table in the Document Outline to the top of the ConfigurationController
class and create an outlet called table:

```
class ConfigurationController: WKInterfaceController {
    @IBOutlet weak var table: WKInterfaceTable!
```

Configuring the Table Rows

Next we need to define what each table row looks like and link each prototype row to its row controller class. We're going to add user interface components to both of the prototype rows in the storyboard and then create outlets for them in their respective row controller classes. We'll start by creating the row controller classes themselves. In the Project Navigator, select the Configuration Table WatchKit Extension group and then select File ➤ New ➤ File... from the menu. In the pop-up that appears, select Swift File from the iOS Source group and click **Next**. Name the file TableRowControllers.swift and click **Create**.

We're going to add two row controller classes to this file: one for the section headers and another for the other rows (which I'll refer to as *body rows* from now on). Make the following changes to TableRowControllers.swift:

```
import Foundation
import WatchKit


class HeaderRowController : NSObject {
}

class BodyRowController : NSObject {
    var attributeValue: AnyObject?
}
```

As you can see, row controller classes are not subclasses of any WatchKit class—they are just plain NSObjects.

Caution   Row controller classes *must* be subclasses of NSObject.

Each body row is associated with a color or a text style, so the BodyRowController class has a property that we'll use to store that value. This property must be declared as optional because the row controller objects are created by WatchKit as part of the initialization of the table, and there is no way for you to provide an initial value for the property.

For this example, I chose to make attributeValue of type AnyObject? so that I can use it to hold either a UIColor or a UIFont object. If you prefer stronger typing, you could define a separate class for each row type (e.g. FontBodyRowController and ColorBodyRowController) and declare their properties to be of type UIFont and UIColor respectively. The downside to that approach is that you would need to add an extra prototype table row in the storyboard and duplicate the row layout for the color and font rows.

Now let's finish the storyboard and add the outlets we need to the row controller classes. Select Interface.storyboard in the Project Navigator and direct your attention to the Document Outline, shown on the left in Figure 6-2. In the node tree for the second interface controller (the one that has the table), you'll see the Table node. Click the disclosure triangle to reveal a further two nodes (labeled Table Row Controller), one for each prototype table row. Expand these nodes and you'll see that they contain a group. You can use this group to add the visual content for the corresponding row type. Let's do that now, starting with the header rows.

> **Tip**   Every prototype table row contains a group. You can use the group's attributes to customize the appearance of the row. For example, you can set its background color (as you'll see in a minute) or change the radius of its rounded corners.

Configuring the Header Rows

Select either of the Table Row Controller nodes, open the Identity Inspector, and, in the Custom Class section, set the class to HeaderRowController. Next, open the Attributes Inspector and set the header row's Identifier attribute to Header; we'll use this identifier when we initialize the table at run time. While we're here, uncheck the Selectable attribute since we don't want the user to be able to select the row header.

The header row is going to display some fixed text, so we need to add a label to the row controller's group. Because you have the row controller selected in the Document Outline, the corresponding table row should be selected in the storyboard. Drag a label from the Object Library and drop it into the table row in the storyboard. The label should be added to the row controller's group, as shown in Figure 6-3.

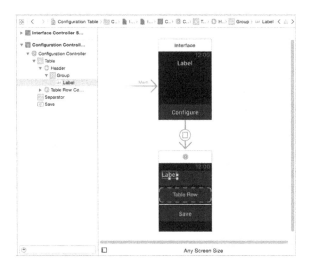

Figure 6-3. *Creating the table header row controller*

In the Attributes Inspector, change the label's `Alignment` attribute to `Center`, its `Vertical` attribute to `Center`, and its `Width` attribute to `Relative to Container`. To make the header visually distinct from the body rows, select its group node in the Document Outline and then use the Attributes Inspector to change its `Color` attribute to `Light Gray Color`. If you look back to Figure 6-1, you'll see that the section header rows are smaller than the body rows. To do that, with the group node still selected, change the `Height` attribute to `Fixed` and enter 24 as the value. If the section header row in the storyboard does not change height when you do this, you probably have the label selected instead of the group.

To complete the header row controller class, we need to add an outlet for the label. Select the label in the Document Outline and then open `TableRowControllers.swift` in the Assistant Editor. If this file is not opened automatically when you open the Assistant Editor, you can open it by selecting `Manual` in the jump bar and then navigating to it. `Control`-drag from the label in the Document Outline to the `HeaderRowController` class in the Assistant Editor and create an outlet called `label`.

> **Note** You may find that Xcode is unable to create an outlet because it has no information about the `HeaderRowController` class. This is an Xcode bug. To work around it, first try cleaning and rebuilding the project (hold down the ⌥ (Option) key, select `Product ➤ Clean Build Folder...` from the menu, and then press ⌘**B**).

Configuring the Body Rows

We'll use a very similar set of steps to configure the body rows, the main difference being that these rows require an image for the check mark that you can see in Figure 6-1 in addition to a label. Select the other Table Row Controller in the Document Outline and open the Identify Inspector. In the Custom Class section, set the Class attribute to BodyRowController to link the row prototype in the storyboard to its row controller class. Next, in the Attributes Inspector, set the Identifier attribute to Body and leave the Selectable attribute checked, because we want to respond to the user tapping a body row by selecting the corresponding color or font.

The row controller's table row in the storyboard should be selected—if not, just select the Body node in the Document Outline. Drag a label object from the Object Library and drop it onto the table row in the storyboard. Then use the Attributes Inspector to set its Vertical attribute to Center. Next, drag an image object and drop it onto the table row. Because the group in the table row is a horizontal one, the image will position itself to the right of the label. We'd like the image to be right-aligned in the row and to have its vertical center aligned with that of the label, so use the Attributes Inspector to set its Horizontal attribute to Right and its Vertical attribute to Center. You'll find the check image in a file called CheckMark@2x.png in the 6 - Configuration Table Images folder of the example source code archive. Select Images. xcassets in the Project Navigator and drag the image into it. Reselect the image object in the Document Outline and use the Attributes Inspector to set the Image attribute to CheckMark and the Mode attribute to Center so that the check mark image is drawn neatly in the center of the space allocated for the image object and is not stretched in either direction.

When WatchKit creates the table rows at run time, it will set their heights based on their content, which means that different rows can have different heights. You can override the calculated height if you want by changing the Height attribute of the row's group object, as we did for the section header rows, but you should not make the height of any selectable row less than 37.5 pt. for the 38mm watch or 40 pt. for the 48mm watch to ensure that the rows are always tall enough for the user to be able to select them accurately. For this example, there is no need to adjust the row heights, so we'll leave the Height attribute unchanged.

Finally, we need to create outlets for the label and the image. Open TableRowControllers.swift in the Assistant Editor. Then Control-drag from the label to the BodyRowController class to create an outlet called label and from the image to the BodyRowController class to create an outlet called checkImage. The storyboard and TableRowControllers.swift file should now be as shown in Figure 6-4.

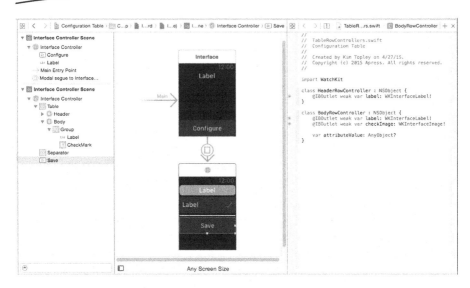

Figure 6-4. *The completed table body row controller*

If you run the application at this point and press the Configure button on the initial interface controller's screen, you'll see that the table in the presented controller is empty. That's because, as I said earlier, all we've done so far is define two row prototypes—we haven't yet given the table any data to display. We'll get around to doing that in a while.

Defining the Interface between the Controllers

This application has two interface controllers: the initial controller and the controller that's presented when the user presses the Configure button. When you push or present a controller, you typically need to add some information to it, and vice versa when control returns to the initial controller. We're going to use the same techniques to pass information between controllers that you saw in Chapter 5—that is, we'll define an object that's passed to the presented controller's awakeWithContext() method which contains everything it needs to initialize itself and a closure that it can call to return information to the initial controller when it's dismissed.

What information do we need to pass between the controllers? The function of the presented controller is to allow the user to select a color and a font that will be applied to the text in the initial controller, so we'll at least need to define an object that encapsulates these attributes. We'll need to use this object in both controllers, so let's put its definition in a separate file to make clear that it is doesn't belong to either controller.

Select the Configuration Table WatchKit Extension group in the Project Navigator and click on File ➤ New ➤ File... in the Xcode menu. In the iOS Source section of the dialog that opens, choose Swift File and click **Next**. Name the file TextAttributes.swift, click **Next**, and save the new file. Select TextAttributes.swift in the Project Navigator and add the following code shown in bold to it:

```
import Foundation
import UIKit

struct TextAttributes {
    let color: UIColor
    let font: UIFont
}
```

Because this object is just a container for information with no associated behavior, I've made it a structure rather than a class. One nice side effect of that decision is that you get a free initializer you can use to set the color and font properties, like this:

```
let attributes = TextAttributes(color: UIColor.redColor(),
        font: UIFont.preferredFontForTextStyle(UIFontTextStyleBody))
```

If you look back at Figure 6-1, you'll see that we allow the user to select from three fixed colors and three fixed text styles (from which we'll derive a font). Rather than hardcode these values in both controllers, we can conveniently define them all as static properties of the TextAttributes structure:

```
struct TextAttributes {
    static let colorNames = ["White", "Yellow", "Green"]
    static let colors = [UIColor.whiteColor(),
                            UIColor.yellowColor(), UIColor.greenColor()]
    static let fontNames = ["Body", "Headline", "Footnote"]
    static let fonts = [
        UIFont.preferredFontForTextStyle(UIFontTextStyleBody),
        UIFont.preferredFontForTextStyle(UIFontTextStyleHeadline),
        UIFont.preferredFontForTextStyle(UIFontTextStyleFootnote)
    ]

    let color: UIColor
    let font: UIFont
}
```

The colorNames and fontNames arrays contain the values that appear in the user interface, whereas the colors and fonts arrays contain the actual values that will be used in the application, in the same order as the corresponding names.

The next step is to define the context object that's passed to the presented controller. This object needs to contain the current text color and font of the label in the main controller's user interface and a closure that will be used to return the user's selected values to the main controller. As noted back in Chapter 5, the context object should be considered to be part of the API of the presented controller, so we'll define it as part of the ConfigurationController class. Select ConfigurationController.swift in the Project Navigator and add the following code shown in bold to it:

```
class ConfigurationController: WKInterfaceController {

    class ControllerContext {
        let textAttributes: TextAttributes
        let callback: (TextAttributes) -> Void

        init(textAttributes: TextAttributes,
            callback: (TextAttributes) -> Void) {
            self.textAttributes = textAttributes
            self.callback = callback
        }
    }
}
```

The textAttributes property supplies the current color and font, and the callback property is the closure that the presented controller will call when it is dismissed, passing another TextAttributes object with the newly selected color and font values.

Implementing the Initial Interface Controller

The job of the initial interface controller is to present the configuration controller when the Configure button is pressed and to set the color and font of the label's text when the application starts and when the configuration controller is dismissed. Let's look at the second of these tasks first and we'll deal with presenting the configuration controller in the next section.

The label's initial color and font could be set in any of the controller's init(), awakeWithContext(), or willActivate() methods. What about updating these attributes when the configuration controller is dismissed? At that point, the configuration controller invokes the callback method that is passed in its context, which we'll implement as part of the initial controller. It would be convenient if we could use the TextAttributes object that we get with that call to update the label in the callback method, but we can't, because when we presented the configuration controller, the initial controller was deactivated, and, as you know, you can't update user interface objects belonging to a controller that's not active. Instead, we have to save the new attributes and wait until the initial controller's willActivate() method is called. So it turns out that setting the label's font and color in the willActivate() method works for both cases (and you may remember that we did the same thing in an example that involved pushing an interface controller back in Chapter 5). Let's add the code to do that.

Select InterfaceController.swift in the Project Navigator and add the following code at the top of the class definition:

```
class InterfaceController: WKInterfaceController {
    @IBOutlet weak var label: WKInterfaceLabel!

    private var textAttributes =
        TextAttributes(color: TextAttributes.colors[0],
                        font: TextAttributes.fonts[0])
    private var attributesChanged = true
    private var text =
        NSMutableAttributedString(string: "Hello, Watch")
```

The textAttributes property is initialized with the font and color that the user will see when the application starts. We could set these in the storyboard, but doing it this way means we don't need to remember to update the storyboard if we ever change the font and color choices. When the configuration controller is presented and dismissed, we'll update this property with the new attributes. The attributesChanged property tells us whether we actually need to update the label's attributes in the willActivate() method. It is possible for the user to open the configuration controller and not change either the selected color or font, or to use the Cancel button in the title bar. In that case, we don't want to waste time by having WatchKit send a message to the watch that just sets the label's attributes to their current values. Finally, the text property is an NSAttributedString that's initialized with the label's text. Why do we need this? We can set the color attribute of a WKInterfaceLabel object at run time by calling its setTextColor() method, but there is no method to change the font. Instead, we have to apply the font that we need to an attributed string and use the label's setAttributedText() method to change it. In fact, we'll use the attributed string to set both the font and the color. To do that, add the following code to the willActivate() method:

```
override func willActivate() {
    if attributesChanged {
        let range = NSMakeRange(0, text.length)
        text.addAttribute(NSForegroundColorAttributeName,
                value: textAttributes.color, range: range)
        text.addAttribute(NSFontAttributeName,
                value: textAttributes.font, range: range)
```

```
        label.setAttributedText(text)
        attributesChanged = false;
    }
    super.willActivate()
}
```

This code should be self-explanatory. Notice that we update the attributes only if the `attributesChanged` property is `true` and, having done so, we reset it to `false`. This property is initially `true` (so we'll set the font and color when the application starts), and we also need to set it to `true` when the presented controller invokes its callback method, provided that either the color or font is changed. To implement that, add the following method to the class definition:

```
func onCallBack(textAttributes: TextAttributes) -> Void {
    if textAttributes.color != self.textAttributes.color
            || textAttributes.font != self.textAttributes.color {
        // Font or color changed
        self.textAttributes = textAttributes
        attributesChanged = true
    }
}
```

Presenting the Configuration Controller

As you've seen, if you run the application and press the `Configure` button, the configuration controller is presented. The presentation happens automatically because we added a modal segue to the `Configure` button in the storyboard. However, at this point, we're not passing context information to the controller. Because the controller is presented by a segue, we can't pass the context object directly to it. Instead, as you saw in Chapter 5, we need to implement the `contextForSegueWithIdentifier()` method in the presenting controller. To do that, add the following code near the bottom of the `InterfaceController` class:

```
override func contextForSegueWithIdentifier(
            segueIdentifier: String) -> AnyObject? {
    return ConfigurationController.ControllerContext(
                    textAttributes: textAttributes,
                    callback: onCallBack)
}

func onCallBack(textAttributes: TextAttributes) -> Void {
```

The context object is an instance of the `ControllerContext` class, which we initialize with the current text attributes from the controller's `textAttributes` property, and a reference to the `onCallBack` method, which the presenting controller will call to pass back the new attributes. To check that this is working, open `ConfigurationController.swift` in the editor and add the following line of code to its `awakeWithContext()` method:

```
override func awakeWithContext(context: AnyObject?) {
    super.awakeWithContext(context)

    // Configure interface objects here.
    println("Context: \(context)")
}
```

Now run the application and press the `Configure` button. When the configuration controller appears, you should see something like this in the Xcode console:

```
Context: Optional(Configuration_Table_WatchKit_Extension.
ConfigurationController.ControllerContext)
```

Implementing the Configuration Controller

Having completed the main interface controller, we now move on to the configuration controller. This is the point where we finally get to use a WatchKit table, so let's look at how the `WKInterfaceTable` class works before we start writing code.

Adding Rows to the Color and Font Table

When we constructed the configuration controller in the storyboard, we added a `WKInterfaceTable` and two prototype rows, but, as you have already seen, just doing this does not produce any visible content in the table. To add content to the table, you need to use one of the following `WKInterfaceTable` methods:

```
func setNumberOfRows(_ numberOfRows: Int,
                    withRowType rowType: String)
func setRowTypes(_ rowTypes: [AnyObject])
func insertRowsAtIndexes(_ rows: NSIndexSet,
                        withRowType rowType: String)
```

Use the first method when you want to initialize the table with a number of rows all of the same type—that is, all created from the same row controller. The `rowType` argument should be the identifier assigned to the row controller in the storyboard. For example, the following code would initialize a table with three rows all created from the Body prototype row:

```
table.setNumberOfRows(3, withRowType: "Body")
```

Add that line of code to the `awakeWithContext()` method in the `ConfigurationController` class, run the example, and press the `Configure` button. You'll see that the table in the presented controller now has three rows, as shown in Figure 6-5.

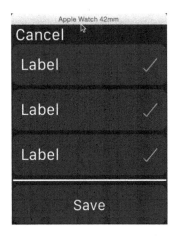

Figure 6-5. A table with three rows of the same type

We haven't yet initialized the three rows with meaningful data, so for the moment they are just copies of the body prototype. We'll take care of initializing the table content shortly. For this example, we need a table with two different row types—some will be headers, others will be body rows. To do that, we construct an array containing the identifiers for the row prototypes in the order in which they should appear in the table and invoke the second method from the list above. Make the following changes to the `awakeWithContext()` method to create a table containing two header rows and two body rows:

```
table.setNumberOfRows(3, withRowType: "Body")
let rowTypes = ["Header", "Body", "Header", "Body"]
table.setRowTypes(rowTypes)
```

The result of running this version of the application is shown in Figure 6-6.

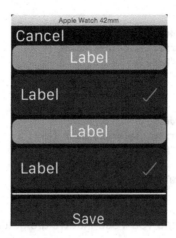

Figure 6-6. *A table with header and body rows*

The setNumberOfRows(_:withRowType:) and setRowTypes() methods remove any table content before adding the new row types. This is appropriate when you first create the table, but you should avoid doing this, if possible, if you need to add or remove rows at run time, because calling either of these methods causes the table to be rebuilt from scratch. To add a row to an existing table, use the insertRowsAtIndexes(_:withRowType:) method, and to remove rows, use the following method:

```
func removeRowsAtIndexes(_ rows: NSIndexSet)
```

For our current example, we don't need to add additional rows or remove rows at run time, but you'll see an example that uses these methods later in this chapter.

The table that we need to create should have two sections, each with a header. The body rows for the first section need to be initialized with the color names taken from the colorNames property of TextAttributes structure. Similarly the rows in the second section should use the font names from the fontNames property. To do that, make the following changes to the awakeWithContext() method:

```
override func awakeWithContext(context: AnyObject?) {
    super.awakeWithContext(context)

    // Configure interface objects here.
    println("Context: \(context)")
    let rowTypes = ["Header", "Body", "Header", "Body"]
    table.setRowTypes(rowTypes)
    var rowTypes = [String]();
```

```
// Color section
rowTypes.append("Header")
for _ in 0..<TextAttributes.colors.count {
    rowTypes.append("Body")
}

// Font section
rowTypes.append("Header")
for _ in 0..<TextAttributes.fonts.count {
    rowTypes.append("Body")
}
table.setRowTypes(rowTypes)
}
```

Run the example again and you'll see that we are getting closer to our goal (see Figure 6-7).

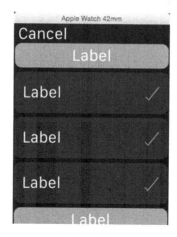

Figure 6-7. The configuration table with header and body rows

Configuring the Table Row Content

The next step is to arrange for the correct text to appear in the header and body rows. When we called setRowTypes(), the table created an instance of the correct row controller class for each row based on the row controller identifier in the rowTypes array. Recall that when we defined the row prototypes in the storyboard, we specified an identifier and the row controller class name for each prototype. Using this information, WatchKit knows that for rows of type Header, it needs to create an instance of the HeaderRowController class and for Body rows it should create

BodyRowController instances. To initialize the table, we can fetch the row controller for each row using the following method:

```
func rowControllerAtIndex(_ index: Int) -> AnyObject?
```

Once we have a reference to a row controller, we can set its properties using the outlets we created when we were building the row prototypes. To do that, add the following code to the awakeWithContext() method:

```
override func awakeWithContext(context: AnyObject?) {
    super.awakeWithContext(context)

    // Configure interface objects here.
    var rowTypes = [String]();

    // Color section
    rowTypes.append("Header")
    for _ in 0..<TextAttributes.colors.count {
        rowTypes.append("Body")
    }

    // Font section
    rowTypes.append("Header")
    for _ in 0..<TextAttributes.fonts.count {
        rowTypes.append("Body")
    }
    table.setRowTypes(rowTypes)

    var inColorSection = false
    var sectionStartIndex = -1
    for index in 0..<table.numberOfRows {
        let controller: AnyObject? = table.rowControllerAtIndex(index)
        if let header = controller as? HeaderRowController {
            inColorSection = index == 0;
            sectionStartIndex = index + 1;
            header.label.setText(inColorSection ? "Color" : "Font")
        } else if let body = controller as? BodyRowController {
            let rowInSectionIndex = index - sectionStartIndex
            switch inColorSection {
            case true:
                let color = TextAttributes.colors[rowInSectionIndex]
                body.attributeValue = color
                body.label.setText(
                        TextAttributes.colorNames[rowInSectionIndex])
                body.label.setTextColor(color)
```

```
            case false:
                let font = TextAttributes.fonts[rowInSectionIndex]
                body.attributeValue = font
                let text = NSAttributedString(
                    string: TextAttributes.fontNames[rowInSectionIndex],
                    attributes: [NSFontAttributeName: font])
                body.label.setAttributedText(text)
                body.checkImage.setHidden(true)

            default:
                fatalError("Invalid index: \(index)")
            }
        }
    }
}
```

This code might seem complex, but it's not as bad as it looks. The for loop iterates over the table rows from first to the last, using the numberOfRows property of WKInterfaceTable to find out how many rows there are. At any given point, we are either in the first section (the color section) or the second section (the font section) and we use the inColorSection variable to keep track of this. Initially, this variable is false because we are not in either section. The sectionStartIndex variable is used to track the index of the first row in the current section. We initialize it to –1 because we need to supply an initializer, but the actual value is not important. Now let's look at what happens in the loop itself.

First, we get the controller object for the current row using the rowControllerAtIndex() method, using the loop index as argument:

```
for index in 0..<table.numberOfRows {
    let controller: AnyObject? = table.rowControllerAtIndex(index)
```

Next, we attempt to cast the controller to HeaderRowController. If this works, we know we are dealing with a header row and we have either entered the color section on the first iteration of the loop or switched to the font section:

```
if let header = controller as? HeaderRowController {
```

Given that we are in a header, we set the inColorSection variable based on whether we are at index 0 (which means we are in the color section) and we set the sectionStartIndex variable to the index of the next row:

```
inColorSection = index == 0;
sectionStartIndex = index + 1;
```

Finally, we use the `label` outlet in the `HeaderRowController` class to set the header text to either `Color` or `Font`:

```
header.label.setText(inColorSection ? "Color" : "Font")
```

That's all we need to do for header rows. The next section of code deals with the body rows. We know we are dealing with a body row if we can successfully cast the row controller object to the type `BodyRowController`. If that is the case, then we set the `rowInSectionIndex` variable to the index of the current body in the current section:

```
} else if let body = controller as? BodyRowController {
    let rowInSectionIndex = index - sectionStartIndex
```

For the first body row in a section, `rowInSectionIndex` will be 0, for the second it will be 1, and so on. We'll use this value to index the arrays in the `TextAttribute` class.

Note   This code makes no assumptions about how many rows there are in each section, even though we know there are three. By avoiding such assumptions, we make it possible to add more colors and/or fonts just by modifying the `TextAttributes` class.

We need to set the text of the row controller's label to either the color or font name. In addition, in the color section we use the current color as the text color and in the font section we set the text from the current font. We use the `inColorSection` variable to distinguish between these two cases. Here's the code that handles rows in the color section:

```
switch inColorSection {
case true:
    let color = TextAttributes.colors[rowInSectionIndex]
    body.attributeValue = color
    body.label.setText(
            TextAttributes.colorNames[rowInSectionIndex])
    body.label.setTextColor(color)
```

Notice that as well as setting the color of the label's text, we also set the row controller's `attributeValue` property to the actual color value. We'll use this later when the user selects a new color. The code that handles the rows in the font section is only a little more complex:

```
case false:
    let font = TextAttributes.fonts[rowInSectionIndex]
    body.attributeValue = font
    let text = NSAttributedString(
            string: TextAttributes.fontNames[rowInSectionIndex],
                attributes: [NSFontAttributeName: font])
    body.label.setAttributedText(text)
```

As before, we set the label's text and the `attributeValue` property but in this case, because we want to apply the font to the text, we first convert it to an attributed string and then use the `setAttributedText()` method. Run the example now and you'll see that the labels in the header and body rows are now correctly configured (see Figure 6-8).

Figure 6-8. *The header and body rows are almost complete*

Showing the Initial Color and Font Selection

There is one more thing we need to do: all the body rows are showing a check mark, but only the rows for the current color and font should be checked. We can easily fix that by looping over each controller and hiding the image for the rows that do not contain the selected color or font. How do we know which color and font are selected? Recall that the context object that's passed to the `awakeWithContext()` method is of type `ControllerContext`, and one of the properties of this object is a

TextAttributes structure that contains the current color and font. It turns out that we will need to use the ControllerContext and the selected color and font elsewhere in our controller implementation, so let's add some properties for them at the top of the ConfigurationController class:

```
class ConfigurationController: WKInterfaceController {
    @IBOutlet weak var table: WKInterfaceTable!
    private var selectedColor: UIColor?
    private var selectedFont: UIFont?
    private var controllerContext: ControllerContext?
```

Now add the code in bold at the end of the awakeWithContext() method:

```
    // Install the selected color and font and update the
    // check marks in the table.
    if let controllerContext = context as? ControllerContext {
        self.controllerContext = controllerContext
        selectedColor = controllerContext.textAttributes.color
        selectedFont = controllerContext.textAttributes.font
        updateCheckMarks()
    }
}
```

This code won't compile yet because we haven't defined the updateCheckMarks() method, which is where we'll actually update the visibility of the check mark images. That code is in a separate method because we'll also need to use it whenever the user taps a table row to change the color or font selection. Add this method to the end of the class definition:

```
// Show or hide the check image for each body row.
private func updateCheckMarks() {
    for index in 0..<table.numberOfRows {
        let controller: AnyObject? = table.rowControllerAtIndex(index)
        var match = false
        if let body = controller as? BodyRowController {
            if let color = body.attributeValue as? UIColor {
                match = color == selectedColor
            } else if let font = body.attributeValue as? UIFont {
                match = font == selectedFont
            }
            body.checkImage.setHidden(!match)
        }
    }
}
```

This code loops over every row in the table. For each body row, it uses the type of the attributeValue property to determine whether it is a color row or a font row and then compares the property value to either the selectedColor or selectedFont property to determine whether there is a match. If there is a match, the check mark image is shown—otherwise, it is hidden. With this change in place, you can now run the application and verify that only the check marks for the selected color and font are visible, as shown in Figure 6-9.

Figure 6-9. The check marks in the body rows are correct

Handling Selection Changes

When the user taps on a body row, we need to change the selected color or font to the one that the user selected and move the check mark from the previously selected row to the new one. We already have a method (updateCheckMarks()) that ensures that the check marks match the selectedColor and selectedFont properties, so we just need to update these properties when the user taps a body row and then call this method. When the user selects a row, WatchKit invokes the following method in its owning interface controller:

```
func table(_ table: WKInterfaceTable,
           didSelectRowAtIndex rowIndex: Int)
```

The rowIndex argument is the index of the row that was tapped and the table argument refers to the table itself, which is useful if your controller's user interface has more than one table. Let's implement this method. Add the following code to the ConfigurationController class:

```
// Handling for row selection change
override func table(table: WKInterfaceTable,
                    didSelectRowAtIndex rowIndex: Int) {
    let controller: AnyObject? = table.rowControllerAtIndex(rowIndex)
    if let body = controller as? BodyRowController {
        if let color = body.attributeValue as? UIColor {
            selectedColor = color
        } else if let font = body.attributeValue as? UIFont {
            selectedFont = font
        }
        updateCheckMarks()
    }
}
```

We use the selected row index to get the row controller object for that row and attempt to cast it BodyRowController so that we can access its attributeValue property. In fact, in this example, this method will only ever be called for taps on body rows, because we unchecked the Selectable check box in the Attributes Inspector for the header row prototype, so we could use the forced cast operator (as!) instead of an if let statement here. Next, we check whether the value of the attributeValue property is a color or a font and assign it to selectedColor or selectedFont respectively. Having done that, we call the updateCheckMarks() method to update the check marks on the screen. That's all we need to do to handle row selection. Run the example now and you'll see that the check marks in both sections move as you tap rows.

Returning Information to the Initial Controller

The code that we have written so far ensures that the user can see the selected color and font and keeps the selectedColor and selectedFont properties up to date as the user makes selections. Now we need to allow the user to dismiss the configuration controller and return the selection information to the initial controller. To make this possible, we first need to link the Save button to an action method in the configuration controller. Select Interface.storyboard in the Project Navigator to open it in the editor and then open ConfigurationController.swift in the Assistant Editor. Control-drag from the Save button in the configuration controller to the ConfigurationController class and create an action method called onSaveButtonClicked()—then add the following code to it:

```
@IBAction func onSaveButtonClicked() {
    if selectedColor != nil && selectedFont != nil {
        let textAttributes =
            TextAttributes(color: selectedColor!, font: selectedFont!)
        controllerContext?.callback(textAttributes)
        dismissController()
    }
}
```

We first check that both a color and a font are selected. It shouldn't really be possible for either selectedColor or selectedFont to be nil unless we have a bug, but we make the check anyway to avoid a crash on the next line of code when we construct a TextAttributes object. Next, we invoke the callback method that the initial controller passed to us via the ControllerContext object, which we stored in the controllerContext property. We know that this will actually call the initial controller's onCallBack() method, which stores the TextAttributes object and returns. Finally, we call dismissController() to remove the presented controller and redisplay the main screen of the application. This causes the initial controller's willActivate() method to be called, and the saved TextAttributes object will be used to update the label, if either the color or font changed.

> **Tip** To remove a presented controller, call dismissController(). To remove a controller that you pushed onto a hierarchical controller stack, use popController() or popToRootController().

That completes our first table-based WatchKit application. If you run it now, you should be able to change the color and font of the text on the initial screen. In passing, note that the user does not have to press the Save button in the presented controller—he could press the Cancel button in the title bar instead. In that case, WatchKit will dismiss the controller, the initial controller's onCallBack() method will not be called, and the label's color and font will not change, which is the correct behavior.

More Table Manipulation

So far, you've seen how to create a table and add rows to it and how to handle row selection events from the table. In this section, you'll create an application that adds and removes rows from a table and also illustrates how to handle events from user interface controls that are part of a table row. The completed application is shown in Figure 6-10.

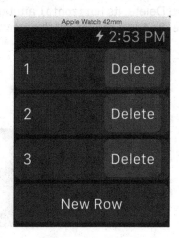

Figure 6-10. A an application that adds and removes table rows

When the application starts, it builds a table with three rows (all of the same type). Each row contains a label with a unique number and a Delete button. When the button in a row is pressed, that row is deleted from the table. To implement that, you need to be able to handle an event from a table row that is not a row selection event. The application also has a New Row button, which adds a new row to the table and scrolls the table so that the new row is visible.

Creating the Application Storyboard

Start by creating a new project called UpdatingTable and add a WatchKit App target to it. Then select Interface.storyboard in the Project Navigator to open the storyboard in the editor. Drag a table from the Object Library, drop it onto the interface controller, and then drag and drop a button below the table. Use the Attributes Inspector to change the button's Title attribute to New Row.

All of the table rows in this example are the same, so we only need one row prototype in the storyboard, which is what we get by default. Each row requires a label and a button. Drag a label from the Object Library and drop it onto the table row in the storyboard. In the Attributes Inspector, set the label's Vertical attribute to Center so that it aligns itself properly with the row. Next, drag and drop a button to the right of the label. The button will initially occupy the whole row, but we need it to take up only as much space as it needs and to be right-aligned in the row. To arrange that, change the button's Title attribute to Delete, its Horizontal attribute to Right, and its Width attribute to Size To Fit Content. At this point, your storyboard should look like Figure 6-11.

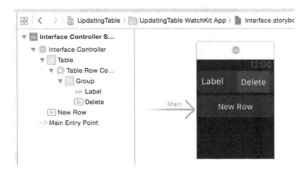

Figure 6-11. The completed application storyboard

Creating the Table Row Controller Class

As you know, each prototype row in a table needs a row controller class. In this example, there is just one prototype row, so we only need one row controller class. Select the UpdatingTable WatchKit Extension group in the Project Navigator and then click on File ➤ New ➤ File... in the Xcode menu. From the iOS Source section in the dialog that appears, select Cocoa Touch Class and click Next. Set the Class name to RowController and make it a subclass of NSObject. Then click Next and save the class, making sure it's added to the UpdatingTable WatchKit Extension group.

To link the row prototype to its controller class, select the storyboard in the Project Navigator and then select the Table Row Controller node in the Document Outline. In the Identity Inspector, set the Class attribute to RowController. We also need to assign an identifier so that we can refer to the prototype row when creating the table. To do that, open the Attributes Inspector and set the Identifier attribute to Row. While you are here, uncheck the Selectable attribute because we are not going to make use of table row selection in this example.

Next, we need to complete the definition of the RowController class, so open the RowController class in the Assistant Editor. Control-drag from the label in the table row prototype to the RowController class in the Assistant Editor and create an outlet called label.

> **Note**   You may find that Xcode won't let you create this outlet. To fix that, close and restart Xcode and try again. If that doesn't work, clean the project build folder, rebuild the project, and repeat the steps above. Once you create the outlet, you'll get a compilation error. We'll fix that shortly.

We'll also need to link an action method to the Delete button. Normally, you would link a button to an action method in its hosting interface controller, but that does not work for buttons (and other active user interface objects like sliders etc) in table rows. To handle events from an object in a table row, you need to connect it to an action method in the table row controller itself, so Control-drag from the Delete button in the storyboard to the RowController class and link it to an action method called onDeleteButtonClicked().

There are a couple more things we need to do before we're finished with the row controller class. First, we need to fix the compilation error for the outlet definition. To do that, delete the import of UIKit and replace it with an import of WatchKit:

```
import UIKit
import WatchKit

class RowController: NSObject {
```

Second, we need to add a reference to the interface controller. As you'll see shortly, we'll need this reference when handling events from the Delete button. Add the line of code shown in bold:

```
import WatchKit

class RowController: NSObject {
    var controller: InterfaceController?

    @IBOutlet weak var label: WKInterfaceLabel!
    @IBAction func onDeleteButtonClicked() {
    }
}
```

That's all we need to do to the RowController class for now, so let's move on to the implementation of the interface controller itself.

Implementing the Interface Controller

Let's start by creating the linkage needed between the interface controller and the storyboard. Select `Interface.storyboard` in the Project Navigator and open `InterfaceController.swift` in the Assistant Editor. Expand the Interface Controller Scene in the Document Outline until you can see the `Table` node and then `Control`-drag from that node to the top of the `InterfaceController` class to create an outlet called `table`. Next, `Control`-drag from the `New Row` button to the bottom of the `InterfaceController` class and create an action method called `onNewRowButtonClicked()`. We'll complete the implementation of this method later.

Now let's add the code to add the initial three rows to the table. As you saw in the previous example, we do that by first telling the table how to create the rows we require and then we loop over the individual rows to initialize them. To do this, add the following code shown in bold to the `InterfaceController` class:

```
class InterfaceController: WKInterfaceController {
    @IBOutlet weak var table: WKInterfaceTable!
    private var nextRowNumber = 1
    private var nextInsertIndex: Int!

    override func awakeWithContext(context: AnyObject?) {
        super.awakeWithContext(context)

        // Configure interface objects here.
        table.setNumberOfRows(3, withRowType: "Row");
        for index in 0..<table.numberOfRows {
            initializeRow(index)
        }
        nextInsertIndex = table.numberOfRows
    }
```

Each row we create has a number that's shown in the label. To keep track of the next available number, we use the `nextRowNumber` property, which we initialize to 1. The `nextInsertIndex` property will be required when we implement the `New Row` button. I'll say more about how it's used shortly.

The new code in the `awakeWithContext()` method first calls the table's `setNumberOfRows()` method:

```
table.setNumberOfRows(3, withRowType: "Row");
```

This causes the table to add three rows to the table, all of them created from the `Row` prototype, which we linked to the `RowController` class when we were building the storyboard. Next, iterate over the newly-created rows to initialize them and, for a reason I'll provide later, set the nextInsertIndex property to the number of rows in the table:

```
for index in 0..<table.numberOfRows {
    initializeRow(index)
}
nextInsertIndex = table.numberOfRows
```

The code to initialize a row is encapsulated in the initializeRow() method, which we haven't written yet, so that we can reuse it when adding new rows to the table. Add the implementation of this method at the bottom of the class definition:

```
    private func initializeRow(rowIndex: Int) {
        let row = table.rowControllerAtIndex(rowIndex) as! RowController
        row.label.setText("\(nextRowNumber++)")
        row.controller = self
    }
}
```

Given the index of the row to initialize, this method gets its RowController object from the table, uses the nextRowNumber variable to initialize the label, and then increments it. The effect of this is that the first row will be labeled 1, the second will be labeled 2, and so on. Finally, we set the RowController's controller variable to self, which is a reference to the interface controller itself.

At this point, you can run the example. You should see three table rows, each with a numbered label and a Delete button, and the New Row button, as shown in Figure 6-10. None of the buttons does anything yet, so let's fix that now.

Implementing the Delete Button

When you press the Delete button in any of the table rows, the onDeleteButtonClicked() method of that row's RowController object is called. This method is currently empty. Add the following code shown in bold to it:

```
class RowController: NSObject {
    var controller: InterfaceController?
    @IBOutlet weak var label: WKInterfaceLabel!

    @IBAction func onDeleteButtonClicked() {
        controller?.rowDeleteClicked(self)
    }
}
```

This code just calls a method (that we haven't yet implemented) in the interface controller, which will perform the actual deletion of the row. The deletion is handled in the interface controller because it's easier to maintain the code when it's all in one place and because it needs to update a property of the interface controller. Add the rowDeleteClicked() method to the InterfaceController class:

```
func rowDeleteClicked(rowController: RowController) {
    for index in 0..<table.numberOfRows {
        if let thisRow = table.rowControllerAtIndex(index)
                         as? RowController {
            if thisRow == rowController {
                table.removeRowsAtIndexes(NSIndexSet(index: index))
                nextInsertIndex = index
                break
            }
        }
    }
}
```

This method is called with a reference to the RowController for the row to be deleted as its argument. To delete the row, we need to call the table's removeRowsAtIndexes() method with the index of the row to be deleted. The row's controller class doesn't know its own row index, so we have to get it by looping over all of the rows in the table until we find the row controller instance for the row that we are trying to delete. We can't optimize this by storing the row's index in its RowController object, because the indices change as we add and delete rows. When we find the correct row controller instance, we do two things:

```
table.removeRowsAtIndexes(NSIndexSet(index: index))
nextInsertIndex =  index
```

The first line performs the actual deletion. As its name suggests, the removeRowsAtIndexes() method can actually delete more than one row, but here we only need to delete one. The second line sets the nextInsertIndex property to the index of the row we are deleting. The effect of this is that when we next add a new row, it will be at the old location of this row (or the next row we delete, if we don't add a new row before deleting another one). We could choose to always add new rows at the end of the table, but doing it this way makes it easy to demonstrate the effect of scrolling to a given table row, as you'll see shortly.

Run the example now and you should be able to delete any row by clicking its Delete button. Notice the nice animation that occurs when you do this.

Implementing the New Row Button

With the code that we already have in place, it's easy to implement the functionality of the New Row button. All we have to do is call the table's insertRowsAtIndexes(_:withRowTypes:) method with appropriate arguments. To do that, add the code in bold below to the onNewRowButtonClicked() method in the InterfaceController class:

```
@IBAction func onNewRowButtonClicked() {
    table.insertRowsAtIndexes(
        NSIndexSet(index: nextInsertIndex), withRowType: "Row")
    initializeRow(nextInsertIndex)
    table.scrollToRowAtIndex(nextInsertIndex)
    nextInsertIndex = nextInsertIndex + 1
}
```

The first line of this method creates the new row using the Row prototype at the location given by the nextInsertIndex property. As you saw earlier, this property is initialized to the number of rows that are initially created and it's updated when any row is deleted. The result is that the new row is either added at the end of the table, or where the last row was deleted. Having created the row, we call the initializeRow() method to initialize it in the same way we initialized the rows that were added to the table in the awakeWithContext() method. We then call the table's scrollToRowAtIndex() method to cause the table to scroll until the newly added row is visible. Finally, we increment the nextInsertIndex property so that the next new row will be added immediately after this one.

The application is now complete. Run it and press the New Row button three times. You'll see that three new rows, numbered 4, 5, and 6, are added at the bottom of the table. Now scroll up to the top of the table and click the Delete button in the first row. The row will be removed, and the other rows move up to take its place. Finally, scroll down to the New Row button and click it again. A new row, labeled 7, is added at the top of the table (which is where the last row was deleted), and the table scrolls automatically to the top so that you can see it.

Menus

Many of the examples in this book use buttons as a way for the user to initiate an operation. In the Configuration Table example earlier in this chapter, a Configure button on the main screen presents a controller to allow the user the change the color and font of the text on the main screen, and a Save button in the presented controller allows the user to save the new configuration. This is fine if there are only a small number of operations that the user can perform, but given the small size of the Apple Watch screen and the size of a button, you can easily run out of space. Fortunately, WatchKit has an alternative: you can use a menu instead of filling the screen with buttons.

To create a menu, you add one to your interface controller in the storyboard and then populate it with up to four menu items, each of which triggers an action in the interface controller, just like a button does. Menu items can be added to the menu in the storyboard at design time, programmatically at run time, or both. The menu is initially invisible; it is activated by the force touch gesture, which is triggered when the user presses on the screen a little more firmly than normal. In the simulator, you press and hold the mouse button to get the same effect. Let's see how menus and menu items work by adding them to the Configuration Table example.

Adding a Menu to an Interface Controller

Start by making a copy of the Configuration Table example that we developed in the first part of this chapter, or make a copy of the 6 - Configuration Table folder in the example source archive and open the project in Xcode. We're going to make the following changes to this project:

- Remove the Configure button from the main interface controller and replace it with a menu item. We'll also add a Reset menu item that resets the label's color and font to their defaults.

- In the presented controller, add a menu with two menu items—one that resets the color and font selections in the configuration table to their initial values and another that selects a random color and a random font.

> **Note** You'll find the completed version of the example we are about to work on in the folder 6 - Menus.

So that you can see both techniques at work, we'll configure the menu for the main interface controller entirely in the storyboard and for the presented controller, we'll add one menu item in the storyboard and the other at run time.

Adding a Menu in the Storyboard

Select Interface.storyboard in the Project Navigator to open the storyboard in the editor and delete the Configure button in the main interface controller. When you do this, the segue to the presented controller will also be removed. We'll fix that when we add the code that responds to the user clicking the menu items. Next, drag a menu from the Object Library and drop it onto the controller. Nothing will change in the storyboard because the menu is invisible, but you'll see that a menu node with a single menu item has been added in the Document Outline, as shown in Figure 6-12.

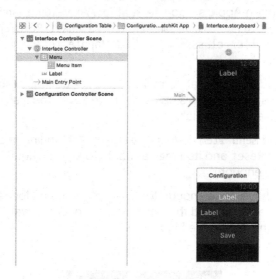

Figure 6-12. Adding a menu to an interface controller

We actually need two menu items. There are two ways to add another menu item: either drag one from the Object Library and drop it below the Menu node in the Document Outline or select the Menu node, open the Attributes Inspector, and change the Items attribute to 2. Add the second menu item and then select the topmost Menu Item node in the Document Outline. In the Attributes Inspector, you'll see that menu items have two attributes: Title and Image (see Figure 6-13).

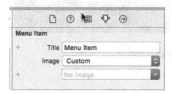

Figure 6-13. The attributes of a menu item

The value of the Title attribute is used as the text that appears below the menu item. You should keep this as short as possible, since there isn't much space available. The text overflows onto a second line, if required, and truncates if there still isn't enough space. Change the value from Menu Item to Configure.

The Image attribute supplies the icon shown above the text. If you click the selector, you will see that there is a list of standard icons that you can choose from, plus Custom, which allows you to use an icon of your own. You can see what all the standard icons look like and how they are intended to be used in the documentation page for the WKInterfaceController class in Xcode, or on Apple's web site at http://developer.apple.com/library/prerelease/ios/documentation/WatchKit/Reference/WKInterfaceController_class/index.html#//apple_ref/c/tdef/WKMenuItemIcon.

There isn't a standard icon that corresponds to the configure action, so we'll just use one that's close—in this case, we'll use More. You'll see in the next section how to use your own icon.

Select the second Menu Item node in the Document Outline and change its Title attribute to Reset and its Image attribute to Repeat (again, not exactly correct, but close enough).

At this point, we have done enough to see what the menu looks like. Run the example. Then press and hold the mouse button over the watch simulator screen to reveal the menu (see Figure 6-14).

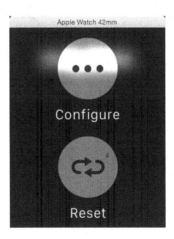

Figure 6-14. A menu with two menu items

At this point, nothing happens when you click either menu item. To fix that, we need to link them to action methods in the interface controller. Select the Interface Controller node in the Document Outline and open the Assistant Editor. You should see the file InterfaceController.swift in the Assistant Editor, but if not, select it manually using the jump bar. Now Control-drag from the Configure menu item in the Document Outline to the bottom of the InterfaceController class in the Assistant Editor and create an action method called onConfigureClicked(). Repeat the process with the Reset menu item to create an action method called onResetClicked(). You should have added two empty methods that look like this:

```
@IBAction func onConfigureClicked() {
}

@IBAction func onResetClicked() {
}
}
```

Now let's add the implementation for both methods.

In the onConfigureClicked() method, we'll present the configuration controller. To do that, we need to invoke the presentControllerWithName(_ :context:) method with the identifier of the configuration controller and the same context information that was passed during the segue in our earlier version of this example. The configuration controller doesn't currently have an identifier, so let's first assign it one. To do that, select the configuration controller in the storyboard, open the Attributes Inspector, and set its Identifier attribute to Configuration. Now add the following code in bold to the onConfigureClicked() method in the InterfaceController class:

```
@IBAction func onConfigureClicked() {
    presentControllerWithName("Configuration",
            context: ConfigurationController.ControllerContext(
                    textAttributes: textAttributes,
                    callback: onCallBack))
}
```

The code that creates the ControllerContext object comes from the contextForSegueWithIdentifier() method. Because we don't need that method any more, you can safely delete it. Now run the example, bring up the menu, and click on the Configure menu item. You'll see the configuration controller appear.

The implementation of the onResetClicked() is also very simple. All we need to do is replace the TextAttributes object in InterfaceController by an instance that has the default color and font and update the label in the same way when the controller is activated. Unfortunately, the code that updates the label is buried in the willActivate() method, so we first need to extract it. To do that, make the following changes to the InterfaceController class:

```
override func willActivate() {
    if attributesChanged {
        let range = NSMakeRange(0, text.length)
        text.addAttribute(NSForegroundColorAttributeName,
                value: textAttributes.color, range: range)
        text.addAttribute(NSFontAttributeName,
                value: textAttributes.font, range: range)
        label.setAttributedText(text)
        updateLabelWithAttributes(textAttributes)
        attributesChanged = false;
    }
    super.willActivate()
}

private func updateLabelWithAttributes(attributes: TextAttributes) {
    let range = NSMakeRange(0, text.length)
    text.addAttribute(NSForegroundColorAttributeName,
                      value: attributes.color, range: range)
    text.addAttribute(NSFontAttributeName,
                      value: attributes.font, range: range)
    label.setAttributedText(text)
}
```

To install the default color and font when the Reset menu item is clicked, add the following code to onResetClicked():

```
@IBAction func onResetClicked() {
    let attributes =
        TextAttributes(color: TextAttributes.colors[0],
                       font: TextAttributes.fonts[0])
    textAttributes = attributes   // set as the current attributes
    updateLabelWithAttributes(attributes)
}
```

Run the example again, use the configuration controller to change the label's color and font, and then show the menu and click the Reset button. The color and font should revert to their initial values.

Adding Menu Items Programmatically

Now let's implement the menu for the configuration controller. We could create this menu in the storyboard in the same way we did for the main controller, but we're going to construct the menu programmatically instead. The WKInterfaceController class has four methods that operate on the controller's menu:

```
func addMenuItemWithItemIcon(_ itemIcon: WKMenuItemIcon,
                title title: String, action action: Selector)
func addMenuItemWithImageNamed(_ imageName: String,
                title title: String, action action: Selector)
func addMenuItemWithImage(_ image: UIImage,
                title title: String, action action: Selector)
func clearAllMenuItems()
```

The first three methods create a new menu item and add it to the menu. As noted earlier in this chapter, a menu can have up to four menu items. The difference between these methods is the way in which the icon is supplied. The first method uses one of the standard icons that come with WatchKit. The other two methods allow you to use a custom icon (which you can include in the asset catalog of the WatchKit App itself and reference by name), or a UIImage object created in the WatchKit extension. As usual, it is best to include the image in the WatchKit App unless it can only be obtained at run time. We'll use the first two methods when adding menu items for this example. The clearAllMenuItems() method is intended to be used when the set of available menu items depends on application state. The next section talks more about this.

Let's go ahead and write some code. The first thing to note is that when you create the menu programmatically, you don't need to drag a Menu from the Object Library to the storyboard, so we can just head straight to the ConfigurationController class and start working.

We're going to add two menu items: one that resets the selected color and font to their values when the controller was presented and another that selects a random color and a random font. Let's handle the reset action first. Add the following code to the end of the awakeWithContext() method in the ConfigurationController class:

```
if let controllerContext = context as? ControllerContext {
    self.controllerContext = controllerContext
    selectedColor = controllerContext.textAttributes.color
    selectedFont = controllerContext.textAttributes.font
    updateCheckMarks()
}
```

```
    // Add menu items
    addMenuItemWithItemIcon(.Repeat, title: "Reset",
                                   action: "onResetClicked")
}
```

Here, we're adding a menu item with title Reset, using the Repeat icon, which is the same one we used for the Reset menu item in the main controller. The standard icons are defined by the WKMenuItemIcon enumeration, which you'll see in the documentation for the WKInterfaceController class. The last argument is a selector for the action method that will be called when the menu item is clicked. Add implementation of this method at the end of the class file:

```
    func onResetClicked() -> Void {
        let color = controllerContext!.textAttributes.color
        let font = controllerContext!.textAttributes.font
        if color != selectedColor || font != selectedFont {
            selectedColor = color
            selectedFont = font
            updateCheckMarks()
        }
    }
}
```

All we're doing here is getting the initial color and font from the controller context, comparing them to the currently selected color and font, and, if either of them is different, resetting the selected values and calling updateCheckMarks() to reflect the change in the table. Run the application and use the Configure menu item to open the configuration controller. The color and font are initially White and Body, respectively. Change one or both of these and then press and hold the mouse button (or force touch on the device) to bring up the menu that we just created and click the Reset menu item. You should see the selected color and font change back to White and Body.

FORCE TOUCH AND TABLE SELECTION

If you force touch the screen over one of the table rows, you'll see that it animates in the same way as it does when you tap the row to select it. This is a little misleading, because the row has not been selected, and no selection event is delivered to your interface controller.

It's quite common in desktop applications (and even in iOS applications) to have a gesture that causes an action to be performed that depends on the point on the screen where the gesture occurred. There is no way to implement this in a WatchKit application because WatchKit does not provide an API that lets you find out where the user's finger was when the force touch gesture was detected. In fact, your WatchKit application can't detect the force touch gesture, or any other user interaction with the screen, such as a swipe. All it can tell is that one of its menu items was activated. If you want the action triggered by the menu item to operate on the selected row of a table, you need to add code to your interface controller to handle table selection events and save the index of the last selected row. Unfortunately, this does not currently result in a good user experience, because the user first has to tap the row to select it and then perform the force touch gesture. That's not at all intuitive, and it's made worse by the fact that the selected table row is only highlighted while the user is tapping it and the fact that the force touch gesture itself gives the incorrect impression that a row is being selected.

Now let's implement the Random menu item. This time, we're going to use a custom icon instead of one of the standard ones. You need to adhere to certain conventions when designing a custom menu icon.

First, you need to create separate icons for the 38mm and 42mm Watches. For the 38mm Watch, the icon must be a 104-pixel square, but you can only use a 72-pixel square region at the center of the icon. For the 42mm Watch, the icon must be 120 × 120 pixels, with a useful area of 80 × 80 pixels at the center. The outer area of the icon must be left blank because WatchKit clips it at run time so that it appears circular. By staying within the prescribed region, you ensure no pixels fall outside the clipping area. For this example, I created suitable icons and put them in the 6 - Menu Images folder of the example source code archive. Figure 6-15 shows an enlarged view of the icon for the 42mm Watch.

Figure 6-15. A custom menu item

The icon is a question mark because the result of using the menu item is that a random color and font are chosen. There is actually a question mark icon in the standard icon set, but I chose not to use it so that I could demonstrate how to create a custom icon.

The outer square is 120 × 120 pixels, as required for the 42mm Watch. The 80-pixel inner square is the area that's available for the icon content. As you can see, the question mark is entirely contained within this area. The area outside this region, which is lightly shaded here for the purpose of illustration but is transparent in the actual icon, is the part of the icon that should be left blank. The 32mm icon is similar, but smaller.

The second thing to bear in mind is that WatchKit uses the image that you supply as a template. That means that it ignores all color information. If you open either of the image files, you'll see that the question mark is actually green, but that's not how it appears on the watch, as you'll see shortly. In fact, pixels in the image that are not opaque appear in the icon, but the color that's used to draw them is fixed (and outside of your control). It follows that when designing your icon, everything apart from the pixels that you want to be visible should be transparent.

Apple provides Photoshop templates that you can use when creating custom menu icons. You'll find a link to these templates in the WatchKit Human Interface Guidelines document at `http://developer.apple.com/watch/human-interface-guidelines/resources`.

Now let's get back to the example application. We need to add the icons to the WatchKit App's asset catalog in such a way that we can use a single name to refer to them independently of which version of the watch the application is running on. In earlier chapters, we did that by configuring a different image name for each watch version. Now you're going to see another way to do the same thing, which requires a little more work when setting up the asset catalog. This technique works for all images, not just for menu item images.

Select `Images.xcassets` in the WatchKit App group and click the + icon at the bottom of the list of icon names in the editor area. In the pop-up that appears, choose New `Image Set` (see Figure 6-16).

Figure 6-16. Adding a new image set to the asset catalog

The image set is initially called Image. Double-click on the name in the name list and change it to RandomMenuIcon. Then right-click on the area to the right of the name column to open another pop-up menu (see Figure 6-17).

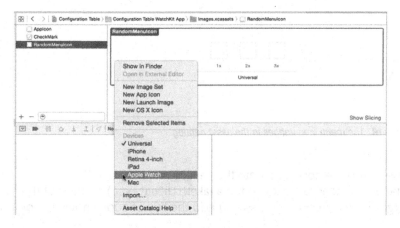

Figure 6-17. Changing the name and type of the image set

You need to change the selection in the Devices area of the pop-up from Universal to Apple Watch. To do that, first click on Apple Watch to select it. The pop-up disappears when you do that, so open it again and click on Universal to deselect it. You should now see three image slots and the subtitle Apple Watch, as shown in Figure 6-18.

Figure 6-18. The image set ready to be configured for Apple Watch

Now drag the file Random_38mm@2x.png from the folder 6 – Menu Images and drop it on the 38mm slot, followed by the file Random_42mm@2x.png onto the 42mm slot. The 2x slot is not currently used. According to Apple, you can use this slot to include an image that will be used if a new Apple Watch with a different screen size is introduced. You can choose to leave this slot empty or drag one of the images into it. The finished result should look like Figure 6-19.

Figure 6-19. The menu icon images in the asset catalog

Now let's add the code to create the Random menu item to the interface controller. Go back to the awakeWithContext() method of the ConfigurationController class and add the line of code shown in bold:

```
    // Add menu items
    addMenuItemWithItemIcon(.Repeat, title: "Reset",
                            action: "onResetClicked")
    addMenuItemWithImageNamed("RandomMenuIcon", title: "Random",
                            action: "onRandomClicked")
}
```

This time, we used the addMenuItemWithImageNamed(_:title:action:) method to add the menu item and we used the name of the image set that we just created as the first argument. When this menu item is clicked, the onRandomClicked() method will be called. Add the following code to implement this method:

```
func onRandomClicked() -> Void {
    let color = TextAttributes.colors[Int(arc4random_uniform(
                    UInt32(TextAttributes.colors.count)))]
    let font = TextAttributes.fonts[Int(arc4random_uniform(
                    UInt32(TextAttributes.fonts.count)))]
    if color != selectedColor || font != selectedFont {
        selectedColor = color
        selectedFont = font
        updateCheckMarks()
    }
}
```

Basically this code is using the arc4random_uniform() function to choose a random index in the range 0 to one less than the number of colors or fonts and then assigning the corresponding color and font to the selectedColor and selectedFont properties. Unfortunately, the code is a little convoluted because Swift does not automatically convert between UInt and UInt32. Having assigned new colors, the code that updates the selected values and the table is the same as in the onResetClicked() method.

That completes this example. You should now be able to run the application and activate the menu in the configuration controller, which should be as shown in Figure 6-20.

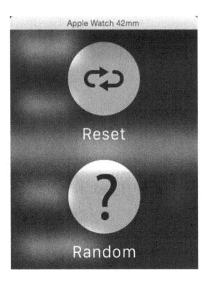

Figure 6-20. A menu with contents added programmatically

Now if you click the Random menu item, you should see the color and font selections in the table change pseudo-randomly.

It's possible to create a menu in the storyboard and then add menu items to it at run time. Why would you do that? Consider the Reset menu item in our example. Strictly speaking, it only needs to be available when the default color and font are not already selected, whereas the Random menu item should always be present. A convenient way to implement this is to create the menu in the storyboard with just the Random menu item and add the Reset menu item programmatically when the selected colors are not the defaults.

We would also need to remove the Reset menu item when the color and font are reset either by the Reset menu item itself or because the user selected both defaults manually. There is no way to remove a specific menu item, but you can remove all the menu items that were added programmatically by calling the clearAllMenuItems() method, which has no effect on anything added to the menu in the storyboard. That's why you should create menu items that always need to be present in the storyboard and add those that sometimes need to be removed at run time. As an exercise, try adding this feature to the configuration controller. Keep in mind that there is no way to find out whether a menu item is currently present in the menu (in fact, there is no class in the WatchKit API that represents either a menu or a menu item), so you'll have to use a property to keep track of whether the Reset menu item is visible or not.

Summary

In this chapter, you learned about the WatchKit tables and menus. Tables are the only way to create a WatchKit layout that is not completely defined in the storyboard. The number of rows in a table can be changed at run time, and each table row can be structured differently, giving you much greater flexibility than you can achieve by other means. Menus allow you to conserve space on the small screen of the Watch by giving you a place to keep functionality that the user does not need permanent access to. You can define fixed menus in the storyboard or you can create them at run time. We'll make good use of both tables and menus in Chapter 7, where we'll build a complete, non-trivial WatchKit application from scratch.

Building a WatchKit App

It's finally time to start building a real-world WatchKit application. As I said in Chapter 1, writing a WatchKit application really means creating an extension to an existing iPhone application. To make your WatchKit application useful, you need to find a way to present the information that your iOS application works with on the Apple Watch, where you have restricted screen space and are limited to interactions that can take place in the time between the user opening your application and lowering his arm—most likely just a few seconds.

Before starting work on your WatchKit app, take some time to decide what it can usefully do and consider how to present the available information in such a way that the user can quickly read it, absorb it, and act on it, if necessary.

In implementation terms, it's unlikely that your WatchKit application will be entirely self-contained—at the very least, it will need to get access to the data that the iOS application itself works with. Fortunately, iOS provides a variety of mechanisms that allow your WatchKit and iOS applications to share data. In the first part of this chapter, you'll get an overview of the iOS application that we're going to extend, the design of the WatchKit app that we'll be building, the forms of communication with the iOS application that we'll need to make it work, and the features of iOS that make that communication possible. We'll then look at the gory details of the implementation. By the time you reach the end of this rather long and detailed chapter, you'll have a fully working WatchKit application, to which you'll add some extra features in Chapter 8.

The WatchKit Weather Application

Let's start by looking at the iOS application we're going to extend onto the watch. You can try it out for yourself by opening and running the project in the folder 7 - LWKWeather - Initial in the example source code archive. Figure 7-1 shows three screenshots from the application.

Figure 7-1. The iOS Weather Application

The application displays weather data for a number of cities chosen by the user. The main screen shows a summary of the current weather and a 5-day weather forecast for one city, as shown on the left in Figure 7-1. By default, the application obtains weather information for New York, Chicago, and Sydney. Press the settings icon in the top part of the display to present a view controller with a table that shows the cities that are currently configured, as shown in the center in Figure 7-1. You can drag the rows of this table around to reorder the pages in the main display. With the configuration shown in Figure 7-1, the page that is displayed when the application starts shows the weather for New York City. You can swipe right to view the weather and forecast for Chicago, one more time for San Francisco, and so on. You can also use the segmented control at the bottom of the page to switch the displayed temperature scale between Celsius and Farenheit.

To change the cities that appear in the settings screen, press the **Add/Remove** button at the top right to get a full list of available cities. Tap any row to add or remove the corrresponding city from the active list. When you are finished with either of the settings screens, press the **Done** button.

There isn't much to this application. That's a deliberate decision—the less functionality there is, the easier it is to show how you can extend it onto the watch. There is just enough functionality here to allow me to illustrate most of the scenarios you are likely to encounter when writing a WatchKit app for your own iOS application.

> **Note**   The forecast data that this application uses is obtained by using an API provided by openweathermap.org. You can find the details of the API, which is very simple and free to use, at http://openweathermap.org/api.

To see the completed WatchKit app we're going to build in this chapter, open and run the completed project in the 7 - LWKWeather - Final folder. Figure 7-2 shows a couple screenshots from this application running on the simulator.

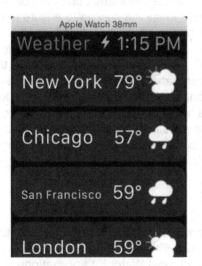

Figure 7-2. The WatchKit weather application

As you can see, the WatchKit application is not just a scaled-down version of the iOS application. When designing a WatchKit application, you need to think about what features of your iOS application the user is likely to want to use most frequently and make those easily accessible. For this application, I decided to show a summary of the weather for all of the user's chosen cities when the application starts. Tapping on any row in this initial screen then shows a slightly more detailed weather summary for the chosen city together with the weather forecast for today and tomorrow, as shown on the right in Figure 7-2.

The iOS application shows up to five days of forecast information, but the WatchKit version shows only two days. I made that choice for two reasons. First, as noted in Chapter 6, Apple recommends that you don't try to display too much information in a table. Each day of weather information requires a row for the date and up to eight more rows for the forecast for each three-hour segment of the day, making a total of nine rows. To represent a full five-day forecast would, therefore, means building a table with up to 45 rows. That's more than double Apple's recommended 20-row limit. Second, the user is most likely to want to see the forecast for today and possibly for tomorrow. It's much less likely that they'll want to quickly look at the weather five days ahead. Of course, if they really want to do that, they can always open the iOS application on their iPhone. For some applications, it might be appropriate to give the user a way to bring more information to the watch. For the sake of simplicity, and because implementing that would not show any functionality that has not been covered elsewhere in this book, I decided not to do that for the WatchKit Weather application.

The WatchKit application will not have any equivalent of the settings screens shown in Figure 7-1. Instead, it will use the same configuration as the iOS application, and we'll implement it in such a way as to ensure that any changes made in the iOS application take effect immediately on the watch. There are other ways to do this, of course. You could, for example, include a settings screen in the WatchKit application or add a feature to the iOS application that lets you maintain separate configurations for the main application and the WatchKit application. Neither of these is difficult to do, but neither of them would demonstrate any new WatchKit features either, so I decided not to show either of those possibilities here. These changes would, however, make a useful coding exercise should you want to extend the application yourself.

Sharing the Data Model

It should be obvious from Figures 7-1 and 7-2 that the WatchKit application will need to use the same data and settings information as its iOS counterpart. That's very likely to be true of most WatchKit applications. Unfortunately, it's not as simple to share information as you might think because, as Chapter 1 makes clear, the executable part of a WatchKit application is implemented in an extension and, at run time, the iOS application and the extension execute in different processes, as shown in Figure 7-3.

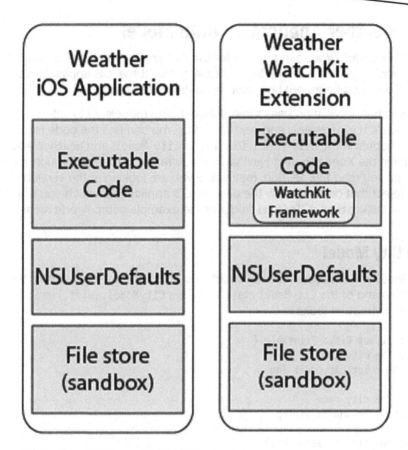

Figure 7-3. An iOS application and its WatchKit extension

The iOS Weather application stores information in files and in its user defaults (NSUserDefaults) object. An extension can also read information from files and from user defaults, but as you can see in Figure 7-3, it s file store and user defaults are separate from those of the iOS application. Consequently, when the WatchKit extension reads from its file store, it's not accessing the same data that the iOS application gets when it reads its own files. Fortunately, iOS 8 added the concept of *app groups,* which allow applications and extensions to share both user defaults and file store. We'll make use of an app group to allow our WatchKit app's extension to read weather information and settings information that were stored by the iOS application. I talk more about how this works in the section "Mechanisms for Sharing" later in this chapter.

The Weather Application Data Model

Now that we know we can arrange for the iOS application and the WatchKit extension to use the same data, let's take a look at the iOS application's data model and figure out how much of it needs to be shared.

The weather application uses three different data models: CityModel, DisplayedCityInfoModel, and WeatherModel. You can find the code for these models in the City Model, Displayed City Model, and Weather Model groups in the Xcode Project Navigator. If you're going to read through the code as you read this section, make sure you are looking at the version of the project that contains only the original iOS application, which you'll find in the 7 - LWKWeather - Initial folder of the example source code archive.

The City Model

CityModel is a collection of City structures. You'll find the definition of this structure and of the CityModel class in the file CityModel.swift. Here's what the City structure looks like:

```
public struct City: Printable {
    // The city code
    public let cityCode: Int

    // The city name
    public let name: String

    // The city timezone name
    public let timezone: String

    // Human-readable description
    public var description: String {
        return "\(name), city code: \(cityCode), TZ: \(timezone)"
    }
}
```

Not surprisingly, there is one instance of City for each city for which the application can display weather information. The cityCode property is a unique number that is used when retrieving forecast data. Because it's unique, it's also used to represent the city in method calls and in other data structures.

The CityModel class contains a list of all the City structures, sorted by city name, and a map that can be used to get the City structure for a given city code. The sorted city list is used to populate the table that you see on the right in Figure 7-1. Here's an extract from the definition of the CityModel class that shows the features of most interest:

```
// Model that holds information for all available cities.
public class CityModel {
    // List of cities, ordered by name.
    public private(set) var cities: [City] = []

    // Map from city code to city data
    private var citiesByCode: [Int: City] = [:]

    // Gets the city with a given code, if one exists
    public func cityForCode(cityCode: Int) -> City? {
        return citiesByCode[cityCode]
    }
}
```

This model is initialized from a file called `cities.plist`, which contains the information required to create `City` structures for a fixed set of cities. You can change the set of cities that the application works with by modifying this file. To add a new city, you'll need to get its city code, which is used in the `openweathermap.org` API calls. You'll find a list of the cities for which you can get forecast details, together with the city code values to be used for, at `http://openweathermap.org/help/city_list.txt`. You'll also need to know the city's timezone, which can easily be found on the Internet.

We need to make sure the `cities.plist` file is available to the extension so that it can create its own copy of the `CityModel`. As you'll see, that happens automatically when we arrange for the code that implements the model to be shared with the extension — a topic covered in the section "Sharing Code," later in this chapter.

The Displayed City Model

The displayed city model holds the ids of the cities that the user actually wants to see forecast information for. This is the list that you see in the middle in Figure 7-1 and it's also the list of cities that are checked on the right in Figure 7-1. In fact, those screens are both concerned with the management of this model. The model also contains a boolean value that determines whether temperatures should be displayed in Farenheit (the default) or Celsius. This value is set from the segmented control that you can see at the bottom of the center screenshot in Figure 7-1.

You'll find the implementation of this model in the file `DisplayedCityInfoModel.swift`. Here's an extract from that file that shows the city list and the temperature display boolean:

```
public class DisplayedCityInfoModel {
    // The delegate for this model.
    public weak var delegate: DisplayedCityInfoModelDelegate?
```

```
// City codes for the cities that are displayed.
public var displayedCities: [Int] = [] {
    // Code not shown
}

// Whether to display temperatures in celsius
public var useCelsius: Bool = false {
    // Code not shown
}
```

Whenever either the city list or the useCelsius property is changed, a call is made to a delegate. This feature is used to keep the user interface in step with the state of the model. The delegate only needs to implement a single method, which is called when either property changes value:

```
public protocol DisplayedCityInfoModelDelegate: class {
    func displayedCityInfoDidChange(model: DisplayedCityInfoModel)
}
```

In the WatchKit weather app, the displayedCities property of this model determines the cities that appear on the main screen of the application (shown on the left in Figure 7-2), and the useCelsius property will be used in the same way as it is in the

iOS application. It follows from this that we'll need to use this model in the WatchKit extension and we'll need to make sure that changes to it made in the iOS application's settings screens are notified to the extension as soon as possible. To do that, we'll need a way to send a message from the iOS application to the extension. You'll see how the model is shared and how changes are notified in the section "Mechanisms for Sharing," later in this chapter.

The Weather Model

The weather model is where the actual weather forecast data is kept. It is basically a map from city code to the forecast data for that city. Here's the basic definition of the model, which comes from the file WeatherModel.swift in the example source code archive:

```
public class WeatherModel {
    // Map from city code to the weather for that city.
    public private(set) var weatherByCity = [Int: CityWeather]()
```

The public private(set) qualifier makes the weather data available to code in any class, but ensures that it can only be modified by code in the WeatherModel.swift file. The rest of the classes used in the model are in a separate file called WeatherData.swift. Figure 7-4 shows the relationships between the four classes that make up the weather model:

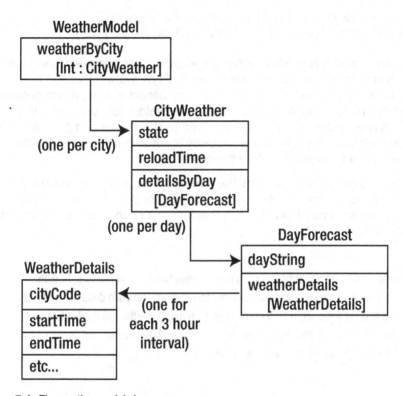

Figure 7-4. *The weather model classes*

The CityWeather class holds the most recently received weather for a city. Here's an extract from the definition of this class (I explain later why it conforms to the NSCoding protocol):

```
public class CityWeather: NSObject, NSCoding {
    // Enumeration of weather details states
    public enum WeatherDetailsState: Int {
        case INIT
        case LOADING
        case LOADED
        case ERROR
    }

    // The city code.
    public let cityCode: Int

    // The state of this data
    public internal(set) var state: WeatherDetailsState
```

```
// Time at which weather details should be reloaded.
public internal(set) var reloadTime: NSDate = NSDate()

// The details for this city, with one entry per day.
public internal(set) var detailsByDay: [DayForecast] = []
```

The state property records whether the weather data has been loaded, is currently being loaded, or has failed to load. Once the weather has been loaded, it is considered to be valid for a fixed period of time, which defaults to an hour in the example source code. For development purposes, it is useful to reduce this time to make the data expire sooner and provoke more frequent reloads. The reloadTime property is set to the time at which the weather should be reloaded from the server.

The detailsByDay property holds the forecast data, with one DayForecast instance for each day. The entries in this array are in ascending order of date, so the first entry holds today's forecast, the second is the forecast for tomorrow, and so on.

> **Note** The openweathermap.org API claims to return five days of forecast data, but in reality it sometimes returns fewer days. The code does not make any assumptions about how many days it should get—the iOS application displays as many days as it receives, but the watch application will never display more than two days of weather.

The forecast data for each day is held in a DayForecast object, which looks like this:

```
public class DayForecast: NSObject, NSCoding {
    // The day for this forecast (e.g. Wednesday, May 27)
    public let dayString: String

    // The weather details for this day.
    public internal(set) var details: [WeatherDetails]

    // Code not shown
}
```

The dayString property is the date for the forecast, in a form that is immediately suitable for display. The value is set when the forecast is received, to avoid having the overhead of formatting a date each time it is used for display. The details of the forecast for the day are held in the details array, in ascending time order. The openweathermap.org API happens to return the forecast in blocks covering three hours, but no use is made of that fact. In the WeatherDetails object for today, only the parts of the forecast that are current and in the future are retained, so it can be assumed that the first entry in this array represents the forecast for the current time, assuming, of course, that the reload time has not passed, in which case the data should be regarded as invalid.

The WeatherDetails object has quite a lot of properties, but very little code. In common with the other objects in the WeatherData.swift file, it is only concerned with holding data and encoding itself to and decoding itself from an archive by conforming to the NSCoding protocol. Here are the properties of the WeatherDetails object, which represent everything that the application could display about the weather for a city:

```
public class WeatherDetails: NSObject, NSCoding {
    public enum WeatherCondition: Int {
        case Thunder
        case Drizzle
        case LightRain
        case Rain
        case HeavyRain
        case FreezingRain
        case Showers
        case LightSnow
        case Snow
        case HeavySnow
        case Sleet
        case Mist
        case Haze
        case Fog
        case Clear
        case FewClouds
        case ScatteredClouds
        case BrokenClouds
        case OvercastClouds
        case Other
    }

    // City to which this weather applies.
    public internal(set) var cityCode: Int

    // Start time for weather.
    public internal(set) var startTime: NSDate

    // End time for weather.
    public internal(set) var endTime: NSDate

    // Day string for these details (e.g. Mon Jan 3)
    public internal(set) var dayString: String?
```

```swift
// Time string for these details, relative to the day (e.g. 3PM)
public internal(set) var timeString: String?

// Actual or forecast weather
public internal(set) var weather: WeatherCondition

// Weather condition summary
public internal(set) var weatherSummary: String?

// Weather condition description
public internal(set) var weatherDescription: String?

// Name of the location.
public internal(set) var locationName: String?

// The lat/long for this weather
public internal(set) var location: CLLocationCoordinate2D?

// Temperature in Celcius
public internal(set) var temperature: Int?

// Pressure in milllibars
public internal(set) var pressure: Float?

// Humidity percentage
public internal(set) var humidity: Int?

// Cloud cover percentage
public internal(set) var clouds: Int?

// Wind speed, miles per hour
public internal(set) var windSpeed: Int?

// Wind direction in degrees: North = 0, East = 90
public internal(set) var windDirection: Int?

// Day or night.
public internal(set) var day: Bool?

    // Code not shown
}
```

If you refer back to the application screenshots in Figure 7-1, you should now be able to figure out where everything on that screen comes from. The name of the city on any given page comes from its City object, which is obtained from the CityModel given the city's code. The same city code is used to get the CityWeather object from the WeatherModel class (using its weatherByCity property). From here, the current weather information is obtained by an expression of the form:

```
cityWeather.detailsByDay.first?.details.first
```

Refer back to Figure 7-4 to see how this expression is derived from the data model. The ?. operator handles the possibility that there is not yet any data available, which is possible while the city's weather is being loaded for the first time. This expression returns either nil or a WeatherDetails object for the current weather, which is used to get the summary (the temperature and the short description of the current conditions) at the top of the screen in Figure 7-1.

The weather forecast table, which is below the summary area, has one section for each DayForecast object in the detailsByDay array. The section header, which shows the date, comes from the dayString property, and each row in the section represents a WeatherDetails object taken from the details array. If you compare what's on the screen to the properties in the data model, you should be able to see the correspondence between them. As you'll see later, there is a similar relationship between the model content and the data on the screens of the WatchKit application.

Weather Model Loading

In the iOS application, the weather model is used by the code in the view controller shown on the left in Figure 7-1. Each instance of this view controller displays the weather for one city. As discussed in the preceding section, it gets the CityWeather object for its city from the weather model's weatherByCity property. If there is not yet an entry for the city in this map, or if an entry is present but its reloadTime has passed, the view controller calls the following method in the model:

```
public func fetchWeatherForCities(cityCodes: [Int], always: Bool)
```

This method requests new data for all the cities in the cityCodes array, but it does not attempt to reload data that is still valid, unless the always argument is true, in which case new data is always requested.

> **Note**   Usually, this method is called with always set to false. When the view
> controller knows that the weather data has expired, it sets always to true to
> avoid the need for the model to check whether the data is still valid.

The fetchWeatherForCities(_:always:) method doesn't return anything, because it doesn't block waiting for new data to arrive. Instead, it locates the CityWeather object for each city for which it's going to load new data (creating it if necessary) and sets its state to LOADING. It then arranges for the weather information to be loaded asynchronously. The weather model itself does not include the code to fetch forecast data from the openweathermap.org server. Instead, it delegates to a loader class that conforms to the following protocol:

```
public protocol WeatherModelLoader {
    func fetchWeatherForCities(cityCodes: [Int])
}
```

The code to request weather data and parse the response into model objects depends on the data source, so having it encapsulated in a separate class makes it possible to get weather from different sources without changing the weather model itself. All that's necessary is to implement a suitable WeatherModelLoader and plug it into the model. In fact, the iOS application does not directly use the WeatherModel class. Instead, it uses a subclass called AppWeatherModel, which simply overrides the createWeatherModelLoader() method of WeatherModel to create an instance of a loader that is specific to the openweathermap.org AP I:

```
// Creates the loader for the weather data. Returns a loader that fetches
// weather data from openweathermap.org
public override func createWeatherModelLoader()
            -> WeatherModelLoader {
    return OpenWeatherMapLoader(model: self)
}
```

You'll find the implementation of the AppWeatherModel and OpenWeatherMapLoader classes in the file AppWeatherModel.swift. I'm not going to discuss the details of the weather loader here because they have nothing to do with writing a WatchKit application, but it's worth reviewing them yourself so that you can see exactly what they do. We'll make use of the fact that we can create WeatherModel subclasses that use different loaders when we extend the application onto the watch.

When the loader receives weather data, it calls the following method in the WeatherModel base class:

```
public func installNewWeatherForCity(cityCode: Int,
            weatherDetails: [WeatherDetails])
```

This method builds a CityWeather object from the given city code and weather details and installs it in the weather model, replacing whatever data currently exists for that city. In the iOS application, the data would have been requested by a view controller, and the model needs to notify it that the data has arrived. It does this by using the default NSNotificationCenter, sending a notification with the name WeatherModelChanged. The user info object of the notification is a dictionary containing single key (cityCodes) for which the value is a list of city codes for which new weather data has been added to the model. The view controller registers as an observer of these notifications, so that it can update its view.

It's possible that the loader will fail to obtain any weather data, perhaps because the iPhone is not connected to a network or because the server is down. In that case, the loader calls the following WeatherModel method:

```
public func notifyWeatherModelLoadFailure(error: NSError,
                    cityCodes: [Int]?)
```

This method changes the state of the CityWeather objects for the cities in the cityCodes argument to ERROR and posts a notification with name WeatherModelLoadFailed and the same user info dictionary as for the WeatherModelChanged notification. The expectation is that the receiving view controllers will update their views to show that there is no current weather available.

> **Note**   You may be wondering why the WeatherModel class uses notifications while the DisplayedCityInfoModel class uses a delegate. The reason is that only one client needs to be notified of changes in the DisplayedCityInfoModel, whereas the WeatherModel has multiple different clients (one view controller for each city for which weather is being displayed), so it could not have a single delegate. Of course, it's possible to create a delegate that delivers notifications to a set of other delegates, but that's effectively what NSNotificationCenter does, so it's an ideal fit for the requirements of the WeatherModel class.

The design of the weather model allows the view controller implementation to be very simple. It needs to first register for notifications and then call the model's fetchWeatherForCities(_:always:) method to get some data. When this method returns, the view controller can assume that there is a CityWeather object for the city or cities for which it requested data and that the state property of that object indicates that the content is valid (value is LOADED), in error (ERROR), or that the forecast data is still being obtained (LOADING). The view controller can use the CityWeather object to make an initial update of its view, and can update it further whenever it receives notifications. You can see exactly how this works by looking at the implementation of the CityWeatherViewController class (in the file CityWeatherViewController.swift), which is responsible for displaying the weather pages like the one shown on the left in Figure 7-1.

The overall sequence of events, from initial request to update of the view controller's view, is shown in Figure 7-5.

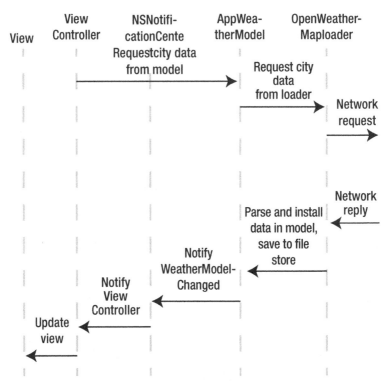

Figure 7-5. Obtaining weather data and updating the view

I mentioned earlier that the reloadTime property of every CityWeather object is set to indicate when new weather data should be requested. Whose responsibility should it be to fetch new data? One approach would be to give that task to the model. Doing it that way would ensure that the model is always as up-to-date as it can be, but there is a disadvantage: data would be reloaded even if it's not currently required. For example, when the user opens the application for the first time, the initial set of view controllers requests weather data for New York, Chicago, and Sydney. Now suppose the user replaces Sydney with San Francisco. The data for Sydney has been loaded and remains valid, but will eventually expire. In these circumstances, there is little point in refreshing it, because it's not going to be displayed anywhere. Instead of reloading expired data itself, the model relies on its clients (the view controllers) to request updated data when they need it, thus ensuring that it only spends the time loading forecasts that are actually going to be used. To honor its side of this contract, the view controller creates an NSTimer, setting its expiry time to the value of the reloadTime property of the CityWeather object for the city that it's linked to and requests new data when the timer fires. You can see the details in the CityWeatherViewController class.

Weather Model Persistence

If the forecast data were only held in memory, it would be lost when the application is terminated, and when the application is next launched, it would have to reload everything from scratch. If the relaunch occurs within an hour, that's a waste of time and network resources, because the forecast data that was fetched earlier might still be valid. To avoid that, the content of the WeatherModel is saved to the application's file store whenever it's modified and is reloaded when the application starts.

You can see the persisted data by running the application on an iPhone and using the Devices window to look at the application's container. To do that, select Window ➤ Devices from Xcode's menu, select your iPhone in the Devices column of the window that opens, and then select the LWKWeather application from the Installed Apps list. Below this list, you'll find a settings icon. Click it to open a pop-up menu and select Show Container. In the sheet that appears, you'll see the content of the application's file store. Navigate to the Library/Caches directory and you'll see another directory inside it called LWKWeather. This is where the WeatherModel class saves its content. Open this folder and you'll see several files, as shown in Figure 7-6.

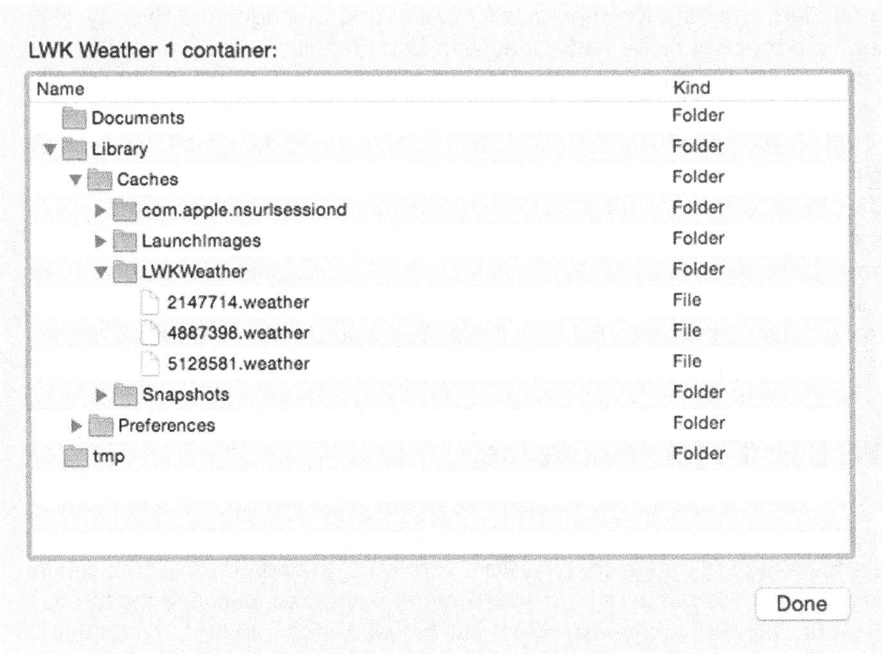

LWK Weather 1 container:

Name	Kind
Documents	Folder
▼ Library	Folder
▼ Caches	Folder
▶ com.apple.nsurlsessiond	Folder
▶ LaunchImages	Folder
▼ LWKWeather	Folder
2147714.weather	File
4887398.weather	File
5128581.weather	File
▶ Snapshots	Folder
▶ Preferences	Folder
tmp	Folder

Done

Figure 7-6. The weather model in the application's container

Each file contains an archived copy of the CityWeather object for one city, created by using the NSKeyedArchiver class, which is why the CityWeather, DayForecast, and WeatherDetails classes need to conform to the NSCoding protocol. The name of the file is its city code, so in Figure 7-6, the model has saved weather for Sydney (city code 2147714), Chicago (4887398), and New York (5128581).

To reload the model when the application starts, the WeatherModel class traverses all the files in the LWKWeather directory, opening them and unarchiving their content to get back a CityWeather object, which is then added to its weatherByCity dictionary. You can see the details of this process in the loadWeatherModel() method of the WeatherModel class. Try adding and removing cities in the settings pages of the application to see how the files in the sandbox are affected. You'll notice that removing a city from display does not remove its saved weather file, because it's still possible to reuse the data if the user adds a city back before its expiry time is reached. In fact, in the current implementation, the data files are never removed. That's not really a problem, because the files are small (around 20K) and there can be at most one for each available city.

Mechanisms for Sharing

You've now seen all the data that the iOS application uses. Now let's look at the iOS features that we'll use to share this data with the WatchKit application.

Sharing Weather Data

Because the WatchKit application displays information derived from the same weather model that the iOS application uses, we need to make that model accessible to it. As you've already seen, the iOS application persists the weather model in files in its local file store. We need the WatchKit extension to be able to access the same persisted information, but you can see by referring back to Figure 7-3 that this is not possible, because the extension does not have access to files stored in the iOS application's file store. You can fix this using an app group. When you create an app group, you also create a container that is shared between all of the applications and extensions that have access to that group, in effect transforming Figure 7-3 into Figure 7-7.

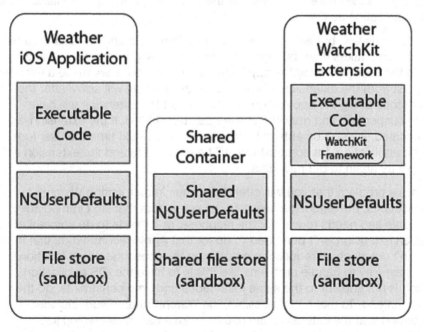

Figure 7-7. Using an app group to provide a container that is shared by the iOS application and the WatchKit extension

To create this setup, we need to create an app group, give the iOS application and the WatchKit extension permission to use it, and change the WeatherModel code so that it persists its state into a file in the shared container instead of in the iOS application's private container. You'll see how to do all these things when we start implementing the WatchKit application a little later in this chapter. Before we can do that, we need to decide how to control access to the shared weather data files—specifically, whether we should allow both the application and the extension to write new data to the shared container.

To make this decision, we need to work out how the WatchKit extension will get the data that it needs. Let's assume that we implement an interface controller in the extension in the same way as the view controller in the application—that is, it will ask the weather model for data when it needs it and will rely on the model to either return the data immediately or fetch it from the openweathermap.org server and notify it when the data is available. With this design, the sequence of events will be the same as shown in Figure 7-5—except that the network request will be made from the extension, the reply will be processed by the extension instead of the iOS application, and the forecast data that the extension has fetched will be persisted to the shared container by the extension, making it available to the iOS application as well.

That sounds OK, but actually there is a problem. Fetching weather data over the network takes time, but the extension can only guarantee to be active while the user is viewing the application on the watch. If we make a network request from the extension, it's possible that the reply will arrive after the user stops using the application, at which point the extension will have been suspended and may even have been terminated. If the extension *is* terminated, it won't be able to handle the reply, so next time the user looks at the application, the forecast will still be out of date and the extension will simply try again to get new data.

This is a problem that you will often face when implementing WatchKi t applications: the extension needs to get some data that isn't immediately available and needs to wait for the response, or it needs to do something that an extension isn't permitted to do (or that Apple recommends that it doesn't do), such as requesting permission to access the user's location. The best way to handle problems like this is to have the iOS application, which is not subject to the same restrictions and time constraints, do the work instead. To make that possible, the WatchKit framework includes a method that the extension can use to make a call to its owning iOS application, starting it if necessary, and to receive a reply from it at some point in the future. We'll use that mechanism to have the AppWeatherModel class in the application load weather data on behalf of the extension and then write it to the file in the shared container, from where the extension can read it and incorporate it into its own in-memory copy of the weather model. The sequence of events would be something like this:

1. At startup, the extension loads the persisted state of the model from the shared container to get the most recent snapshot of forecast data. This data could be current, or it could be partly or completely expired.

2. When an interface controller needs the weather data for a city, it first checks the weatherByCity dictionary in its in-memory copy of the model. If the data that it needs is available and current, nothing else needs to be done.

3. Otherwise, the interface controller calls the model's fetchWeatherForCities(_:always:) method, just like the view controller in the iOS application does. In the AppWeatherModel, this method delegates to a method in the loader class that sends a message to the openweathermap.org server. But in the extension's implementation of the model, we'll make use of the fact that we can plug in our own loader by implementing one that passes the request from the extension to the iOS application.

4. When the iOS application receives the request, it immediately returns the data if it's present, but if not, it makes a call to the AppWeatherModel fetchWeathe rForCities(_:always:) method, which causes the data to be requested asynchronously from the server.

5. When the data arrives, AppWeatherModel does its usual thing: it updates its in-memory model, writes the new data to the shared container, and posts a notification using NSNotificationCenter. The code in the iOS application that received the request from the extension in step 4 observes WeatherModelChanged notifications and sends a message back to the extension to tell it that new weather data is available when one is received.

6. On receipt of this message, the weather model in the extension reads the new data from the shared container and updates its own in-memory state. In so doing, it causes a notification to be posted.

7. The notification is received by the interface controller, which can now update the screen.

For the moment, I've glossed over the details of sending a request from the extension to the iOS application (step 3) and how to send a message back to the extension (step 5). Later in this chapter, I cover the iOS features we'll use to do those things. Meanwhile, we've now answered the design question that we posed earlier in this section about management of the shared container file store: the iOS application will be responsible for writing new forecast data to the shared container, and the extension will just read from it when required.

Sharing Displayed City Info

We decided earlier that the cities that appear on the WatchKit application's main screen (on the left in Figure 7-2) should be the same ones that the iOS application displays. That means the WatchKit extension needs to load the data in the DisplayedCityInfoModel and be notified when the user changes it. The iOS application persists this model in its NSUserDefaults object, which is in its private container and is not accessible to the extension. Fortunately, every shared container also contains an NSUserDefaults object (see Figure 7-7), so to make the DisplayedCityInfoModel available to the extension, we can change the iOS application to persist it in this shared NSUserDefaults object. That still leaves the problem of how to notify the extension when the content of the DisplayedCityInfoModel changes, which happens when the user adds cities to, removes cities from, or changes the order of items in the displayed city list using the settings screens in Figure 7-1. It may seem that this should not be a problem, because NSUserDefaults posts a notification when its content changes. Unfortunately, that notification does not work for shared NSUserDeaults objects. Instead, we'll use the same mechanism to send a notification from the application to the extension that we use to report updates to the weather model.

Sharing Code

I've mentioned how we're going to share the persisted state of the weather application's data model, but I haven't yet discussed how we're going to share the code. We need to use the same classes and structures in the iOS application and the WatchKit extension. That's not quite trivial because they are compiled and linked by two different targets in Xcode, and these targets produce two distinct executables. To share the weather model, we need to arrange for the code that we need to share to appear in both executables. There are a couple of less-than-ideal ways we can do this:

1. We could simply copy and paste the code from the iOS application target into the WatchKit extension target.

2. We could leave the code where it is and simply add the code files to the WatchKit extension target. That will give us what we need: the model classes will be compiled twiced and will be linked into both executables.

> **Tip**   Wondering how to assign one source file to more than one Xcode target? It's easy. Just select the file in the Project Navigator and then open the File Inspector (⌥⌘1). In the Target Membership section, you'll see a list of all the targets together with a check box. To assign the file to a target, just select the target's check box.

The first option is obviously bad, but what about the second one? That would ensure that we wouldn't have any code duplication and it would, without doubt, work for some applications. But for this application there is still a problem. The problem occurs because the iOS application and the extension need to share not only the code of the weather model classes, but also their archived forms. That's an issue because the archiver (NSKeyedArchiver) includes in an archive the full class name for every class that it saves. The full name of a class includes its module name, which is (at least by default) the name of the Xcode target from which it was compiled. That means that classes archived by the iOS application, which is compiled from the LWK Weather target, will have names like LWKWeather.CityWeather. When the archive is read by the WatchKit extension, the unarchiver (NSKeyedUnarchiver) will try to unpack the data and create classes with the module name LWKWeather. It won't find any such classes, because the versions that are linked into the extension were compiled from a target called LWK Weather WatchKit Extension and have names like LWK_Weather_WatchKit_Extension.CityWeather. There is a way to work around this, but there's also a better way that doesn't require any kind of workaround: you can use an *embedded framework*. The ability to use embedded frameworks was added in iOS 8, and Xcode makes it really easy to do. You'll see the details during the course of the implementation, but the basic idea is that the framework has a target of its own, and we'll move all the code we want to share into that target. The classes and structures in the framework target are all in the same module, so they'll have a unique full class name, which neatly solves the archiving problem. It's also better for maintenance and understanding, because all the shared code is conveniently grouped together in the Xcode Project Navigator. We'll also move the cities.plist file to the framework target so that it's copied to both the application and extension bundles, because they both need access to it.

Sending a Request to an iOS Application

I mentioned that there are a couple of iOS features that we're going to use to communicate between the iOS application and the WatchKit extension without showing you the details. Now it's time to look at the details and finally write some code that we'll eventually use in the WatchKit weather application.

Let's start with sending a request from the extension to the iOS application. To do that, we'll use the following method of the WKInterfaceController class:

```
class func openParentApplication(
     _ userInfo: [NSObject : AnyObject],
      reply reply: (([NSObject : AnyObject]!,NSError!) -> Void)?
  ) -> Bool
```

The request is sent in the userInfo dictionary. You can include anything in this dictionary as long as it could be stored in a property list file. In practice, that means you'll need to convert anything other than numbers, strings, and dates (and arrays and dictionaries containing those types) to an NSData object, typically by implementing NSCoding and using an NSKeyedArchiver. The reply argument is a function (or closure) that accepts a map of key/value pairs that make up the response to the request and an NSError object that can be set to indicate an error. The openParentApplication(_:reply:) method returns true if the request was successfully sent to the application and false if not.

Here's how the process works:

1. If (and only if) the iOS application is not running when the request is made, it is started in the background and its application delegate's application(_:will FinishLaunchingWithOptions:) and application(_: didFinishLaunchingWithOptions:) methods are called, as usual. There is nothing in the options dictionary that indicates that the application is being started to service a WatchKit extension request.

2. The application delegate's `application(_:handle WatchKitExtensionRequest:reply:)` method is called and receives the request that the extension passed to `openParentApplication(_:reply:)`

3. The application should do whatever is necessary to complete the request and then, either immediately or some time later, it must call the `reply` closure that was passed to the application delegate's `application(_: handleWatchKitExtensionRequest:reply:)` method. The application has a finite period of time within which it must reply, or the request will time out.

4. At some point, the closure or function that the WatchKit extension passed as the `reply` argument to `openParentApplication(_:reply:)` will be called, in the extension's main thread. If the application did not reply in a timely manner, the reply closure is called with the `error` argument set to an appropriate value. But if a reply was received, `error` will be `nil`.

That all sounds straightforward. But as you'll see, you need to be careful when writing the code that runs in the iOS application.

Let's write a simple example that demonstrates how this works. We're going to build a user interface with a button and a label. When the button is clicked, the WatchKit extension calls the iOS application with a request containing the current date and time. The iOS application adds 30 seconds to the date and time that it received and sends it back to the extension as its reply, where it will be used to set the `text` attribute of the label.

Open Xcode and create a new Single View application called `Messaging` and add a WatchKit application target to it. Select `Interface.storyboard` and drag a button and a label onto it. Change the `Title` attribute of the button to `Call Application`, then set the `Width` attribute of the label to `Relative to Container`, its `Alignment` attribute to `Center`, its `Text` attribute to `No Reply Yet`, and its `Lines` attribute to 0. Open `InterfaceController.swift` in the Assistant Editor and Control-drag from the button to create an action method called `onButtonClicked()` and from the label (which is most easily located in the Document Outline) to create an outlet called `label`. That's everything you need to do to hook the storyboard up to the interface controller.

When the button is clicked, we need to open the iOS application and send it a dictionary containing the key time and the current time (as an NSDate object) as its value. We'll also need to provide a method or closure that will be called when the reply is received. Add the following code to the onButtonClicked() method in InterfaceController.swift:

```
@IBAction func onButtonClicked() {
    let userInfo = ["time" : NSDate()]
    let result = WKInterfaceController.openParentApplication(userInfo,
        reply: { (response, error) in
            if let error = error {
                self.label.setText("Error: \(error)")
                println("\(error)")
            } else if let time: NSDate = response["time"] as? NSDate {
                self.label.setText("\(time)")
            } else {
                self.label.setText("No time received")
            }
        }
    )
    println("Result = \(result)")
}
```

This code builds the request in the userInfo dictionary and uses openPare ntApplication(_:reply:) to send it to the iOS application. When the reply closure is called, it first checks whether there was an error. If not, it gets the return value from the response dictionary and uses it to set the label's Text attribute. If there was an error, the label shows an error message, which is also written to the Xcode console.

We haven't written the code that handles the request in the iOS application yet, but it's interesting to see what happens if we try this code right now. Run the WatchKit application in the simulator and click the button. Immediately, you'll see the text Result = true in the Xcode console, indicating that the request was sent successfully. After a very brief pause, you'll also see an error message in the console and in the WatchKit app:

```
Error Domain=com.apple.watchkit.errors Code=2 "The UIApplicationDelegate
in the iPhone App never called reply() in -[UIApplicationDelegate appli
cation:handleWatchKitExtensionRequest:reply:]" UserInfo=0x60800006db40
{NSLocalizedDescription=The UIApplicationDelegate in the iPhone App never
called reply() in -[UIApplicationDelegate application:handleWatchKit
ExtensionRequest:reply:]}
```

That's pretty clear—the iOS application didn't reply to the request. In this case, that's obviously because we haven't implemented the request handler yet, but you may find that you see this message even if you have a request handler. When that happens, you can be pretty sure there is a bug in your code. The most common reason for seeing this message unexpectedly is that the iOS application crashed while handling the request. You can diagnose that by setting breakpoints in your request handler, or, if you're testing on a real watch, you might also find some useful information in the iPhone device log. You can look at the log in Xcode by opening the Devices window (Window ➤ Devices) and selecting the iPhone in the Devices column on the left.

> **Caution** Sometimes when the iOS application fails to respond, the extension does not see any reply at all to the openParentApplication(_:always:) method. In my experience, this only happens when running on a real watch—I have never seen this when using the simulator.

Now let's switch over to the iOS application and implement the request handler. As I said earlier, the request is delivered to the application delegate in its application(_:handleWatchKitExtensionRequest:reply:) method. Open AppDelegate.swift in Xcode and add the following code to it:

```
func application(application: UIApplication,
    handleWatchKitExtensionRequest userInfo: [NSObject : AnyObject]?,
    reply: (([NSObject : AnyObject]!) -> Void)!) {
    var result = [NSObject : AnyObject]()

    NSLog("application(_:handleWatchKitExtensionRequest) was called")
    if let startTime = userInfo?["time"] as? NSDate {
        let endTime = startTime.dateByAddingTimeInterval(30)
        result["time"] = endTime
    }

    NSLog("Reply is \(result)")

    reply(result)
}
```

This code is very straightforward. The result variable is the dictionary that will be sent as the response to the request. Initially it's empty, but if the userInfo dictionary from the request contains a key called time and its value is an NSDate object, a value with the same key and an updated NSDate value is stored in the result dictionary. The result dictionary is then returned to the extension by calling the reply closure that's passed in.

> **Note**   Keep in mind that the extension and the iOS application are executing in
> different processes, so the call to the `application(_:handleWatchKit`
> `ExtensionRequest:reply:)` method is not made directly from the
> extension's `openParentApplication(_:always:)` call. Similarly, when
> the iOS application calls the reply closure, this does not directly call the reply
> handler in the extension.

Run the updated example on the simulator or an a real watch, press the
`Call Application` button, and you should shortly see the label update with a
time value.

DEBUGGING THE REQUEST HANDLER CODE IN THE IOS APPLICATION

What if your request handler has a bug? How would you diagnose it? In the preceding code,
I included some `NSLog()` statements to indicate when the request handler is called and
when it sends its reply. When you run the example, you won't see that output in Xcode.
Whether you run the example on the simulator or on a watch, the Xcode console shows the
output from the WatchKit extension, not the iOS application. However, there is a way to see
the output from the `NSLog()` statements in the iOS application. On the simulator, you can
do that by opening the simulator log file by selecting Debug ➤ Open System Log...
from the simulator's menu. It's important to note, however, that this only works if you use
`NSLog()` for logging—Swift's `println()` function does not send output to the simulator
log. If you're running on a real iPhone and Watch, you can view the output by opening the
Xcode `Devices` window and selecting the iPhone. You'll see the `NSLog()` output among all
the other console messages at the bottom of the screen.

If logging is not enough to help you figure out what's wrong with the code in the iOS
application, you can attach the Xcode debugger to it by starting the WatchKit application in
the normal way and then launching the iOS application, attaching the Xcode debugger to it,
and setting breakpoints if necessary, as you saw in the section "Debugging the WatchKit App
Extension and the iOS Application Together" in Chapter 2. This technique works on both the
simulator and a real device.

The code in the `application(_:handleWatchKitExtensionRequest:reply:)`
method is enough to demonstrate how a request handler is supposed to
work, but it is over-simplified and it may not always work. In reality, it's
unlikely that the iOS application will be able to send an immediate reply to

the WatchKit extension. Most likely, it'll have to do some asynchronous work and send the reply later. Let's change the example code to do that. Make the changes shown in bold:

```
func application(application: UIApplication,
    handleWatchKitExtensionRequest userInfo: [NSObject : AnyObject]?,
    reply: (([NSObject : AnyObject]!) -> Void)!) {
    var result = [NSObject : AnyObject]()

    NSLog("application(_:handleWatchKitExtensionRequest) was called")
    if let startTime = userInfo?["time"] as? NSDate {
        let endTime = startTime.dateByAddingTimeInterval(30)
        result["time"] = endTime
        dispatch_async(dispatch_get_global_queue(
                        DISPATCH_QUEUE_PRIORITY_DEFAULT, 0), {
            NSLog("Handling request in background thread")
            NSThread.sleepForTimeInterval(1)

            let endTime = startTime.dateByAddingTimeInterval(30)
            result["time"] = endTime

            NSLog("Reply is \(result)")
            reply(result)
        })
        return
    }

    NSLog("Reply is \(result)")

    reply(result)
}
```

Now instead of sending a reply immediately, the handler uses dispatch_ async() to send the reply from a background thread and, to increase the realism a little, puts the thread to sleep for a second before doing so. Run this modified version of the example and you'll find that it still works on the simulator, but you may find that it sometimes doesn't work on the watch. The problem is that iOS starts your application in the background to service the extension's request and an application that's in the background could be suspended or terminated at any time, including while it's waiting to get data from the network that it needs before it can reply to your request. To avoid that, Apple suggests that you tell iOS that your application needs background time by immediately calling the UIApplication beginBackgroundTaskWithExpirationHandler() method. When your handler has finished its work, it must call the endBackgroundTask() method. To put that into practice, make the changes shown in bold to the request handler:

```
func application(application: UIApplication,
    handleWatchKitExtensionRequest userInfo: [NSObject : AnyObject]?,
    reply: (([NSObject : AnyObject]!) -> Void)!) {
    var taskId: UIBackgroundTaskIdentifier = 0
    taskId = application.beginBackgroundTaskWithExpirationHandler({
        // Called if the handler does not call endBackgroundTask()
        // before the allocated background time expires.
        reply(nil)
    })
    var result = [NSObject : AnyObject]()

    NSLog("application(_:handleWatchKitExtensionRequest) was called")
    if let startTime = userInfo?["time"] as? NSDate {
        dispatch_async(dispatch_get_global_queue(
                        DISPATCH_QUEUE_PRIORITY_DEFAULT, 0), {
            NSLog("Handling request in background thread")
            NSThread.sleepForTimeInterval(1)

            let endTime = startTime.dateByAddingTimeInterval(30)
            result["time"] = endTime

            NSLog("Reply is \(result)")
            reply(result)

            self.endTaskIn2Seconds(application, taskId: taskId)
        })
        return
    }

    reply(result)

    endTaskIn2Seconds(application, taskId: taskId)
}

private func endTaskIn2Seconds(application: UIApplication,
            taskId: UIBackgroundTaskIdentifier) {
    let endTaskTime = dispatch_time(DISPATCH_TIME_NOW,
                            Int64(2 * NSEC_PER_SEC))
    dispatch_after(endTaskTime, dispatch_get_main_queue(), {
        application.endBackgroundTask(taskId)
    })
}
```

The first thing that the application(_:handleWatchKitExtensionRequest: reply:) method does is call beginBackgroundTaskWithExpirationHandler(). This ensures that the iOS application will have a period of time in the background where it is not in danger of being terminated before it completes its work. To balance this, we need to call the endBackgroundTask() method whenever we leave the handler, passing it the background task id that we got when we started the background task. I added a method called endTaskIn2Seconds(_:taskId) to take care of that. This method waits for two seconds before ending the background task. This delay is a workaround (suggested by Apple) for a timing problem: it turns out that if we end the task immediately, it's possible that the reply message will not be sent to the watch. This risk exists even if we are able to send a reply immediately, as we did in the first version of this code. For that reason, you should always include this workaround in your request handler.

Sending a Notification to the WatchKit Extension

If you look back at our discussion of how we plan to load data in the iOS application on request from the WatchKit extension, which you can find in the earlier section "Sharing Weather Data," you'll see that at step 5, when the iOS application receives new weather data, it needs to send a notification to the extension. Normally, notifications are sent using the NSNotificationCenter class. That won't work in this case because the application and the extension are in different processes, but NSNotificationCenter only works when the sender and receiver are in the same process. To send this notification, we'll need to use the lower-level CFNotificationCenter API from Core Foundation. Here's a summary of how that API works—refer to the documentation page for CFNotificationCenter in the Xcode API Reference for the details:

- To add an observer for a notification, use the CFNotificationAddObserver() function to link the notification (by name and source) to a callback function.

- To send a notification, call the CFNotificationCenterPostNotification() or CFNotificationCenterPostNotificationWithOptions() function, supplying the notification name and some associated data, among other things.

This is very similar to the way that NSNotificationCenter works, so you are probably wondering why we should use this lower-level, C language API instead. The reason is that it allows us to use a notification center—the *Darwin notification center*—that can deliver notifications between processes, which is exactly what we need. All we need to do is pass a reference to the

Darwin notification center when registering our observer and when posting notifications. Getting the Darwin notification center reference is just one line of code:

```
let center = CFNotificationCenterGetDarwinNotifyCenter()
```

The downside is that we need to work with a C-language API. Using C code from Swift is usually very easy, but in this case, there is a problem with the CFNotificationCenterAddObserver() function. Here's the declaration of that function:

```
func CFNotificationCenterAddObserver(
        _ center: CFNotificationCenter!,
        _ observer: UnsafePointer<Void>,
        _ callBack: CFNotificationCallback,
        _ name: CFString!,
        _ object: UnsafePointer<Void>,
        _ suspensionBehavior: CFNotificationSuspensionBehavior)
```

The problem is the callBack argument, which supplies a reference to the function to be called when a notification is received. It's declared like this:

```
typealias CFNotificationCallback =
    CFunctionPointer<((CFNotificationCenter!,
                      UnsafeMutablePointer<Void>,
                      CFString!,
                      UnsafePointer<Void>, CFDictionary!) -> Void)>
```

This declaration says that CFNotificationCallback is a pointer to a C function. Unfortunately, there is no way to convert a Swift function or method reference to a C function pointer. However, we *can* declare a C function in an Objective-C source file, so we can solve this problem by writing an Objective-C wrapper class that we can call from our Swift code instead of trying to interface directly with the Darwin notification center. Let's do that now and, as we do so, prove to ourselves that we can use the Darwin notification center to send a message from an iOS application to a WatchKit extension.

Create a new Single View Application project called DarwinBridge and add a WatchKit target to it. We're going to build a simple user interface on the iPhone that consists of just a button. When the button is pressed, we'll send a Darwin notification center notification to the WatchKit extension. When the notification is received, we'll display some text on the screen of the watch. Before we write the code to do this, let's build the user interfaces we'll need.

We'll start with the iOS application. Select Main.storyboard in the Project Navigator and drag a button onto the storyboard, placing it somewhere near the center. Change the button's text to Send Notification. With the button selected, click the Pin icon at the bottom right of the storyboard and, in the pop-up that opens, check Horizontal Center in Container and Vertical Center in Container. Then click the Add 2 Constraints button. Next, click the Resolve Auto Layout Issues icon and click Update Frames in the pop-up (if Update Frames is grayed out, click the button in the storyboard and try again). The button should now move to the center of the view in the storyboard.

Open ViewController.swift in the Assistant Editor and Control-drag from the button to the class definition to create an action method called onButtonClicked(). That's all we need to do in the iOS application for now, so let's switch over to the WatchKit application. Select Interface. storyboard in the Project Navigator and then drag and drop a label and a button from the Object Library onto it.

> **Tip** Sometimes you'll find that the Object Library does not update to show the correct set of objects when you switch between iOS and WatchKit storyboards. If that happens to you, you can fix it by clicking the Show the Media Library button above the Object Library and then clicking the Show the Object Library button.

Select the label and change its Text attribute to No Message, its Alignment attribute to Center, its Lines attribute to 0, and its Width attribute to Relative to Container. Select the button and change its Title attribute to Clear. Next, open InterfaceController.swift in the Assistant Editor (it should already be open) and Control-drag from the label to the class definition to create an outlet called label and from the button to the class definition to create an action method called onButtonClicked(). Add the following code to this method, to reset the label's text when the button is pressed:

```
@IBAction func onButtonClicked() {
    label.setText("No Message")
}
```

Now let's build the Objective-C bridge we'll need to access the Darwin notification center from Swift. Strictly speaking, we only need to wrap the CFNotificationCenterAddObserver() function, but we're actually going to build wrapper functions for all the CFNotificationCenter functions that we'll be using, to keep our Swift code as simple as possible.

> **Note** There is an open source library called MMWormHole that provides similar functionality to the bridge that we're about to develop, which you can find at https://github.com/mutualmobile/MMWormhole. It's free and easy to use, but I decided not to use it in the WatchKit weather application because I think it's useful to demonstrate how to write a bridge from Swift code to a Core Foundation API and to show exactly how the notification process works.

We're going to need to use the bridge in both the iOS application and the WatchKit extension, so we'll put the code in an embedded framework. To do that, select File ➤ New ➤ Target... from Xcode's menu. Choose Framework and Library in the iOS section of the dialog that appears, followed by Cocoa Touch Framwork, and click Next. On the next page of the dialog, set Product Name to DarwinBridgeCode and click Finish to add the new target to the project (see Figure 7-8).

Figure 7-8. Adding a shared framework target to the project

Notice that the framework includes a header file called DarwinBridgeCode.h. This is called the framework's *umbrella header*. Code that uses the framework must import its umbrella header file.

Now let's implement the bridge itself as an Objective-C class. To do that, right-click the DarwinBridgeCode group and select New File... from the pop-up. Choose Cocoa Class from the iOS Source section of the dialog that appears and click Next. In the next page of the dialog, change the Class to DarwinNotificationCenterBridge and make it a subclass of NSObject. Finally, change the language to Objective-C, click Next, and save the new class in the DarwinBridgeCode group.

Let's start by defining the API for the bridge. To do that, open Darwin NotificationCenterBridge.h in the editor and add the following code shown in bold to it:

```
#import <Foundation/Foundation.h>

@protocol DarwinNotificationObserver

- (void)onNotificationReceived:(NSString *)name;

@end

@interface DarwinNotificationCenterBridge : NSObject

+ (void)postNotificationForName:(NSString *)name;
+ (void)addObserver:(id<DarwinNotificationObserver>)observer
                  forName:(NSString *)name;
+ (void)removeObserver:(id<DarwinNotificationObserver>)observer
                  forName:(NSString *)name;

@end
```

The postNotificationForName: method is the one that code in the iOS application will call to send a notification to the WatchKit extension. The other two methods are used in the extension to register and remove an observer for named notifications. The observer is required to conform to the DarwinNotificationObserver protocol, which is also defined in this header file.

Note You may have noticed that these methods are all class methods. That's because we only need one logical instance of the bridge. You could implement them as instance methods and then create a singleton bridge instance, but that would require more code both in the implementation and in the application itself. Feel free to change the implementation if you prefer an instance-based solution.

The Darwin notification center supports only a single observer for each notification name. However, we'll need to be able to support multiple observers. To make that possible, the DarwinNotificationCenterBridge class will keep a set of observers for each name and will register itself with the Darwin notification center as the single observer for each name. Whenever a notification for a given name is received, it will pass the notification on to all the observers that registered with it for that name.

Now let's implement the DarwinNotificationCenterBridge class, starting with the class initializer. Add the code in bold to DarwinNotificationCenter Bridge.m:

```
#import "DarwinNotificationCenterBridge.h"

static NSMutableDictionary *nameToObserversMap;

@implementation DarwinNotificationCenterBridge

+ (void)initialize {
    if (nameToObserversMap== NULL) {
        nameToObserversMap= [[NSMutableDictionary alloc] init];
    }
}
```

The nameToObserversMap is used to hold the registered observers for each notification name. The key to this map is the notification name (a string), and its value is an NSMutableSet containing the observers for that notification, all of which are of type id<DarwinNotificationObserver>.

Next, we'll implement the postNotificationForName: method. This is just a direct pass-through to the CFNotificationCenterPostNotification WithOptions() function. Add the code shown in bold:

```
+ (void)initialize {
    if (nameToObserversMap == NULL) {
        nameToObserversMap = [[NSMutableDictionary alloc] init];
    }
}

// Posts a notification for a given name.
+ (void)postNotificationForName:(NSString *)name {
    CFNotificationCenterPostNotificationWithOptions(
            CFNotificationCenterGetDarwinNotifyCenter(),
            (__bridge CFStringRef)name,
            NULL, NULL,
```

```
        kCFNotificationDeliverImmediately |
            kCFNotificationPostToAllSessions);
}
```

@end

If you check the declaration of the CFNotificationCenterPostNotification WithOptions() function in the API documentation, you'll see that you can specify the notification name, the source of the notification, and a dictionary to be passed to observers. Here, however, we have used the value NULL for the object (that is, the source) and userInfo (the dictionary) arguments, because these arguments are not supported by the Darwin notification center. That means we can deliver a notification to a given name, but we can't send any additional information along with the notification. Fortunately, as you'll see later, that's enough for the WatchKit Weather application.

Now let's add the implementation of the addObserver:forName: method. This requires a little more code because we need to allow more than one observer for each notification name. Add the following code to DarwinNotificationCenterBridge.m:

```
// Adds an observer for a notification with a given name.
+ (void)addObserver:(id<DarwinNotificationObserver>)observer
                    forName:(NSString *)name {
    BOOL needRegister = NO;
    NSMutableSet *observers =
        (NSMutableSet *)[nameToObserversMap objectForKey:name];
    if (observers == nil) {
        observers = [[NSMutableSet alloc] init];
        [nameToObserversMap setObject:observers forKey:name];
        needRegister = YES;
    }
    [observers addObject:observer];

    if (needRegister) {
        CFNotificationCenterAddObserver(
            CFNotificationCenterGetDarwinNotifyCenter(),
            (const void *)self,
            onNotificationCallback,
            (__bridge CFStringRef)name,
            NULL,
            CFNotificationSuspensionBehaviorDeliverImmediately);
    }
}
```

The first part of this function sets the needRegister variable to YES and adds an NSMutableSet to the nameToObserversMap if this is the first observer for the given notification name. The observer is then added to the set, and if needRegister is YES, the CFNotificationCenterAddObserver() function is called to register with the Darwin notification center. There is a compilation error for this call, because the callBack argument references a function that we haven't yet added. Add the definition of that function using the following code:

```
// Callback from Darwin Notification Center.
void onNotificationCallback(CFNotificationCenterRef center,
                            void *observer, CFStringRef name,
                            const void *object,
                            CFDictionaryRef userInfo) {
    NSString *notificationName = (__bridge NSString *)name;
    NSArray *observers =
            [nameToObserversMap objectForKey:notificationName];
    if (observers != NULL) {
        for (id<DarwinNotificationObserver> observer in observers) {
            [observer onNotificationReceived:notificationName];
        }
    }
}
```

This code is very straightforward. The notification name is cast from CFStringRef to NSString and then used to get the set of observers for that notification from the nameToObserversMap. If there are any observers, their onNotificationReceived: methods are called with the notification name as argument.

> **Note**   Notifications from CFNotificationCenter are always delivered on the main thread.

Finally, we need to implement the removeObserver:forName: method. This just reverses the steps in the addObserver:forName: method. Add this code to DarwinNotificationCenterBridge.m:

```
// Removes an observer for a notification with a given name.
+ (void)removeObserver:(id<DarwinNotificationObserver>)observer
                 forName:(NSString *)name {
    BOOL needUnregister = NO;
    NSMutableSet *observers =
            (NSMutableSet *)[nameToObserversMap objectForKey:name];
    if ([observers containsObject:observer]) {
        [observers removeObject:observer];
```

```
    if (observers.count == 0) {
        [nameToObserversMap removeObjectForKey:name];
        needUnregister = YES;
    }
}

if (needUnregister) {
    CFNotificationCenterRemoveObserver(
        CFNotificationCenterGetDarwinNotifyCenter(),
        (const void *)self,
        (__bridge CFStringRef)name,
        NULL);
}
}
```

That completes the implementation of the Darwin notification center bridge. Now let's try to make use of it in our example application. Open ViewController.swift and add the following code to the onButtonClicked() method to send a notification with name TestNotification when the button in the iOS application is clicked:

```
@IBAction func onButtonClicked(sender: AnyObject) {
    DarwinNotificationCenterBridge.postNotificationForName(
        "TestNotification")
}
```

This doesn't compile because the identifier DarwinNotificationCenterBridge is unknown. To fix that, we need to import the framework:

```
import UIKit
import DarwinBridgeCode

class ViewController: UIViewController {
```

This still doesn't work, because we have a couple of steps to complete back in the framework itself. Select the framework's umbrella header (DarwinBridgeCode.h) and add an import line for DarwinNotificationCenter Bridge.h:

```
#import <UIKit/UIKit.h>
#import "DarwinNotificationCenterBridge.h"

//! Project version number for DarwinBridgeCode.
FOUNDATION_EXPORT double DarwinBridgeCodeVersionNumber;
```

This makes the definitions in DarwinNotificationCenterBridge.h available to users of the framework (provided that they import its umbrella header, of course), but there is still a problem beacsue the header is private to the framework. We need to make it public. To do that, select DarwinNotification CenterBridge.h in the Project Navigator and open the File Inspector (⌥⌘1). In the Target Membership area, you'll see that the file is assigned to the DarwinBridgeCode target, but its visibility is currently Project. Change this to Public, as shown in Figure 7-9.

Figure 7-9. Making a framework header public

Now rebuild the project, and the compilation error should go away.

Next, we need to register to receive notifications with name TestNotification from the Darwin notification center whenever the interface controller of the WatchKit app is active. To do that, we first need to import the DarwinBridgeCode framework and conform the interface controller class to the DarwinNotificationObserver protocol. To do that, add the following code in bold to InterfaceController.swift:

```
import WatchKit
import Foundation
import DarwinBridgeCode

class InterfaceController:
        WKInterfaceController, DarwinNotificationObserver {
    @IBOutlet weak var label: WKInterfaceLabel!

    func onNotificationReceived(name: String!) {
        label.setText("Received notification")
    }
```

Finally, we need to register as an observer for this notification when the interface controller is activated and unregister when it's deactivated. We can do each of these things with a call to methods in our new framework:

```
override func willActivate() {
    super.willActivate()
    DarwinNotificationCenterBridge.addObserver(self,
                            forName: "TestNotification")
}

override func didDeactivate() {
    super.didDeactivate()
    DarwinNotificationCenterBridge.removeObserver(self,
                            forName: "TestNotification")
}
```

That's it. Now run the WatchKit application from Xcode and then launch the iOS application from the home screen of the simulator (or the iPhone if you are using real hardware). Press the Send Notification button, and you should see the message Received notification appear in the WatchKit app, as shown in Figure 7-10.

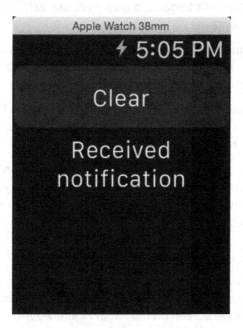

Figure 7-10. WatchKit extension receiving a notification from the iOS application

Press the Clear button to reset the label in the WatchKit user interface and check that you can send as many notifications as you want.

Building the WatchKit Weather App

We now have everything we need to start implementing the WatchKit Weather application. We're going to use the Xcode project for the iOS Weather application as the starting point and enhance it in stages, as follows:

1. Add an embedded framework for the classes that need to be shared between the iOS application and the WatchKit extension.

2. Add the Darwin notification center bridge we developed in the preceding section to the framework and move the model classes that need to be shared into it.

3. Create an app group and change the shared model classes to persist their state into the group's shared container. At this point, we'll be able to run the iOS application again and verify that it still works.

4. Add a WatchKit target and give it access to the shared container.

5. Modify the DisplayedCityInfoModel class to notify changes made in the iOS application's configuration screens to the WatchKit extension.

6. Add code to the iOS application that will handle the WatchKit extension's openParentApplication(_: reply:) method calls.

7. Create a subclass of WeatherModel for the extension that will use the openParentApplication(_:reply:) method to request new forecast details from the iOS application.

8. Implement the main interface controller of the WatchKit app, to show a summary of the current weather for the cities configured in the DisplayedInfoCityModel. This interface controller provides the screen on the left in Figure 7-2.

9. Implement the WatchKit app's detail screen, to show the details of the forecast for one city. This is the screen on the right in Figure 7-2.

Take a copy of the 7 - LWKWeather - Initial folder from the example source code archive and open it in Xcode. Build the project and run it on the simulator or an iPhone to check you have a good starting point for the changes we are about to make. Let's start by moving the code that we need to share to an embedded framework.

Moving Shared Code to a Framework

With the Weather application project open in Xcode, create an embedded framework using the same steps we used in the last section. Select File ➤ New ➤ Target... from the menu, in the iOS Framework & Library section of the dialog, choose Cocoa Touch Framework, and click Next. On the next page use SharedCode as the Product Name and make sure the language is Swift. Click Finish to create the framework.

After Xcode creates the framework, select the LWKWeather node at the top of the Project Navigator to display the project info and build settings in the editor area. In the Info section, select the LWKWeather project and take a note of the value of the iOS Deployment Target setting (it's probably 8.0). Select the SharedCode target and make sure the General tab is showing. We need to change two settings in the Deployment Info section of this tab. First, make sure the Deployment Target matches the value of the iOS Deployment Target on the LWKWeather project page, which probably means changing it to 8.0. Second, check the Allow app extension API only check box. Because the framework is going to be used in an extension, we need to make sure it doesn't make use of APIs that extensions are not allowed to use. Enabling this setting causes the compiler to flag an error if you try to use an API that is not safe for use in an extension. Your settings should now be as shown in Figure 7-11.

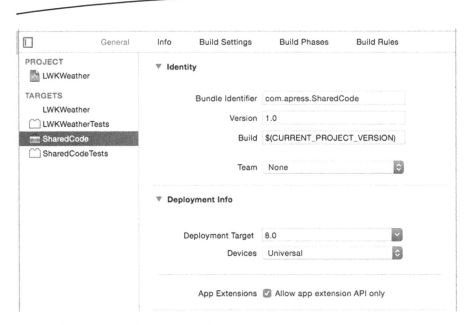

Figure 7-11. Configuring the SharedCode framework

Adding the Darwin Bridge to the Framework

Our first task is to add the code for the Darwin Bridge to the framework. When Xcode added the shared framework target, it also added two new groups called SharedCode and SharedCodeTests in the Project Navigator. Right-click the SharedCode group and add a new group nested beneath it called Darwin Notifications. Locate the DarwinNotificationCenterBridge.h and DarwinNotificationCenterBridge.m files from the framework that we created earlier and drag and drop them under the Darwin Notifications group, making sure that the Copy items if needed check box is selected in the dialog that appears before the copy occurs.

> **Tip**   You can find these files in the 7 - DarwinBridge/DarwinBridgeCode folder of the example source code archive.

Select DarwinNotificationCenterBridge.h, open the File Inspector, and change the visibility of the file in the Target Membership section from Project to Public. Finally, open the SharedCode.h header file and add the following line at the end of the file, to make the declarations in `Darwin NotificationCenterBridge.h` visible to code that imports the framework's umbrella header:

```
#import <SharedCode/DarwinNotificationCenterBridge.h>
```

You now have an embedded framework that includes the Darwin Bridge functionality.

Moving the Shared Model Classes

Next, we'll move the model classes that we need to share into the framework. Start by creating a new group called `Weather Model` under the `SharedCode` group. Drag and drop the files `WeatherModel.swift` and `WeatherData.swift` from the `Weather Model` group in the iOS application into it. Select the `Displayed City Model` group, drag it into the `SharedCode` group, and then do the same with the `City Model` group. The last file we need to move is `WeatherUtilities.swift`. This file doesn't really fit under any of the existing groups, so create a group called `Utilities` under `SharedCode` and drag `WeatherUtilities.swift` into it.

Even though we've moved all the model files, they are not yet part of the embedded framework because they still belong to the `LWKWeather` target. To fix that, open the File Inspector, select each file in the `SharedCode` group in the Project Navigator individually then, and in the Target Membership section of the File Inspector, uncheck `LWKWeather` and check `SharedCode`. If you've done this correctly, you should see a lot of compilation errors reported in the Activity View, because the classes that you've just moved are no longer visible to the code in the `LWKWeather` target. If you open the Issue Navigator (⌘4), you'll see that this change has affected six files: `AppWeatherModel. swift`, `WeatherPageViewController.swift`, `CityWeatherViewController. swift`, `CityListViewController.swift`, `AppDelegate.swift`, and `SettingsViewController.swift`. Open each of these files and add the following line after the existing imports:

import SharedCode

Now rebuild, and all should be well. If you try running the application on the simulator, you may find that almost immediately after it starts, it crashes. This only happens if you ran the application at least once before we started making changes to it. The reason it crashes is that the weather data from the earlier run of the application is archived using different class names. When it was part of the `LWKWeather` project, the full name of the `CityWeather` class was `LWKWeather.CityWeather`, but now it has changed to `SharedCode.CityWeather`. When the application tried to load the weather model, it crashed because the NSKeyedUnarchiver cannot find a class called LWKWeather.CityWeather. I referred to a similar problem that arises when you try to archive files that belong to more than one target in the section "Shared Code" earlier in this chapter. Here, we get the problem because the application is trying to make sense of data stored by a previous, incompatible version. You can fix that immediately by deleting the application from the simulator and then running it again. Everything will work, but you will have lost any configuration changes that you made. If you were making a change like this to an application that's already in the App Store, you wouldn't be able to get away with telling your users to uninstall and reinstall and then manually restore their settings. Fortunately, there is an easy way to make the application work with archives generated by the previous version: you just have to tell NSKeyedUnarchiver what to do when it finds references to classes that it doesn't know about. To do that, add the following lines of code shown in bold to AppDelegate.swift:

```
func application(application: UIApplication,
            didFinishLaunchingWithOptions launchOptions:
                [NSObject: AnyObject]?) -> Bool {
    // Load cached weather.
    NSKeyedUnarchiver.setClass(CityWeather.self,
                        forClassName: "LWKWeather.CityWeather")
    NSKeyedUnarchiver.setClass(DayForecast.self,
                        forClassName: "LWKWeather.DayForecast")
    NSKeyedUnarchiver.setClass(WeatherDetails.self,
                        forClassName: "LWKWeather.WeatherDetails")

    AppWeatherModel.sharedInstance().loadWeatherModel()

    return true
}
```

The setClass(_:forClassName:) method tells NSKeyedUnarchiver to use the class given by its first argument whenever it needs to unarchive data for a class with the name given by its second argument. You should now be able to successfully run the application.

Adding the WatchKit Extension and Creating the App Group

The next step is a simple one and one that you are, by now, very familiar with. Add a WatchKit App target to the project in the usual way, making sure to choose Swift as the language and to exclude the notification and glance scenes.

If you build the project at this point, you may see the error "WatchKit apps must have a deployment target equal to iOS 8.2." It's not obvious why Xcode should force you to downgrade the deployment target for your Watch app to iOS 8.2, but if you get this error, you have no choice but to do so. To do that, select LWKWeather in the Project Navigator. Select the LWK Weather WatchKit App target in the editor area and open the Build Settings tab. In the Deployment section, you'll see that the iOS Deployment Target is set to iOS 8.3 (or iOS 8.4 or higher, depending on when you read this). Change that setting to iOS 8.2, as shown in the bottom right corner of Figure 7-12, and build again.

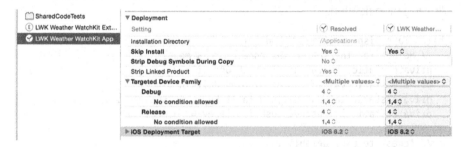

Figure 7-12. Changing the iOS Deployment Target for the WatchKit extension

The WatchKit extension is automatically given access to the code in the SharedCode framework—to prove that, add the following import line in bold to InterfaceController.swift and rebuild:

```
import WatchKit
import Foundation
import SharedCode
```

Now let's see if the extension can use the weather data model. Add this code to the awakeWithContext() method in InterfaceController.swift:

```
override func awakeWithContext(context: AnyObject?) {
    super.awakeWithContext(context)

    let model = DisplayedCityInfoModel.sharedInstance()
    println(model.displayedCities)
}
```

This code should print the city codes for the cities that are configured in the settings screen of the iOS application. Run the WatchKit app and look at the Xcode console—you'll see that it appears to have worked:

```
[5128581, 4887398, 2147714]
```

Unfortunately, those are actually the city codes for the cities that are used by default if no persisted state was found. Why did that happen? Because when we initialized the DisplayedCityInfoModel in the awakeWithContext() method, it retrieved the displayed city list from NSUserDefaults—but that's the NSUserDefaults object in the extension's container, not the one in the iOS application's container, which is where the displayed city list is persisted (refer back to Figure 7-7 if you need some clarification on this point). Moving the code to the shared framework was not enough—as I said in the section "Sharing Displayed City Info" earlier in this chapter, we need to change the model so that it uses the shared NSUserDefaults objects. Making that change is very simple: open DisplayedCityInfoModel.swift and make the following modification:

```
public class DisplayedCityInfoModel {
    // Holder for the shared instance of this model.
    private static var token: dispatch_once:t = 0
    private static var instance: DisplayedCityInfoModel?
    private static let userCitiesDefaultsKey = "displayedCityInfo"
    private static let useCelsiusDefaultsKey = "useCelsius"

    // Access to user defaults.
    private let userDefaults = NSUserDefaults.standardUserDefaults()
    private let userDefaults =
        NSUserDefaults(suiteName: "group.com.apress.lwkweathertest")!
```

Here, we're using the NSUserDefaults initializer that looks for the user defaults object in the shared container for an app group called group.com. apress.lwkweathertest. The name of the app group is required to start with "group.", but the rest of the name is up to you. It's made globally unique because Xcode prepends to it your iOS developer program team id, which means that if you use the same app group name as I did, your use of it won't clash with mine. You can, of course, choose a different group name if you want to, as long as you use the same name everywhere.

We need to make a similar change in the implementation of the weather data model. To do that, open WeatherModel.swift and make the following change to the init() method:

```
public init() {
    let baseURL = NSFileManager.defaultManager().URLsForDirectory(
                        NSSearchPathDirectory.CachesDirectory,
                        inDomains: .UserDomainMask)[0] as! NSURL
    weatherDirURL = baseURL.URLByAppendingPathComponent("LWKWeather")
    let baseURL = NSFileManager.defaultManager().
            containerURLForSecurityApplicationGroupIdentifier(
                    "group.com.apress.lwkweathertest")!
    weatherDirURL = baseURL.URLByAppendingPathComponent("LWKWeather")
```

The containerURLForSecurityApplicationGroupIdentifier() method of NSFileManager returns a URL that refers to the shared container for the app group passed as its argument (the one labeled "Shared Container" in Figure 7-7). With this change, the weather model code in the iOS application and in the extension will look for their persisted data in the same place.

There's one more thing we need to do before we can test whether these changes work. By default, your application and WatchKit extension are not permitted to use app groups. To fix that, you'll need to add the App Group capability to both the application and extension targets. You can only do that if you have a paid iOS developer program membership. If you don't have one yet, you'll need to sign up and wait until you are approved.

To add the App Group capability to the iOS application, select the LWKWeather node at the top of the Project Navigator and then the LWKWeather target in the left column in the editor area.

> **Caution**   Be sure to select the LWKWeather node in the Targets section, not the one in Project section.

Select the Capabilities tab, and a little way down the screen you'll see the App Groups section and a segmented control that indicates that the App Groups capability is currently turned off for this target (see Figure 7-13).

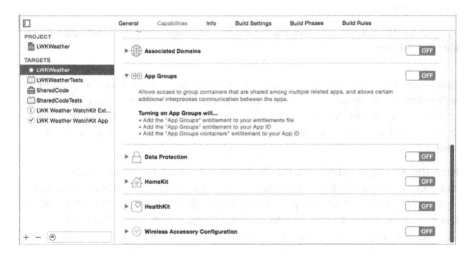

Figure 7-13. Configuring App Groups for the iOS application target

Toggle the segmented control to the ON position, and Xcode will prompt you to choose your development team. Choose your team (if you are individual developer, you only have one), and Xcode will do some work and then show you the list of App Groups that your development team has already created, which may be empty. Click the + icon under the group id list, and Xcode will open a dialog that lets you enter a new group id. Enter the group name that you want to use (choose com.apress.lwkweathertest if that's what you used in DisplayedCityInfoModel.swift and WeatherModel.swift) and click OK. Xcode will add the app group you chose to your developer account and update the display to show that the group is active, as shown in Figure 7-14.

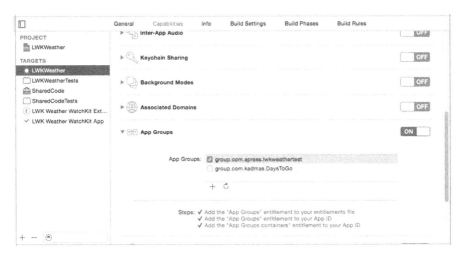

Figure 7-14. The app group has been created and the App Groups capability is enabled for the iOS application

Now you need to repeat the process to enable App Groups for the WatchKit extension. Start by selecting LWK Weather WatchKit Extension in the Targets section and then follow the same steps as before. This time, you'll find that the group id you need is already in the group id list, so you'll just have to select it.

Now the iOS application and the WatchKit extension both have access to the shared container, but, of course, there's no useful data there to recover. In a production application, you would write code to migrate the data from the iOS application's container to the shared container when the user upgrades to the version of your application that contains the WatchKit app.

I'm not going to describe in detail how to do that here because the details depend on how your data is persisted. For the weather application, two simple steps would be required:

- Copy the relevant values from the NSUserDefaults object in the application's container to the one in the shared container.

- Copy the files containing persisted weather data from the iOS application's LWKWeather directory in the application's container to the corresponding directory in the shared container.

To demonstrate that we can now share data between the application and the WatchKit extension, run the iOS application in the simulator (by choosing the LWKWeather scheme) and add San Francisco to the list of displayed cities. Stop the iOS application and use the LWK Weather WatchKit App scheme to run the WatchKit app. Now, the code we added to InterfaceController. swift will load the displayed city list from the shared NSUserDefaults object, and you should see four city codes in the Xcode console:

```
[5128581, 4887398, 2147714, 5391959]
```

Updating the DisplayedCityInfoModel Class

As you saw earlier in this chapter, the DisplayedCityInfoModel class contains the list of cities for which the user wants to see weather data and the setting that controls whether temperatures are shown in Farenheit or Celsius. The content of this model is persisted in the shared NSUserDefaults object, so it's accessible to both the iOS application and the WatchKit extension. The model state can be changed by using the iOS application's settings screens. When any changes are made in these screens, we would like the WatchKit app to update itself immediately to reflect those changes, if it's active. Usually, a notification is sent for changes to an NSUserDefaults object, but that does not happen for a shared NSUserDefaults object, so we'll have to handle the notification ourselves. We'll do that by using the Darwin bridge.

Here's a summary of the modifications we'll need to make to the
DisplayedCityInfoModel class:

- Whenever the value of its displayedCities or useCelsius
  property changes, we'll send a notification via the Darwin
  bridge. We'll also change the code that saves the new
  property value to the NSUserDefaults object so that it does
  nothing if the change is made in the extension. The code
  in the extension that uses the DisplayedCityInfoModel
  class doesn't actually change these properties, but we'll
  make this change anyway, to guarantee that changes can
  be only persisted in the iOS application.

- When it's used in the extension, the
  DisplayedCityInfoModel class will register to receive
  notifications from the Darwin bridge. When it receives
  a notification that a change has been made in the iOS
  application's version of the model, it will update itself
  from the state in the shared container and notify its
  delegate that something has changed. As you'll see later,
  in the extension, the model's delegate will be an interface
  controller, so the effect of this will be to cause the user
  interface to update to reflect whatever the user changed.

Open DisplayedCityInfoModel.swift in the editor and let's start working on
these changes. The first thing we need to do is make the class conform to
the DarwinNotificationObserver protocol so that it can receive notifications
sent over the Darwin bridge. To do that, make the changes shown in bold:

```swift
public class DisplayedCityInfoModel: DarwinNotificationObserver {
    // Code not shown

    // Notifies the delegate of a change in the model. This call is
    // always made in the main thread.
    private func notifyDelegate() {
        delegate?.displayedCityInfoDidChange(self)
    }

    // DarwinNotificationReceiver protocol conformance.
    // Handles notification of a change made in the iOS app.
    // Update the model state. As a side-effect, this will
    // notify the delegate if anything actually changes.
    @objc public func onNotificationReceived(name: String) {
        loadDisplayedCities()
        loadUseCelsius()
    }
}
```

> **Note**   If you're wondering why the onNotificationReceived() method
> has the @objc attribute, it's because it needs to be called from an Objective-C
> method in the Foundation framework. To make that possible, you need to either
> tag the method with @objc or make the class a subclass (directly or indirectly)
> of NSObject. Here, the class is not derived from NSObject, so the @objc
> attribute is required.

When a message is received from the Darwin bridge, the
onNotificationRecieved() method is called, which in turn calls the
(existing) loadDisplayedCities() and loadUseCelsius() methods.
These methods update the model state from the shared NSUserDefaults
object and, if anything actually changes, notify the registered
DisplayedCityInfoModelDelegate.

Next, we need to register the model to receive Darwin bridge notifications,
but only if it's running in the extension. The following code takes care of that:

```
public class DisplayedCityInfoModel: DarwinNotificationObserver {
    // Holder for the shared instance of this model.
    private static var token: dispatch_once:t = 0
    private static var instance: DisplayedCityInfoModel?
    private static let userCitiesDefaultsKey = "displayedCityInfo"
    private static let useCelsiusDefaultsKey = "useCelsius"
    private static let inExtension: Bool =
            NSBundle.mainBundle().bundleIdentifier?.hasSuffix(
                    "watchkitextension") ?? false
    private static let darwinPath = "DisplayedCityInfoModel"

    // Code not shown

    // Private initializer. Initializes the displayed cities
    // and use celsius properties from user defaults or to default values.
    private init() {
        loadDisplayedCities()
        loadUseCelsius()

        if (DisplayedCityInfoModel.inExtension) {
            DarwinNotificationCenterBridge.addObserver(self,
                    forName: DisplayedCityInfoModel.darwinPath)
        }
    }
}
```

We set the inExtension property to true if the code is executing in an extension. There is no direct way to know that's the case, so we use an indirect way—the bundle identifier of a WatchKit extension has the suffix watchkitextension, so we can tell we are running in an extension by looking at the identifier of the bundle in which the code was packaged.

> **Tip**   To see the bundle identifier for the WatchKit extension, open the Info. plist file in the LWK Weather WatchKit Extension group and check the value of the Bundle Identifier key.

We use the value of the inExtension property in several places in this class, including in the initializer, shown previously, where we register to receive Darwin notifications that have the name given by the darwinPath property, which we initialize with the string DisplayedInfoCityModel. We can safely define the notification name as a local constant because this class contains both the sender and the observer of these notifications.

Next, we need to ensure that changes are saved to the NSUserDefaults object only when they occur in the iOS application. To do that, update the saveDisplayedCities() and saveUseCelsius() methods as shown here:

```
// Saves the updated displayed cities to the user defaults.
private func saveDisplayedCities() {
    if (!DisplayedCityInfoModel.inExtension) {
        userDefaults.setObject(displayedCities,
                forKey: DisplayedCityInfoModel.userCitiesDefaultsKey)
        userDefaults.synchronize()
    }
}

// Loads the use-celsius value from the user defaults.
private func loadUseCelsius() {
    useCelsius = userDefaults.boolForKey(
            DisplayedCityInfoModel.useCelsiusDefaultsKey)
}

// Saves the useCelsius value to the user defaults.
private func saveUseCelsius() {
    if (!DisplayedCityInfoModel.inExtension) {
        userDefaults.setBool(useCelsius,
                forKey: DisplayedCityInfoModel.useCelsiusDefaultsKey)
        userDefaults.synchronize()
    }
}
```

In both cases, we change the code so that the updates are saved only if the inExtension property is false, indicating that the code is running in the iOS application. Notice that we also call the synchronize() method to make sure that the iOS application's change has been persisted before we send a notification to the extension. To send that notification, we'll add some code to the notifyDelegate() method, which is always called to inform the model's delegate of a change after either of the two methods that we just modified have been called:

```
// Notifies the delegate of a change in the model. This call is
// always made in the main thread.
private func notifyDelegate() {
    delegate?.displayedCityInfoDidChange(self)
    if (!DisplayedCityInfoModel.inExtension)
        // Notify extension across Darwin bridge
        DarwinNotificationCenterBridge.postNotificationForName(
                DisplayedCityInfoModel.darwinPath)
    }
}
```

Once again, we use the inExtension property to ensure that the notification can only be sent from the iOS application to the extension and not vice versa.

That completes our work in the DisplayedCityInfoModel class. Let's run a quick test to make sure that the code works. Open InterfaceController. swift and add the following code in bold:

```
class InterfaceController: WKInterfaceController {
    var delegate: DisplayedCityInfoModelDelegate?

    override func awakeWithContext(context: AnyObject?) {
        super.awakeWithContext(context)

        let model = DisplayedCityInfoModel.sharedInstance()
        println(model.displayedCities)

        class ModelDelegate: DisplayedCityInfoModelDelegate {
            func displayedCityInfoDidChange(model: DisplayedCityInfoModel) {
                println("Displayed cities: \(model.displayedCities)")
                println("Use celsius: \(model.useCelsius)")
            }
        }
        delegate = ModelDelegate()
        model.delegate = delegate
    }
```

We create an internal class called ModelDelegate that conforms to the DisplayedCityInfoModelDelegate protocol and assign an instance of it to be the delegate of the DisplayedCityInfoModel. Any changes that are reported to this class are printed to the console.

Notice that we also save a reference to the delegate in the delegate property of the InterfaceController class. That's necessary because DisplayedCityInfoModel keeps only a weak reference to its delegate (which is the correct way to manage delegates). If we didn't keep a strong reference to it in the delegate property, the ModelDelegate instance would be deallocated as soon as the awakeWithContext() method returns control to its caller.

Now run the WatchKit application on the simulator, start the iOS application manually from the iPhone simulator's main screen, and open the settings screen (the screen in the center in Figure 7-1). If you toggle the temperature setting between Celsius and Farenheit, you should see the change reported in the console, indicating that it's being reflected in the extension's copy of the DisplayedCityInfoModel. You should also see changes to the displayed cities reported if you reorder the cities in the list at the top of the screen, or press the Add/Remove button and change the population of the displayed cities list.

Updating the Weather Model Classes

We discussed the changes that we would need to make to share weather data between the iOS application and the extension in the section "Sharing Weather Data" earlier in this chapter. The idea is that the extension will load its in-memory copy of the weather model with the current state from the shared container. When it needs to get updated data, the extension will send a request to the iOS application, using the WKInterfaceController openPar entApplication(_:reply:) method. Whenever the iOS application updates the model, either in response to a request from the extension or because it needed to use forecast data that had expired, it first persists the update and then sends a message over the Darwin bridge, to which the extension responds by getting updated data from the shared container and installing it in its own copy of the model. In this section, we'll implement the extension's implementation of the weather model.

Recall that the WeatherModel class is a base class that contains all the weather data and some common code used to manage it. The iOS application uses a concrete subclass called AppWeatherModel, together with a loader class called OpenWeatherMapLoader, to fetch forecast data from openweathermap.org and install it in the model. For the extension, we'll create a new subclass of WeatherModel and a new loader that requests updated data from the iOS application instead of over the Internet.

In the Project Explorer, create a new group under LWK Weather WatchKit Extension and call it Watch Weather Model. Right-click on the new

group and select New File.... In the dialog that appears, select Cocoa
Touch Class from the iOS Source section. Click Next, name the class
WatchAppWeatherModel, and make it a subclass of WeatherModel. Ensure that
the language is Swift, click Next, and save the new class. You'll immediately
be confronted with a compilation error because the WeatherModel base class
is in the shared framework. To fix that, make the following change at the top
of WatchAppWeatherModel.swift:

```
import UIKit
import WatchKit
import SharedCode
```

Now make the changes shown here in bold in the same file, to implement
the WatchAppWeatherModel class:

```
// MARK: -
// MARK: WATCH APP WEATHER MODEL

// The Watch App implementation of the weather model.
class WatchAppWeatherModel : WeatherModel {
    // Holder for the shared instance of this model.
    private static var token: dispatch_once:t = 0
    private static var instance: WatchAppWeatherModel?

    // Determines whether this model can update the persistent storage.
    // Overrides the default to not allow updates.
    override var readOnly: Bool {
        return false
    }

    // Gets the shared instance of this model.
    class func sharedInstance() -> WeatherModel {
        dispatch_once(&token) {
            self.instance = WatchAppWeatherModel()
        }
        return instance!
    }

    // Creates the loader for the weather data. Returns a
    // loader that fetches weather data from the iOS application
    override func createWeatherModelLoader() -> WeatherModelLoader {
        return WatchAppWeatherModelLoader(model: self)
    }
}
```

There are only two things worth commenting on in this code. The first is the
createWeatherModelLoader() method, which is called from the base class
when the model's loader is required for the first time. It creates and returns an

instance of the WatchAppWeatherModelLoader class, which doesn't exist yet, so there should be a compilation error for this code. The other point of interest is the readOnly property. This property determines whether new model data will be persisted into the shared container. We only want the iOS application to persist model data, so in the AppWeatherModel class this property is always true, but here we override the property definition so that it's always false.

Now let's implement the loader class. Add the following code at the bottom of the same file:

```
// MARK: -
// MARK: WATCH APP WEATHER MODEL LOADER
private class WatchAppWeatherModelLoader:
            WeatherModelLoader, DarwinNotificationObserver {
    // The model for which this class will load data.
    private let model: WeatherModel
    private var registeredCityCodes = Set<Int>()

    init(model: WeatherModel) {
        self.model = model
    }

    // Requests that the loader obtain weather details for a given
    // set of cities. This method is always called on the main thread.
    func fetchWeatherForCities(cityCodes: [Int]) {
        let userInfo: [NSObject: AnyObject] =
            [WatchAppWeatherInterface.LoadWeatherCommandName : cityCodes]
        for cityCode in cityCodes {
            if !registeredCityCodes.contains(cityCode) {
                registeredCityCodes.insert(cityCode)
                DarwinNotificationCenterBridge.addObserver(self,
                                forName: "\(cityCode)")
            }
        }
        let result = WKInterfaceController.openParentApplication(
                userInfo, reply: { (results, error) in
            if let replyData = results?[
              WatchAppWeatherInterface.LoadWeatherReplyName] as? NSData {
                if let cityWeatherItems =
                    NSKeyedUnarchiver.unarchiveObjectWithData(replyData)
                            as? [CityWeather] {
                    for cityWeather in cityWeatherItems {
                        let cityCode = cityWeather.cityCode
                        self.model.installNewWeatherForCity(cityCode,
                            detailsByDay: cityWeather.detailsByDay)
                    }
                }
            }
        })
    }
}
```

```
// Handles notification of data received for a city. The
// name is the city code as a string
@objc func onNotificationReceived(name: String) {
    if let cityCode = name.toInt(),
        let cityWeather = model.getArchivedWeatherForCity(cityCode) {
        model.installNewWeatherForCity(cityCode,
                          detailsByDay: cityWeather.detailsByDay)
    }
}
}
```

The core of this class is in the fetchWeatherForCities() method, which is called when forecast data is required, but the data is either not currently in the model or is out of date. In this case, we need to delegate the task of getting new data to the iOS application by calling the openParentApplicatio n(_:reply:) method of WKInterfaceController. The iOS application figures out what it's being asked to do from the information in a dictionary that's passed with the call. Here, we're creating the dictionary and initializing it with an array containing the city codes for the cities we need data for, using the key LoadWeatherCommandName. That key is not defined in this class because it also needs to be used by the code in the iOS application that handles the request. Instead, it's in a small class called WatchAppWeatherInterface, which we'll create shortly.

The next block of code deserves a little explanation:

```
for cityCode in cityCodes {
    if !registeredCityCodes.contains(cityCode) {
        registeredCityCodes.insert(cityCode)
        DarwinNotificationCenterBridge.addObserver(self,
                            forName: "\(cityCode)")
    }
}
```

The iOS application informs us that new data is available by sending a notification over the Darwin bridge using the string form of the city code as the notification name. We need to register as an observer of the Darwin bridge for each city we request data for, but we only need to do that the first time we request data for any given city. To ensure that we don't register more than once, we keep the city codes we have registered for in the registeredCityCodes array. Once we have registered, we never unregister. There is little reason to unregister—the model is a singleton that should remain alive as long as the extension is active, and staying registered means that we'll also be updated if the iOS application fetches new weather data for itself, which could save a round trip if the extension needs that same data at some future point (which is likely, because the iOS application and the WatchKit application always display forcasts for the same cities).

Next, we make the call to the iOS application, passing a closure that processes the reply and the dictionary containing the command and the array of city codes

```
let result = WKInterfaceController.openParentApplication(
        userInfo, reply: { (results, error) in
    if let replyData = results?[
      WatchAppWeatherInterface.LoadWeatherReplyName] as? NSData {
        if let cityWeatherItems =
          NSKeyedUnarchiver.unarchiveObjectWithData(replyData)
                            as? [CityWeather] {
            for cityWeather in cityWeatherItems {
                let cityCode = cityWeather.cityCode
                self.model.installNewWeatherForCity(cityCode,
                        detailsByDay: cityWeather.detailsByDay)
            }
        }
    }
})
```

We'll implement the handler code in the iOS application that processes this request in the next section, so for now, I'll just describe what it does. When it's called, the handler checks whether it already has current data for any of the cities in the request that it received. It collects the CityWeather objects for each city for which current data is available into an array, serializes the array into an NSData object using NSKeyedArchiver, and places it into a dictionary under the key LoadWeatherReplyName, which is (or rather, soon will be) defined in the WatchAppWeatherInterface class and returns that dictionary by calling the reply closure that's passed to it along with the request. The closure in the previous code is invoked when the reply is received in the extension. It checks whether the reply data contains a key called LoadWeatherReplyName with a value of type NSData, and if it does, the closure tries to unarchive it into an array of CityWeather objects. If this works, it uses the WeatherModel's inst allNewWeatherForCity(_:detailsByDay:) method to add the forecast data to the in-memory copy of the model. This will cause notifications to be delivered to registered observers of the model in the usual way.

It's more likely that the iOS application does not have the weather data that was requested, in which case the handler will request it. When it arrives, it sends a notification over the Darwin bridge, which will be delivered to the WatchAppWeatherModelLoader class since we registered it to receive these notifications earlier in the implementation of this method. We still need to add the method that handles the notification. To do that, add the following code at the end of the class:

```
// Handles notification of data received for a city. The
// name is the city code as a string
@objc func onNotificationReceived(name: String) {
    if let cityCode = name.toInt(),
        let cityWeather = model.getArchivedWeatherForCity(cityCode) {
            model.installNewWeatherForCity(cityCode,
                    detailsByDay: cityWeather.detailsByDay)
    }
}
```

The notification name is the city code for the city new data is available for, in string form, which is first converted to an Int. The data itself cannot be sent over the Darwin bridge along with the notification. Instead, it will have been written to the shared container. To get it, we call the getArchivedWeatherForCity() method, passing the city's code. You'll find the implementation of this method, which is not discussed here, in the WeatherModel class. If the data is present (and it should be, because it's just been updated), the getArchivedWeatherForCity() method returns it as a CityWeather object, and we use the WeatherModel installNewWeatherFor City(_:detailsByDay:) method to add it to the local, in-memory copy of the model, just as we did with data that was returned directly from the call to the iOS application. Adding the data causes a notification to be sent. The observers are actually interface controllers, so this notification will cause the user interface to be updated with the new data.

The only thing left to do is create the WatchAppWeatherInterface class containing the constants that are used in the informal API between the extension and the iOS application. Because it's used in both places, this class needs to be in the embedded framework, so right-click the Weather Model group under the SharedCode group and select New File.... From the iOS Source section of the dialog, choose Swift File and click Next. Name the file WatchAppWeatherInterface and save it. When the file opens in the editor, add the following code in bold to it:

```
public class WatchAppWeatherInterface {
    // Command used to request loading of weather for cities.
    // Data must be an array of city codes.
    public static let LoadWeatherCommandName = "LoadWeatherCommand"

    // Reply used to return city weather data. Data is an array
    // of CityWeather objects, archived as NSData.
    public static let LoadWeatherReplyName = "LoadWeatherReply"
}
```

You should now be able to build the project without any compilation errors.

Adding the WatchKit Request Handler

As you just saw, the WatchAppWeatherModelLoader class requests forecast information from the iOS application by using the openParentApplicatio n(_:reply:) method of WKInterfaceController. For this to work, the iOS application's UIApplicationDelegate needs to implement the application(_ :handleWatchKitExtensionRequest:reply:) method. In "Sending a Request to an iOS Application" earlier in this chapter, you saw how this application delegate method is typically implemented. For the weather application, we're going to use the same basic code that you saw earlier to implement the application(_:handleWatchKitExtensionRequest:reply:) method, but the logic that is specific to the weather application will be in a separate class. To get started, open the file AppDelegate.swift in the editor and add the following code just above the closing brace:

```
// MARK: -
// MARK: Handler for requests from the WatchKit extension
func application(application: UIApplication,
        handleWatchKitExtensionRequest userInfo: [NSObject : AnyObject]?,
        reply: (([NSObject : AnyObject]!) -> Void)!) {
    var taskId: UIBackgroundTaskIdentifier = 0
    taskId = application.beginBackgroundTaskWithExpirationHandler({
        // Out of time -- just send a nil reply.
        reply(nil)
        application.endBackgroundTask(taskId)
    })

    dispatch_async(dispatch_get_main_queue(), {
        let results =
            WatchAppWeatherRequestHandler.sharedInstance().
                    handleWatchExtensionRequest(userInfo!)
        reply(results)

        let endTime = dispatch_time(DISPATCH_TIME_NOW,
                                    Int64(2 * NSEC_PER_SEC))
        dispatch_after(endTime, dispatch_get_main_queue(), {
            application.endBackgroundTask(taskId);
        })
    });
    }
}
```

You should recognize most of this code from our earlier discussion. The part that's specific to the weather application is bracketed by the dispatch_async() call, where we call the handleWatchExtensionRequest() method of the WatchAppWeatherRequestHandler class, which we'll create shortly. We decided what this method needs to do during the implementation of the WatchAppWeatherModelLoader class in the previous section: if it has current forecast data for any of the cities in the request from the extension, it should return it in the form of an array of CityWeather objects. Whatever is returned is sent back to the WatchKit extension by calling the reply closure. For the other cities, it needs to request a new forecast and send notifications via the Darwin bridge when it arrives.

Now let's implement the WatchAppWeatherRequestHandler class. Select the LWKWeather group in the Project Navigator, right-click, and add a nested group called Watch Communication. Right-click on the new group, select New File..., and then select Swift File from the iOS Source section of the dialog that appears. Click Next, name the file WatchAppWeatherRequestHandler.swift, and save it.

This class is going to be a singleton, so let's first add the boilerplate code that's needed to implement a sharedInstance() method that returns the singleton instance:

```
import Foundation
import SharedCode

public class WatchAppWeatherRequestHandler {
    // Holder for the shared instance of this class.
    private static var token: dispatch_once:t = 0
    private static var instance: WatchAppWeatherRequestHandler?

    // Gets the shared instance of this class.
    public class func sharedInstance() -> WatchAppWeatherRequestHandler {
        dispatch_once(&token) {
            self.instance = WatchAppWeatherRequestHandler()
        }
        return instance!
    }
}
```

From our earlier discussions about the way in which this class should work, we know that it needs to register itself as an observer of the iOS application's in-memory weather model so that it can notify the extension when the model changes. The natural place to register for this notification is in an initializer. Add the code for the initializer and a method that handles the notifications:

```
// Gets the shared instance of this class.
public class func sharedInstance() -> WatchAppWeatherRequestHandler {
    dispatch_once(&token) {
        self.instance = WatchAppWeatherRequestHandler()
    }
    return instance!
}

// Private initializer to ensure a single instance
private init() {
    // Register for notifications of weather changes/load errors.
    NSNotificationCenter.defaultCenter().addObserver(self,
            selector: "onNotification:",
            name: nil, object: AppWeatherModel.sharedInstance())
}


// Handler for notifications from the iOS app weather model.
@objc public func onNotification(notification: NSNotification) {
    if notification.name ==
            WeatherModel.NotificationNames.weatherModelChanged
        || notification.name ==
            WeatherModel.NotificationNames.weatherModelLoadFailed {
        // Notification that weather data has been loaded or
        // load failed. Send to WatchKit extension via Darwin
        // notification center, if the expected payload is present.
        if let userInfo = notification.userInfo,
            let cityCodes = userInfo["cityCodes"] as? [Int] {
            for cityCode in cityCodes {
                // Send a Darwin center notification using the
                // city code as the name.
                DarwinNotificationCenterBridge.
                        postNotificationForName("\(cityCode)")
            }
        }
    }
}
```

The notification from the model (which is the application's AppWeatherModel instance) will report either a change in the model due to the arrival of new forecast data, or a failure to load updated weather. In either case, the notification should include the city or cities to which it relates as an array of city codes stored in the userInfo directionary under the key cityCodes.

If it does, the onNotification() method sends over the Darwin bridge one notification for each city, with the city code (in string form) as the notification name. You've already seen the code that receives and handles these messages—it's in the onNotificationReceived() method in the WatchAppWeatherModel class. Review the code or the description of it in "Updating the Weather Model Classes" if you have forgotten how these notifications are processed in the WatchKit extension.

Finally, we need to implement the handleWatchKitExtensionRequest() method. Add the following code to the WatchAppWeatherRequestHandler class:

```
// Handles a request from the Watch extension. The command name
// is extracted from the request dictionary, the request is handled
// and the reply is stored in a new dictionary, which is returned to
// the caller. This method must be called in the main thread.
public func handleWatchExtensionRequest(
        request: [NSObject : AnyObject]) -> [NSObject : AnyObject] {
    assert(NSThread.isMainThread())

    // Create the reply dictionary.
    var reply = [NSObject : AnyObject]()

    // Get the city codes for which we need to get weather data.
    if let cityCodes = request
        [WatchAppWeatherInterface.LoadWeatherCommandName] as? [Int] {
        let timeNow = NSDate()
        var citiesToLoad = [Int]()

        // For each requested city, get the current weather state. If
        // there is none or if the weather is old, request a reload.
        for cityCode in cityCodes {
            let currentWeather = AppWeatherModel.sharedInstance().
                                        weatherByCity[cityCode]
            if currentWeather == nil || currentWeather!.shouldReload {
                // No weather or the weather is out of date
                citiesToLoad.append(cityCode)
            }
        }

        // Initiate load for any cities for which we do not have
        // current data. Later, we will get notification of success or
        // failure from the notification center and we will send a message
        // to the WatchKit extension as a Darwin notification
        if !citiesToLoad.isEmpty {
            AppWeatherModel.sharedInstance().fetchWeatherForCities(
                    citiesToLoad, always: false)
        }
```

```
        // Now get the current state for each requested city.
        var cityWeatherList = [CityWeather]()
        for cityCode in cityCodes {
            if let currentWeather = AppWeatherModel.sharedInstance().
                                    weatherByCity[cityCode] {
                cityWeatherList.append(currentWeather)
            }
        }

        // Encode the reply data as NSData and add it to the reply map.
        let data = NSKeyedArchiver.archivedDataWithRootObject(
                                    cityWeatherList)
        reply[WatchAppWeatherInterface.LoadWeatherReplyName] = data
    }

    return reply
}
```

You already know what this method does, so let's briefly go through how it does it. The first few lines get the array of city codes for which weather data is required from the request dictionary. For each city, the AppWeatherModel's weatherByCity dictionary is checked to see if there is current data. If there isn't, the city code is added to the citiesToLoad array. Once all of the requested cities have been checked, if this array is not empty, it is passed to the AppWeatherModel's fetchWeatherForCities() method, which will arrange for new data for each city to be requested from the openweathermap. org server. That data will arrive at some time in the future, and its arrival will be notified to the WatchKit extension by the code in the onNotification() method that we just added to this class.

Next, the CityWeather objects for *all* the cities that were in the request dictionary passed to the method are added to the cityWeatherList array, which is then archived into an NSData object and returned to the caller of this method. For those cities for which current data is available, the CityWeather object that is sent to the extension will contain the weather data and will be in the LOADED state. For the cities for which weather data has not yet been loaded or has expired, the CityWeather object will be in LOADING state and will contain the expired data, if there is any.

That completes the implementation of the WatchAppWeatherRequestHandler class. All that remains is to implement the two interface controllers for the WatchKit application screens, which is our task for the final two sections of this chapter.

> **Note**   You'll find a copy of the source code for the project in its current state in the folder 7 - LWKWeather - Interim in the example source code archive.

Implementing the Main Interface Controller

Finally, we are going to start building the user interface of our WatchKit weather application. We'll start, logically enough, with the main interface controller, the screen that the user sees when the application is launched. A typical example of this is shown in Figure 7-15.

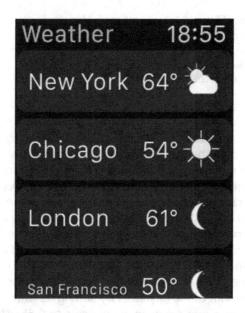

Figure 7-15. The main interface controller

This screen consists of a table that displays the cities that are configured in the DisplayedCityInfoModel. The rows in the table map one-to-one to the city codes in the model's displayedCities property. Because the rows are all of the same type, we're going to need only one table row controller class, which will contain three user interface objects: two labels to display the city name and the temperature and an image that displays an icon that represents the forecast weather. We can get the city name from the city's City object in the CityModel, and the weather information will come from the WatchAppWeatherModel class. Let's start by building the table row controller in the storyboard and then we'll discuss how to create and manage the table itself.

Adding the Table to the Storyboard

Select Interface.storyboard in the Project Navigator to open the storyboard in the editor. Then drag a table from the Object Library and drop it onto the empty interface controller that Xcode gave us when we created the project. Open InterfaceController.swift in the Assistant Editor and Control-drag from the table to the top of the class definition to create an outlet called table. While we have this file open, delete the delegate property and the test code that we added to the awakeWithContext() method earlier. When you've done that, the top of the class definition should look like this:

```
class InterfaceController: WKInterfaceController {
    @IBOutlet weak var table: WKInterfaceTable!

    override func awakeWithContext(context: AnyObject?) {
        super.awakeWithContext(context)

    }
}
```

Now let's construct the table row controller. Drag a label from the Object Library and drop it onto the table row in the storyboard. This is the label that will display the city name, so we want it to always be aligned to the left of the row, which is the default. We would also like it to be vertically centered, so change the Vertical attribute to Center. City names vary considerably in width, from Paris at one extreme to Bridgetown, Barbados at the other. It's not really going to be possible to always fit the whole name in the space available on the screen, especially given that we also need to include the temperature and an icon. Furthermore, we don't want a long city name to steal space from the other two items in the row. To stop that from happening, fix the width of the city label by setting its Width attribute to Relative to Container and the associated value to 0.55. We'll also allow WatchKit to reduce the font size a little so that the user can see as much as possible of the city name even if it's quite long. To do that, set the Min Scale attribute to 0.6. You can see the effect of this in the row for San Francisco in Figure 7-15.

> **Note**   Instead of allowing the font to scale, we could set the Lines attribute to 0 to allow long names to overflow onto a second line. That has the effect of automatically making the table row taller to match, but unfortunately, it doesn't look very appealing—try it and see for yourself.

Now let's add the temperature label. Drag another label onto the row controller and drop it to the right of the city name label. To position it properly, set its Horizontal attribute to Right and its Vertical attribute to Center. To get an idea of how wide it's going to be at run time, change its text to 82.

Finally, drag and drop an image object to the right of the temperature label. If you have difficulty positioning it properly, drag it over the Document Outline instead and drop it below the temperature label (which shows up as 82). Set its Mode attribute to Center, its Horizontal attribute to Right, and its Vertical attribute to Center. At the moment, the image is taking up too much space in the storyboard and it's hiding the temperature label. That's because it's set to fit its content, and the storyboard editor has no idea how large the image that it contains will be. In fact, the weather icons are all 24-point squares, so we might as well use that fact to make the storyboard look like it will at run time. To do that, change the Width and Height attributes of the image to Fixed and set their associated values to 24. The row controller should now look like the one shown in Figure 7-16.

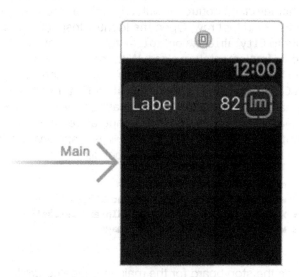

Figure 7-16. The table row controller for the main interface controller

Our next task is to create the row controller class and add outlets that are linked to the user interface objects that we just added in the storyboard. In the Project Navigator, right-click the LWK Weather WatchKit Extension group and in the pop-up, select New Group. Change the group's name to Main Interface Controller. We're going to use this group to keep the code for the main interface controller in one place, so drag the file InterfaceController.swift into it. Right-click on the group and select New File... from the pop-up. In the dialog that appears, choose Swift File from the iOS Source section and click Next. Name the file

CityTableRowController.swift and save it. With the file open in the editor, add the import statement and the following empty class definition to it:

```
import Foundation
import WatchKit

class CityTableRowController : NSObject {
}
```

Now switch back to Interface.storyboard and select the table row controller in the Document Outline. In the Attributes Inspector, set the Identifier attribute to CityTableRowController and leave the Selectable attribute checked because we want the user to be able to tap on a row to push another interface controller with a more detailed view of the weather for the city in that row. Open the Identity Inspector and set the Class attribute to CityTableRowController to link the row controller in the storyboard to its implementation class. With the link made, we can create outlets for the three user interface objects in the row controller. Open CityTableRowController.swift in the Assistant Editor and Control-drag from the city name label to the top of the class definition to create an outlet called cityLabel. Do the same with the temperature label and the image, naming the outlets temperatureLabel and image respectively. When you've done that, the row controller class should look like this:

```
class CityTableRowController : NSObject {
    @IBOutlet weak var cityLabel: WKInterfaceLabel!
    @IBOutlet weak var temperatureLabel: WKInterfaceLabel!
    @IBOutlet weak var image: WKInterfaceImage!
}
```

That completes the storyboard for the main interface controller. We're almost ready to write the controller code. The last thing we need to do is add the weather icons for the image object. You'll find these icons in the 7 - LWKWeather Images folder. Select Images.xcassets in the LWK Weather WatchKit App group and then drag all the images apart from AppIcon40@2x. png into it. The image you didn't drag is the application's home screen icon. To install that, select the AppIcon image set and drag AppIcon40@2x.png into the slot labeled Home Screen (All), as shown in Figure 7-17.

Figure 7-17. The asset catalog with the home screen icon installed

Building and Maintaining the Table

All the code in the interface controller is concerned with constructing the table based on the content of the DisplayedCityInfoModel and the WatchKit extension's copy of the weather model and keeping it up to date with changes in either of those models. Here's the overall plan:

▨ We'll build the initial set of table rows when the controller's awakeWithContext() method is called. Because the extension may not have been active for some time (or at all, if this is the first time the user has started the WatchKit app), some or all of the weather data that is available may not be current, so we'll request updated data if necessary.

▨ When the interface controller is activated, we'll check whether the table is still displaying current data. This is necessary because while the controller was inactive, the user could have changed the list of displayed cities or the temperature display preference, and some or all of the weather data may have expired. In order to be notified when new weather data arrives, we'll register as an observer of the weather model.

▨ Although it's unlikely, weather data may expire while the controller is active. To handle that, we'll run a timer that's set to expire when the oldest data in the table passes its reload time. When this happens, we'll refresh the data and restart the timer.

▨ Also while the controller is active, the user may use the iOS application's configuration screens to change the list of displayed cities or the temperature display preference. To keep track of this, we'll register as an observer of the DisplayedCityInfoModel and we'll update the table if any changes are notified.

■ Finally, the iOS application may fetch new weather data at any time. When it does so, it will send a message over the Darwin bridge. If the WatchKit app is active (that is, not suspended and not terminated) when this happens, it will update its copy of the weather model, and we'll need to show the new data. This will happen automatically, because the interface controller is already an observer of the weather model for the purpose of receiving new data in responses to its own requests.

As you can see, most of the logic is going to be concerned with building and updating the table rows. We'll implement this logic in two methods:

■ The updateTable() method will assume that the current set of table row controllers matches the list of cities in the DisplayedCityInfoModel and will update the user interface objects in each row based on the data that's currently in the WatchKit app's copy of the weather model. As it does so, it will check the reloadTime in the CityWeather object for each city in the table and set a timer to expire at the earliest reload time, at which point new data will be requested if it hasn't already been received.

■ The checkAndRebuildTable() method will compare the cities in the table row controllers to the list of displayed cities in the DisplayedCityInfoModel. If they don't match, the table will be rebuilt, and the updateTable() method will then be called to install the data in each row.

We'll start by implementing these two methods. Once we've done so, it will be a simple task to write the rest of the code. First, let's add some properties that these methods need. Add the following code shown in bold at the top of the InterfaceController class:

```
class InterfaceController: WKInterfaceController {
    @IBOutlet weak var table: WKInterfaceTable!

    // The cities for which data is currently displayed.
    private var displayedCityCodes = [Int]()

    // Timer used to reload weather.
    private var reloadTimer: NSTimer?

    // Next city for which data should be reloaded.
    private var reloadCityCode: Int?
```

The reloadTimer property keeps a reference to the timer that will fire when the oldest weather data in the table expires and the reloadCityCode property is the city code of the city for that row. The displayedCityCodes array keeps the city codes for each row in the table, in display order. In the checkAndRebuildTable() method, we'll compare this array to the displayedCities property of the DisplayedCityInfoModel to determine whether we need to rebuild the table.

Next, add an initializer:

```
private var reloadCityCode: Int?

// MARK: -
// MARK: Initialization
override init() {
    super.init()
    WatchAppWeatherModel.sharedInstance().loadWeatherModel()
}
```

The initializer just loads the WatchAppWeatherModel from the persisted state in the shared container. It's possible that neither the WatchKit application nor the iOS application has been used for some time, in which case some or all of the data that was loaded may have expired. We'll find out whether this is the case when we call checkAndRebuildTable() in the awakeWithContext() method.

Now add the implementation of the checkAndRebuildTable() method:

```
// MARK: -
// MARK: Table construction
// Rebuilds the table rows if the displayed cities list
// changes and recreates the table data if so.
private func checkAndRebuildTable() {
    DisplayedCityInfoModel.sharedInstance().loadDisplayedCities()
    let cityCodes =
            DisplayedCityInfoModel.sharedInstance().displayedCities;
    let citiesChanged = cityCodes != displayedCityCodes
    if citiesChanged {
        // Cities changing.
        displayedCityCodes = cityCodes
        table.setNumberOfRows(displayedCityCodes.count,
                            withRowType: "CityTableRowController")
        WatchAppWeatherModel.sharedInstance()
            .fetchWeatherForCities(displayedCityCodes, always: false)
    }
}
```

This method first loads the list of displayed cities from the shared container, to be sure it is up to date. Then the list of cities in its displayedCityCodes is compared to cityCodes, the property we just added to hold the list of city codes that are in the table. If these are the same, then the table already has the correct set of rows (although their content may be out of date). If they are not the same, we update the cityCodes variable and then call the setNumberOfRows(_:withRowTypes:) method of the table to replace the existing rows (if any) with the correct number of new ones, all using the row controller with identifier CityTableRowController. We then call the fetchWe atherForCities(_:always:) method of WatchAppWeatherModel to get up-to-date weather data for all the cities in the table. This will only actually request new data for a city if the data that is already in the model has expired, so it's possible that this call will not actually need to do anything.

The checkAndRebuildTable() method makes sure that the table contains the correct rows, but it does not populate those rows with any data. That's the function of the updateTable() method, which loops over all the table rows, installing the forecast data for each city. Add the implementation shown here to the InterfaceController class:

```
// MARK: -
// MARK: Table updates
// Updates the table based on the current weather data.
private func updateTable() {
    var reloadTime = NSDate.distantFuture() as! NSDate
    reloadCityCode = nil;
    for index in 0..<displayedCityCodes.count {
        var imageName: String?
        var temperature = ""
        let rowController = table.rowControllerAtIndex(index)
                                as! CityTableRowController
        let cityCode = displayedCityCodes[index]
        let cityName = CityModel.sharedInstance().cityForCode(
                            cityCode)?.name ?? "Unknown City"
        if let cityWeather = WatchAppWeatherModel.sharedInstance().
                                weatherByCity[cityCode],
            let weatherDetails = cityWeather.currentWeather
                where cityWeather.state == .LOADED {
                if let temp = weatherDetails.temperature {
                    temperature = WeatherUtilities.temperatureString(temp)
                }
                imageName = WeatherUtilities.selectWeatherImage(
                                weatherDetails.weather,
                                day: weatherDetails.day ?? true)

                // Update the reloadTime to the earliest reload time
                // encountered so far
```

```
            let thisReloadTime = cityWeather.reloadTime
            if thisReloadTime.compare(reloadTime) == .OrderedAscending {
                reloadTime = thisReloadTime
                reloadCityCode = cityCode
            }
        }

        rowController.cityLabel.setText(cityName)
        rowController.temperatureLabel.setText(temperature)
        rowController.image.setImageNamed(imageName)
    }

    // Start a timer so that the weather is reloaded when it expires.
    if (reloadCityCode != nil) {
        if (reloadTimer == nil || !reloadTimer!.valid ||
                reloadTimer!.fireDate.compare(reloadTime)
                                == .OrderedDescending) {
            reloadTimer?.invalidate()
            reloadTimer = NSTimer(fireDate: reloadTime, interval: 0,
                        target: self, selector: "reloadWeather:",
                        userInfo: nil, repeats: false)
            NSRunLoop.currentRunLoop().addTimer(reloadTimer!,
                            forMode: NSDefaultRunLoopMode)
        }
    }
}
```

The city code for row N in the table can be obtained from the entry with index N in the displayedCityCodes property, which will have been set by the checkAndRebuildTable() method. The updateTable() method loops over this property, getting the city code and the row controller for the current row. Given the city code, the city name can be obtained from the City object in the CityModel and the weather information from the weatherByCity dictionary of the weather model. If the weather data exists and it's in loaded state, the temperature is converted to string form and an image that represents the current weather condition is obtained by calling the selectWeatherImage(_:day:) method in the WeatherUtilities class, which is shared with the iOS application. I'm not going to show that method here because it's just a big switch statement that maps a weather condition (of type WeatherDetails.WeatherCondition, such as Thunder, Drizzle, and so on) to the name of one of the images we added to the Images.xcassets file of the WatchKit App target. The only slight twist is that there are two different images for each different weather condition: one to be used when it's daytime, the other for the night, selected by the value of the day argument. If there is no weather data available or the weather is still being loaded, the temperature string will be empty and the image is nil. Finally, the city name, temperature, and weather icon are installed in the two labels and the image in the row controller for the current row.

Once all the table rows have been updated, a timer is started that will expire at the earliest reloadTime of all the items of weather data in the table. The rather complicated if statement at the end of the method ensures that a timer is not started if there's already a timer running that expires at the same time, or if none of the table rows contains valid data. When the timer expires, the reloadWeather() method will be called. Here's the code for that method, which you should add to the class:

```
// Reloads data for the all cities for which the weather
// data has expired.
func reloadWeather(_: NSTimer) {
    var citiesToReload = [Int]()
    let cityCodes = DisplayedCityInfoModel.sharedInstance().displayedCities
    for cityCode in cityCodes {
        if let cityWeather = WatchAppWeatherModel.sharedInstance().
                weatherByCity[cityCode] {
            if cityWeather.shouldReload {
                citiesToReload.append(cityCode)
            }
        }
    }

    if citiesToReload.count > 0 {
        WatchAppWeatherModel.sharedInstance().
                fetchWeatherForCities(citiesToReload, always: true)
    }
}
```

This method is another loop over all the displayed cities, checking whether its weather data needs to be reloaded by inspecting the shouldReload property of its CityWeather object. This is a computed property that returns true if the reload time has passed and the weather data is not currently being reloaded. The city codes of all the cities for which this property is true are added to the citiesToReload array, which is then passed to the fetchWea therForCities(_:always:) method of the WatchAppWeatherModel class, with which you should by now be very familiar.

We've almost completed the implementation of this class. All we need to do now is handle the interface controller's lifecycle events and the notifications that are delivered when the weather model or the DisplayedCityInfoModel changes. Let's start with the lifecycle methods. Add the code shown in bold to awakeWithContext(), willActivate(), and didDeactivate():

```
override func awakeWithContext(context: AnyObject?) {
    super.awakeWithContext(context)

    setTitle("Weather")
```

```swift
    // Configure interface objects here.
    // Build the table based on the current displayed
    // cities.
    checkAndRebuildTable()
}

override func willActivate() {
    super.willActivate()

    // Listen to changes in the displayed city list and
    // the celsius/farenheit setting.
    DisplayedCityInfoModel.sharedInstance().delegate = self

    // Rebuild the table if the displayed cities list or the
    // temperature setting has changed. Update based on the
    // current weather data.
    checkAndRebuildTable()
    updateTable()

    // Observe notification of weather model changes.
    NSNotificationCenter.defaultCenter().addObserver(self,
                    selector: "onNotification:", name: nil,
                    object: WatchAppWeatherModel.sharedInstance())
}

override func didDeactivate() {
    DisplayedCityInfoModel.sharedInstance().delegate = nil
    NSNotificationCenter.defaultCenter().removeObserver(self)
    reloadTimer?.invalidate()
}
```

We've already mentioned what needs to be done in these methods, so this code should not contain any surprises. In the awakeWithContext() method, we set the controller title (although we could also have set that in the storyboard) and call the checkAndRebuildTable() method to make sure that table has the correct initial set of rows.

In willActivate(), we register ourselves as the delegate of the DisplayedCityInfoModel so that we are notified when the user changes any configuration information. At the moment, there is a compilation error for this code because the InterfaceController class does not yet conform to the delegate protocol. We'll fix that shortly. Next, we call checkAndRebuildTable() and updateTable() to install the most current data in the table, and finally we register for notifications of changes in the weather model.

The didDeactivate() method simply reverses some of the steps we took in willActivate(), unregistering as the delegate of the DisplayedCityInfoModel and for notifications from the model.

Now let's add the conformance to the `DisplayedCityInfoModel` delegate protocol. Start by declaring conformance in the class definition:

```
class InterfaceController:
        WKInterfaceController, DisplayedCityInfoModelDelegate {
```

Then, add the method that's called to report changes in the model:

```
// MARK: -
// MARK: DisplayedCityInfoModelDelegate implementation
// Method called when the list of displayed cities or the temperature
// setting changes. Rebuild the table if necessary and update the
// table content.
func displayedCityInfoDidChange(model: DisplayedCityInfoModel) {
    checkAndRebuildTable()
    updateTable()
}
```

If this method is called, then either the user has switched between Celsius and Farenheit or the list of displayed cities has changed. We handle both cases by calling checkAndRebuildTable() followed by updateTable().

> **Note** Theoretically, if the user switched between Celsius and Farenheit, we only need to call updateTable(). We could add information or a second delegate method so that these cases can be distinguished, but there's little point because neither of these will happen very frequently.

Finally, add the following method to handle notifications from the weather model:

```
// MARK: -
// MARK: Notification handling
// Handles a notification, which means that some data
// in the weather model has changed. If it affects any of
// the cities that we are displaying, update the table.
func onNotification(notification: NSNotification) {
    if let userInfo = notification.userInfo,
        let cityCodes = userInfo["cityCodes"] as? [Int] {
        for cityCode in cityCodes {
            if find(displayedCityCodes, cityCode) != nil {
                updateTable()
                break
            }
        }
    }
}
```

All notifications from this model include a key with the name `cityCodes`, the value of which is an array containing the codes for the cities that are affected by the notification (typically, new forecast data has been received). This method checks whether any of the cities in the notification are in the interface controller's table and, if so, calls `updateTable()` to redisplay everything.

> **Note**   Again, we could make this more efficient by only updating rows for the cities that are affected by the notification. However, the benefit of doing so is minimal because new forecast data is only obtained once per hour, by default.

That's it! Now you should be able to run the WatchKit application and see the weather for your configured cities appear, as shown in Figure 7-15. With the WatchKit app running, start the iOS application by tapping its icon on the home screen and open its configuration screen. If you change the order of cities by dragging up and down, you should see the changes reflected immediately on the watch. This happens because the iOS instance of the `DisplayedInfoCityModel` class sends a notification of the change over the Darwin bridge. The notification is received by the WatchKit application's instance of the model, which reloads itself from the shared `NSUserDefaults` and then notifies its delegate, which, as you've just seen, is the `InterfaceController`. Similarly, if you add or remove cities, you'll see that change take effect immediately on the watch, and, after a short delay, the weather for a newly added city will appear.

Implement the Forecast Detail Interface Controller

When the user taps on a row in the main interface controller, we're going to push another controller to display the forecast for that city for today and tomorrow. Figure 7-18 shows what that interface controller looks like.

Figure 7-18. The forecast detail interface controller

The interface consists of a summary area at the top and a table with the detailed forecast information, broken down into three-hour blocks. The summary information is taken from the city's CityWeather object, and the data to populate the table comes from the first two DayForecast entries in its detailsByDay property. As we did with the main interface controller, we'll start by configuring the new controller in the storyboard and then we'll write the code.

Adding the Controller to the Storyboard

Let's start by creating the new controller's implementation class. Add a new group called Details Interface Controller nested inside the LWK Weather WatchKit Extension group, right-click the new group, and select New File... from the pop-up that appears. From the iOS Source section of the dialog, choose Cocoa Touch Class and press Next. Name the class DetailsInterfaceController, make it a subclass of WKInterfaceController, click Next, and save it. Now open the storyboard by selecting Interface. storyboard in the Project Navigator. Drag an interface controller from the Object Library, drop it next to the main interface controller, and in the Identity Inspector, set the new controller's class name to DetailsInterfaceController.

The summary information at the top of the controller has three parts: at the top and bottom are labels that show the city name and the weather summary, and in the middle is a horizontal group containing an image for the current weather condition and a label for the temperature. To create this layout, drag a label, a group, and another label onto the controller and configure the labels as follows:

- For the top label, change the Text attribute to City, set the font to Headline so that it stands out a little, and set the Alignment to center and the Width attribute to Relative to Container.

- For the bottom label, change the Text attribute to Summary, the Text Color to Light Gray, Alignment to center, and Width to Relative to Container.

Next, we'll add an image and a label to the group. Drag an image onto the group and then select the group again and drag a label onto it, dropping it to the right of the image. Select the image and set its Mode to Center, its Vertical attribute to Center, its Width to Relative to Container with an associated value of 0.5 so that it takes up exactly half of the available width, and its Height to Fixed with a value of 24 points. Now select the label, set its Text attribute to 82, its Alignment to center, its Vertical attribute to Center, and its Width to Relative to Container with a value of 0.5.

Between the summary and the table, we need to add a separator, but we don't want it to completely fill the width of the screen. To create a little space on the left and right of the separator, we'll place it in a group and set the group's insets. Drag a group from the Object Library and drop it below the Summary label. In the Attributes Inspector, set its Layout attribute to Vertical, its Insets attribute to Custom and set the Top, Bottom, Left, and Right inset values to 2, 2, 8, and 8 respectively. Then drag a separator and drop it into the group. You should see the effect of the group's insets to the left and right of the separator. Change the separator's Color attribute to Dark Gray. At this point, the interface controller should look like Figure 7-19.

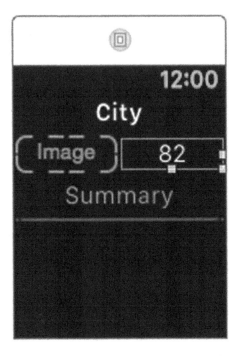

Figure 7-19. The summary area of the forecast detail interface controller in the storyboard

The last piece of the controller's interface is the table. Drag a table from the Object Library and drop it below the group containing the separator. This table needs two different row styles—one will act as a section header and will show a date, and the other will display weather information. That means we'll need two different row controllers, so set the table's Rows attribute to 2.

Before we start work on the row controllers, let's create the outlets in the DetailsInterfaceController class for the user interface objects that we've already added. Open DetailsInterfaceController.swift in the Assistant Editor and create outlets as follows:

- Control-drag from the City label to the top of the DetailsInterfaceController class and create an outlet called cityNameLabel.

- Control-drag from the image to create an outlet called image.

- Control-drag from the temperature label, creating an outlet called tempLabel.

- Control-drag from the summary label and call the outlet summaryLabel.

- Finally, Control-drag from the table to create an outlet called table.

Next, let's create the table's row controller classes so that we can link the user interface objects in the storyboard to outlets as we create them. In the Details Interface Controller group, add a new Swift file called Details TableRowControllers.swift, open that file in the editor, and add these two empty class definitions:

```
import Foundation
import WatchKit

// Table row that contains the date.
public class DateRowController : NSObject {
}

// Table row that contains the weather details for
// part of a day.
public class DetailsRowController : NSObject {
}
```

Now go back to Interface.storyboard and select the top table row. In the Attributes Inspector, set its Identifier to DateRowController. Select the second row controller and set its Identifier to DetailsRowController.

Now open DetailsTableRowControllers.swift in the Assistant Editor so that you can easily access it when creating outlets. Select the top table row in the storyboard, open the Identity Inspector, and set the Class attribute to DateRowController. If you are having trouble doing this, it's probably because you selected the group inside the table row. You can fix that by selecting the row in the Document Outline instead. Once you've done that, select the other table row and set its Class to DetailsRowController.

The top row controller will be used to display a date, so we just need to add a label to it. Drag a label from the Object Library and drop it onto the table row in the storyboard. In the Attributes Inspector, set its Text attribute to Date and its Font to Caption 2. Next, select the table row's group and set its Insets attribute to Custom. Leave all four inset values at 0 so that the row occupies as little space as possible. Also set the group's Color attribute to something that's a little lighter than the background, but not too light—you'll probably find the RGB values (55, 55, 55) work well. Finally, set the Height attribute to Size To Fit Content.

This table row requires just one outlet. Control-drag from the label to the DateRowController class and create an outlet called dateLabel.

The bottom table row requires two labels and an image. Drag and drop two labels and then an image into the table row and use the Attributes Inspector to set their attributes as follows:

- For the first label, set the Text Color to Light Gray and the Vertical attribute to Center.

- For the second label, again set the Text Color to Light Gray and the Vertical attribute to Center. Also set the Horizontal attribute to Right. When you do that, the label will temporarily move to the other side of the image.

- For the image, set the Mode to Center, the Horizontal attribute to Right (which will make it move back to the right side of the second label), the Vertical attribute to Center, and the Width and Height attributes to Fixed with a value of 24.

To complete this row, select the row's group in the Document Outline and change its Insets attribute to Custom, set the Left and Right inset values to 4 and 2 respectively, and set the Height attribute to Size To Fit Content.

To create the outlets, Control-drag from the left label to the DetailsViewController to create an outlet called timeLabel. Then create an outlet called tempLabel for the second label and another called image for the image.

There's only one more thing to do in the storyboard: arrange for the DetailsViewController to be pushed when the user taps a table row in the main interface controller. We can do that in code by handling the table row selection event, but here we're going to use a storyboard segue instead. In the Document Outline, select the table row for the main interface controller (the node labeled CityTableRowController) and Control-drag from it to the Details interface controller (either in the Document Outline or in the storyboard). To create the segue, release the mouse button and choose push from the pop-up that appears. When you've done that, your storyboard is complete, and it should look like Figure 7-20.

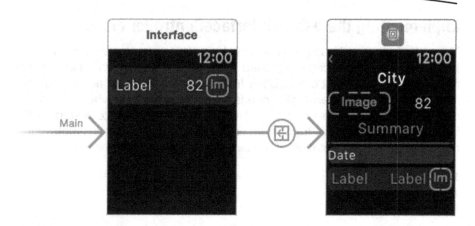

Figure 7-20. The completed storyboard

If you run the WatchKit application now and tap on a city in the main interface controller, you'll see that the details interface controller is pushed, but it does not yet display any useful information. We'll take care of that in the next section. Before we do so, we'll need to arrange for the city code of the city whose weather the details interface controller should display to be passed to it. As discussed in Chapter 5, the way to do that is to supply the city code as the context argument of the details interface controller's awakeWithContext() method. When, as here, a controller is pushed as a result of a storyboard segue, the initiating controller is required to supply the context by overriding a method of the WKInterfaceController class. In the case of a segue from a table row, we need to override the contextForSegueW ithIdentifier(_:inTable:rowIndex) method. To do that, add the following code to the InterfaceController class:

```
// Gets the context for the segue from a table row.
override func contextForSegueWithIdentifier(segueIdentifier: String,
                inTable table: WKInterfaceTable,
                rowIndex: Int) -> AnyObject? {
    return DisplayedCityInfoModel.sharedInstance().displayedCities[rowIndex]
}
```

This method obtains the city code for the row that was tapped by using the row number that's passed to it as an index into the DisplayedCityInfoModel's displayedCities array, which is in one-to-one correspondence with the rows in the table. If you now run the WatchKit example again with a breakpoint on the details interface controller's awakeWithContext() method, you'll see that it receives the correct city code when it is pushed.

Implementing the DetailsInterfaceController class

The task of the DetailsInterfaceController class is to display the data for the city whose city code is passed to its awakeWithContext() method. It needs to get the current city weather from the weather model and update itself if that data changes. It also needs to request new data when the data that it currently has expires, or if it has already expired. Let's start by importing the SharedCode framework and adding some properties that we'll need and the implementation of the awakeWithContext() method:

```
import WatchKit
import Foundation
import SharedCode

class DetailsInterfaceController: WKInterfaceController {
    @IBOutlet weak var cityNameLabel: WKInterfaceLabel!
    @IBOutlet weak var image: WKInterfaceImage!
    @IBOutlet weak var tempLabel: WKInterfaceLabel!
    @IBOutlet weak var summaryLabel: WKInterfaceLabel!
    @IBOutlet weak var table: WKInterfaceTable!

    // Maximum number of days of weather to display
    private static let maxDays = 2
    private var cityCode: Int!
    private var reloadTimer: NSTimer?

    override func awakeWithContext(context: AnyObject?) {
        super.awakeWithContext(context)

        // Configure interface objects here.
        setTitle("Weather")

        cityCode = context as! Int
        let cityName = CityModel.sharedInstance().cityForCode(
                        cityCode)?.name ?? "Unknown City"
        cityNameLabel.setText(cityName)
    }
```

In the awakeForContext() method, we set the controller's title and get the city code by casting the context value to an Int and then store it in the cityCode property. Given the city code, we get the city name from the CityModel object and use it to set the Text property of the city name label. In the (very unlikely) case that we don't find an entry for the city in the CityModel, we use the text Unknown City instead. This should only happen if there is programming error, or if the city has not been included in the cities.plist file. If you run the example now, you can verify that the correct city name is shown when you tap a row of the main interface controller.

Now add the following code in bold to the willActivate() and didDeactivate() methods:

```
override func willActivate() {
    super.willActivate()

    // Update the view and arrange to reload weather
    // when it expires.
    updateDetails()

    // Observe notification of weather model changes.
    NSNotificationCenter.defaultCenter().addObserver(self,
        selector: "onNotification:", name: nil,
        object: WatchAppWeatherModel.sharedInstance())
}

override func didDeactivate() {
    super.didDeactivate()
    NSNotificationCenter.defaultCenter().removeObserver(self)
    reloadTimer?.invalidate()
}
```

In willActivate(), we first invoke a method called updateDetails() that we haven't yet implemented (so there is a compilation error for this line at the moment). This method updates the summary information at the top of the interface controller and, if necessary, it also populates (or repopulates) the forecast table. You'll see the implementation of this method shortly. We also register for notifications from the weather model so that we can keep the user interface up to date when the city's weather forecast changes. The didDeactivate() method removes this registration and also invalidates the reload timer, which is used to request new data when the current data expires.

Next, add the onNotification() method, which is called when a notification from the weather model is received:

```
// Method called when weather updates are received. Updates the
// view if the current city weather has been updated.
func onNotification(notification: NSNotification) {
    if let cityCodes = notification.userInfo?["cityCodes"] as? [Int] {
        if find(cityCodes, cityCode) != nil {
            updateDetails()
        }
    }
}
```

The notification's payload is an array of city codes for which the forecast data has changed. This method checks whether the array includes the city code for the controller's city and, if so, it calls the updateDetails() method, thus making sure that the controller is always displaying the most up-to-date data. Here's the code for that method, which you should add to the controller class:

```
// Updates the view from the current model state
private func updateDetails() {
    var updateTable = false
    if let cityWeather = WatchAppWeatherModel.sharedInstance().
                            weatherByCity[cityCode] {
        var temperature = " "
        var imageName: String?
        var condition = " "

        switch cityWeather.state {
        case .INIT:
            // Nothing to do
            break
        case .LOADING:
            condition = "Loading Weather"

        case .ERROR:
            condition = "Failed to Load Weather"

        case .LOADED:
            if let weatherDetails = cityWeather.currentWeather {
                let reloadTime = cityWeather.reloadTime
                if reloadTime.compare(NSDate()) == .OrderedDescending {
                    // All data is available
                    updateTable = true
                    if let temp = weatherDetails.temperature {
                        temperature = WeatherUtilities.
                                    temperatureString(temp)
                    }

                    if let cond = weatherDetails.weatherDescription {
                        condition = cond
                    }
                    imageName = WeatherUtilities.selectWeatherImage(
                                weatherDetails.weather,
                                day: weatherDetails.day ?? true)
                }
            }
        }
        tempLabel.setText(temperature)
        image.setImageNamed(imageName)
        summaryLabel.setText(condition)
```

```
        // Start a timer to reload the weather data when it expires.
        reloadTimer?.invalidate()
        reloadTimer = NSTimer(fireDate: cityWeather.reloadTime,
                    interval: 0, target: self,
                    selector: "reloadWeather:", userInfo: nil,
                    repeats: false)
        NSRunLoop.currentRunLoop().addTimer(reloadTimer!,
                            forMode: NSDefaultRunLoopMode)
    } else {
        image.setImage(nil)
        tempLabel.setText(" ")
        summaryLabel.setText("No weather available")
    }

    if updateTable {
        // Update the table content from the current weather.
        updateTableContent()
    } else {
        // Clear the table.
        table.setRowTypes([String]())
    }
}
```

The first part of this method gets the CityWeather object for the controller's city from the weather model and uses it to update the summary information at the top of the screen. If there is no CityWeather object, the weather image and temperature are cleared and the condition label shows the text No Weather Available. This is a transient state that occurs before the city's weather has been loaded for the first time. In practice, it's not likely that you'll ever see this because this controller is always reached from the main interface controller, which will have already attempted to load the weather details.

When there is a CityWeather object, what happens depends on its state. If the state is INIT, there is nothing more to display. If it's LOADING, the summary label is set to Loading Weather and everything else is blanked out. Similarly, if the state is ERROR, the text Failed to Load Weather will be displayed and everything else will be blank. In the LOADED state, assuming that the weather data has not expired, we get the current weather and use it to set the temperature label and the weather image. The code that's used here is the same code you saw in our discussion of the main interface controller earlier in this chapter.

Next, a timer is started to trigger a reload of the weather data when its reload time is reached. This timer may or may not expire while the controller is active. If it does not, then, as you have already seen, it is cancelled in the didDeactivate() method. If the timer does fire, the reloadWeather() method is called. Add the code for that method, which simply requests updated forecast data, to the DetailsInterfaceController class:

```
// Reloads weather data when the current data has expired.
func reloadWeather(_: NSTimer) {
    WatchAppWeatherModel.sharedInstance().
                fetchWeatherForCities([cityCode], always: true)
}
```

Returning to the updateDetails() method, you'll see the following code at the end:

```
    if updateTable {
        // Update the table content from the current weather.
        updateTableContent()
    } else {
        // Clear the table.
        table.setRowTypes([String]())
    }
```

The updateTable variable is true only if there is valid weather data (that is, the CityWeather object exists and it is in the LOADED state). If this is the case, then we need to populate the table with the forecast information—otherwise, we call the WKInterfaceTable setRowTypes() method with an empty array, which has the effect of removing all rows from the table. The table is populated by the updateTableContent() method, shown here:

```
// Updates the table from the current weather information.
private func updateTableContent() {
    // Define the row controller types
    var rowTypes = [String]()
    var dayCount = 0
    if let cityWeather = WatchAppWeatherModel.sharedInstance().
                            weatherByCity[cityCode] {
        dayCount = min(cityWeather.detailsByDay.count,
                    DetailsInterfaceController.maxDays)
        for dayIndex in 0..<dayCount {
            let dayForecast = cityWeather.detailsByDay[dayIndex]
            rowTypes.append("DateRowController")
            for weatherDetails in dayForecast.details {
                rowTypes.append("DetailsRowController")
            }
        }
    }
    table.setRowTypes(rowTypes)
```

```
// Configure each row
if let cityWeather = WatchAppWeatherModel.sharedInstance().
                          weatherByCity[cityCode] {
    var rowIndex = 0
    for dayIndex in 0..<dayCount {
        let dateController = table.rowControllerAtIndex(rowIndex++)
                              as! DateRowController
        let dayForecast = cityWeather.detailsByDay[dayIndex]
        dateController.dateLabel.setText(dayForecast.dayString)
        for weatherDetails in dayForecast.details {
            let detailsController =
                    table.rowControllerAtIndex(rowIndex++) as!
                        DetailsRowController
            detailsController.timeLabel.setText(
                          weatherDetails.timeString ?? "")

            var temperature = ""
            if let temp = weatherDetails.temperature {
                temperature = WeatherUtilities.temperatureString(temp)
            }
            detailsController.tempLabel.setText(temperature)

            let imageName = WeatherUtilities.selectWeatherImage(
                            weatherDetails.weather,
                            day: weatherDetails.day ?? true)
            detailsController.image.setImageNamed(imageName)
        }
    }
}
}
```

The first section of this method constructs the array of row controller types for the WKInterfaceTable setRowTypes() method. As discussed earlier, there are two controller types: one for each day and which acts as a section header, the other for the weather information rows for a given day. The following code adds the correct row controller identifiers to the rowTypes array:

```
dayCount = min(cityWeather.detailsByDay.count,
                DetailsInterfaceController.maxDays)
for dayIndex in 0..<dayCount {
    let dayForecast = cityWeather.detailsByDay[dayIndex]
    rowTypes.append("DateRowController")
    for weatherDetails in dayForecast.details {
            rowTypes.append("DetailsRowController")
        }
    }
}
```

The dayCount variable is set to the smaller of the number of days for which there is forecast data and the constant maxDays, which is set to 2. This ensures that no more than two days of weather will be shown. The forecast data for each day is held in a DayForecast object in the CityWeather's detailsByDay array. The loop iterates over this array dayCount times. On each pass, it first adds row type DateRowController to generate the date row and then adds row type DetailsRowController for each block of weather details that we have for that day. The openweathermap.org server returns forecaset data in blocks covering three hours, so there will be eight weather blocks in a full day. Each of these blocks is represented by an object of type WeatherDetails in the details array of the DayForecast object for the day that it corresponds to. Suppose this method were running at 6 p.m. on a particular day. At this point, there would be two WeatherDetails objects in today's DayForecast (covering the period 6 p.m.–9 p.m. and 9 p.m.–midnight) and eight WeatherDetails objects for tomorrow. The resulting rowTypes array would contain these values:

```
DateRowController  (for today)
DetailsRowController  (for the 6pm - 9pm forecast)
DetailsRowController  (for the 9pm - midnight forecast)
DateRowController   (for tomorrow)
DetailsRowController (for the 12am to 3am forecast)
DetailsRowController (for the 3am to 6am forecast)
DetailsRowController  etc...
DetailsRowController
DetailsRowController
DetailsRowController
DetailsRowController
DetailsRowController
```

Having populated the rowTypes array, we call the setRowTypes() method to create the controller instances:

```
table.setRowTypes(rowTypes)
```

The rest of the method retrieves each of the newly created row controller instance and populates its user interface objects. The details are very similar to code that you have already seen, so let's just concentrate on the part that determines which data should be used for each row. Here's the code that does that:

```
var rowIndex = 0
for dayIndex in 0..<dayCount {
    let dateController =
            table.rowControllerAtIndex(rowIndex++) as! DateRowController
    let dayForecast = cityWeather.detailsByDay[dayIndex]
    dateController.dateLabel.setText(dayForecast.dayString)
```

```
for weatherDetails in dayForecast.details {
    let detailsController =
        table.rowControllerAtIndex(rowIndex++) as! DetailsRowController

    // Code not shown
}
}
```

The rowIndex variable is initialized to 0 and will track the index of the row controller that we're working with. The outer loop processes each day of the forecast. The row that corresponds to each day is always of type DateRowController, so it's always safe to cast the controller that we get from the rowControllerAtIndex() method at the top of this loop to DateRowController. The dateLabel in this controller is populated from the DayForecast object for the day that we're handling and then we iterate over the WeatherDetails objects in its details array. We know that we have created a row controller of type DetailsRowController for each of these objects, so we can call rowControllerAtIndex() again and cast the returned controller to DetailsRowController before populating it. If it's still not clear to you how this code works, try setting a breakpoint and stepping through it yourself.

We've now finished writing the WatchKit weather application. Run the finished product to make sure it works. If you weren't typing in the code as you were reading, you'll find a snapshot of the completed source code in the folder 7 - LWKWeather - Final.

Summary

In this very long chapter, we put together everything we learned in the first six chapters of this book to develop a complete, non-trivial WatchKit application. In the process, you saw how to modify the design of the original iOS application to make it usable in the restricted screen space of the watch. You also saw how to use an embedded framework to share code and how to move code from the application into the framework. It's important to be able to share data as well as code, and we looked at how to create a shared container and how to use it to share both data and user defaults. For our simple application, we made use of flat binary files, but for more sophisticated applications that use Core Data, it's equally possible to move the data store to the shared container so that both the iOS and WatchKit applications can access it.

In addition to code and data sharing, it's also useful to be able to communicate by sending messages. We looked at two ways to do this: the Darwin bridge and the `WKInterfaceController` `openParentApplication(_:reply:)` method. I recommend that you make use of the example source code for this chapter to experiment with both of these mechanisms to see what can be done with them.

With this long chapter behind us, let's move on to something simpler and look at how to add a glance to our new weather application.

Chapter 8

Glances, Settings, and Handoff

One of the first things I discovered when I got my Apple Watch is how difficult it can be to launch an application. Starting from the watch face, you have to press the digital crown to open the home screen. That's where the problems start. It's easy to miss the digital crown and touch the screen instead, or you might touch the digital crown in the wrong place, causing it to rotate. On some watch faces (including Astronomy, which is my favorite), either of these actions starts an animation. To stop the animation, you need to press the digital crown to get back to where you started and then you need to press it again to reach the home screen. Once you're on the home screen, your next task is to move the screen around to find the icon for the application you want to launch. Having done that, you may need to move it to the center, to make it large enough to hit reliably, and then touch it. That doesn't sound so bad, but it can be frustratingly difficult to do, especially if you are on the move and also trying to see what's in front of you.

Contrast that with how much easier it is to launch a glance—all you have to do is swipe up from the bottom of the watch face then swipe right until you find the glance that you're looking for. Once you've found the glance and seen enough, you can swipe down to hide it. What's more, next time you swipe up, the same glance will be the first thing you see. Swiping is much easier than trying to click the digital crown! Any WatchKit application can implement a glance, and the good news is that it's easy to do.

In the first part of this chapter, we'll add a glance to the Weather app we developed in Chapter 7. Initially, we'll have the glance show the weather for whichever city the user last viewed in the WatchKit application, but that's not the only possibility. In the second part of the chapter, we'll add a couple more options along with a settings bundle to the WatchKit app, allowing the user to configure the behavior of the glance in the iPhone's Apple Watch application.

By default, touching a glance opens its owning WatchKit application and shows its initial interface controller, or whichever screen the user was last viewing if the WatchKit application is already running. To close the chapter, we'll improve on that behavior by using handoff to make the WatchKit application switch immediately to the weather details for the city that the user was viewing in the glance.

Glances

A glance is your opportunity to give the user a quick and easy way to view and open your application. What you put in your glance depends entirely on what your application does, but you need to choose wisely because you can only have one glance, and its size is limited to that of the screen—no scrolling is allowed. Furthermore, glances are passive—you can't include user interface objects like buttons and sliders that allow the user to interact with your application. However, passive does not mean static; as you'll see later in this chapter, it's possible for the content of the glance to change over time or even while the user is looking at it. It's a good idea to make the content relevant and useful, because the user is at liberty to remove your glance from his glance list if he doesn't find it to be of value.

Adding a Glance to a Project

In this chapter, we'll add the glance shown in Figure 8-1 to the Weather application.

Figure 8-1. The glance for the Weather application

Like all screens in a WatchKit application, a glance is configured in the storyboard and is managed by an interface controller. Let's get started by taking a copy of the WatchKit weather application that we developed in Chapter 7 and adding a glance to it. Make a copy of the folder 7 - LWKWeather - Final and open the copied project in Xcode. When you add a WatchKit app extension target to a project, Xcode offers to include a glance scene in the storyboard, as shown in Figure 8-2.

Choose options for your new target:

Product Name:	TestGlances WatchKit App
Organization Name:	Apress
Organization Identifier:	com.apress.TestGlances
Bundle Identifier:	com.apress.TestGlances.watchkitapp
Language:	Swift
	☑ Include Notification Scene
	☐ Include Glance Scene
Project:	📄 TestGlances
Embed in Application:	Ａ TestGlances

Cancel   Previous   Finish

Figure 8-2. The glance and notification scene check boxes in Xcode

In all of the examples so far in this book, we have left the Glance Scene check box unchecked because we didn't need a glance. We did just that when we started working with project for the Weather application, so now we'll have to add the glance manually. Fortunately, that only requires a few simple steps. Start by right-clicking on LWK Weather WatchKit Extension in the Project Navigator and adding a nested group called Glance Controller. Right-click on the new group, select New File..., and then choose Cocoa Touch Class from the iOS Source section. Click Next. Name the class LWKWeatherGlanceController, make it a subclass of WKInterfaceController, and save it. Open the class in the editor and add the following code shown in bold so that we can observe the glance controller's lifecycle events:

```
class LWKWeatherGlanceController: WKInterfaceController {
    override func awakeWithContext(context: AnyObject?) {
        super.awakeWithContext(context)
        println("awakeWithContext called")
    }

    override func willActivate() {
        super.willActivate()
        println("willActivate called")
    }

    override func didDeactivate() {
        super.didDeactivate()
        println("didDeactivate called")
    }
}
```

Next, select Interface.storyboard to open the storyboard in the editor. Drag a glance interface controller from the Object Library and drop it somewhere near the other two interface controllers. As you can see, a glance controller is different from an ordinary controller in a couple of ways: it has a glance entry point arrow linked to it, and it's pre-populated with two groups (see Figure 8-3).

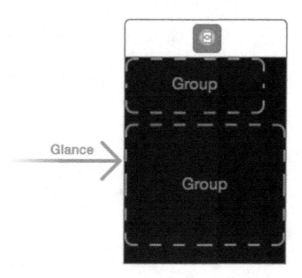

Figure 8-3. Adding a glance interface controller to the storyboard

As you'll see, you can't add arbitrary content to a glance—you have to use the layout templates that are included in Xcode, which restricts your freedom of choice, but ensures that there is some degree of consistency between applications in the way that glances appear. We'll choose the templates that we'll use for the Weather application's glance after we've finished constructing the glance itself.

With the glance controller selected in the storyboard, open the Identity Inspector and set the `Class` attribute to `LWKWeatherGlanceController` to create the linkage between the storyboard and the controller's implementation class.

Running the Glance

Now let's see how the glance looks in the simulator. To do that, we need to add a scheme that will launch the glance instead of the watch application. Had we elected to include a glance scene when we added the WatchKit app target, Xcode would have done that for us. Because we didn't, we need to add the scheme manually. To do that, select the `LWK Weather WatchKit App` scheme in the scheme selector, click on it, and choose `Edit Scheme...` from the pop-up to open the scheme editor, shown in Figure 8-4.

Figure 8-4. The Xcode scheme editor

Click the Duplicate Scheme button on the bottom left of the editor to create a new scheme based on the one we just opened. Change the scheme name in the input field at the top left to Glance - LWK Weather WatchKit App (see Figure 8-5) and click Close to create the scheme.

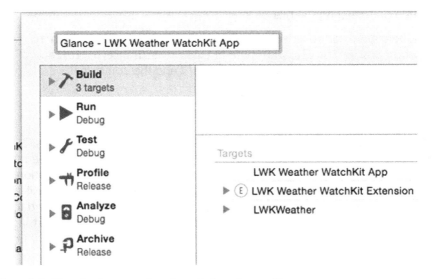

Figure 8-5. Changing the name of a scheme in the scheme editor

The new scheme should now be selected in the scheme selector. Click it and select Edit Scheme... again to reopen the scheme editor. In the middle of the editor, you'll see a control labeled Watch Interface, which is currently set to Main. Change it to Glance to cause the glance to be started instead of the watch application when we run the scheme (see Figure 8-6). Then click Close.

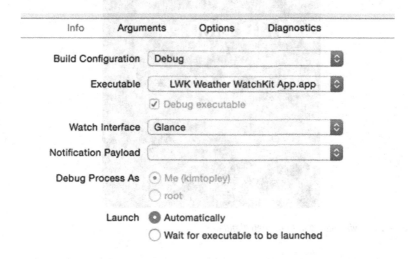

Figure 8-6. *Selecting Glance as the Watch Interface to be launched*

Now we're ready to try out the glance in the simulator. At the moment, though, the glance scene is empty, so drag a date object from the Object Library and drop it into one of the groups in the glance interface controller in the storyboard, so that we can see when the glance has been activated. Make sure the Xcode console is open (View ➤ Debug Area ➤ Activate Console) and that the glance scheme is selected and press the Run button. You should see our skeleton glance appear in the watch simulator display (see Figure 8-7).

Figure 8-7. A trivial glance in the watch simulator

If you look at the Xcode console, you'll see some output from the debug statements we added to the controller class:

```
awakeWithContext called
willActivate called
```

The lifecycle of a glance is similar to that of any other interface controller, except that it's created and its awakeWithContext() method is called as soon as the watch application is installed on the watch. As you might expect, the willActivate() method is called when the glance is made visible. There's no way on the simulator to simulate swiping up and down to make the glance appear and disappear, but there is one more thing we can do: use the mouse to tap the glance. This launches the application and deactivates the glance, so in the console, you'll see this:

```
didDeactivate called
```

It's important to realize that the lifecycle of the glance is not linked at all to the lifecycle of the interface controllers in the application itself, or even to the lifecycle of the application. The easiest way to see this is to run this example on a real watch, which you can do by using the same scheme in Xcode, selecting the iPhone that's paired to your watch as the device instead of the simulator, and then clicking the Run button.

> **Caution**   You may find that this doesn't work. The first time I tried this on my watch, the application failed to start properly. If that happens to you, uninstall the application from the iPhone and try again.

In the Xcode console, you should see that the glance controller was created immediately, even though it hasn't been brought into view yet:

```
awakeWithContext called
```

Now go to the watch face and swipe up from the bottom of the screen to show your glances. You should see our glance in there somewhere—it's probably the first one but if not, swipe sideways until you find it. If you don't see the glance at all, open the Apple Watch app on the iPhone, scroll down until you find the entry for LWKWeather, and tap on it to open the page for the Weather app. Make sure the Show in Glances switch is in the on position as shown in Figure 8-8.

Figure 8-8. The LWKWeather page in the iPhone Apple Watch app

Because the glance controller has now been activated, you'll see this in the Xcode console:

```
willActivate called
```

Lower your wrist or wait a few seconds for the display to time out, and the Xcode console will show this:

```
didDeactivate called
```

Raise your wrist and swipe up from the bottom of the screen again to reveal the glance. Then swipe right to show the previous glance. As our glance moves offscreen, it's deactivated.

While your glance remains in the user's configured glance list, the watch uses the same glance controller instance. The controller is discarded if the user removes it from the glance list. To prove that, open the LWKWeather page in the Apple Watch app on the iPhone (Figure 8-8), make sure the glance is visible on the watch, Move the Show in Glances switch to the off position and then move it back to on. You'll see the following in the Xcode console:

```
didDeactivate called
awakeWithContext called
willActivate called
```

When you moved the switch to the off position, the glance was deactivated and its controller was discarded. When you moved the switch back to the on position, a new glance controller instance was created and its awakeWithContext() method was called, followed by willActivate() as it became visible. All of this is independent of what is happening to the other interface controllers in your application.

Implementing the Weather App Glance

Now that you've seen how to add a glance scene to your project and how to run it, let's implement the glance for the Weather application. We'll start by creating the glance user interface in the storyboard, we'll link the user interface objects to outlets in the controller, and then we'll implement the controller itself.

Building the Glance Interface

Let's first remove the date object we added for testing purposes by selecting Interface.storyboard in the Project Navigator, clicking on the date object, and pressing the delete key. This returns the glance controller to its initial state.

As I said earlier, you don't have full control over your glance's user interface. Apple has created template layouts for the top and bottom parts of the glance, and you have to stick with them. You can see all the available templates by selecting the glance interface controller in the storyboard and opening the Attributes Inspector. Initially, you'll see the layout that's selected by default, which consists of two empty groups; the lower group is a little more than twice the height of the one at the top (Figure 8-9).

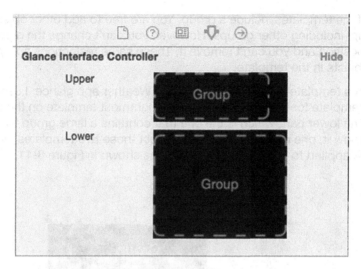

Figure 8-9. The default glance template selection in the Attributes Inspector

If you click on either group, you'll see the templates that are available for that part of the interface, as shown in Figure 8-10.

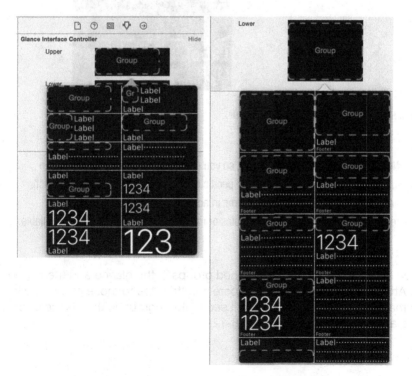

Figure 8-10. The glance layout templates

Some of the templates include a group. You are free to add other objects to the group, including other groups. However, you can't change the group's size or position and you can't remove it. These same restrictions apply to all of the objects in the template.

To select a template, just click on it. For the Weather app glance, I used the default template for the upper part and the rightmost template on the top row for the lower part, which is the one that contains a large group with two labels below it, one marked as a footer. Select those two templates, and they'll be applied to your glance controller, as shown in Figure 8-11.

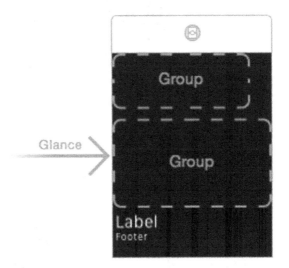

Figure 8-11. The Weather app glance layout

> **Note**   Glances are not interactive, so you can't add objects that the user can interact with to the user interface. Specifically, if you try to add a button, switch, or slider, you'll get a compilation error. In addition to these restrictions, Apple recommends that you don't use tables or maps due to the limited space available.

If you select either of the pre-defined groups in the glance and then open the Attributes Inspector and compare its attributes to those of a group in the main interface controller, you'll see that the group in the glance does not have a Size attribute (see Figure 8-12).

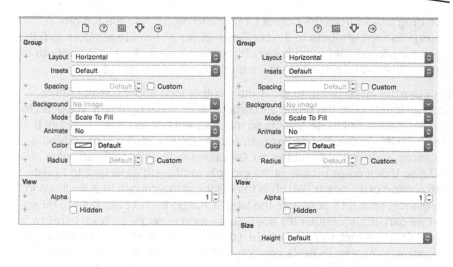

Figure 8-12. A group in a glance (left) and in the main interface controller (right)

If you do the same with one of the labels in the glance and compare its attributes with those of a label in one of the other controllers, you'll see that there are even more attributes missing from the label in the glance. These attributes are missing because you're not allowed to do anything that would change the overall layout of the template.

Now let's start building the glance user interface that you saw in Figure 8-1. For ease of reference, you can see the layout we're aiming for in Figure 8-13.

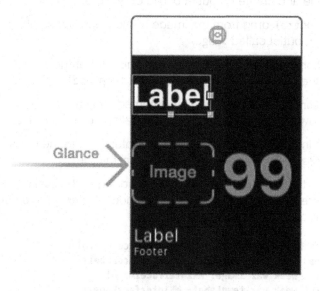

Figure 8-13. The glance user interface in the storyboard

First drag a label from the Object Library and drop it into the top group. Change its Font attribute to System Bold 26, its Min Scale attribute to 0.6 (so that it can adjust for the larger city names), and its Vertical attribute to Bottom. That's all we need to do for the top part of the layout.

We'll use the lower group to show the weather icon and the temperature. Drop an image onto the group and drop a label to the right of it. We need to set the attributes of these objects so that they appear as shown in Figure 8-13. Start with the image. Set its Mode attribute to Center, its Vertical attribute to Center, its Width to Relative to Container with an associated value of 0.5 so that it takes up half of the group's width, and its Height to Fixed with a value of 48 points, which is the height of the images that we'll use in the glance. Now let's configure the label. Change its Text attribute to 99 so that we can judge whether it's going to be wide enough, its Text Color to Light Gray, its Font to System Bold 50, its Min Scale attribute to 0.6, and its Alignment to center. To fix its position and size, set its Horizontal attribute to Right, its Vertical attribute to Center, and its Width attribute to Relative to Container with a value of 0.5. Your storyboard should now look like Figure 8-13, and you can see that the temperature value fits neatly in the space available, so we don't need to adjust its font size any further.

Now let's go through the usual routine to create outlets for the user interface objects in the glance that we'll need to access. Open LWKWeatherGlanceController.swift in the Assistant Editor and do the following:

- Control-drag from the label in the top group to the class file and create an outlet called cityLabel.

- Control-drag from the image to the class file, creating an outlet called image.

- Control-drag from the label on the right of the image to the class file and name the outlet tempLabel.

- Control-drag from the label immediately below the lower group to create an outlet called conditionLabel.

- Finally, Control-drag from the footer label to the class file and create an outlet called footerLabel.

Next, delete the three debug lines that we added to the awakeWithContext(), willActivate(), and didDeactivate() methods. When you've done that, the glance controller class should look like this:

```
class LWKWeatherGlanceController: WKInterfaceController {
    @IBOutlet weak var cityLabel: WKInterfaceLabel!
    @IBOutlet weak var image: WKInterfaceImage!
    @IBOutlet weak var tempLabel: WKInterfaceLabel!
```

```
@IBOutlet weak var conditionLabel: WKInterfaceLabel!
@IBOutlet weak var footerLabel: WKInterfaceLabel!

override func awakeWithContext(context: AnyObject?) {
    super.awakeWithContext(context)
    println("awakeWithContext called")
}

override func willActivate() {
    super.willActivate()
    println("willActivate called")
}

override func didDeactivate() {
    super.didDeactivate()
    println("didDeactivate called")
    }
}
```

We are now ready to start adding code to the glance interface controller.

Implementing the Glance Interface Controller

The glance interface is very much like the Weather app's detail screen (Figure 7-18, so the implementation is also very similar. We'll need to get the weather details for a city from the weather model and use them to populate the screen. We'll need to observe notifications from the model so that we can update the interface if new data is received while the glance is visible, and we also need to respond if the user changes the temperature scale from Celsius to Farenheit, or vice versa. You've seen most of this code before—I won't describe it in any great detail.

Let's start by importing the SharedCode framework at the top of the LWKWeatherGlanceController class, adding a few properties that we'll need and making the class conform to the DisplayedCityInfoModelDelegate protocol so that we can respond to temperature scale changes:

```
import WatchKit
import Foundation
import SharedCode

class LWKWeatherGlanceController:
        WKInterfaceController, DisplayedCityInfoModelDelegate {
    @IBOutlet weak var cityLabel: WKInterfaceLabel!
    @IBOutlet weak var image: WKInterfaceImage!
    @IBOutlet weak var tempLabel: WKInterfaceLabel!
    @IBOutlet weak var conditionLabel: WKInterfaceLabel!
    @IBOutlet weak var footerLabel: WKInterfaceLabel!
```

```
private var cityCode = 0 { // Will be set by selectCity()
    didSet {
        if (cityCode != oldValue) {
            // Fetch the weather, if we don't already have it.
            WatchAppWeatherModel.sharedInstance().
                fetchWeatherForCities([cityCode], always: false)
        }
    }
}

// Whether we are using celsius for display.
private var usingCelsius = false

// Timer used to reload weather.
private var reloadTimer: NSTimer?
```

Note that because we haven't yet implemented the method that's required by the `DisplayedCityInfoModelDelegate` protocol, you'll see a compilation error in this code, which we'll fix in due course.

The `cityCode` property is the code for the city whose weather the glance is displaying. Initially, we're going to use the last city that the user viewed in the WatchKit app's weather detail screen, but in the next section we'll add a setting that will allow the user to choose from a couple of other options. The code that selects the city is encapsulated in a method called `selectCity()` that you'll see shortly. When the value of this property changes, we use the weather model's `fetchWeatherForCities(_:always:)` method to start loading its forecast data. Recall from our discussion of this method in Chapter 7 that this method does nothing if the data we require is already loaded.

The `usingCelsius` property records whether the temperature that's currently displayed is in Celsius. We'll use this property to update the screen if the user changes that preference. Finally, the `reloadTimer` is used to reload the weather data when its expiry time is reached.

A glance is loaded and initialized when its watch application is first installed and when the watch boots, so that it is immediately available when the user swipes up from the bottom of the screen. To maximize the chances that we have data available when this happens, we need to load the weather model from the file store, select the city that we're going to be displaying the weather for, and then start fetching the most recent forecast data for it as soon as the glance is initialized. To do that, add the following code shown in bold to the awakeWithContext() method:

```
override func awakeWithContext(context: AnyObject?) {
    super.awakeWithContext(context)

    // Load the weather model
    WatchAppWeatherModel.sharedInstance().loadWeatherModel()

    // Select the city based on current state
    selectCity()
}
```

Now let's implement the selectCity() method. Add the following code to the class definition:

```
private func selectCity() {
    var newCityCode: Int?

    // Use the last city that the user viewed.
    let userDefaults =
        NSUserDefaults(suiteName: "group.com.apress.lwkweathertest")
    if let lastCityCode =
        userDefaults?.integerForKey("LastViewedCityCode")
        where lastCityCode != 0 {
        newCityCode = lastCityCode
    }
    cityCode = newCityCode ?? 5128581
                // By default, show New York weather
}
```

We start by getting the code for the city that the user last viewed, which is stored under the key LastViewedCity in the shared user defaults object. There is, of course, no code that saves the last viewed city in the user defaults at the moment. We'll fix that later. If the LastViewedCity key is present (which we can only detect by checking whether the value returned from the integerForKey() method is nonzero), we'll use it. Otherwise, we default to showing the weather for New York City.

Now let's implement the glance lifecycle methods. Add the following code in bold to the willActivate() method:

```
override func willActivate() {
    super.willActivate()

    // Observe notification of weather model changes.
    NSNotificationCenter.defaultCenter().addObserver(self,
        selector: "onNotification:", name: nil,
        object: WatchAppWeatherModel.sharedInstance())
```

```
    // Become the delegate of the DisplayedCityInfoModel
    DisplayedCityInfoModel.sharedInstance().delegate = self

    // Set whether we are using celsius.
    usingCelsius = DisplayedCityInfoModel.sharedInstance().useCelsius

    // Update the city in case the user used the app
    selectCity()

    // Update the view
    updateDetails()
}
```

We start by registering as an observer of the weather model and as the delegate of the DisplayedCityInfoModel class. I've already explained why this is required. Next, we set the useCelsius property from the same property of the DisplayedCityInfoModel, so that the code in the delegate method (which we'll add shortly) can detect when it changes. Next, we use the selectCity() method to choose the city that we're going to show in the glance. We need to do this whenever the glance is activated because the user could have used the WatchKit Weather app to view the weather for a different city since the glance was last visible. Finally, we call the updateDetails() method to populate the glance with weather data. Before we implement the updateDetails() method, let's add the code we need in the didDeactivate() method:

```
override func didDeactivate() {
    super.didDeactivate()

    reloadTimer?.invalidate()
    NSNotificationCenter.defaultCenter().removeObserver(self)
    DisplayedCityInfoModel.sharedInstance().delegate = nil
}
```

Here, we are just tidying up by stopping the reload timer and removing ourselves as an observer of the weather model and as the delegate of the DisplayedCityInfoModel.

The code that populates the glance is in the updateDetails() method. Add this code to the class definition:

```
private func updateDetails() {
    var imageName: String? = nil
    var temperature = "- -"
    var condition = ""
    var state = "Loading..."
    var reloadTime: NSDate?
```

```
let cityName =
        CityModel.sharedInstance().cityForCode(cityCode)?.name
        ?? "Unknown City"
cityLabel.setText(cityName)

if let cityWeather = WatchAppWeatherModel.sharedInstance().
                          weatherByCity[cityCode],
    let weatherDetails = cityWeather.currentWeather
    where cityWeather.state == .LOADED {
        reloadTime = cityWeather.reloadTime
        if reloadTime!.compare(NSDate()) == .OrderedDescending {
            // Data has not expired...use it
            if let temp = weatherDetails.temperature {
                temperature = WeatherUtilities.temperatureString(temp)
            }
            imageName = WeatherUtilities.selectWeatherImage(
                        weatherDetails.weather,
                        day: weatherDetails.day ?? true,
                        glance: true)
            condition = weatherDetails.weatherDescription ?? ""
            state = ""
        }
}

image.setImageNamed(nil) // Workaround for WatchKit bug
image.setImageNamed(imageName)
tempLabel.setText(temperature)
conditionLabel.setText(condition)
footerLabel.setText(state)

reloadTimer?.invalidate()
if let reloadTime = reloadTime {
    reloadTimer = NSTimer(fireDate: reloadTime, interval: 0,
                        target: self, selector: "reloadWeather:",
                        userInfo: nil, repeats: false)
    NSRunLoop.currentRunLoop().addTimer(reloadTimer!,
                        forMode: NSDefaultRunLoopMode)
}
}
```

The first part of this method gets the city's weather data and uses it to update the five user objects on the screen if it's valid. If we don't have valid data, we blank out the weather image, change the temperature to two dashes, and set the footer label to Loading.... The second part creates and starts the reloadTimer so that the weather data will be reloaded when it expires. We only need to do this if we currently have valid data.

> **Note**   The line `image.setImageNamed(nil)` really shouldn't be required, but without it, the image that's installed by the following line of code sometimes doesn't show up. It's a bug in the version of WatchKit included in (at least) iOS 8.3.

You'll currently have a compilation error for the call to the `selectWeatherImage()` method in the `WeatherUtilities` class. We created this method in Chapter 7 to return the weather image for a given weather condition. The images that we used in Chapter 7 are all 24 points square, but that's too small for the space allocated to the image in the glance, so we're going to use 48-point images instead. Rather than duplicate the code in the `selectWeatherImage()` method, I added a `glance` argument to it, which requests the glance image instead of the normal image if its value is `true`. Open the file `WeatherUtilities.swift` and make the following change to the definition of the `selectWeatherImage()` method:

```
public static func selectWeatherImage(
        condition: WeatherDetails.WeatherCondition,
        day: Bool, glance: Bool = false) -> String {
```

The `glance` argument has a default value of `false`, so that existing calls work as they did before. The other change that's required is to the `return` statement at the end of the method:

```
        return imageName
    return glance ? imageName + "Glance" : imageName
}
```

This simple change works because the names of the glance images in the asset catalog are the same as those of the oridinary images with the string `Glance` appended. With this change, the compilation error for this method in the glance controller should go away.

> **Note**   You may find that the compilation error does not go away, even after you rebuild. To fix that, hold down the option key and select `Product` ➤ `Clean Build Folder...` from Xcode's menu. Click `Clean` when prompted and build again.

While we're dealing with the glance images, let's add them to the asset catalog. To do that, select `Images.xcassets` in the `LWK Weather WatchKit App` group in the Project Navigator to open it in the editor area and then drag and drop all of the images from the folder `8 - LWKWeather Glance Images` onto it.

Now let's go back to the LWKWeatherGlanceController class and finish it up. We just need to add a few more simple methods:

```
// DisplayedCityInfoModelDelegate conformance.
// Redisplay everything if we switched temperature scale.
func displayedCityInfoDidChange(model: DisplayedCityInfoModel) {
    if DisplayedCityInfoModel.sharedInstance().useCelsius != usingCelsius {
        usingCelsius = !usingCelsius
        updateDetails()
    }
}

// Method called when weather updates are received. Updates the
// view if the current city weather has been updated.
func onNotification(notification: NSNotification) {
    if let cityCodes = notification.userInfo?["cityCodes"] as? [Int] {
        if find(cityCodes, cityCode) != nil {
            updateDetails()
        }
    }
}

func reloadWeather(_: NSTimer) {
    WatchAppWeatherModel.sharedInstance().
            fetchWeatherForCities([cityCode], always: false)
    updateDetails()
}
```

The displayedCityInfoDidChange() method is required by the DisplayedCityInfoModelDelegate protocol. It's called if the user changes the list of displayed cities or switches the preferred temperature display scale. We're only interested in the latter case, which we detect by comparing the value of the model's useCelsius propery to our saved value. If they differ, we save the new value and call updateDetails() to update the screen.

The onNotificationMethod() method handles notification of a change in the weather model. If the change is to the data for the city being displayed in the glance, the updateDetails() method is called to update the screen. Finally, the reloadWeather() method handles the expiry of the reload timer. It requests new data and updates the screen, in case new data is available because the iPhone Weather app has already loaded it.

The glance controller implementation is now complete, but there's one more thing to do. The selectCity() method expects the code for the last city for which the user viewed detailed weather to be available in the shared user defaults object. To make that happen, add the following

bold code to the awakeWithContext() method of the WatchKit app's
DetailsInterfaceController class:

```
override func awakeWithContext(context: AnyObject?) {
    super.awakeWithContext(context)

    // Configure interface objects here.
    setTitle("Weather")

    cityCode = context as! Int
    let cityName = CityModel.sharedInstance().
            cityForCode(cityCode)?.name ?? "Unknown City"
    cityNameLabel.setText(cityName)

    let userDefaults = NSUserDefaults(
                suiteName: "group.com.apress.lwkweathertest")
    userDefaults?.setInteger(cityCode, forKey: "LastViewedCityCode")
    userDefaults?.synchronize()
}
```

To do the same thing when the user views weather on the iPhone, add
similar code to the iPhone app's CityWeatherViewController class:

```
override func viewWillAppear(animated: Bool) {
    super.viewWillAppear(animated)
    installWeatherForCityCode(cityCode)

    let userDefaults = NSUserDefaults(
                suiteName: "group.com.apress.lwkweathertest")
    userDefaults?.setInteger(cityCode, forKey: "LastViewedCityCode")
    userDefaults?.synchronize()
}
```

With this change, the glance will show a weather summary for the city for
which the user last viewed weather details on the watch or on the iPhone,
although in the latter case the glance won't update itself automatically if it is
visible while the user is swiping through the weather screens, because there
is no notification when the user defaults are updated. As an exercise, you
could add this by using the Darwin notification center to send a message
from the iPhone application to the glance controller in the viewWillAppear()
method.

Now build and run the application on the simulator using the Glance - LWK
Weather WatchKit App scheme to verify that the code works.

> **Note**   If you haven't been following the step-by-step instructions, you can find
> a snapshot of the current state of the application in the folder 8 - Glance
> Part 1 in the example source code archive.

Use the mouse to tap the glance interface and you'll see that the WatchKit
app is launched. Once you're convinced that everything is working, run
the code on a real watch, switch to the watch face, and swipe up from the
bottom to see the glance. Tap the glance to switch to the application then
tap a row to view a different city. Press the digital crown to return to the
watch face and swipe up again. You should see the glance reappear and
switch to show the city that you just viewed in the application.

Using Watch App Settings

Right now, the glance always shows the weather for the last city that
was viewed in the watch app's detailed weather screen or in the iPhone
application. It would be nice to allow the user some other choices, such
as showing the weather for a random city, or rotating through all of the
cities that are selected in the displayed cities list. Implementing those other
choices is not difficult, but what about the configuration screen that we'll
need to make them available to the user? We could implement that as part
of the watch app or the iPhone app, but in this section we're going to use a
feature of the iPhone Apple Watch app that allows an iOS application with
an embedded WatchKit app to supply a settings bundle for it. If the iPhone
Apple Watch app finds such a bundle, it includes the settings in its page for
that watch app.

Creating the Watch App Settings Bundle

Let's start by adding the settings bundle for the WatchKit app. It's important
to note that this bundle has to be embedded in the iOS application, not in
the WatchKit app, and it must be called Settings-Watch.bundle. To create
the bundle, right-click on the LWKWeather group in the Project Navigator and
select New File.... In the dialog that appears, choose WatchKit Settings
Bundle from the iOS Apple Watch section and click Next. On the next screen,
make sure that name is Settings-Watch.bundle and click Create.

In the Project Navigator, expand the Settings-Watch.bundle node and
you'll see that it contains a nested group called en.lproj (which is used for
localization) and a file called Root.plist. Click on Root.plist to open it in
the editor (see Figure 8-14).

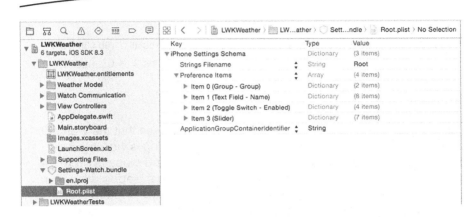

Figure 8-14. *The watch settings bundle*

Click on the disclosure triangle next to the Preference Items entry and you'll see four default items that Xcode added for us. We're only going to use the first of them, so let's delete the other three. To do that, select the row for Item 1, press the delete key, and then repeat for Item 2 and Item 3. Next, click the disclosure triangle next to Item 0 to expose two nested items called Type and Title. Change the value of the Title item to Glance Configuration.

We are now going to add a multivalue item. A multivalue allows us to present a set of options to the user, from which only one can be chosen. Each option will represent one way to configure the glance. Click the disclosure triangle next to Item 0 to close it and then press return. Xcode adds a new item and pops up a chooser to allow the item type to be selected (see Figure 8-15). Choose Multi Value.

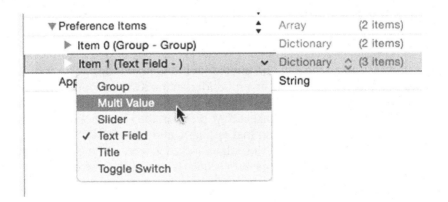

Figure 8-15. *Adding a multivalue item to the watch settings bundle*

Click the disclosure triangle of the multivalue item to open it and you'll see four nested items. Change the value of the Title item to Glance Content, the value of the Identifier item to GlancePreference, and the value of the Default Value item to 0. Now we need to add the three options that the user will be able to choose from. Each option will be mapped to a value. When the user selects one of the options, the corresponding value will be saved to the user defaults under the key given by the Identifier item, which we just changed to GlancePreference.

To configure each option, we need to provide a title, which the user will see, and a value. The titles and values are actually configured in separate lists. Let's create the titles list first. To do that, select the Default Value row and press return. Xcode adds a new row and opens a pop-up to let you select its type, from which you should choose Titles. The item that was just added is a list, which is currently empty. Click its disclosure triangle so that it points downward and press return. A new row will be added, and Xcode helpfully opens an editor so that you can enter its value. Set the value to Last Viewed City and press return. Now in the Key column of the same row, you'll see + and - icons. Click the + icon twice to add two more icons, labeled Item 1 and Item 2. Set the value of the Item 1 row to Random City and the value of the Item 2 row to Rotate Through Cities.

We've added all the option titles—now we need to add the values. Click the disclosure triangle on the Titles row to close it, select that row, press the return key, and select Values from the pop-up that appears in the new row. Click the disclosure triangle on the newly added row to open it—it's empty, so you won't see anything new appear. With the new row selected, click the + icon to add a new nested row and set its value to 0. This is the value that will be stored in the user defaults for the Last Viewed City option. Select the same row and click the + icon twice more to add two more rows. Set their values to 1 (for Item 1) and 2 (for Item 2).

We have one more thing to do: we need to arrange for the user's selections to be stored in the user defaults object that's shared between the iOS application and the WatchKit application. By default, they will be stored in the iOS application's user defaults. To change that, set the value for the ApplicationGroupContainerIdentifier key, which is the last row of the editor, to group.com.apress.lwkweathertest, the identifier of the app group that contains the shared user defaults object. When you have done that, your settings bundle should be as shown in Figure 8-16. Before proceeding, check and correct any errors.

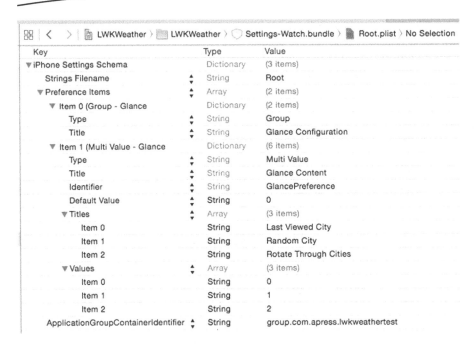

Key		Type	Value
▼ iPhone Settings Schema		Dictionary	(3 items)
Strings Filename	⬍	String	Root
▼ Preference Items	⬍	Array	(2 items)
▼ Item 0 (Group - Glance)		Dictionary	(2 items)
Type	⬍	String	Group
Title	⬍	String	Glance Configuration
▼ Item 1 (Multi Value - Glance)		Dictionary	(6 items)
Type	⬍	String	Multi Value
Title	⬍	String	Glance Content
Identifier	⬍	String	GlancePreference
Default Value	⬍	String	0
▼ Titles	⬍	Array	(3 items)
Item 0		String	Last Viewed City
Item 1		String	Random City
Item 2		String	Rotate Through Cities
▼ Values	⬍	Array	(3 items)
Item 0		String	0
Item 1		String	1
Item 2		String	2
ApplicationGroupContainerIdentifier	⬍	String	group.com.apress.lwkweathertest

Figure 8-16. The completed watch settings bundle

> **Note**   You can read more about settings bundles in the *Preferences and Settings Programming Guide*, which you'll find at https://developer.apple.com/ library/ios/documentation/Cocoa/Conceptual/UserDefaults/ AboutPreferenceDomains/AboutPreferenceDomains.html.

You can check that the settings bundle works as expected by running the WatchKit app and then opening the Apple Watch application on the iPhone and selecting the page for the LWKWeather application. It should be as shown on the left in Figure 8-17. Tap on the Glance Content row to expose the three available choices, as shown on the right in Figure 8-17. As you can see, the first entry (the one configured as the default in the settings bundle) is currently checked.

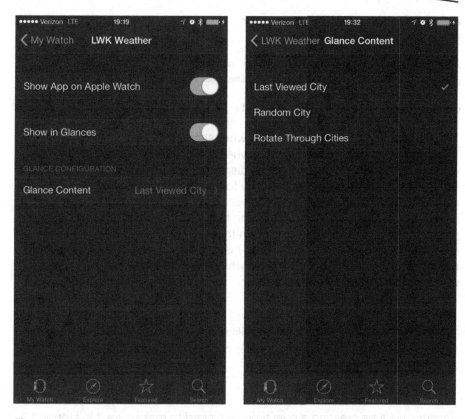

Figure 8-17. The watch app configuration pages in the Apple Watch application

Implementing the Glance View Options

Now that we've built the settings bundle, we can add the code we need in the glance controller. The idea is to modify the selectCity() method so that it sets the cityCode property based on the value of the GlancePreference key in the shared user defaults object. This is the key that we configured in the settings bundle to store the user's choice from the multivalue item. The value will be 0, 1, or 2, depending on which option the user selected.

Select LWKWeatherGlanceController.swift in the Project Navigator and add the properties shown in bold before the awakeWithContext() method:

```
// Timer used to reload weather.
private var reloadTimer: NSTimer?

// Timer used for rotating through cities
private var cityCycleTimer: NSTimer?
```

```
// Index for the next city in rotation
private var nextCityIndex = 0

// Time between cities in rotation, in seconds
private let rotatingCityInterval: NSTimeInterval = 1
```

```
override func awakeWithContext(context: AnyObject?) {
```

These three new properties are used when the user selects the Rotate Through Cities option. In this case, when the glance is activated, the weather for the first city in the user's displayed city list is shown. Then, one second later, it is replaced by the data for the second city, and so on. This continues until the glance is deactivated. The cityCycleTimer property refers to the timer used to switch to the next city, the nextCityIndex property is the index of the next city in the DisplayedCityInfoModel's displayedCities list for which weather is to be displayed in the glance, and rotatingCityInterval is the time for which each city's details are shown, which is hard-coded to one second.

> **Note**   The time interval could be another user-settable preference. As an exercise, you could try adding this preference to the settings bundle and modifying the controller code to use it.

Because we'll be creating a new timer, we need to make sure it is stopped when the glance is deactiveated. To do that, add the following bold code to awakeWithContext():

```
override func didDeactivate() {
    super.didDeactivate()

    cityCycleTimer?.invalidate()
    cityCycleTimer = nil
    reloadTimer?.invalidate()
    NSNotificationCenter.defaultCenter().removeObserver(self)
    DisplayedCityInfoModel.sharedInstance().delegate = nil
}
```

Most of the work for this feature is done in the selectCity() method.
The changes to this method are such that it is easier to remove it completely
and then replace it with the following code than to try to show how to edit it
in place:

```
private func selectCity() {
    var newCityCode: Int?

    cityCycleTimer?.invalidate()
    let userDefaults =
            NSUserDefaults(suiteName: "group.com.apress.lwkweathertest")
    if let preference =
            userDefaults?.integerForKey("GlancePreference") {
        switch (preference) {
        case 0:  // Last viewed city
            if let lastCityCode =
                    userDefaults?.integerForKey("LastViewedCityCode")
                    where lastCityCode != 0 {
                newCityCode = lastCityCode
            }

        case 1:  // Random city
            let cityCount = DisplayedCityInfoModel.sharedInstance().
                            displayedCities.count
            let index = Int(arc4random()) % cityCount
            newCityCode = DisplayedCityInfoModel.sharedInstance().
                            displayedCities[index]

        case 2:  // Rotate through all cities
            displayNextCity()
            return

        default:
            println("Unexpected glance preference value: \(preference)")
        }
    }

    cityCode = newCityCode ?? 5128581 // By default, show New York weather
}
```

The first part of this code gets the value stored for the key
GlancePreferences in the shared user defaults, defaulting it to 0 if it's not
present (since 0 is the value returned by the integerForKey() method if no

value is found). Next, we enter a switch statement based on the value we just retrieved. Here's what the four cases in this switch do:

- The first case, corresponding to the Last Viewed City option, is the same code we used in the original version of this method, setting the newCityCode variable from the last city the user viewed.

- The second case is entered when the user chooses the Random City option. It generates a random number from 0 to the number of entries in the user's displayed city list minus 1 and then uses that as an index in the displayed city list to get a city code.

- The third case corresponds to Rotate Through Cities. This option requires too much code to be embedded here, so it's implemented in another method called displayNextCity() that you'll see shortly. In this case, the displayNextCity() method is going to set the cityCode property, so we return immediately after calling it to avoid having the value overwritten by the code at the end of the method.

- The default case should never be triggered, and we just write a debug line if it is. In this case, the newCityCode variable won't be set, so the weather for New York City will be displayed.

Finally, the value of the newCityCode variable is assigned to the cityCode property. If this variable was not set (which happens when the glance is used for the first time), then the city code for New York City will be used instead.

Because we are using the arc4random() function to generate random numbers, we'll get a better result if we give it a chance to set itself to a random initial value. To do that, add the following code to the willActivate() method:

```
override func willActivate() {
    super.willActivate()

    // Stir up the random number generator
    arc4random_stir()
```

Next, let's add the displayNextCity() method together with a helper method that it needs, both of which are shown here:

```
private func displayNextCity() {
    let cityCount = DisplayedCityInfoModel.sharedInstance().
                            displayedCities.count
    let index = min(nextCityIndex, cityCount - 1)
    nextCityIndex = (nextCityIndex + 1) % cityCount
    cityCode = DisplayedCityInfoModel.sharedInstance().
                            displayedCities[index]
    updateDetails()

    // Schedule a timer for the next city, if we don't have one.
    if cityCycleTimer == nil {
        cityCycleTimer = NSTimer.scheduledTimerWithTimeInterval(
                        rotatingCityInterval,
                        target: self, selector: "onNextCityTimer:",
                        userInfo: nil, repeats: true)
    }
}

func onNextCityTimer(_: NSTimer) {
    displayNextCity()
}
```

The first part of the displayNextCity() method uses the value of the nextCityIndex property to get the code for the next city to be displayed from the DisplayedCityInfoModel's displayedCities property, making sure that the index is within the bounds of the array, and then increments nextCityIndex modulo the length of the array, ready for next time. The city code is assigned to the cityCode property, and the updateDetails() method is called to display the weather for the new city on the screen.

> **Note** We need to bounds check the nextCityIndex property because the user could remove an entry from the displayed cities list by using the iPhone application's configuration screens while the glance is displayed.

Finally, the first time this method is called, we create a repeating timer that will fire every rotatingCityInterval seconds (which, as you have seen, is actually 1 second). When the timer fires, the onNextCityTimer() method is called. That method just calls displayNextCity() to display the details for the next city.

You now have all the code. You can test these changes either on the simulator or on a device, but it's easier to do so on a real watch. After installing the application on the watch, open the Apple Watch app on the iPhone and use the settings screens that we added to select and then try out all three possible glance configurations. When you are testing the Rotate Through Cities option, keep your wrist raised so that the screen doesn't go blank while you are cycling through the city list. If it does, you should be able to swipe up to redisplay the glance, and the cycle should continue from where it left off.

> **Note**   You'll find a copy of the project that contains all the code that you've seen so far in the folder 8 - Glance Part 2 in the example source code archive.

The Rotate Through Cities option demonstrates that although glances are not interactive, they do not need to be static. Of course, you shouldn't make your glance do so much work that it starts using a significant amount of battery power.

Implementing Handoff

In iOS 8, Apple added the handoff feature, which allows the user to start an activity on one device and continue it on another. WatchKit provides a very easy way to use handoff to allow you to react to state sent to the WatchKit application when it is launched as a result of the user tapping on the glance. Let's see how to use this feature in the context of the Weather application.

What will happen is this: when the user taps on the glance, the WatchKit application will launch and then push the detail interface controller for the city that the user was viewing in the glance. This means, for example, that the user can configure the glance to show a random city and then tap on it to immediately see the two-day forecast for that city in the main application. Implementing this turns out to be very easy.

The key to handoff is the concept of a *user activity.* What this means depends entirely on the application. In the case of the weather application, there is really only one activity and that is viewing weather for a city. The activity needs to be assigned a type, which is a name that is conventionally a reversed-DNS designator such as com.apress.lwkweather.viewcityweather.

Whenever the interface controller starts an activity, it needs to call the following method in its base class:

```
func updateUserActivity(_ type: String,
            userInfo userInfo: [NSObject : AnyObject]?,
            webpageURL webpageURL: NSURL?)
```

The userInfo argument is a dictionary that holds information that describes the activity. It is used by whatever picks up the handed-off activity. The webPageURL argument can be used to pass the URL of a web page to open in a browser. We're not going to use that feature here. If, at any point, the user activity ends, the controller should call the invalidateUserActivity() method.

When the application is launched from the glance, if the glance has called the updateUserActivity(_:userInfo:webPageURL:) method, the following method of the WatchKit application's initial interface controller is called some time shortly after it is launched:

```
func handleUserActivity(_ userInfo: [NSObject : AnyObject]?)
```

The userInfo argument references a dictionary containing the values that the glance supplied to updateUserActivity(_:userInfo:webPageURL:).

To implement handoff between the glance and the WatchKit Weather application, all we need to do is follow the rules just given, passing the city code for the city being viewed in the glance in the userInfo dictionary. Let's go through the implementation.

Open the LWKWeatherGlanceController class and add the following code in bold to the property observer for the cityCode property:

```
private var cityCode = 0 { // Will be set by selectCity()
    didSet {
        if (cityCode != oldValue) {
            // Fetch the weather, if we don't already have it.
            WatchAppWeatherModel.sharedInstance().
                    fetchWeatherForCities([cityCode], always: false)

            // Handoff
            if cityCode != 0 {
                updateUserActivity(
                    "com.apress.lwkweather.viewcityweather",
                    userInfo: ["cityCode": cityCode],
                    webpageURL: nil)
            }
        }
    }
}
```

Whenever the code for the city being viewed in the glance changes, the user activity will be updated with a dictionary containing the city code stored under the key `cityCode`. We also need to invalidate the activity when the glance is deactivated. To do that, we need to add just additional line of code in the `didDeactivate()` method:

```
override func didDeactivate() {
    super.didDeactivate()

    cityCycleTimer?.invalidate()
    cityCycleTimer = nil
    reloadTimer?.invalidate()
    NSNotificationCenter.defaultCenter().removeObserver(self)
    DisplayedCityInfoModel.sharedInstance().delegate = nil

    invalidateUserActivity()
}
```

Note that we supply the user activity type `com.apress.lwkweather.viewcityweather` as the first argument when we called the `updateUser Activity(_:userInfo:webPageURL:)` method. In the main interface controller of the WatchKit extension, we need to add the code that handles this activity type. Open `InterfaceController.swift` and add this override of the `handleUserActivity(_:)` method to it:

```
// MARK: -
// MARK: HANDOFF
override func handleUserActivity(userInfo: [NSObject : AnyObject]?) {
    if let dictionary = userInfo as? [String: AnyObject],
        let cityCode = dictionary["cityCode"] as? Int {
        pushControllerWithName("DetailsInterfaceController",
                               context: cityCode)
    }
}
```

This code gets the `cityCode` value from the dictionary of information set when the activity was created, if there is one, and uses it to push the weather details interface controller. Recall from the last chapter that this controller's `awakeWithContext()` method expects to get the city code as its context argument, so we pass it as the second argument to `pushController WithName(_:context:)` method.

There's just one more change to make. In the WatchKit weather application, the details interface controller is pushed by WatchKit code as a result of the user tapping a row in the table in the main interface controller, which triggers a segue. The link between the two controllers is made in the storyboard, so there was no need to give the details controller an identifier. Now, however, we need to push the same controller in code, so an identifier *is* required. To assign one, open `Interface.storyboard` in the editor and select the details interface controller. Open the Attributes Inspector and set the `Identifier` field to `DetailsInterfaceController`, the same value we used when calling `pushControllerwithName(:context:)` in the code above.

Now build and run the application on a real watch (you can't test handoff in the simulator).

> **Note** You'll find a copy of the completed project in the folder 8 - Glance Part 3 in the example source code archive.

Use the Apple Watch app on the iPhone to configure the glance to rotate through cities and then open the iPhone Weather application and add a few more cities to the displayed cities list. When you've done that, swipe up on the watch screen to reveal the glance. As the glance cycles through the cities in the displayed cities list, tap the screen and you'll see the application launch, and then the details screen for the city that you tapped on will be pushed almost immediately. That's handoff in action!

Summary

Glances provide a convenient way for the user to see your application's state and a quicker and less error-prone way to launch it than going through the watch's home screen. In this chapter, you saw how easy it is to implement a glance. Although applications are not required to have one, I recommend that you implement a glance if you have data that you could usefully present to the user while your application is not running.

This chapter also introduced the watch application settings bundle. Although we used it here to tailor the Weather application's glance, you can use it to configure any aspect of your watchkit application's behavior.

Finally, you saw how to implement handoff from the glance to the WatchKit application. Although the handoff functionality provided by WatchKit is very simple, you can use it to implement a shortcut into your application's user interface that will save the user time and frustration.

Notifications

One of the best features of Apple Watch is that it can handle local and remote notifications for your iOS application even if you haven't bundled a WatchKit application with it. It's entirely possible that the default notification handling is good enough, in which case you don't need to add a watch application—and even if you have added one, you still may not need to enhance it to work with notifications. In the first part of this chapter, you'll see how notifications are handled when your application does not have a WatchKit app.

If the default notification handling does not meet your requirements, you can customize it in your WatchKit app. There are two levels of customization you can choose from: the most basic form is configured entirely in the storyboard and requires no code; the other gives you a great deal more flexibility but requires you to create a specialized interface controller. You'll see how to customize the appearance of notifications in the second part of this chapter.

> **Note** This chapter assumes that you are familiar with the concepts behind local and remote notifications in iOS. Although there is some introductory material in the first part of the chapter, this is not a notifications tutorial. If you need more information on notifications, refer to Apple's *Local and Remote Notification Programming Guide*, which you can find at `http://developer.apple.com/library/ios/documentation/NetworkingInternet/Conceptual/RemoteNotificationsPG/Introduction.html`.

Default Notification Handling

As far as the user is concerned, Apple Watch makes no distinction between local and remote notifications. As you'll see later in this chapter, the same is true when you add notification handling to your watch application. However, if you have an Apple Watch, it's easy to see what happens when an application schedules a local notification. If you don't have a watch, there is no way to see what the default notification handling gives you because the iOS simulator does not support it—your only option is to add a WatchKit application with a simulated remote notification payload. You'll see how to do this in the section "Handling Notifications in Your WatchKit App" later in this chapter. The rest of this section assumes that you have an Apple Watch available for testing.

> **Note**   If you want a way to deliver remote notifications to your phone for test purposes, take a look at the NWPusher project on GitHub at `http://github.com/noodlewerk/NWPusher`.

Let's build a simple iOS application that schedules a local notification and see what happens when we force it to be delivered first on the iPhone and then on the watch. Our application will have a simple user interface that consists of a single button. When the button is pressed, we'll schedule a local notification to be delivered a short time into the future and we'll see how that looks on the watch.

Start by creating a new Single View application called `DefaultNotifications`, but don't add a WatchKit application target to it, because in this section we're experimenting with what happens when you don't customize notification handling.

Select `Main.storyboard` in the Project Navigator and drag a button from the Object Library to the center of the view, adjusting its position until you see blue horizontal and vertical guides indicating that it is centered. Then drop it and select Editor ➤ Resolve Auto Layout Issues ➤ Add Missing Constraints from Xcode's menu to add Auto Layout constraints that pin it to the center of the view. Change the button's text to Schedule Notification and then select Editor ➤ Resolve Auto Layout Issues ➤ Update Frames from the menu to adjust its size (if this menu item is not enabled, make sure the button is selected in the storyboard and try again). Next, open `ViewController.swift` in the Assistant Editor and Control-drag from the button to the class definition to create an action method called `onButtonClicked()`. We're going to use this method to create and schedule a local notification, but first we have to get the user's permission to do so.

As you probably already know, beginning with iOS 8, an application cannot schedule or handle notifications unless it declares that it intends to do so. The first time it does this, iOS prompts the user to give permission for the application to use notifications. If the user declines, the application will not be allowed to schedule local notifications or receive remote notifications. To declare that our application needs to work with notifications, add the following code shown in bold to the application(_:didFinishLaunchingWith Options:) method in AppDelegate.swift:

```
func application(application: UIApplication,
        didFinishLaunchingWithOptions launchOptions:
        [NSObject: AnyObject]?) -> Bool {
    let settings = UIUserNotificationSettings(
            forTypes: .Badge | .Alert | .Sound, categories: nil)
    application.registerUserNotificationSettings(settings)

    return true
}
```

The UIUserNotificationSettings object that we're creating says that we may include an alert message in our notifications and we may also badge the application's icon and/or play a sound. The nil categories value indicates that we're not going to include any action buttons. Later in this section, you'll see what happens when we add action buttons to a notification.

Let's give the app a simple icon. Open the folder 9 - DefaultNotifications - Images in the finder. Then select Images.xcassets in the Project Navigator to open the asset catalog in the editor and select the AppIcon image set. Drag the file AppIcon@2x.png onto the iPhone App 2x slot at the top right of the catalog and AppIcon@3x.png onto the iPhone App 3x slot. Now run this application on your iPhone. The first time you run it, iOS prompts for permission for the application to use notifications, as shown in Figure 9-1.

Figure 9-1. Getting permission to use notifications

This prompt only appears once, so click OK so that we'll be able to use notifications next time we launch it. In a real application, the user can deny permission, or can initially grant permission and then revoke it in the Settings app. We're not concerned with such complications here, since our only concern is to demonstrate what happens when notifications are enabled.

While we're working in the AppDelegate.swift file, add the following method to it:

```
func application(application: UIApplication,
    didReceiveLocalNotification notification: UILocalNotification) {
  println("Received local notification: \(notification)")
}
```

This method is called instead of displaying an alert if the application is in the foreground when the notification is delivered. It's also called if the application is in the background and the user taps on the notification alert when it's displayed. In either case, we write a message to the console so that we can see that the notification was delivered.

Now let's add the code to schedule a notification. Back in ViewController. swift, add the following code to the onButtonClicked() method:

```
@IBAction func onButtonClicked(sender: AnyObject) {
    let notification = UILocalNotification()
    notification.fireDate = NSDate().dateByAddingTimeInterval(5)
    notification.alertTitle = "Alert!"
    notification.alertBody = "Local notification!"
    notification.soundName = UILocalNotificationDefaultSoundName
    notification.hasAction = true
    notification.alertAction = "Do Something"
    UIApplication.sharedApplication().
                    scheduleLocalNotification(notification)
}
```

This code schedules a local notification to be delivered five seconds into the future.

Local Notifications on the iPhone

Run the application again and press the Schedule Notification button. After five seconds, you should see a message in the Xcode console indicating that the notification was delivered. Now press the button again and immediately press the iPhone's Home button to force the application into the background. This time, the notification is not delivered to the application—instead it's shown in a banner at the top of the screen, as shown in Figure 9-2.

Figure 9-2. A notification displayed as a banner on the iPhone

If you tap the banner, the notification is delivered to the application, as you can see from the Xcode console.

In the onButtonClicked() method, we set the hasAction property to true and the alertAction propery to Do Something, but we don't see any evidence of this in the banner in Figure 9-2. In fact, the alert action is only shown if the user uses the Settings application to elect to receive notifications as alerts. To try that out, open Settings, select Notifications, and then select the row for DefaultNotifications. At the bottom of the screen that appears, select Alerts instead of Banners. Then return to our application, schedule another notification, and press the Home button. This time, the notification is delivered as an alert, including a button labeled Do Something (see Figure 9-3).

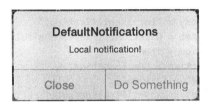

Figure 9-3. A notification displayed as an alert on the iPhone

You can easily verify that the notification is delivered to the application if you click the Do Something button, and that it is not delivered if you press Close. The Do Something is not displayed when the notification is displayed as a banner, because tapping the banner has the same effect.

Local Notifications on the Watch

Now let's see what happens when we deliver the same local notification on the watch. To force the notification to be delivered to the watch, you just need to lock the iPhone.

> **Note** The user can stop the notification from being delivered on the watch by opening the Apple Watch application on the iPhone, going to the Notifications screen, finding the entry for your application under "MIRROR IPHONE ALERTS FROM," and moving the enablement switch to the off position. In that case, the system delivers the notification on the phone instead. The notification is also delivered on the phone if the watch is not available for any reason.

Run the application again, press the Schedule Notification button, and then quickly lock the iPhone's screen. After a few seconds, you'll see the notification pop up on the watch. First, you'll see a simplified version of the notification, called the *short look notification*, which contains the application's icon, the text from the alertTitle property, and the application name, as shown on the left in Figure 9-4.

Figure 9-4. The short look (left) and long look (right) notifications

After a short time, the short look notification transitions to the long look notification, a larger version that contains everything that is in the short look notification plus the text from the `alertBody` property and a `Dismiss` button. The long look notification is shown on the right in Figure 9-4.

> **Note**   If the user enables Notification Privacy on the Notifications page in the Apple Watch application on the iPhone, the long look notification is not shown until the user taps on the short look screen.

Tapping on the `Dismiss` button or swiping down from the top of the screen clears the notification. Tapping anywhere else has no effect, and if you do nothing, the notification will be removed but will remain in the watch's notification center. The user can reveal a shorter version of the notification by swiping down from the top of the screen and can then choose to delete it or tap on it to bring back the long look version. As you can easily verify by looking at the Xcode console, whatever the user does, the notification is not delivered to the iOS application.

Notifications with Actions

Notifications can be configured with one or more custom action buttons that are displayed along with the other elements of the notification when it's delivered on the iPhone or on the watch. Let's add a couple of buttons to the notification in our test application to see how this looks. Start by making

the changes shown in bold in the application(_:didFinishLaunchingWith
Options:) method in AppDelegate.swift:

```
func application(application: UIApplication,
        didFinishLaunchingWithOptions launchOptions:
        [NSObject: AnyObject]?) -> Bool {
    let action1 = UIMutableUserNotificationAction()
    action1.identifier = "ACTION1"
    action1.title = "Action 1"
    action1.destructive = false
    action1.authenticationRequired = false
    action1.activationMode = .Background

    let action2 = UIMutableUserNotificationAction()
    action2.identifier = "ACTION2"
    action2.title = "Action 2"
    action2.destructive = true
    action2.authenticationRequired = false
    action2.activationMode = .Background

    let action3 = UIMutableUserNotificationAction()
    action3.identifier = "ACTION3"
    action3.title = "Action 3"
    action3.destructive = false
    action3.authenticationRequired = false
    action3.activationMode = .Foreground

    let actionCategory = UIMutableUserNotificationCategory()
    actionCategory.identifier = "BasicActions"
    actionCategory.setActions([action1, action2, action3],
                forContext: UIUserNotificationActionContext.Default)
    actionCategory.setActions([action1, action2],
                forContext: UIUserNotificationActionContext.Minimal)

    let settings = UIUserNotificationSettings(
                forTypes: .Badge | .Alert | .Sound, categories: nil)
    let settings = UIUserNotificationSettings(
                forTypes: .Badge | .Alert | .Sound,
                categories: Set([actionCategory]))
    application.registerUserNotificationSettings(settings)

    return true
}
```

This code creates three actions with identifiers ACTION1, ACTION2, and
ACTION3 and groups them into a category called BasicActions by calling the
category's setActions(_:forContext:) method. The first call registers all
three actions for the default notification context. This context is used when

there is enough screen space available to display up to four actions, such as when the notification is displayed in an alert. The second call registers two of the actions for use in the minimal context, which is used when there is limited space, such as when the notification is displayed in a banner or on the phone's lock screen. Having created the actions and linked them to a category, we have to include them in the UIUserNotificationSettings object that we use to register the application's notification requirements. Here, we have only one category, but you can declare as many as you need.

Also in AppDelegate.swift, add the following new method:

```
func application(application: UIApplication,
            handleActionWithIdentifier identifier: String?,
            forLocalNotification notification: UILocalNotification,
            completionHandler: () -> Void) {
    println("Handling action id \(identifier)")
    completionHandler()
}
```

Each action is represented in the user interface by a button. This method is called when the user presses one of those buttons. It receives the identifier from the action and the entire local notification. There is a similar method that handles actions created from remote notifications. Here, we just print the action identifier and then call the completion handler that is passed to this method, which we are required to do.

To associate a set of custom actions with a notification, just set its category property. To do that, add the line shown here in bold to the onButtonClicked() method in ViewController.swift:

```
@IBAction func onButtonClicked(sender: AnyObject) {
    let notification = UILocalNotification()
    notification.fireDate = NSDate().dateByAddingTimeInterval(5)
    notification.alertTitle = "Alert!"
    notification.alertBody = "Local notification!"
    notification.soundName = UILocalNotificationDefaultSoundName
    notification.hasAction = true
    notification.alertAction = "Do Something"
    notification.category = "BasicActions"
    UIApplication.sharedApplication().
                scheduleLocalNotification(notification)
}
```

Now run the application again, press the Schedule Notification button, and lock the iPhone's screen to force the notification to be delivered on the watch. When the notification arrives on the watch, you'll see that the short look version is unchanged, but the long look notification includes two of the action buttons, as shown in Figure 9-5.

Figure 9-5. A long look notification with custom actions

Why are only two actions shown on the watch, whereas all three would be shown on the iPhone? The long look notification is a default context, so it is able to present up to four actions. The reason the third action is not shown is because its activationMode property is set to Foreground:

```
let action3 = UIMutableUserNotificationAction()
action3.identifier = "ACTION3"
action3.title = "Action 3"
action3.destructive = false
action3.authenticationRequired = false
action3.activationMode = .Foreground
```

On the iPhone, this property determines whether the iOS application is launched in the foreground or background to handle the action if the associated button is pressed. The watch interprets this slightly differently—when the user presses a button created from a foreground action, the main interface controller of the WatchKit application is expected to handle it, while background actions are handled by the UIApplicationDelegate of the iOS application. Because we don't have a WatchKit application, the foreground action cannot be handled, so it's not displayed.

With the long look notification ion displayed, press one of the action buttons and you'll see that the message we're printing from the application(_:handle ActionWithIdentifier:forLocalNotification:completionHandler:) method appears in the console, confirming that background actions are handled by the iPhone even when the notification was delivered to the watch.

Handling Notifications in Your WatchKit App

When you add a WatchKit app to your application, you have three additional options for handling notifications. Your first option is to just add the WatchKit app and use the notification support that WatchKit gives you by default. If that isn't enough, you can add a notification scene to your storyboard, which leaves the short look notification unchanged, but gives you two further options for the long look notification—you can use the simpler static form, which must be configured entirely in the storyboard, or you can choose the dynamic version, which requires an additional interface controller and some code. This section explores all three options.

Default WatchKit Notification Handling

Let's start by doing nothing more than adding a WatchKit app target to our simple notifications application. I made a copy of the project we have been working with and changed its name to WatchNotifications so that it's clear that we're now working with WatchKit notifications. You'll find the copied project in the 9 - WatchNotifications - Start folder of the example source code archive. Open this project and make a couple of changes to it.

First, add a WatchKit target in the usual way, *remembering not to create a Notifications scene*—we'll add that scene ourselves in the next section. Second, select Images.xcassets in the WatchNotifications WatchKit App group in the Project Navigator, select the AppIcon image set in the left column of the editor area, and delete it. Then open the folder 9 - WatchNotifications - Images in the example source code archive and drag the folder Appicon.appiconset that you'll find there onto the editor area in Xcode. We've just added a full set of icons to the WatchKit app. So that we can distinguish these icons from the ones we are using for the iOS application, I used a copy of the Sun icon from our weather application. Your asset catalog should now be as shown in Figure 9-6.

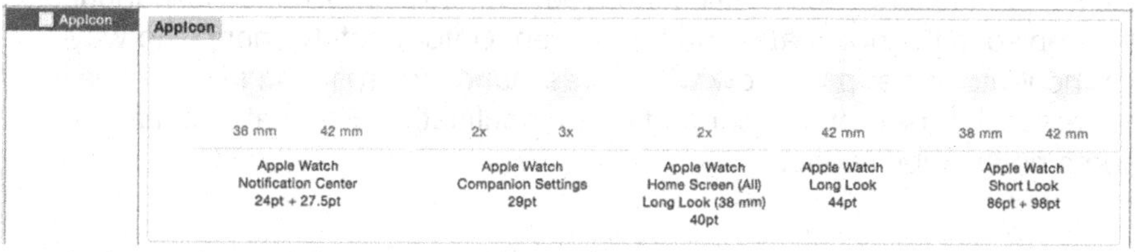

Figure 9-6. Icons for the WatchKit notifications test application

Note that a fully configured WatchKit application needs eight different icons. Fortunately, it's easy to create these if you use a vector graphics-based editor such as Adobe Illustrator. By searching, you can easily find various web-based services that will create icon sets for you.

Run the application on your iPhone. When it starts, press the `Schedule Notification` button and quickly lock the screen so the notification is delivered on the watch. After five seconds, the short look notification appears, followed by the long look version. These are shown in Figure 9-7.

Figure 9-7. *The short and long look notifications when there is a WatchKit app*

If you compare Figure 9-7 with Figure 9-4, you'll see that the only difference is that the WatchKit App's icon is used instead of the iOS application's icon. In practice, you would probably use the same icon for both applications, so this would not be an important distinction. What about the action buttons? You'll recall that the notification uses a category that has three actions, but previously only two of them were shown in the long look notification because the third had foreground activation mode. If you scroll the long look notification screen, you'll see that there are still only two buttons. So far, we don't seem to have gained anything, but that's not quite true—if you tap the icon in the long look notification, your WatchKit application is launched and replaces the notification on the screen. Unfortunately, there's no way for the WatchKit app to know why it was launched, so it can't customize its appearance based on the content of the notification. For that, you have to add a notification scene.

Adding the Static Long Look Notification Scene

In every example in this book so far, we have politely declined Xcode's offer to include a notification scene in the storyboard when adding a WatchKit target to our projects. Now, finally, we are going to use a notification scene.

Because our project already exists, we can't have Xcode add the scene for us, but it's easy enough to do it ourselves, just as it was when we were working with glances in Chapter 8. Open Interface.storyboard in the editor, drag a *Notification Interface Controller* from the Object Library, and drop it onto the storyboard. The controller is pre-initialized with a Dismiss button and a sash that contains the WatchKit app's title and icon, as shown in Figure 9-8.

Figure 9-8. The static long look notification

The controller we just added is an example of a static long look notification. It's presented instead of the default notification shown on the right in Figure 9-7 when a notification with a category that matches the one that it's configured with is received. If you run the iPhone application now and schedule a notification to be delivered on the watch, you'll see that the watch uses our new controller and populates the label with the alertBody property from the notification (see Figure 9-9).

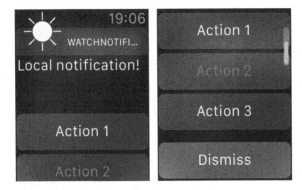

Figure 9-9. Our static long look notification in use

If you scroll down a little, you'll see that there are three action buttons, as shown on the right in Figure 9-9. Recall that the default static long look notification presentation (Figure 9-5) did not include the third button, because its action is configured with foreground activation mode. I say more about this in the section "Action Handling" later in this chapter.

Configuring the Static Notification

It's very easy to use the static long look notification—you just have to add a controller to your storyboard and you don't have to write any code to manage it. In fact, you can't write any customization code because, unlike all the other WatchKit interface controllers, the static long look notification controller is not backed by a class. On the flip side, the layout of the static long look notification is very simple, and it can only display the text in the notification's alertBody property in the pre-configured label. If you need to display additional information from your notification, you'll need to add a long look notification controller, which I cover shortly. There are three different sets of attributes that you can use to customize the short look controller. Select the controller in the storyboard and open the Attributes Inspector to reveal the interface controller's attributes (see Figure 9-10).

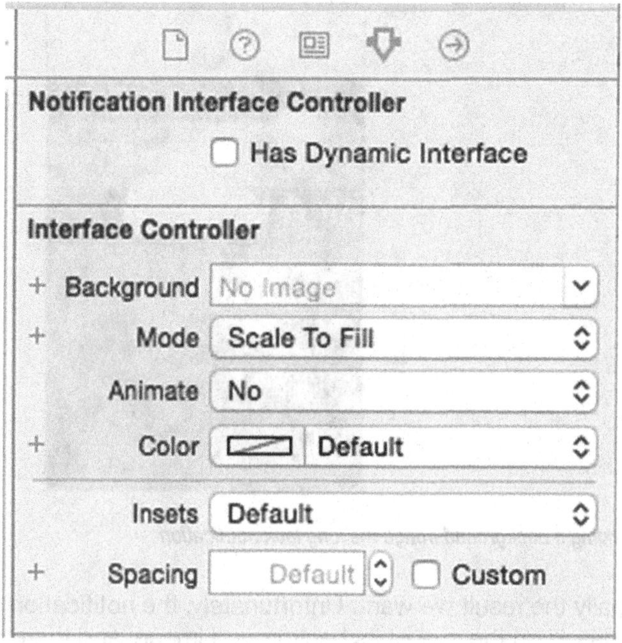

Figure 9-10. *Static long look notification controller attributes*

Leave the Has Dynamic Interface Controller attribute unchecked for now because we're not concerned with the dynamic controller in this section. The remainder of the attributes should look familiar to you—they are very similar to the attributes of a group. You can use them to configure the background of the area of the controller in which your notification information is presented. This is the area that contains the label in Figure 9-9. As you can see, it has a plain black background by default. Let's make that a little more interesting by adding an image and changing the background color.

Select Images.xcassets from the WatchNotification WatchKit App group in the Project Navigator to open the asset catalog in the editor then drop onto it the two images that you'll find in the folder 9 - WatchNotifications - Backgrounds in the example source code archive. Now go back to the storyboard and select the controller again. In the Interface Controller section of the Attributes Inspector, click the + icon next to the Background attribute (see Figure 9-10) and add an input field for the 42mm watch. Select the image CloudAndSun38 in the original Background input field and CloudAndSun42 for the 42mm watch. The image will look squashed in the storyboard, because it's being resized to fit the space available. Change the Mode attribute to Center so that it's shown at its correct size, as shown in Figure 9-11.

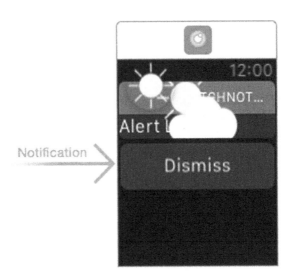

Figure 9-11. Adding a background image the long look notification

That's not really the result we want. Unfortunately, the notification does not resize itself based on the size of its background image, and there's no way to directly set its size. Maybe we can work around it by using the notification controller's insets? Let's try. Set the Insets field to Custom and then try increasing the Top and/or Bottom insets. This has the effect of making the notification area smaller, but the image is always vertically centered. Changing the Top inset value to 50 gives the result shown in Figure 9-12.

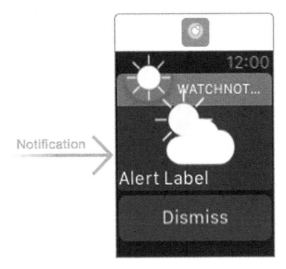

Figure 9-12. Changing the notification controller insets

That's a little better, but it still isn't quite right. Also, increasing the top insets has pushed the alert label to the bottom of the notification area, which may not be what you want. Although you can probably make this work for some images, it's not working in this case. Luckily, there is another way to fix this. We can add a group to the notification controller, set the image as the background of the group, and fix the group's height based on the image size. We can then move the label inside the group and position it according to our requirements. The downside of this approach is that you can't get the image to cover any of the area behind the sash. If you need to do that, you can use a hybrid approach where you put the label in a group, fix the group's height, and then design your image so that it's exactly the same height as the group plus the height of the sash and use it as the background of the notification controller. Of couse, you'll need to make sure this works properly for both watch sizes.

> **Note** You are free to add interface objects to the notification controller, as long as you don't add an interactive object (such as a button) or remove the alert label. Like glances, notification controllers are not interactive.

Go back to the storyboard, reset the Insets attribute to Default, clear the Background attribute, and press the X icon next to the 42mm input field. Now drag a group from the Object Library and drop it directly above the label. In the Document Outline, drag the label so that it's nested inside the group. When you've done that, your Document Outline should look like Figure 9-13.

Figure 9-13. Wrapping the alert label in a group

Now we need to set the height of the group based on the image sizes. The 38mm image is 80 pts high, and the 42mm image is 100 pts high. Select the group, change its `Height` attribute to `Fixed`, and set the value in the field that appear underneath it to 80. Press the + icon next to it to add an input field for the 42mm watch and set its value to 100. To set the background images, select `CloudAndSun38` as the `Background` attribute and then press the + icon next to it, add a field for the 42mm watch and set its value to `CloudAndSun42`. Finally, set the `Mode` to `Center`. Your controller should now look like Figure 9-14.

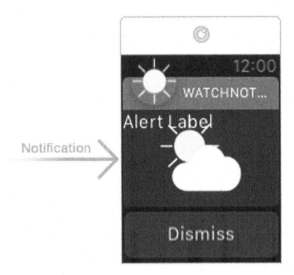

Figure 9-14. The group with the background image added

That black background doesn't look right with the bright sun. Select the interface controller and set its `Color` attribute to a nice sky blue (RGB values 70, 150, 200 give a nice result). Now your controller is beginning to look much nicer (see Figure 9-15).

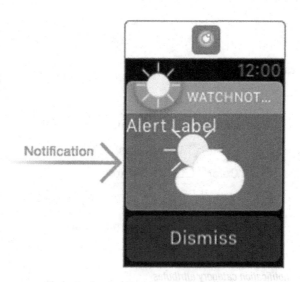

Figure 9-15. The group with the background image and color set

Next, let's configure the alert label. This is just a standard label, so you can configure it any way you need to. I recommend that you set the Lines attribute to 0 to allow the notification text to wrap if necessary. Select the label and do that now. For this example, we also need to choose a text color that works well with the blue background and the white clouds. Any dark color would be acceptable. I chose to use black and I set the font to Headline for better readability. You can use the usual attributes to change the position of the label relative to its enclosing group. Change the Vertical attribute to Bottom to move it to the bottom of the group.

There are a few more configuration items that we can play with. To see them, select the Notification Category item in the Document Outline and then look at the Attributes Inspector (see Figure 9-16).

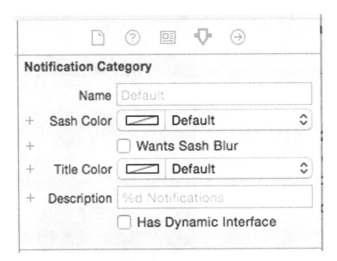

Figure 9-16. The notification category attributes

Ignore the Name attribute for now—that's covered in the section "Notification Categories" later in this chapter. The Sash Color attribute sets the color of the sash, which is the translucent band at the top of the notification area. The Wants Sash Blur attribute, as its name suggests, applies a blur to the content beneath the sash. Similarly, the Title Color attribute sets the color of the text in the sash, which is the application name. Experiment with all these attributes to see how they work, change the Sash Color attribute to Clear Color, and select the Wants Sash Blur attribute.

Before we run the application again, let's make a small change to the code that creates our test notification. Open ViewController.swift and change the value of the alertBody property as shown here in bold:

```
@IBAction func onButtonClicked(sender: AnyObject) {
    let notification = UILocalNotification()
    notification.fireDate = NSDate().dateByAddingTimeInterval(5)
    notification.alertTitle = "Alert!"
    notification.alertBody = "It's Sunny!"
    notification.soundName = UILocalNotificationDefaultSoundName
    notification.hasAction = true
    notification.alertAction = "Do Something"
    notification.category = "BasicActions"
    UIApplication.sharedApplication().
                  scheduleLocalNotification(notification)
}
```

Now run the application on the iPhone, press the Schedule Notification button, and lock the screen. The static long look notification, when it appears, should be as shown in Figure 9-17.

Figure 9-17. A customized static long look notification

Action Handling

When you add a notification scene to your WatchKit app, you gain the ability to handle the foreground actions that are configured for that notification's category. When we defined the BasicActions category that we are currently using for all our notifications, we include three actions, two of which were background and one foreground. As you've already seen, background actions are handled by launching the iPhone application in the background and calling the application(_:handleActionWithIdentifier:forLocal Notification:completionHandler:) method (or a similarly named method for a remote notification) of its iPhone app's application delegate. When you tap the button for a foreground action, your WatchKit app is launched, and the handleActionWithIdentifier(_:forLocalNotification:) method in your WatchKit Extension's main interface controller (or the handleActionWith Identifier(_:forRemoteNotification:) method for a remote notification) is called is to allow you to save state information that you can use to update your user interface. Let's modify the WatchNotifications WatchKit app to demonstrate how this works.

Open Interface.storyboard in the editor and drop a label onto your main interface controller (*not* the notification scene). In the Attributes Inspector, set the label's Lines attribute to 0 to allow text to wrap onto subsequent lines, if necessary. Open InterfaceController.swift in the Assistant Editor and Control-drag to it from the label to create an outlet called label.

Then add a property called userInfo that we'll use to save the user info dictionary from the notification when we receive it:

```
class InterfaceController: WKInterfaceController {
    @IBOutlet weak var label: WKInterfaceLabel!
    private var userInfo: [NSObject: AnyObject]?
```

Now add the code shown here in bold to the willActivate() method:

```
override func willActivate() {
    super.willActivate()

    let text = userInfo?.description ?? "No notification payload"
    label.setText(text)
    userInfo = nil
}
```

This code uses the content of the userInfo dictionary, if it exists, to set the text property of the label and installs a default message otherwise. Then it clears the userInfo property for next time. Now add the following code to the class:

```
override func handleActionWithIdentifier(identifier: String?,
        forLocalNotification localNotification: UILocalNotification) {
    userInfo = localNotification.userInfo
}
```

This is the method that is called when a button created from a foreground action of a local notification is pressed. We extract the userInfo dictionary from the notification and save it in the controller's userInfo property, where it is used by the willActivate() method. Notice that we don't call the superclass implementation of this method—it's not necessary to do so because the documentation says that it does nothing. Now run the application on the iPhone, schedule a notification, and lock the screen. When the long look notification appears on the watch, scroll down and press the button labeled Action 3, which is the one that's created from a foreground action. The WatchKit application will be launched, and you'll see the text No notification payload on the screen. There's no payload because we didn't set the userInfo property when we scheduled the notification. Let's fix that and try again. Open ViewController.swift in the WatchNotifications group and add the following bold code to the onButtonClicked() method:

```
    notification.userInfo = ["Time" : NSDate()]
    UIApplication.sharedApplication().
                scheduleLocalNotification(notification)
}
```

Now run the same test again. This time, you'll see the notification payload on the screen, as shown in Figure 9-18.

19:47

[Time: 2015-06-17
23:46:55 +0000]

Figure 9-18. Handling a foreground action from a static long notification

Notification Categories

Earlier, I mentioned that when a notification arrives, WatchKit looks in the storyboard for a notification scene with a category that matches the category property of the notification. The category property of the notification that we have been using to test has the value BasicActions, but we haven't actually set the category attribute of our notification scene— we would set it by using the Name field shown in Figure 9-16. If WatchKit can't find a notification scene with a matching category name, it tries to find one that does not have a category name. That's why our notification scene is being used even though its category name does not match that of the notification. The idea behind this is to allow you to present a different interface based on the category of the incoming notification. You can add a separate notification scene for each different category that your application uses, setting the controller's category property appropriately.

What happens if there is no scene with the correct category for a notification and there also is no default scene? To find out, open Interface.storyboard and select the Notification Category node in the Document Outline (refer back to Figure 9-13 if you have forgotten where that node is). In the Attributes Inspector, set the Name attribute to NO_MATCH (or anything other than BasicActions), run the application again, and schedule a notification.

This time, WatchKit won't find a notification scene for category `BasicActions` and there is no longer a default scene, so it just uses the default long look controller, the same one that it used before we added the notification scene to the storyboard (see Figure 9-7). Before moving on, reset the notification category's `Name` attribute to blank.

Adding the Dynamic Long Look Notification Scene

As you've seen, you can customize the static long look notification to make it look a little more attractive than the default, but the only information you can display from the notification is the value of the `alertBody` property. To do anything more sophisticated, you need to add a dynamic long look scene. Unlike the static version, the dynamic scene requires a controller class, and you can add code to this class to customize the controller's user interface, using information from the notification, before it's shown to the user.

Adding the Dynamic Controller to the Storyboard

Let's add a dynamic long look notification scene to our example application. To do that, open `Interface.storyboard` in the editor, select the static notification controller in the Document Outline, and check the `Has Dynamic Interface` check box in the Attributes Inspector (refer back to Figure 9-10 for the location of this check box).

Xcode adds the long look notification controller to the storyboard and links it to the static controller using a segue arrow (which is just for presentation since you can't do anything with it), as shown in Figure 9-19.

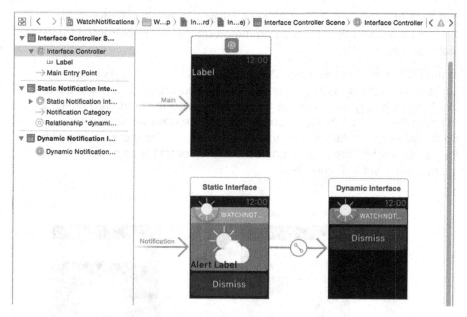

Figure 9-19. The long look notification scene in the storyboard

Next, we need to add a controller class that will be linked to the scene. Right-click the WatchNotifications WatchKit Extension group in the Project Navigator and select New File... from the pop-up. From the iOS Source section of the dialog that appears, select Cocoa Touch Class and click Next. Name the new class BasicActionsNotificationController and make it a subclass of WKUserNotificationInterfaceController, click Next, and save the new class. Notice that notifications use a different controller base class. WKUserNotificationInterfaceController is a subclass of WKInterfaceController with two additional methods that you can override to construct the notification's user interface. You can see skeleton versions of these methods in the source file that Xcode added to the project—one for local and another for remote notifications—and you'll see a typical implementation of one of them shortly.

To link the controller class to the dynamic long look scene in the storyboard, open Interface.storyboard again, select the Dynamic Notification Interface Controller node in the Document Outline, open the Identity Inspector, and set the Class attribute to BasicActionsNotificationController.

Next, let's construct the user interface we want. We're going to add a group to display the same image that we are using in the static controller, and we're going to add three labels to it. We'll use these labels to display information that we'll get from the notification. Building the interface is a mechanical process that you're very familiar with by now. Fortunately, we can save some time by copying the group that we constructed for the static scene.

In the Document Outline, open the Static Notification Interface Controller node so that you can see the nested Group node. Hold down the ⌥ (option) key and drag the Group node onto the storyboard until it's over the dynamic controller scene (which will be obvious because the controller will be outlined in blue) and then drop it. The group, along with its background image, will be copied into the content area of the dynamic scene, as shown in Figure 9-20.

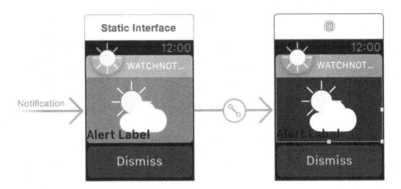

Figure 9-20. Copying a group from the static scene to the dynamic scene

Select the dynamic controller scene by clicking on its sash. Open the Attributes Inspector and set its Color attribute to the same color that you used for the group in the static scene.

> **Note** You can't explicitly set the attributes of the sash in the dynamic controller scene—they are inherited from the static controller.

When you copied the group, you also copied the alert label, which you can see at the bottom of the group. We need three labels stacked one above the other, aligned at the top of the group. Select the group and change its Layout attribute to Vertical so that the labels will be arranged in a column. To move the alert label to the top, select it and change its Vertical attribute to Top. Next, select the label, hold down the ⌥ (option) key, and drag the label down to create a copy and drop it. Do the same thing again to create the third label, as shown in Figure 9-21.

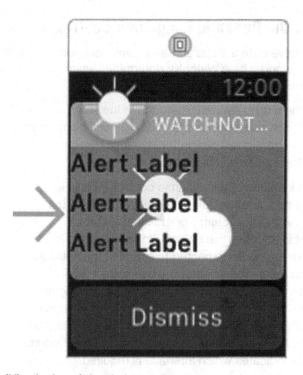

Figure 9-21. Building the dynamic long look controller scene

Next, we need to create outlets for the labels. Open BasicActions
NotificationController.swift in the Assistant Editor. Then Control-drag
from each label in turn to the top of the class file, creating outlets called
alertBodyLabel for the top label, cityLabel for the middle label, and
tempLabel for the bottom label, as shown here in bold:

```
class BasicActionsNotificationController:
            WKUserNotificationInterfaceController {
    @IBOutlet weak var alertBodyLabel: WKInterfaceLabel!
    @IBOutlet weak var cityLabel: WKInterfaceLabel!
    @IBOutlet weak var tempLabel: WKInterfaceLabel!
```

That's all we need to do in the WatchKit app storyboard.

Implement the Dynamic Long Look Controller

Now that we have both a static and a dynamic long look controller, it's reasonable to wonder how WatchKit determines which one it should use. Here's how the decision is made:

1. If there is no dynamic interface in the storyboard, or WatchKit determines that there is insufficient power to warrant constructing the dynamic interface, the static interface is used.

2. An instance of the dynamic controller class is created, and its didReceiveLocalNotification (_:withCompletion:) or didReceiveRemote Notification(_:withCompletion:) method is called. This method is expected to examine the notification and determine whether the dynamic or static interface would be more appropriate. Having made this determination, it should customize the dynamic controller interface (if it's going to be used) and then call the completion handler method with an argument that indicates which interface is required.

3. If the completion handler was called in a timely manner, WatchKit displays either the static or dynamic interface based on the argument that was passed to it. If the completion handler is not called quickly enough, the static interface is used and the dynamic controller instance is discarded.

Let's try this out by enhancing the iPhone part of the application so that it sends the additional notification fields that we need to populate the dynamic interface. To make it more interesting, we'll add a control to the iPhone application so that we can decide which notification interface to trigger.

Open Main.storyboard in the editor, drag a segmented control from the Object Library, and drop it a little way below the button that's already there. Change the text in the left segment to Static and the text in the right segment to Dynamic then drag the control horizontally to center it. With segmented control selected, select Editor ➤ Resolve Auto Layout Issues ➤ Add Missing Constraints in Xcode's menu to complete the layout.

Open ViewController.swift in the Assistant Editor and Control-drag from the segmented control to the class file to create an outlet called typeSelector:

```
class ViewController: UIViewController {
    @IBOutlet weak var typeSelector: UISegmentedControl!
```

Now make the following changes to the onButtonClicked() method in ViewController.swift:

```
@IBAction func onButtonClicked(sender: AnyObject) {
    let notification = UILocalNotification()
    notification.fireDate = NSDate().dateByAddingTimeInterval(5)
    notification.alertTitle = "Alert!"
    notification.alertBody = "It's Sunny!"
    notification.soundName = UILocalNotificationDefaultSoundName
    notification.hasAction = true
    notification.alertAction = "Do Something"
    notification.category = "BasicActions"
    notification.userInfo = ["Time" : NSDate()]
    if typeSelector.selectedSegmentIndex == 1 {
        // Dynamic interface selected
        notification.userInfo = [
            "cityLabel": "New York",
            "tempLabel": "82\u{00B0}"
        ]
    }
    UIApplication.sharedApplication().
                scheduleLocalNotification(notification)
}
```

The effect of this change is to add a userInfo dictionary with values defined for the cityLabel and tempLabel keys if the dynamic interface is selected in the segmented control. We'll use the presence of these values to decide whether to show the dynamic interface.

Now switch back to the WatchKit extension and open BasicActions NotificationController.swift in the editor. Then add the following code:

```
override func didReceiveLocalNotification(
            localNotification: UILocalNotification, '
            withCompletion completionHandler:
                ((WKUserNotificationInterfaceType) -> Void)) {
    var interfaceType = WKUserNotificationInterfaceType.Default
```

```
if let userInfo = localNotification.userInfo,
    let cityText = userInfo["cityLabel"] as? String,
    let tempText = userInfo["tempLabel"] as? String {
    alertBodyLabel.setText(localNotification.alertBody)
    cityLabel.setText(cityText)
    tempLabel.setText(tempText)
    interfaceType = .Custom
}

completionHandler(interfaceType)
}
```

WatchKit calls this method when it receives a local notification (handling for a remote notification is identical, but the method name is different). Recall from our earlier discussion that this method needs to decide which interface should be displayed, configure the dynamic interface if necessary, and then call the completion handler method, the signature of which is as follows:

```
(WKUserNotificationInterfaceType) -> Void
```

The argument tells WatchKit that it should display the static interface if its value is .Default and the dynamic interface if it is .Custom.

In the code just shown, we initialize the interfaceType variable to .Default and then inspect the notification. If the notification includes a userInfo dictionary *and* both the cityLabel and tempLabel keys are present and their values are both strings, we use their values, along with the value of the alertBody property of the notification, to configure the labels and set interfaceType to .Custom. Finally, we call the completion handler, passing it the value of the interfaceType variable. The effect of all this should be that the selection of interface depends on the content of the notification's userInfo dictionary, which in turn depends on the segmented control selection. That's all the code we need to write.

> **Note** You'll find a copy of the completed WatchNotifications project in the folder 9 - WatchNotifications - Final in the example source code archive.

Let's try it out! Run the application on the iPhone. Leave the Static section of the segmented control selected, schedule a notification, and lock the screen. You should see the static interface on the watch. Now unlock the iPhone screen, toggle the segmented control to Dynamic, press the Schedule Notification button again, and lock the screen. This time, you'll see that the dynamic long look notification is used, and it should be as shown in Figure 9-22.

Figure 9-22. The dynamic long look controller in action

Notifications and the Simulator

Throughout this chapter, we have been testing by scheduling local notifications on a real iPhone and handling them on a real watch. Testing *remote* applications on a real device is a little more difficult—unless you already have your application's push service in place, you'll have to do a lot of setup and then use something like the NWPusher client I referred to earlier to push notification payloads to your application. However, you can do limited testing of remote notifications using the simulator. Let's see how that works by using the simulator to test sending remote notifications to our WeatherNotifications application.

Start by taking a copy of the WeatherNotifications project to another folder. If you haven't been following the step-by-step instructions, you can take a copy of the folder 9 - WatchNotifications - Final to use as your starting point. Testing remote notifications in the simulator is just like testing glances: to have the simulator show your notification user interface instead of running your WatchKit app, you need to create a new scheme. If you want to test both your static and dynamic interfaces, you need to create two schemes.

> **Note** There is no way to test the short look notification interface in the simulator. That's not really an issue because the short look notification interface is provided automatically for you by WatchKit itself.

Open your new project and select WatchNotifications WatchKit App and a simulator in the scheme selector. Click on the scheme name and select Edit Scheme. When the scheme editor opens, click on Duplicate Scheme, change the scheme name to Static Notification - WatchNotifications WatchKit App, and click Close. Edit the new scheme, select Static Notification in the Watch Interface selector, and then click Close. To create the scheme for the dynamic notification, repeat the process starting with the static notification scheme, but this time set its name to Dynamic Notification - WatchNotifications WatchKit App and choose Dynamic Notification as the Watch Interface type.

To test a remote notification, you need to create a file containing a simulated remote notification payload in JSON format. The easiest way to do that is to allow Xcode to create one for you and then modify it to suit your requirements. Xcode creates a payload file when you add a notification scene at the same time that you add a WatchKit app target to your project. So, create a new Single View project and add a WatchKit App target to it, making sure you select the Include Notification Scene checkbox. In the Project Navigator, open the group for the WatchKit extension followed by the nested Supporting Files group. There, you'll a file called PushNotificationPayload.apns. Drag this file and drop it into the Supporting Files group under the WatchNotifications WatchKit Extension group in your original project, making sure you select the option to copy the file when prompted.

Open PushNotificationPayload.apns in the editor to show the initial remote notification payload (see Figure 9-23).

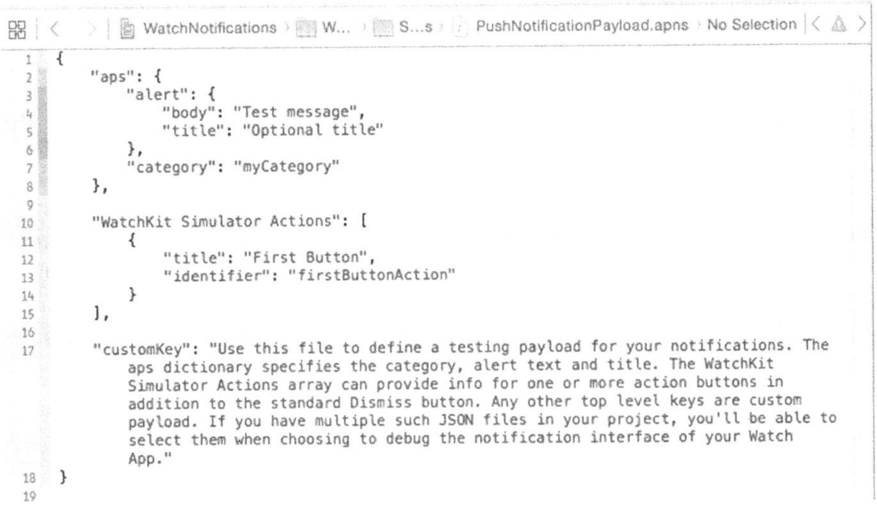

```
     {
 1
 2        "aps": {
 3            "alert": {
 4                "body": "Test message",
 5                "title": "Optional title"
 6            },
 7            "category": "myCategory"
 8        },
 9
10        "WatchKit Simulator Actions": [
11            {
12                "title": "First Button",
13                "identifier": "firstButtonAction"
14            }
15        ],
16
17        "customKey": "Use this file to define a testing payload for your notifications. The
          aps dictionary specifies the category, alert text and title. The WatchKit
          Simulator Actions array can provide info for one or more action buttons in
          addition to the standard Dismiss button. Any other top level keys are custom
          payload. If you have multiple such JSON files in your project, you'll be able to
          select them when choosing to debug the notification interface of your Watch
          App."
18    }
19
```

Figure 9-23. A remote notification payload file

You can read about the format of this file and the keys you can use in Apple's *Local and Remote Notification Programming Guide*. Let's make some changes to it that will allow us to use it with the notification scene in our WatchNotifications project. Modify the file as shown here:

```
{
    "aps": {
        "alert": {
            "body": "It's Sunny!",
            "title": "Optional title"
        },
        "category": "BasicActions"
    },

    "WatchKit Simulator Actions": [
        {
            "title": "First Button",
            "identifier": "firstButtonAction"
        }
        {
            "title": "Action 1",
            "identifier": "ACTION1"
        },
        {
            "title": "Action 2",
            "identifier": "ACTION2"
        },
        {
            "title": "Action 3",
            "identifier": "ACTION3"
        }
    ],

    "customKey": "Use this file to define a testing payload for your notifications. The aps dictionary specifies the category, alert text and title. The WatchKit Simulator Actions array can provide info for one or more action buttons in addition to the standard Dismiss button. Any other top level keys are custom payload. If you have multiple such JSON files in your project, you'll be able to select them when choosing to debug the notification interface of your Watch App."

    "cityLabel": "New York",
    "tempLabel": "82"
}
```

The basic details of the notification are in the aps section. The only part of this that the simulator uses is the value of the body key, which we set to the same value as the alertBody propery in our local notification. Next, there's an array called WatchKit Simulator Actions. The simulator does not run your iOS application before showing the notification scene, so it doesn't know what notification action categories you would register. Instead, you need to configure the buttons that you want in this section, giving the action title and identifier for each of them. Here, we've specified the same three actions that we configure in our iOS application. Finally, we added entries for the keys cityLabel and tempLabel that were included in the userInfo dictionary in our local notification. These are used only for the dynamic notification.

Now run the Static Notification - WatchNotifications WatchKit App scheme, making sure that you have a simulator selected as the target. You should see the static long look notification in the simulator window, as shown in Figure 9-24. If you don't see the alert text in the notification and there's an error message in the Xcode console telling you to add a remote notification payload, then either you didn't copy the payload file to the correct location or there is a syntax error in the JSON in the file.

Figure 9-24. The static long look notification in the simulator

> **Note**   The simulator only displays the long look notification. The only way to see the short look notification is to use a real watch.

Now run the Dynamic Notification - WatchNotifications WatchKit App scheme. You probably expect to see the dynamic notification scheme, but in fact you'll just see the static notification scheme again. The reason is that the simulator uses the same process to decide whether to show the static or dynamic notification scheme that the real device does, but because we are now testing a remote notification, not a local one, the notification interface controller needs to implement the didReceiveRemoteNotificatio n(_:completionHandler:) method in addition to didReceiveLocalNotifica tion((_:completionHandler:). To do that, add the code in bold here to the BasicActionsNotificationController class:

```
override func didReceiveRemoteNotification(
            remoteNotification: [NSObject : AnyObject],
            withCompletion completionHandler:
                    ((WKUserNotificationInterfaceType) -> Void)) {
    var interfaceType = WKUserNotificationInterfaceType.Default

    if let cityText = remoteNotification["cityLabel"] as? String,
          let tempText = remoteNotification["tempLabel"] as? String {
        let aps = remoteNotification["aps"] as? [NSObject : AnyObject]
        let alert = aps?["alert"] as? [NSObject : AnyObject]
        alertBodyLabel.setText(alert?["body"] as? String)
        cityLabel.setText(cityText)
        tempLabel.setText(tempText)
        interfaceType = .Custom
    }

    completionHandler(interfaceType)
}
```

This method does the same as didReceiveLocalNotification ((_:completionHandler:), except that it gets the notification in the form of nested dictionaries built from the JSON payload instead of as a UILocalNotification object. So, to get the cityText and tempText properties, we directly read the values with those keys from the payload dictionary. It's slightly harder to get the body text, because it's nested inside the alert section, which is in turn nested inside the aps section. Each nesting level in the JSON corresponds to a nested dictionary, so we need a couple levels of indirection to access the value that we need. Once we have all the values, we configure the interface in the same way that we did for the local notification.

Run the Dynamic Notification - WatchNotifications WatchKit App scheme again and you will now see the dynamic notification interface (see Figure 9-25).

Figure 9-25. The dynamic long look notification in the simulator

Note   You'll find the source code for the completed version of this project in the folder 9 - WatchNotifications – Simulator in the example source code archive.

Tip   If you want to see what happens if you take too long to initialize the dynamic notification controller, place a breakpoint at the start of the didReceive RemoteNotification(_:completionHandler:) method and run the dynamic notification scheme again. When the breakpoint is hit, do nothing and you'll see a message in the Xcode console indicating that the controller took too long to initialize and the static notification will be shown instead.

Summary

Notifications are, without doubt, one of the Apple Watch's best features. In this chapter, you saw how the watch handles notifications with and without assistance from your WatchKit application. And you saw the differences between the short look notification and the static and dynamic long look notifications. Finally, we looked at how to use the simulator to test remote notifications.

Index

X, Y, Z

Get the eBook for only $5!

Why limit yourself?

Now you can take the weightless companion with you wherever you go and access your content on your PC, phone, tablet, or reader.

Since you've purchased this print book, we're happy to offer you the eBook in all 3 formats for just $5.

Convenient and fully searchable, the PDF version enables you to easily find and copy code—or perform examples by quickly toggling between instructions and applications. The MOBI format is ideal for your Kindle, while the ePUB can be utilized on a variety of mobile devices.

To learn more, go to www.apress.com/companion or contact support@apress.com.

Printed in the United States
By Bookmasters